Mestizo Democracy

NUMBER EIGHT
Rio Grande/Río Bravo
Borderlands Culture and Traditions Series
Norma E. Cantú, General Editor

Mestizo Democracy

The Politics
of Crossing Borders

• • •

BY JOHN FRANCIS BURKE

Foreword by Virgilio Elizondo

Texas A&M University Press   •   College Station

Library of Congress Cataloging-in-Publication Data

Burke, John Francis, 1957–
    Mestizo democracy : the politics of crossing borders / by John
Francis Burke ; foreword by Virgilio Elizondo. — 1st ed.
        p. cm. — (Rio Grande/Río Bravo : borderlands culture and
traditions ; no. 8)
    Includes bibliographical references and index.
    ISBN 1–58544–208–9 (cloth : alk. paper)
    ISBN 1–58544–346–8 (pbk.)
    1. Multiculturalism—United States.   2. Democracy—United
States.   3. Americanization.   4. Political culture—United States.
5. United States—Emigration and immigration.   I. Title.   II. Rio
Grande/Río Bravo ; no. 8.
    E184.A1 B8985   2002
    305.8'00973'090511—dc21   2002006061

To the teachers in my life
who have selflessly dedicated themselves
to the edification of others through education
—especially my parents, Patricia and Jack Burke,
and my wife, Mary Jane.

• • •

Contents

. . .

Foreword by Virgilio Elizondo, ix
Preface, xi

INTRODUCTION   Enriching Community through Diversity, 3

PART I   *Mestizaje as Political Theory*

1. Moving beyond the Either/Or of *Unum* v. *Pluribus*, 19
2. Mestizaje as Holistic Engagement of Multiple Cultures, 52
3. Attributes of a Mestizo Democracy, 83

PART II   *The Politics of Multiculturalism*

4. A *Post*-liberation Philosophy and Theology, 115
5. Reconciling Multiculturalism with Democracy, 146

PART III   *Practical Applications*

6. Fostering Unity-in-Diversity, 179
7. Crossing Borders as Public Policy, 204

CONCLUSION   Embracing the Future of Mestizo Democracy, 246

Notes, 261
Bibliography, 283
Index, 295

Foreword

• • •

You don't have to be a political scientist to recognize that the face of our country is rapidly becoming a composite of faces from the entire world. The old racial and ethnic categories of identification are rapidly becoming obsolete. Will we become a new disunited tower of Babel with no possibility of communication, or will we become an ever-more united humanity, a unity as radical a breakthrough in the history of humanity as was the very foundation of the United States over two centuries ago? John Burke dares to tackle this fascinating challenge of the twenty-first century.

Being a Mexican American mestizo and having studied and written extensively on the subject in order to know and understand myself and my people, it was with a great deal of enthusiasm that I read *Mestizo Democracy: The Politics of Crossing Borders* by John Francis Burke. It is truly a ground-breaking work that dares to explore the universal *mestizaje* taking place in the United States and its effects on our body politic. I do not know of another political theory in the United States dealing with this all-important topic. The term *mestizo*, originally used in Latin America to categorize the children of Native American and European parents, is now being applied to any person of racially or ethnically mixed origins.

From the old and separate ethnic and racial ghettos of the United States is arising a new phoenix, the new human person in whose very body and soul are contained the blood and spirit of every human race upon the earth. A new humanity is emerging. This universal mestizaje is a natural product of the society started by the founders of this country who postulated as a foundation stone of this new government that all are created equal! If all are equal, all equally have the right to procreate and raise families.

How can mestizaje not be part of a truly democratic society? In a society where all men and women are truly equal, friendships will develop beyond any race or ethnic barrier, love affairs will flourish, and children will be born. This is the natural product of a truly multicultural and multiracial democratic society. It is happening and will take place at an ever-increasing pace. It was condemned in the past, somewhat tolerated in the present, but, I dare to say, will be celebrated in the future. Yet to my knowledge no one has studied the effects and challenges of this cultural mixing.

John Burke tackles the mestizo outcome of the growing multiculturalism and multiracialism of the United States that very few are willing to explore or even to recognize. Until recent times racial and even ethnic mixture was frowned upon and even forbidden. Only in 1967 did the United States Supreme Court declare as unconstitutional U.S. laws against miscegenation. Yet today more and more young people are identifying themselves, with great pride, as products of two or more races. My students in various universities speak with great pride, but also with many examples of great pain, of experiences with the different ethnic sides of their families. Mestizo reality is not only becoming more and more common but is also being discussed by young people without any negative slurs.

Among the many great merits of this book is the fact that the author is an engaging scholar. Not only has he been studying the subject for many years, but, more importantly, he has been living the reality of mestizaje, along with his wife, Mary Jane De La Rosa, and their children, Sean and Francisco. He lives and works in the mestizo reality of Texas and thus brings a unique perspective to the subject. He is a rare scholar because he not only bridges serious academic theory and grassroots involvement, but brings out how these different activities enrich each other. In addition to his contributions as a scholar, Burke is a dedicated church member who has put his ideas into practice, especially by fashioning outstanding multicultural and multilingual offerings by church choirs. Beyond his church work, he has been intensely involved in community-organizing projects and other works of the community.

The twenty-first century will be characterized by the capacity to juxtapose identities. We therefore need to envision transnational and national political schemes that move beyond the territorial scripting of identity so as to realize dynamic and just democratic interaction. Mestizaje, in ethical terms, is a vital cultural resource upon which to draw for realizing this end. *Mestizo Democracy* opens the doors to this fascinating adventure and challenge of the twenty-first century.

—Virgilio Elizondo

Preface

• • •

This book is the culmination of ongoing research I have been doing on multicultural relations for the past dozen years. Even in the early 1990s the United States was clearly becoming a more culturally diverse nation, but this reality has become unequivocal today. Yet, our discourse on multiculturalism, whether in the academy or society at large, seems incapable of envisioning a recognizable universality among the nation's diverse cultures while also allowing for the intrinsic distinctiveness of each culture. My observations suggest that we tend either to insist that some uniform vision of being "American" should be shared in common or to revel in the uniqueness of each cultural community without much regard for what unites us as a political people.

My initial forays beyond this either/or approach to multicultural relations were largely abstract considerations of the models of assimilation and separatism within political theory. Indeed, much of chapter 1 is informed by some of my earliest engagements with multicultural relations in terms of U.S. American and European political theory. However, the more I became attuned to the increasing Latino presence that is part and parcel of my life in Texas, the more I came to appreciate that the Latino heritage of *mestizaje* offers a concrete compass for effecting both a political theory of "unity-in-diversity" and constructive multicultural relations at the grassroots level.

As I did more research on mestizaje—the dynamic mixing of African, indigenous, and European cultures in Latin America—I became intrigued by the argument of some Chicano and Latino scholars that *un mestizaje nuevo*—a new mixing of cultures—was developing, especially in the U.S. Southwest, between the long-standing European American and Latino cultures but also encompassing the African American, Asian American, and other cultural communities increasingly integral to that region. Beyond just acknowledging empirical biological and cultural mixing, this scholarship was recasting mestizaje into an ethical argument that cultures can intersect and combine in a fashion that enriches both personal and community well-being.

At the same time, as captivated as I was by this ethos, I found that it actually confirmed my concrete experiences in political and religious communities that have an extensive Latino presence. Academic scholarship notwithstanding, my keen interest in mestizaje finds its origins in my personal and intuitional experiences in Texas over the past two decades. This practical sensibility may not endear parts of this text to academics who prefer to deliberate over politics and multiculturalism in a rather detached fashion, but consonant with the personalist tradition I feel that ideas lack merit and verve apart from their relevance to transforming particular lives and communities in a just fashion.

This book therefore synthesizes my long-standing scholarly interest in multicultural relations and my grassroots engagement with these issues. I contend that a mestizo democracy can effect a unity-in-diversity that enables diverse cultural heritages not only to intersect but also to transform one another in ways that enrich their particular identities and revitalize the overarching political community. Indeed, although I draw the ethos of my argument from contemporary Latino theology, my real contribution lies in recasting this ethos of "crossing borders" as a democratic political theory relevant to communities, from the local to the transnational level, wrestling with the challenges of multiculturalism.

Admittedly, most of the ensuing discourse is written for an audience composed of political theorists and theologians. Still, consonant with the above ethos of integrating theory and practice, I hope that my articulation of a mestizo democracy will interest all those wrestling with the challenges of multicultural relations in their particular social sector or locale. Effecting just multicultural relations is much too crucial to the future of democracy to be relegated exclusively to the deliberations of the academic salon.

I recall reviewing a work over a decade ago in which the author had assembled an anthology of his previous writings. He indicated at the outset that although he had been tempted to revise some of the articles for the book, he chose instead to leave them intact, essentially so that the reader would engage them in their original contexts. I have done just the opposite: although sections of this text have been published in earlier forms, I have quite consciously rewritten this text from start to finish so as to provide coherent transitions from chapter to chapter and to manifest the inclusive, holistic ethos that informs my substantive arguments. Even in those chapters that mirror most closely previously published articles, especially 5 and 6, I have still done substantial revision both to update my arguments and to integrate those chapters as seamlessly as possible with the rest of the text.

Given the number of academic disciplines from which I have drawn to prepare this text and the range of topics I cover, different readers will undoubtedly be attracted to different parts of the text. Political theorists should be drawn especially to chapters 1 through 5 and to the conclusion, and political theologians to chapters 2 through 4. Pastoral theologians will find chapter 6 of interest. Scholars in the field of public administration and policy, as well as practitioners in the public, private, and nonprofit sectors, will gravitate to chapter 7. Finally, scholars in the areas of Chicano, indigenous, Latino, and postmodern studies should be attracted to issues throughout the text.

One of the challenges that comes with writing about multiculturalism, especially within the context of Latino studies, is choosing appropriate terminology to depict culture, ethnicity, and race. In the eighteenth century, race was treated as a form of taxonomic classification, that is, races could be scientifically distinguished and identified. Contemporary science, instead, has abandoned such inquiry, and, therefore, the examination and discussion of race is now largely a matter for the social sciences. Consistent with this development, throughout this text I use race as a rather fluid category, as engaged by the methodology of cultural hermeneutics, not positivistic science. Therefore, in my presentation, ethnicity and race are mutually related concepts. Culture is a more encompassing notion only insofar as I also include religious traditions under its purview.

The most common umbrella terms employed in the United States for labeling persons whose heritage is from Spain or Latin America are *Hispanic* or *Latino*. *Hispanic* is a term largely generated by the U.S. Government for the census and other purposes. Many Latinos and Latino scholars object to *Hispanic* because it stresses the Spanish over the indigenous side of the peoples of Latin America and because the term did not originate from within the culture. Thus, *Hispanic* privileges Spanish, whereas *Latino* more broadly covers under its umbrella other Romance or Latinate languages, such as French, in the case of persons of Haitian origins, and Portuguese, in the case of Brazilians. Nevertheless, many Spanish-dominant Latinos actually do use the umbrella term *Hispanio*.

Most Latino scholars prefer *Latino*, although as illustrated above, it, too, has a European lineage. Moreover, in Spanish, *Latino* features the masculine ending, leading many Latina scholars to move back and forth in their texts between *Latina* and *Latino* or to employ the forms *Latino/a* and *Latina/o*. Although I am sympathetic to this gender-related concern, adopting *Latina/ o* and *Latino/a* can prove cumbersome. Other Latino scholars even argue for terms like *la raza* or, in the case of Mexican Americans, *Chicano* or the *people of Atzlán*, but these terms are too time-bound or quixotic to communicate the overarching Latino heritage to non-Latinos. The linguistic issue becomes even more complicated when one tries to distinguish Latinos living in the United States from Latin Americans in other parts of Latin America.

I have therefore chosen to use *Latino(s)*—primarily because it is the umbrella term that has the widest popular use today—to refer to persons of Spanish and/or Latin American heritage living in the United States and *Latin American(s)* to refer to persons living outside the United States in the countries of Latin America. Although much of my discussion of mestizaje will be drawn from the legacy of Mexican Americans living in the U.S. Southwest, I still use the term *Latinos* most of the time, for even in the major cities of this region an increasing number of Central Americans, South Americans, as well as persons from the Caribbean also comprise the Latino population. I only use *Mexican American* when the point being made specifically refers to the cultural context of Mexican Americans. Occasionally, I employ the term *Chicano* when I am talking specifically about the Mexican American civil rights movement of the 1960s and 1970s. However, when I use the term *Mexican,* I am referring to Mexico.

Finally, when I use the terms *African Americans, Asian Americans,* and *European Americans* I am referring to people of those cultural heritages living in the United States. Although it is tempting to use the term *Anglo* to refer to European Americans because the term is so widely used in the U.S. Southwest, I have kept its use to a minimum, for readers in other parts of the United States may not have the same familiarity with the term or may associate it exclusively with the people and culture of England. In the case of the original peoples of the Americas, I most often use the term *indigenous,* but when referring more specifically to the indigenous peoples within what is now the United States, I sometimes use the term *Native American,* consistent with popular usage. Similarly, I employ *Latino* rather than the term *Latino American* because the latter term has almost no popular usage. At the same time, to distinguish all the people in the United States from the peoples of the rest of the Americas, I use the term *U.S. Americans,* as awkward as that might seem to some readers.

I am indebted to a number of persons who have contributed substantially in a variety of ways to the realization of this book. I would like to thank Mary Dietz, Don Lutz, and Ed Portis for providing me with forums at which I could try out some of my ideas, especially those important to the book's genesis. Beyond that, their discourses with me regarding political theory, and on democracy in particular, have been of inestimable value. In terms of the Latino issues integral to my argument, I am indebted to the spirited conversations I have had with Debra Andrist, Esmeralda Cervantes, and María Pilar Aquino Vargas, and again for the venues they provided for featuring my work. I would also like to thank Adolfo Santos for his collaboration in generating some of the empirical information and analysis in chapter 2. Finally, I would be remiss if I failed to thank Guadalupe Solano; her attentive friendship both with my family and me has been *pura mexicana* and has facilitated this work in countless unseen ways.

In terms of the substantive direction of the book, I will be forever indebted to Clarke Cochran and Tim Matovina for their superb reviews of the initial draft. Clarke, in particular, was willing to step in at a moment's notice without complaint to become an additional reviewer—testimony to his moral and professional integrity that I and others in the political science profession have come to know so well.

With regard to the actual production of this text, I am grateful to the University of St. Thomas for allowing me a measure of released time in my teaching schedule in both the fall and spring semesters of the 1999–2000 academic year. I would like to thank Valerie Alberto, Kayleen Clements, Arthur Pronin, Barbara Sandoval, and Jason Vasquez, who attended to tasks such as clarifying sources, retyping previous drafts, and proofreading. I especially want to thank both Patricia Cunningham and Cheryl Wegscheid, whose professional diligence, boundless energy, and painstaking attention to detail during the final stages of editing the manuscript have given it a polished finish.

Finally, I could never have written this book without the patient endurance and support shown especially by my wife, Mary Jane, over the past several years. Because I wrote this book without any sabbatical leaves or outside research grants—a strategy I would recommend to no one—I gave up enormous amounts of time with her and our sons, Sean and Francisco. Mary Jane frequently kept our sons engaged with any number of activities to give me the time and space to work on the book. In addition, she was my principal resource regarding my use of Spanish in the text. I am so grateful for her sacrifices and indulgence. Despite the various obstacles I faced in the writing of this text, the vivacity of my young sons, who indeed are *mestizos nuevos,* provided me with more than enough energy and inspiration to bring this long-standing project to fruition. ¡*Gracias á todos!*

Mestizo Democracy

Introduction

Enriching Community through Diversity

*T*he capacity to cross geographic and figurative borders will be one of the political virtues of the twenty-first century. Increasingly across the United States, each of us is encountering 'others' supposedly different from oneself in terms of race, religion, ethnicity, and language, among other categories. More and more of us are mingling with diverse people in our neighborhoods, schools, workplaces, shopping sites, civic forums, and places of worship. The dramatic increases in the Asian American and Latino populations in the United States over the past decade noted in the 2000 U.S. Census testify to this increasing diversity. Indeed, more Latinos now reside in the United States than African Americans. Further, the global economy is meshing our destinies with those of other peoples and cultures. Our children are less likely than we to lead a life beyond the touch of people and places far afield. Even if they never leave their hometowns, they will keep in touch with people across the globe through their jobs, personal interests, contacts, and friendships and via the Internet and other forms of advanced telecommunications.

Unfortunately, some voices in the United States have expressed great alarm in recent years over the impact of non-European American cultures on the U.S. American "way of life." Texts such as Peter Brimelow's *Alien Nation* contend in an alarmist fashion that European Americans will be moving to the heartland of the United States to escape the ongoing "invasion" of foreign peoples and cultures. Additionally, California's Propositions 187 (ending state support of undocumented aliens), 209 (ending affirmative action), and 227 (ending bilingual education) have cast a xenophobic shadow over the rest of the country.

The U.S. Southwest, in particular, has become a flash point in this contemporary politics of migration and multiculturalism. Even though migrants and immigrants are coming to the United States from every part of the world and arrive through entry points throughout the country, the border between the United States and Mexico has become the frontline for trying to curtail illegal immigration. In the same decade that Canada, Mexico, and the United States concluded the North American Free Trade Agreement (NAFTA), the United States simultaneously intensified efforts to thwart the migration of undocumented workers across the U.S.-Mexican border. This border, which distinguishes the developed from developing worlds in the Western Hemisphere and U.S. American and Canadian culture from that of Latin America, seems to focus the anxieties of those who feel that the rising numbers of non-Europeans, in particular Latinos, threaten to alter our nation's destiny.

The current extensive migration of Mexicans and Central Americans has brought renewed attention to the U.S. Southwest. The truth is, however, that border crossings have been a way of life in this region for well over two centuries. Although these migrants are technically entering the United States, they are also entering a region that has deep indigenous and Latino cultural roots. Latinos dwelled in parts of California, New Mexico, and Texas well before the western migration of European Americans to this region began in the 1820s. Most immigrants to the United States in the seventeenth, eighteenth, and nineteenth centuries had little choice but to make a geographic and cultural break with their countries of origin. By contrast Latin Americans coming to the U.S. Southwest, an area acquired from Mexico in the war of 1846–1848, enter a region with extensive historical and cultural connections to Mexico and Latin America. Ongoing advances in telecommunication and transportation systems, in turn, enable contemporary Latinos to sustain even stronger ties with the rest of Latin America.

These observations will hardly warm the hearts of nativists and xenophobes in the United States. Still, whether such critics like it or not, the interaction of multiple cultures plays a significant part in the daily lives of most U.S. Americans. This is not a cause, a fad, or a theory but reality. The question is not whether we have to deal with multiple cultures in the United States, but how to do so in a democratic, inclusive fashion.

Unfortunately, so much of the debate over multiculturalism in everyday conversation, television talk shows, and even in scholarly debates proves to be polemical rather than constructive. Zealous partisans of multiculturalism advocate celebrating distinct cultural communities at the expense of the overall civic community while the equally zealous critics on the other side would have us believe that multiculturalism is the nadir of Western civilization. Instead, we need to envision a set of democratic relations between diverse cultural groups that culminates neither in the predominance of one culture over all others in the name of assimilation nor, conversely, in utter separatism and stark antagonism between cultural groups.

Instead of berating the U.S. Southwest and its growing Latino presence as emblematic of supposed social ills in the United States today, we need to look at this region with new eyes, recognizing that its long-standing heritage of mixing cultures—*mestizaje*—offers valuable insights for the challenges posed by the growing intersection of multiple cultures throughout the United States and across the globe. This work focuses on how the normative recasting of mestizaje in Latino theology as a lateral mixing of multiple cultures—a mixing that does not culminate in assimilation—offers a basis for realizing a democracy that articulates and practices collaborative multicultural relations.

Conceptual Impasses That Thwart the Engagement of Unity-in-Diversity

Although the debate over reconciling the nation's many cultural groups to a substantive sense of political community extends back to the founding of the United States, that debate has become particularly salient since the African American civil rights movement of the 1950s and 1960s. In 1960, against the backdrop of the heated campaign issue over whether John Kennedy as a Catholic could faithfully serve in the office of president without compromising either his church or his country, John Courtney Murray confidently claimed that in spite of diverse moral and cultural traditions U.S. Americans held fundamental truths in common. Indeed, he insisted that these truths served as "articles of peace" enabling multiple religious groups to pursue and contest differing moralities and cultures in a peaceful fashion.[1]

Murray's argument is a masterful reconciliation of the First Amendment to the U.S. Constitution with the Catholic natural-law tradition. But more importantly, as Robert Bellah points out, Murray's work is "an opening salvo in a cultural revolution" in which participants in minority, gender, religious, or sexual-preference movements have sought inclusion in the political community without having to sacrifice their cultural mores.[2] Prior to these initiatives the predominant white Anglo-Saxon Protestant (WASP) culture had been pluralistic only to the extent that other races, ethnicities, and creeds were tolerated as minority subcultures. The expectation was that these subcultures in time would either assimilate or remain subordinate. However, underneath the "religious issue" of the 1960 presidential campaign lay the more crucial question, pinpointed by *Commonweal,* a Catholic lay periodical: were we to have "a pluralistic society with a strong Protestant tradition rather than a Protestant society with pluralistic tradition"?[3]

Would that matters were as simple as they were in 1960. Whereas Murray could invoke a Judeo-Christian heritage underlying the U.S. political compact, today Islam and non-Western religions are rapidly expanding in the United States. Increasingly, minorities and immigrants constitute new entrants into the labor force. Whereas prior to 1960 immigration into the United States had primarily been from Europe, since then immigrants have been coming more commonly from Asia, Africa, Latin America, and other regions of the globe. In states with rapidly rising Asian American and Latino populations, minorities in combination will soon represent a majority of the population. In major cities such as Houston, Los Angeles, and San Antonio, Latinos are the largest if not the majority group. If historically the racial divide in the United States has been overwhelmingly addressed as black *v.* white, the rising tide of Asian American, Latino and other ethnic, linguistic, racial, and religious groups has made this divide kaleidoscopic in color and character.

Unfortunately, our conceptual framework for envisioning and realizing a democratic "unity-in-diversity" between diverse cultural groups is surely wanting. Two conceptual divides in particular hinder the articulation of a substantive pluralism in which the contributions of diverse groups both transform one another's perspective and reconfigure the ethos of the political community. First, both in some social-science outlooks and in our everyday perspectives, individuality is somehow antagonistic to group, community, or collective life.[4] According to this conventional wisdom, individual freedom entails not being controlled by community or group mores, whereas group life entails and even rewards assimilation and conformity. To the contrary, as suggested by Sarah Lawrence Lightfoot, we can project and practice a community life comprised of the mutual sharing of diverse gifts:

There can be a difficult but harmonious coming together—the building of a rich community and individual expression. As a matter of fact, if we would let some of those individual gifts thrive, there would be more possibility for a rich community life.[5]

The conventional opposition between individuality and community or group life overlooks the intersubjective basis of human relations. Indeed, our personal distinctiveness—our gifts in Lightfoot's terms—is disclosed and cultivated through our interactions with others.

Seen from this standpoint of public intersubjective relations, politics is more than just a set of disconnected individuals, each pursuing his or her self-interest or, conversely, a monistic community in which some shared characteristic—ethnicity, language, race, or religion among other possibilities—automatically excludes others. Personal freedom and dignity are realized to the degree that we are able to participate as equals with other human beings in public interaction. Additionally, from the communal perspective, a vibrant community comes about through the interchange of heterogeneous perspectives. Engaging and dismantling the obstacles that deter full political participation by any person or group enable a much wider diversity of gifts to enrich the community.

However, in the case of multiculturalism, one is not dealing just with diverse individuals versus a community, but particular cultural groups vis-à-vis the larger political community. In this case, a second conceptual divide—assimilation *v.* separatism—preempts any discussion of how cultural groups can mutually contribute both to each other's development and to that of the political community without either group losing its particular distinctiveness.

In assimilation—"the melting pot"—individuals are expected to shed their past cultures and to clothe themselves in a universal U.S. American culture. Just as previous generations of especially European American immigrants became more American than European in orientation, the expectation is that today's immigrants from Africa, Asia, Latin America, and other places should make the same transition to becoming U.S. American. In this fashion, a shared language—English—and a shared U.S. American culture supposedly enable a civil if not harmonious discourse between what had been a diverse, if not divisive, set of tongues and cultures.

Proponents of separatism counter that the United States is comprised of so many diverse cultures that attempts to realize a universal U.S. American culture actually culminate in one powerful particular culture—WASP culture, for instance—masquerading as a universal and subordinating all other cultural groups. Separatists point especially to the historical record: African Americans have never been effectively assimilated, and Native Americans, by and large, have been eliminated not assimilated. In addition, they remind us that most other nascent cultural groups have had to endure extensive discrimination while reaching for the brass ring of assimilation: recall the "No Irish Need Apply" signs of a century ago. Given this tainted record and the underlying deep differences between cultures, separatists contend that the only way cultural groups can sustain integrity is by establishing and preserving separate cultural enclaves.

If separatists claim that the so-called melting pot is actually just the imposition of an amalgamated European American culture on all other cultural groups, assimilationists counter that the separatists' prescriptions would rend political communities along tribal lines, in the manner of Lebanon in the 1980s or the Balkans in the 1990s. Institutionalization of cultural-group rights would supposedly lead to a return of the incessant feudal wars characteristic of the Europe from which the early colonists chose to escape.

As was the case with the individual *v.* community dichotomy, assimilationism *v.* separatism presumes there are only two possibilities—a universal, uniform community identity or particular intense cultural identities. Behind this presumption lies the notion of cultural identity as a possession to be preserved and not as a fluid relationship in which a culture is both affected by constant new influences and, reciprocally, affects or shapes those influences. Just as the intersubjective basis of human relations dissovles the wall between the individual and the community, so the logic of distinguishing a universal generic community from particular dense cultures disintegrates once we acknowledge that cultures continually interpenetrate and transform one another and that any articulation of a universal political community is connected to this vibrant interchange among its particular cultural groups.

If we insist upon the cherished melting-pot notion as the principal formula for coping with multiculturalism in the United States, cultural tensions and conflicts may very well escalate to the dire proportions posed by Brimelow's *Alien Nation*. Rather than envisioning culture as a possession that separates one culture from another, and therefore to assimilate means giving up one's culture, we must seek an experiential and conceptual framework that suggests in relational terms how diverse cultures can intersect and engender a new culture that reflects the contributing cultures yet is distinct from them. Instead of engaging multiculturalism as a zero-sum game—assimilation or separatism—we need to draw upon a U.S. cultural heritage that considers engagement with diverse 'others' as intrinsic to cultural formation. This intersubjective rendering of cultural transformation then provides a basis for articulating a democratic political theory that integrates the assimilationist's emphasis on unity with the separatist's concern with cultural integrity.

The Import of Mestizaje for Effecting Democratic Multicultural Relations

Specifically, *mestizaje* is a long-standing heritage of the U.S. Southwest that concretely illustrates how cultures can combine without any one necessarily becoming dominant or hegemonic. Historically, *mestizaje* initially refers to the mixing of the African, indigenous, and Spanish peoples during the Spanish conquest of the Americas. *Una nueva raza*—a new race—emerged from this intersection—the mestizos. Although in Mexico the mestizaje is primarily between the indigenous and Spanish peoples, contrary to conventional wisdom an African presence also permeates Mexican history and culture, especially in the Veracruz region and in the mining towns.[6] To be Mexican is to be of a culture that is part African, part indigenous, and part Spanish but that did not exist prior to the mixing of these groups in the sixteenth century in Mexico and in most of the other countries of Latin America.

Consequently, unlike the waves of European immigrants who crossed the sea to colonize what would become the United States and Canada, Mexican Americans are from the U.S. Southwest. Most of this region prior to 1848 was part of Mexico and, prior to that, part of the Spanish New World going back to the 1520s. Some Latino families in Texas, New Mexico, and California can trace their residency in these regions to decades before the military and legal acquisition of these lands by the United States after 1848. Applying the word *immigrant* to Mexican Americans, consequently, does not capture the reality that they were present in the U.S. Southwest before "Americans" came to colonize that region. In turn, although generations of Mexicans and other Latinos have crossed into the territorial U.S. since 1848, especially during the twentieth century, they have been migrants to a region that has a rich history of Latino culture.

The objection will be made that Mexican Americans are still partially Spanish in ancestry and therefore simply colonized the U.S. Southwest prior to the expansion of European Americans into this territory. The key word here is *partially*. Due to mestizaje, Mexican Americans and other Latinos are also indigenous in terms of their racial and cultural background. Latino culture is a combination of the cultures of the Spanish conquerors and the conquered indigenous people that cannot be rendered accurately by the notions of either assimilation or separatism. Especially in terms of their indigenous heritage, Latinos have ties to the U.S. Southwest that reach back generations before the U.S. American colonization of the region.

Over the past century and a half, *un mestizaje nuevo* has emerged among European Americans, Latinos, and other types of Americans in the U.S. Southwest. Mexican American identity, in particular, is situated "in-between" long-standing Mexican and U.S. American cultures; it is shaped by both cultures yet possesses neither culture in its entirety. This experience of cultural combination that recognizes the contributions of the intersecting cultures yet does not culminate in assimilation suggests a framework by which the nation's multiple groups in a heterogeneous age can mutually engage one another as equals and can contribute to the overarching political consensus without having to shed their heritages as the price of participation. Moreover, contrary to the motif of conquest that sullies the original mestizaje in Mexico, Latino theologians in the United States have recast this Latino heritage of "crossing borders" as an ethical capacity to mix and match seeming opposites in terms that challenge and extirpate conqueror-conquered political relationships. The mestizo, conventionally rejected as a half-breed, becomes the basis for realizing an inclusive, albeit at times agonal, pursuit of multicultural relations.

By rendering cultural identity as an ongoing fluid combination of multiple cultures, rather than as a possession either to be kept isolated from other cultures or superimposed upon other cultures, mestizaje conceptually moves beyond the *unum-pluribus* divide. Cultures can engage each other and engender new cultures that reflect the contributing cultures, yet are new and distinct in their own right. Mestizaje is not about preserving cultural enclaves or assimilating immigrants or colonized peoples into a hegemonic universal culture. Contrary to the argument of separatists, *mestizaje* suggests that culture is not a possession to be petrified. Counter to the static universal identity of assimilationists, mestizaje affirms plurality as intrinsic to cultural formation. But most importantly, the heritage of mestizaje in the U.S. Southwest offers an experiential basis for pursuing a substantive unity-in-diversity between the growing, not diminishing, cornucopia of cultural groups that make up the United States in the twenty-first century— the aim that ignited Murray's "salvo" four decades ago.

The remainder of my argument pursues and illustrates the content and contours of a mestizo democracy. Mestizaje has been well researched as a cultural phenomenon in Latino and Latin American studies, and its ethical implications, as already mentioned, are being elucidated by Latino theologians. However, the import of mestizaje for political theory, especially in the United States, has not been previously pursued. Given that mainstream political theory has become preoccupied with "difference" in recent years, it makes sense to move beyond the boundaries of European and European-American political theory to engage a perspective that for over five centuries has been emerging from the encounter among African, indigenous, and European perspectives. I contend that mestizaje can effect a democracy among diverse cultures in which unity and diversity, community and individuality, and universals and particulars are integral, not antithetical, to each other.

Organization of the Text

I have divided my presentation into three sections. In the initial section, I develop a political theory steeped in the Latino heritage of mestizaje, especially as communicated by Latino theologians. In chapter 1 I expand upon how the prevailing either/or of assimilation *v.* separatism paralyzes the debate over multicultural relations in the United States. In lieu of that approach I propose a vision of unity-in-diversity in which cultures intersect and transform one another without necessarily culminating in the triumph of one hegemonic culture. In particular, I illustrate how mestizaje provides an *affective* engagement of democratic multicultural relations that moves beyond the *unum-pluribus* divide.

In chapter 2 I delve more extensively into both the empirical bases for developing mestizaje into a political theory that articulates unity-in-diversity. Beginning with José Vasconcelos's recasting of mestizaje as *la raza cosmica,* I review how *un mestizaje nuevo* is developing, because of the growing Latino presence, not only in the U.S. Southwest but also throughout much of the United States. Specifically, I pinpoint the ecstatic and agonal dimensions of this concrete juxtaposition of cultures through the work of Virgil Elizondo and Gloria Anzaldúa.

In chapter 3 I set forth the specific characteristics of a mestizo democracy, especially as contained in the work of Latino theologians. In particular I emphasize that with regard to "crossing borders" these characteristics call our attention both to the means—those more inclusive forms and processes of community building—and to the ends—a more just set of political, social, and economic policies and outcomes, especially for those traditionally marginalized: the poor and racial/cultural minorities. Although this argument to some may seem like warmed-over liberation theology, I emphasize instead how the grassroots character of this holistic Latino spirituality, especially as manifested in popular religion, has the potential for building salient multiracial political coalitions in the United States.

In the second section of the text I situate my rendering of a mestizo democracy in ongoing debates within contemporary political theory. In chapter 4, largely through Enrique Dussel's contention that modernity is "invented" through the European conquest of the Americas, I explore the very basis for universal communication through diverse cultures. If in previous chapters I steer between the poles of assimilation and separatism, in this case I pinpoint how a mestizo democracy challenges both the sanguine hope of modernists and the relativist despair of postmodernists. In turn, by disclosing, through the work of Octavio Paz, the lingering Eurocentrism in Dussel's project of liberation, I likewise project a basis for a *post*-liberation theology that engages the preferential option for the poor in terms that reflect a mixture of European and indigenous standpoints.

In chapter 5 I place mestizo democracy within the liberal-communitarian debate over multiculturalism. In addition to contrasting the engagement of multiculturalism in Canada with that of the U.S. Southwest, I point out that a mestizo democracy is distinct from both Will Kymlicka's liberal articulation of cultural rights and Charles Taylor and Michael Walzer's more communitarian articulation of a "deep diversity" because a mestizo democracy accents how cultures can mutually transform one another without leading to one culture dominating others. Subsequent comparisons between my articulation of mestizaje with concordant ideas in the work of Jeremy Waldron, Iris Young, and Homi Bhabha then enable me to compare and contrast the virtues of a mestizo democracy to the claims made by liberalism, communitarianism, postmodernism, and tribalism.

In the third section of the text, I provide a couple practical applications of a mestizo democracy. Chapter 6 is a case study of the principles and practices of a multicultural relations committee that I coordinated in a faith-based community in the 1990s. Although the parochial focus of this case study limits its relevance to more secular forums, the positive and negative lessons learned from this concrete experience will be of interest to anyone in the private, public, and nonprofit sectors seeking to realize diverse yet synergistic workplaces and decision-making bodies. The content of this case study also provides a microcosm of the contending rationalities and spiritualities that animate the theoretical discussions of chapters 2 through 4.

While chapter 6 focuses on the processes of multicultural engagement, chapter 7 examines six public policy issues that I consider consonant with a mestizo democracy—multilingualism, political participation, equal education and employment opportunity, housing, migration, and globalization. By choosing to focus on these issues I am not suggesting that they are the only ones relevant to a mestizo democracy. However, these specific policy analyses embrace a holistic approach that can juxtapose and combine multiple identities in a way essential for contending with the policy challenges of the coming century and in a fashion that counters conventional zero-sum thinking.

Finally, in the concluding chapter I argue that a mestizo democracy is animated by a practical rationality that is both more affective and effective for realizing a just set of multicultural relations than other long-standing U.S. political languages or Aristotelian or Kantian alternatives within the European canon. At the same time, I contend that this mestizo practical rationality manifests the creative spirit of James Madison's seminal engagement of pluralism, and does so by envisioning democratic schemes that integrate multiple cultures from the local to the transnational level.

The Contribution of Spiritual Language For Effecting Political Community

To articulate a mestizo democracy, I draw extensively on the insights of Latino theologians. Some critics would suggest that this invocation of theological arguments is inappropriate for a pluralistic discussion of democracy in a nation that prides itself on the separation of church and state. For at least four reasons I find this contention unconvincing if not misbegotten.

First, as stressed by Robert Bellah, in the United States there have been at least three different discourses that have animated our public discourse—Lockean individualism, Biblical thought, and civic republicanism.[7] Although Lockean individualism has been the prevailing discourse, Bellah and others have illustrated the degree to which spiritual and religious arguments have cultivated the political perspectives of U.S. Americans past and present. Despite the best efforts of what Stephen Carter has labeled "the culture of disbelief" to exclude spiritual and religious justifications from political and public-policy debates, those justifications have played a vital role throughout U.S. history and in particular in the debates over slavery and civil rights.[8] Indeed, at least three different prevailing models of "the role of religion in public life" espouse some entanglement of religious and political perspectives.[9] Carter, for instance, boldly claims that the Establishment Clause seeks separation of church and state precisely to enable religious groups to have equal access to the political and policy debates without fear that any one of them would become the established church. In essence, the Establishment Clause actually enables faith communities to participate in politics.[10] Clearly, both in experiential and conceptual terms, spiritual language has played an integral role in U.S. political debates.

Second, over the past two centuries theorists of modernization have contended that as economic development increases and incites a transition from an agricultural to an industrial society, people define their identities no longer by spirituality or religion but by their economic role—"as owners, workers, small businessmen, and so forth."[11] To the contrary, at the outset of the twenty-first century in the United States spiritual and religious identities continue to flourish and, if anything, have intensified their impact on the political and social discourse. The rise of the Christian Coalition over the past two decades is the most notable example. Given the important role that spirituality and religion play in how people define their personal lives and political responsibilities, it would be capricious to exclude theological arguments in favor of secular philosophical approaches in academic studies of the nexus of culture, politics, and religion.

Third, especially in the Latino worldview, no clear demarcation exists between spirituality and everyday life. Modern rationality tends to depict reason as cold and calculative and relegates considerations of spirituality and aesthetics to the realms of emotion, if not irrationality. In contrast, one cannot grasp the ethos of mestizaje apart from a holistic, aesthetic rationality drawn from African, indigenous, and medieval Christian traditions that neither compartmentalize spirituality as just one of life's distinct activities nor disconnect one's current life from the afterworld or other dimensions of being. At marches and rallies of the United Farm Workers, banners of Our Lady of Guadalupe are usually very prominent. This spiritual symbol is not superficial or pietistic but draws from a strongly felt Mexican heritage in which Guadalupe stands on the side of the poor, the oppressed, and the marginalized. Indeed, one cannot grasp fully why César Chávez used the tactics of pilgrimage and fasting in his moblizing of the United Farm Workers without understanding the sacramental outlook that informs Catholic social teaching.[12] Discussing mestizaje without engaging how African, indigenous, and Christian spiritualities contribute to it is to miss the heart of the matter.

Finally, recalling Murray's endeavor to pinpoint a "minimum of agreement" between U.S. religious traditions that enables us to confront directly "the painful conflicts in American society,"[13] I would argue that the Western casting of U.S. interreligious discourse is increasingly dated. In the United States of the twenty-first century, interreligious dialogue will not be just among atheists, Catholics, Jews, and Protestants, but between the Judeo-Christian tradition and other world religions—especially Buddhism, Hinduism, and Islam. It makes perfect sense, therefore, to probe the juxtapositions of spiritual traditions that inform mestizaje, because this capacity to combine opposites will be vital for anticipating and negotiating the increasing impact these religions and spiritualities will have on future U.S. and transnational politics. If the pervasiveness of religious groups in U.S. politics rejects the modernization thesis of the Enlightenment, the growing diversity of these groups moves us beyond stale sectarian polemics within the Judeo-Christian tradition.

Pursuing a Just Mestizo Democracy

The future of the United States and much of the rest of the world will be a multicultural intersection of ethnic, linguistic, racial, and religious groups. Beyond just the traditional association of mestizaje with the historic mingling of cultures in Mexico and the U.S. Southwest, I present in the remainder of this text how the conceptual articulation of unity-in-diversity in mestizaje moves beyond a possessive, tight scripting of cultural identities to engage and foster the intersection of multiple cultural groups in an inclusive, democratic fashion.

Anyone living in the U.S. Southwest cannot help but experience this incessant mixing of cultures that does not culminate in a melting pot. This region of the country is not just African American, Asian American, European American, Latino, or Native American but rather manifests a mixing of these heritages that has been underway for well over five centuries. One senses an engagement of cultural identity that does not rush quickly to tightly scripted categories, but pursues intriguing combinations of cultures without abandoning the quest for political community.

At the same time, extolling the virtues of mestizaje in the U.S. Southwest can easily become an idyllic idolization of Latino culture that hides the legacy of racism and discrimination experienced by Native Americans, Latinos, and other minority groups in this region. To the contrary, this historical experience of subjugation intimately connects mestizaje to the issues of justice experienced by people on the margin.

A just unity-in-diversity thus entails the pursuit of the following two questions. What are the conditions under which diverse cultural groups can even begin to dialogue? How can marginalized groups gain genuine access—without emasculating their respective cultures in the process—to the political, social, and economic decision-making structures that in large part affect their destinies? Given the import of such questions, a mestizo democracy is hardly a saccharine celebration of multiculturalism. Rather it is a politics of "crossing borders" that considers how cultures can realize their respective distinctiveness in interaction with other cultures while simultaneously engendering a just, substantive political community in which the dignity of 'others' is not marginalized.

Part I

Mestizaje as Political Theory

CHAPTER 1

Moving Beyond
the Either/Or
of *Unum* v. *Pluribus*

*A*t present most commentaries on the growing multicultural character of the United States fall into two camps: assimilationists and separatists. Assimilationists contend that multiculturalism treads upon the very ideals of Western civilization; they maintain that there has to be a universal American identity held by everyone for the sake of political civility and order. Separatists, on the other hand, contend that there is little hope for constituting and sustaining a substantive common ground among different cultural groups, that our cultural identities are so autonomous that the best we can do is guarantee the integrity of each enclave. In terms of the long-standing American appeal to *e pluribus unum,* assimilationists are fixated on *unum* and separatists on *pluribus.*

Confronting the multicultural reality of the United States does not have to lead to sacrificing diversity for the sake of unity or vice versa. Political theory that focuses on the intersubjective relations between people and between cultures suggests that if we take *e pluribus unum* seriously, unity and diversity are actually entwined. In this chapter, I review not only the shortsightedness of the assimilationist and separatist positions but suggest that both outlooks suffer from the same epistemological problem: an inability to envision how the concepts of universal community and particular cultural groups can be complementary, not antithetical to each other.

To depict the key characteristics of both the assimilation and separatist camps, I initially examine the positions of multiculturalism offered by Georgie Anne Geyer and Arthur Schlesinger, Jr., on the one hand, and Vine Deloria, Jr., on the other. I then assess the degree to which Benjamin Barber's call for acultural democratic practices that move between the alternatives of an assimilationist "McWorld" and a separatist "jihad" offers a credible engagement of multiculturalism.

Having canvased these prevailing outlooks toward multiculturalism in the United States, I turn to phenomenology and hermeneutics to depict the intersubjective character of human relationships and then to suggest—in contrast to the possessive rendering of cultural identity in assimilation and separatism—that cultures in like fashion can intersect and transform one another without having to lead to the hegemonic control of one culture over others. In illustrating this unity-in-diversity, I principally rely on the thought of Hannah Arendt, Hans-Georg Gadamer, and Maurice Merleau-Ponty. In so doing, I suggest how my articulation of unity-in-diversity simultaneously converges with and yet critiques the key concerns of postmodernism. Most importantly, I contend that if we are to engage the 'other' at the center of the debate over multiculturalism, we need to move beyond the Eurocentric hangover that still permeates these discussions.

Indeed, to move beyond Eurocentric castings of multiculturalism and to reveal an experiential basis for realizing unity-in-diversity within the United States, I conclude by addressing why the Latino experience of mestizaje, reconceptualized as political theory, is preferable to mainstream communitarian discourses such as Robert Bellah's. Although Bellah argues that one's language of discourse must resonate in the body politic to effect political community, his own recourse to the political languages of Biblical thought and civic republicanism ignores the degree to which non-European outlooks are integral to the culture of the United States. By way of contrast I suggest that a mestizo democracy, informed by the Latino heritage of mixing cultures, offers a much more fertile basis for realizing a unity-in-diversity in the U.S. experience.

Assimilation v. Separatism: Opposite Sides of the Same Coin

Assimilationists contend there is a prevailing culture that immigrants and minorities must adopt in order to be U.S. Americans. In this "melting pot," the diversity of cultures and creeds coming to the United States blend together to comprise a culture whose historical antecedents are largely, though not exclusively, Anglo-Saxon. An identifiable Western intellectual tradition reaching back to the ancient Greeks and Romans informs this blending with regard to public policies, educational programs, and social interaction. In effect, the immigrant's cultural background is stripped and replaced with a shared universal identity of what it means to be "American." Past cultural values and mores as the modus vivendi for human relations give way to a contractual outlook on rights and public responsibilities. The melting pot is a unity that ultimately aspires to uniformity.

Separatists, in contrast, maintain that an overarching culture in the United States to which all groups should assent simply does not exist and that instead the autonomy of each particular cultural group must be sustained. They argue that a hegemonic tradition in the United States has superimposed its culture at the expense of all others—a universal by power, not by truth. To counter this cultural oppression, the separatist's task becomes to ensure that

- all cultural groups enjoy political representation and in some instances sovereignty;
- education curricula give each culture its just due alongside the formerly hegemonic culture;
- educational and workplace systems direct their recruitment and advancement efforts to cultural groups either historically subjugated in U.S. history or blatantly underrepresented in public- and private-sector power structures.

Although capable of empowering voices previously marginalized in the United States, separatism conversely maintains that the differences distinguishing diverse cultures are so fundamental that any attempt to cultivate "a shared commitment to common ideals" is inherently hegemonic.[1]

Assimilationists do not recognize how easily a dominant culture through its command of the prevailing political and economic power structures becomes "universal." Indeed, the assimilationist claim of a clearly identifiable intellectual tradition sustaining the prevailing culture suggests that this legacy from the past is static and that it can simply apply to anyone at any time in the same way, without any sense that interpretation, from the past or present, is essential to communicating this legacy. To the contrary, the "great books" themselves were influenced by multiple cultures in the past, and their significance—whether for past, present, or future—cannot be understood apart from the cultural and historical milieus in which they were written or from the cultural and historical milieus of subsequent interpreters.

Conversely, separatists do not recognize that distinctiveness of cultures is realized in relationship to other cultures and that the possibility therefore arises for a unity that links and transcends the particularity of cultures. Moreover, the particular cultures of separatists are no more static than the overarching "tradition" appealed to by assimilationists; cultures change through interaction with other cultures. Consequently, a basis exists for suggesting that diverse cultures share traditions that are precisely revealed through cross-cultural exploration. The separatist insistence on expanding U.S. education curricula to include a wide range of cultural traditions meets the problem of a pseudo-universalism; however, if this culminates in educational enclaves that focus solely on each group's cultural "possessions," then democratic discourse becomes Balkanized. Each cultural enclave becomes a mini-version of the static-tradition argument, refusing acknowledgment of how other cultures have contributed to one's own and of how the activity of interpretation enables one culture to communicate itself, albeit imperfectly, to another.

Neither assimilationist nor separatist schemes offer a constructive direction for dealing with multiculturalism because both render cultural identity as a possession, not a set of relations. In the case of the melting-pot theory, a universal identity is imposed on each member of the community in the name of assimilation. In the case of separatism, relativist identities tear the citizenry apart and preempt any universal bond. Neither alternative allows that cultures can intersect and mutually transform each other; neither renders political community as an intersubjective undertaking in which citizens mutually interact through their respective cultures.

AMERICANS NO MORE?

In the past few years a bevy of books has warned of the perils that multicultural and immigration trends pose to American identity, such as Peter Brimelow's *Alien Nation* and Chilton Williamson's *The Immigration Mystique*. To illustrate the assimilation perspective, I will focus on Georgie Anne Geyer's *Americans No More* and Arthur Schlesinger, Jr.'s *The Disuniting of America*. Geyer's work raises sensible concerns about how changes in U.S. immigration policy and in the process for obtaining U.S. citizenship have watered down the substantive content of what it means to be a U.S.

citizen. Schlesinger points out how the contemporary excesses of ethno-centrism are eroding this substantive notion of citizenship.

According to Geyer what has traditionally set the United States apart from other countries is an articulation of political citizenship that is open to all varieties of peoples and cultures. In contrast to the ascriptive citizenship of "the Old World" in which political membership was connected to one's social station, the U.S. notion of citizenship depends on the citizen's voluntary consent to join the body politic, regardless of background—a *radical individualism.*[2] All citizens are peers in this latter political community, with individual rights to protect them from the tyranny of government and with personal responsibilities to participate and support the common well-being of the polity. This integral combination of personal rights and responsibilities among equal citizens has, according to Geyer, enabled the United States to flourish as a political democracy with economic liberty.[3]

Geyer traces the evolution of U.S. radical individualism to the Western European heritage. She traces from the ancient Greeks the citizen's demand to be an integral player in the debate over public issues and to serve the polity as a defender when under attack; "the Aristotelian idea of a democracy," by Geyer's reckoning, is that of an "an office-holder-in-waiting."[4] This commitment to public participation and well-being was then adopted by the Romans and eventually expanded across the Empire—the *Pax Romana.* But anticipating her critique of the current infatuation with multiculturalism in the U.S., Geyer argues that the Romans' extension of citizenship to too many "uncommitted people and peoples" ultimately eroded the greatness of the Empire.[5]

The "modern-day realization" of Aristotle's notion of citizenship, by Geyer's account, occurred only with the development of radical individualism at the core of the Protestant Reformation, the Enlightenment, and the onset of capitalism from the seventeenth through nineteenth centuries, especially in England.[6] In turn, the "civic spirit" that comes to animate U.S. democracy derives from this Anglo-Saxon heritage. The founding of the United States, according to Geyer, recast the legacies of Greece, Rome, and Reformation England into a vision of voluntary political and economic participation that transcends the ancient fetters of tribal and clan strife.

As Geyer quite rightly stresses, in the United States political citizenship has been passed on to immigrants through civics courses that culminate in a citizenship test—a right of passage from the ways of the Old World to that of the New. For instance, she effectively recounts the poignancy of a citizenship oath ceremony on July 4 at Jefferson's Monticello, replete with an address by the historian David McCullough, recounting the special significance of U.S. heritage.[7]

Geyer fears that changes in U.S. immigration policy over the past four decades, as well as the onset of multiculturalism, are undermining this exceptional notion of U.S. citizenship, "the cornerstone of all the other commitments—marriage, baptism, school, university—that people make."[8] In like fashion, Schlesinger stresses how the ongoing fixation with ethnicity and race in the debate over multiculturalism undermines the United States' need for unifying ideals and a common culture:

> The multiethnic dogma abandons historic purposes, replacing assimilation by fragmentation, integration by separatism. It belittles *unum* and glorifies *pluribus.*[9]

In particular he takes to task the African-centrist movement in public and higher education. He demonstrates that many of the historical claims of this movement—such as "ancient Egypt was essentially a black African country"—are false.[10] In fact, the movement twists history to fit this particular community's political agenda and to raise the self-esteem of its children. Be it these practices or their precedents in European American ethnic chauvinism, Schlesinger argues that "history as a weapon is an abuse of history."[11]

Most of Geyer's text, though, illustrates specific practices that threaten any democracy seeking to effect a unity-in-diversity. She pinpoints how both future citizens as well as the polity as a whole are being cheated by the current "watered-down" character of the citizenship process; for instance, immigrants are given so many chances to pass an increasingly simpler test that the test becomes meaningless. She reviews how some minority and cultural activist groups are largely financed by private foundations and government grants and do not have a large grassroots base, begging the question addressing on whose behalf they can legitimately speak. Finally, her chapter "California: The Way America Will Be" forecasts how the economic and cultural dynamics of California over the past four decades will soon be the issues and realities that most parts of the United States will wrestle with in the twenty-first century.[12]

One can concur with Geyer's and Schlesinger's call for a resuscitation of the participatory character of U.S. citizenship without placing its demise on the backs of non-European Americans. Geyer's argument becomes problematic when she dwells on how the federal immigration reform of 1965 has opened up the floodgates through which mostly non-Europeans have sub-sequently passed. Are the recent Hispanic and Asian arrivals of the past three decades really "without the prospect of real assimilation training or socialization into American life," as she contends?[13] The very time frame that Geyer focuses on as the demise of the U.S. citizenship framework—the latter half of the twentieth century—is actually the very period during which persecuted and discriminated groups in the U.S. finally gained national rec-ognition of their plight and, consequently, considerable access to political and economic decision-making structures.

Other than a parenthetical reference claiming that the problems of race were supposedly overcome by the Civil Rights movement of the 1960s, Geyer offers no recognition that this "sweet land of liberty" might seem rather bitter to peoples who were not beneficiaries of the white Anglo-Saxon–Protestant heritage she links to U.S. citizenship. African Americans still have to wrestle with the repercussions of slavery, a system imposed by presumably enlight-ened U.S. citizens. How much confidence do Native Americans place in the agreements and promises engendered by the political consensus Geyer ac-cents, given that their ancestors were gradually exterminated as one treaty after another was violated by the U.S. Government? Why should Mexican Americans have much confidence in Geyer's "civic spirit" when their ances-tors were essentially conquered through the Treaty of Guadalupe-Hidalgo of 1848 and subsequently had to endure a system of segregation in the U.S. Southwest parallel to that of African Americans in the U.S. South? Would Chinese Americans necessarily take heart in Geyer's articulation of citizen-ship, given that their ancestors were denied legal access to the United States for the better part of a century by the Chinese Exclusion Act of 1882? Finally, lest we forget, Japanese Americans—not German or Italian Americans—lost their homes and businesses during World War II when they were in-terned in camps by the U.S. Government. It is therefore unlikely that many people of color in the United States would view the conditions of the pre-1965 United States as the "good old days."

Likewise, as cogent as Schlesinger's critique of ethnocentrism is, he offers little in the way of an alternative that genuinely moves between the assimi-lation and separatism alternatives. *Unum* is so consistently weighted over *pluribus* in Schlesinger's *Disuniting of America* that his invocation of "one people" is utterly abstract.[14] Schlesinger's only hint at a cultural pluralism distinct from assimilation and ethnocentrism is his evocation of Horace Kallen's 1915 essay "Democracy versus the Melting Pot." Kallen, he points out, pinpoints that "the melting pot" is invalid either as an ideal or as a reality and that Kallen instead emphasizes that ethnic diversity actually enriches the overall nation.[15] But besides noting how the work of Diane Ravitch amplifies cultural pluralism today, Schlesinger's elaboration of this alternative always returns to his stress on unifying ideals and a common culture.[16]

On a theoretical level Geyer provides an excellent rendering of U.S. citizenship as moving beyond the ascriptive character of political and economic power networks of the Old World. Indeed, on the one hand, as the Indian American author Bharati Mukherjee contends, being U.S. American is the capacity for dreaming new lives free from past traditional cultural restraints.[17] On the other hand, intrinsic flaws are observable in Geyer's and Schlesinger's recourse to European heritage for their articulation of U.S. citizenship. Athenian democracy, after all, was supported by a household system of slaves. Roman citizenship was spread through an empire, not a democracy. The ideals of the Reformation and the Enlightenment, though noteworthy, certainly in practice did not apply to women and, in turn, provided the justification for extending European civilization to the rest of the world through colonialism. In Schlesinger's case, by insisting, as does Geyer, that the ideals of political rights and cultural freedom are "European," he ends up practicing the very ethnocentrism that he chastises in the work of African centrists.[18] He plays right into the hands of non-Europeans who contend at human rights conferences that such "European" rights are irrelevant to their own cultures and countries—a position used to justify oppression.

In the U.S. context, the various civil rights movements of the past five decades and the more recent emphases on multiculturalism make plain that one cannot completely separate political citizenship from the cultural dispositions of the diverse peoples that comprise the country. Indeed, a merit system of achievement is a commendable goal, but as proponents of affirmative action stress, the prevailing systems of recruitment and advancement in political, economic, and social networks still favor European Americans. The universal citizenship Geyer cherishes is all too often achieved by disabling the cultural heritages of non-European groups. Although Schlesinger recognizes the contributions of the various civil rights movements to the American consensus, he does not seem to appreciate how these movements recast in cultural terms the long-standing ideals he so cherishes. At best he leaves us with "melting pot lite."

Geyer's argument gains cogency when she illustrates how the global economy is eroding people's capacity to feel connected to one another at a local or even national level. Geyer contrasts the ethos, felt by some past U.S. leaders, of civic responsibility to local, state, and national communities to the ethos of the new generation of power elite, the executives of multinational corporations who feel no particular loyalty to any nation. In particular, she notes, they continually hopscotch across the globe to mingle with their consociates, who are equally void of national ties. The rest of us become merely consumers of market goods and services, not citizens engaging our fellow citizens over the destiny and well-being of our communities.

She especially emphasizes how the market has undermined what De Tocqueville termed intermediate institutions—civic and voluntary associations lying between government and the market. These associations, from De Tocqueville's time to the present, have been the vehicles for shaping national citizenship. In like fashion, her indictment of the fact that U.S. elections are primarily characterized by money raising activities, television spots, and direct mail, bereft of citizen participation, is compelling. This eclipse of U.S. civil society, she adds, ultimately undermines the nation-state's capacity to provide a sense of stability in international politics.

However, Geyer's indictment of the deleterious consequences of the global economy for cultivating citizenship and democracy could have been made without her caricature of immigrants or multiculturalism. Had she titled her work "Citizens No More," it would have been much more compelling. Her critique of the challenges of immigration and multiculturalism, though, illustrates the prevailing divide of the assimilation-separatism debate: one either has radical individualism or tribalism, liberal democracy or cultural democracy, with the former in each case being preferable. Ultimately, she cannot envision a democratic citizenship fostered through the intersection of the plural cultures of the public world—an *unum* yes, but through *pluribus*.

In conclusion, contrary to Geyer and Schlesinger, the democratic citizenship they seek to promote cannot be accomplished simply by assimilating what they portray as ideals stemming from ancient Greece and Rome and Reformation/Enlightenment Europe. The challenge before us is to admit the intrinsic role that ethnic, linguistic, racial, and religious cultures play in political, economic, and social relationships and consider how the mixing rather than the extirpation of these cultures can lead to networks of collaboration, rather than of domination.

BETTER RED THAN DEAD?

Examples abound within the U.S. American experience on which one could focus to illustrate separatism: black nationalism—especially the Garveyites and the Black Muslims, the Chicano movement's celebration of the mythical Aztlán as the homeland of the Aztecs, religious separatism—as in the communal practices of the Amish or Hasidic Jews, and white supremacy groups that reject assimilation and miscegenation.[19] However, I will dwell upon the separatism articulated over the past four decades by the very provocative Native American scholar, Vine Deloria, Jr. His holistic and systematic articulation of his indigenous worldview poses a strong challenge to the Eurocentric casting of U.S. American identity by the Geyers and the Schlesingers. Given that mestizaje is historically steeped in the spiritualities and traditions of the indigenous peoples of the Americas, it will be crucial ultimately to distinguish the differences between mestizaje and Deloria's rendering of this heritage.

The case of Native Americans for separate political sovereignty and cultural rights is very strong, given they were the peoples of the Americas who were conquered by the European colonizers and their descendants. Canadian jurisprudence, for instance, has explored at great length the rights and procedures guaranteeing cultural survival of Canada's indigenous peoples. In chapter 5 I review the claim that such cultural rights are compatible with liberal democracy. Moving beyond this atonement motif, Deloria clearly articulates the tribal way of life as being rooted in a natural, land-based spirituality and makes a devastating critique of the individualistic and Reformation-derived conception of U.S. citizenship that Geyer and Schlesinger cherish.

Deloria's principal contention is that the Native American tribes are nature-based peoples whose spiritualities are deeply rooted in specific geographic places: "American Indians hold their lands—places—as having the highest possible meaning, and all their statements are made with this reference point in mind."[20] These sacred lands unite tribal members with their ancestors, for the latter upon their death do not go to another realm but remain spiritually in the same spatial location. The cultural and religious understanding of each tribe, Deloria shows, is intimately joined to its sacred lands.[21]

In terms of everyday community life of the tribe, this natural spirituality leads tribal members to focus more on their connection and responsibilities to the other members of the tribe, including the ancestors and those yet to be. According to Deloria, tribal ethics is always oriented toward the ongoing events and practices of the community rather than toward an individualistic sense of self. Ceremonies and symbols, thus, are "rooted in real events in specific locations."[22] This sense of ethical connection, in turn, extends to the birds, animals, and plants—"the 'other peoples' of creation."[23] In contrast to a materialistic appropriation of nature for human desires, the rhythms of sacred places reveal how creation's entities are vividly related: "We are not larger than nature and . . . we have responsibilities to the rest of the natural world that transcend our personal desires and wishes."[24]

Deloria contrastingly characterizes most U.S. Americans as a hybrid people whose spiritual origins are connected to Christianity's attempt to rise from the land-based Jewish tradition to provide a universal outlook that transcends place in an attempt to bind diverse peoples together. As opposed to a consonance with the rhythms of nature and a cyclical view of time, the focus of hybrid peoples on history, he contends, leads them to measure and control events in a chronological way.

In fact Deloria criticizes most of the Western heritages that Geyer sees as so constitutive of citizenship. The immortality of the soul in ancient Greek philosophy and the resurrection of the body in Christianity, he suggests, lead to a distancing of the person from the natural world.[25] Deloria argues that with the conjoining of Christianity to the Roman Empire, Christian spirituality was channeled into an ecclesiastical hierarchy that became preoccupied with maintaining political and economic power. The Reformation, in turn, created not Geyer's moral citizens but "self-centered individuals" whose quest for a religious universality will only lead to the "exploitation of land, people, and life itself" in the Americas.[26] Given the deep divide in Western thinking between the intellect and experience, and Christianity's abstract universal rendering of spirituality, Deloria, borrowing from Chief Luther Standing Bear of the Sioux tribe, maintains that the European American in the United States, even after four centuries, remains "a foreigner and an alien."[27]

What are the ethical consequences of this political and economic triumph of a hybrid people in the United States, according to Deloria? Besides the obvious elimination of most Native Americans, he contends that the results have been and will be the constant bickering and strife among Christian groups, the divorce of ethics from the actual practices of geographically situated peoples, the elimination of genuine community in the endeavor to unite diverse peoples and places, and the destruction of the natural environment. Exploitation of other human beings and of natural places accordingly is inevitable without the emphasis on land, ethnicity, and healing intrinsic to the spiritual worldview of Native American tribes.[28] Deloria stresses that place-based tribes foster a substantive community and holistically integrate the religious, political, economic, social, and intellectual spheres separated in the Western worldview.[29] Indeed, he finds commonality with the Amish and the Mormons insofar as these groups stress the nexus between the land, community, and spirituality.[30]

Ironically, Deloria comes to many of the same conclusions as Geyer and Schlesinger regarding the demise of substantive community life in which each person feels a strong responsibility to neighbor and to the common good. But whereas Geyer and Schlesinger connect the demise of citizenship to the tribalism encouraged by multiculturalism, Deloria contends that it is the detached, abstract individualism and universalism espoused in the Western tradition that prevents full personal development in rich place-based communities. Cultivating a sense of personal responsibility to the community, to nature, and to the transcendent accordingly can only ensue in tribes rooted in particular sacred lands. Consequently, from Deloria's vantage point, Geyer's bemoaning of the erosion of national citizenship by the global economy is inappropriate because that erosion is the logical culmination of the Western Christian ethos.

Although Deloria cogently articulates the normative sense of community and spirituality realized in specific land-based tribes, he does not discuss the conflicts that ensued among indigenous tribes in the Americas before and during the conquest by Europeans and European Americans. Nor does he engage with the fact that the Aztecs and Incas, in the preconquest Americas, had created civilizations whose scope was much more expansive than that of nomadic tribes and whose power and influence, in the preconquest Americas, resembled that of nation-states. His lack of concern for how "thick" communities can be suffocating to personal development is also disturbing. By "thick" I mean dense, tightly scripted substantive articulations of community life as opposed to a more "thin" sense of shared moral or political values, as in the procedural articulation of interest-group pluralism or the more universal morality that is shared among civilizations as suggested by Michael Walzer.[31]

Despite his evocative portrait of the land-based character of Native American spirituality, Deloria seems unable to discern that attempts to provide a sense of unity across cultures and places need not jeopardize the integrity of the heritages of particular peoples if such attempts ensue through a mutual lateral interpenetration of cultures. Deloria's separatism simply will not come to grips with examples of how indigenous, European, and other cultures have intersected and transformed one another over the past five centuries without culminating in an abstract and oppressive universalism uprooted from specific sacred lands. Separatist schemes, in their endeavor to avoid the tyranny of universalism at the expense of diversity, end up cultivating the anarchy of diverse cultural communities standing utterly distinct from each other.

In conclusion, Geyer and Schlesinger, on the one hand, and Deloria, on the other, represent the polarities of the *unum-pluribus* divide. Whereas the former stress how the radical individualism and democratic universalism of the United States is being undermined by growing diverse cultural loyalties, the latter insists that the United States is a history of how particular land-based communities have been overwhelmed, if not exterminated, by a misbegotten hybrid universal spirituality. Neither scheme—assimilation nor separatism—entertains the notion that multiple cultural hertitages can shape and be integral to both person and community identities. Thus, neither pole of this divide, is capable of articulating a unity-in-diversity that moves beyond the possessive scripting of identity. If the citizenship celebrated by *unum* renders cultural identities as divisive to one's national identity, the "thick" tribalism of *pluribus* abandons any hope for a substantive connection between persons, cultures, or peoples beyond parochial locales.

ARE WE FATED TO JIHAD V. MCWORLD?

On the international scale, Benjamin Barber has quite aptly characterized the opposition between separatism and assimilation as "Jihad *v.* McWorld."[32] Barber's analysis provides a dense description of these two prevailing alternatives for approaching multicultural relations. At the same time, his call for a rejuvenation of a civic nation-state illustrates what is wrong in some ongoing attempts to move beyond *unum* v. *pluribus*: in reaction to the rise of cultural arguments they extract any consideration of culture from their articulation of democracy.

"McWorld" is the spread of the global economy. According to Barber the transgressing of national boundaries by contemporary "communications, information, entertainment, and commerce" is melding all nation-states "into one homogeneous global theme park."[33] But being universal and homogeneous is not necessarily being democratic, for in McWorld the responsibilities of the citizen are replaced by the wants and needs of mere consumers.

"Jihad," in reaction to this economic globalization, emphasizes narrow particular cultures, tribes, and religions that reject any form of international economic interdependence or modern advances in technology that bring diverse peoples together. In particular Barber examines the ethnic tensions that have arisen in Western Europe, along the Pacific Rim, in the transitional democracies of Eastern Europe, and in religious fundamental-ism, especially as exemplified in certain strains of Islam. As opposed to the civil plurality of democracy or the myriad choices of capitalistic McWorld, jihad promises a return to a "depluralized, monocultural, unskepticized, reenenchanted" world.[34]

Overall, as Barber argues, neither McWorld's emphasis on the consumer nor jihad's stress on tribal or sectarian identities encourages citizens who can engage deliberatively in democracy:

> Jihad pursues a bloody politics of identity and McWorld a bloodless economics of profit. Belonging by default to McWorld, everyone is a consumer; seeking a repository for identity, everyone belongs to the same tribe. But no one is a citizen. Without citizens, how can there be democracy?[35]

Indeed, though opposites on the surface, Barber insists that McWorld and jihad mutually undermine democratic civil society and its institutions in nation-states.[36]

For Barber, borrowing from John Dewey, democracy is not just a type of government but "a way of life."[37] The citizen in a democracy is not just someone who expresses consumer preferences or is preoccupied with the particulars of personal identity, but can engage in rational discourse and debate with other citizens in the public realm. Civil society—the place of citizens—is a set of mediating institutions and voluntary associations that temper the excesses of governments and markets. Both McWorld and jihad erode this vital civil society.

Barber particularly rejects the notion in vogue these days that democ-racy and capitalism—especially of a neoliberal variety—are the same. The marketplace, albeit important, he contends, cannot ensure the following four responsibilities of democracy:

(1) to educate citizens how to use markets wisely and correct the excesses of markets;
(2) to engender moral values and a common substantive culture besides consumerism;
(3) to create institutions and policies that prevent both anarchy and monopoly;
(4) to engender an articulation of the common good that tempers "the inadvertent social consequences of individual choosing."[38]

At the same time, vis-à-vis fundamentalist political states, the contribution of a democratic civil society, he maintains, is its commitment to the equality of human beings and a broad scope of individual liberty. A democracy is an open community in which inclusiveness is a virtue and personal identity is not too narrowly circumscribed by the state.

Overall, Barber wants to resuscitate the idea of a public of deliberative citizens as opposed to McWorld's "politics of commodity" and jihad's "politics of resentment."[39] Although democracy in one form or another has been cultivated in some modern nation-states over the past three to four centuries, in view of the expanse of the global economy Barber quite rightly concludes that we need to cultivate a transnational civil society that can serve as a foundation for a transnational democratic government.[40]

Barber's persuasive critique of the eclipsing of democratic citizenship and civil society by McWorld and jihad on a global level parallels the contrast that I have been drawing between the alternatives of assimilation and separatism for dealing with multicultural relations in the United States. Neither McWorld or assimilation, on the one hand, nor jihad or separatism, on the other, is capable of envisioning a democracy in which personal liberty and communal well-being are realized through the interaction of diverse cultures with one another in an atmosphere of mutuality. In fact the McWorld *v.* jihad and assimilation *v.* separatism frameworks reduce political identity to either a radical materialistic individualism that eschews cultural backgrounds—"the universalism of the profit motive"—or a strong sense of community at the expense of personal freedom and diverse cultural groups—"the parochialism of ethnic identity."[41]

Barber's argument on the global level parallels much of Geyer's perspective regarding the demise of citizenship in the United States. Like Geyer, Barber traces the rise of democratic civil society and government to developments in Western Europe in the seventeenth and eighteenth centuries that precede the rise of capitalism. Although there is a link between democracy and capitalism, both Barber and Geyer delineate crucial differences between democracy and capitalism regarding political deliberation and orientation toward the common good. Furthermore, Barber and Geyer both raise crucial concerns regarding the threats posed by both the global economy and by cultural parochialism to cultivating citizenship and democracy.

Barber's critique, though, is stronger than Geyer's on two counts. First, whereas Barber presents jihad as a reaction to McWorld and never loses sight of the fact that the global economy is the main threat to democracy, Geyer, in a jingoistic fashion, becomes fixated on the threats posed by multiculturalism. Second, Barber more carefully articulates how civil society and the democratic way of life is distinct from government and market activities. Whereas Geyer gets mired in what is wrong with contemporary U.S. immigration policies and practices, Barber throughout his text gives ample illustrations of the type of institutions and practices that he sees as representative of democratic citizenship. Barber's presentation recasts much of Geyer's argument in a positive vein.

Nevertheless, as much as Barber's argument is more compelling than Geyer's, it retains an element of assimilation reminiscent of Geyer's and Schlesinger's positions. In striving to avoid the parochialism of jihad, Barber's articulation of citizenship and civil society does not admit that cultural identities have an important part to play in the shaping of personal civic participation and the cultivation of a substantive common good. For Barber, culture, especially of the ethnic, linguistic, racial, and religious varieties, is not something constitutive of citizens. In this regard the persona of the citizen in Barber's account resembles more the universal abstract individual of the marketplace than the tightly scripted cultural identity of tribal communities.

Deloria's vibrant description of community life and the sense of the tribal member's responsibility to it, however, does not just disappear by rendering it as a vestige of jihad. Barber never takes up the challenge posed by Deloria that the ethos of community fostered in tribal relations is not necessarily antithetical to the norms of civil participation and the pursuit of the common good emphasized by Barber. But Barber fails to appreciate Deloria's evocation of the depth and impact of communal norms upon tribal members, even should they eventually choose to leave the tribe. Barber's attempt to move beyond jihad and McWorld through a civic democracy still anesthetizes culture, much in the way the values of religious traditions are dismissed by some political theorists as lacking merit for the deliberations of liberal democracies. Barber's articulation of an acultural democracy may be preferable to the anti-cultural diatribes of Geyer or Schlesinger, but it does not deal substantively with the multicultural relations that increasingly comprise contemporary democracies.

All is not lost. One can move beyond the either/ors presented by assimilation *v.* separatism and McWorld *v.* jihad by engaging personal and cultural identity not as a possession but as a dynamic, ongoing set of relations steeped in intersubjectivity and entailing engagement, not disparagement of the 'other.' Geyer's, Schlesinger's, and Barber's call for a renewal of democratic citizenship is appropriate, but their respective frameworks do not capture and develop how multiple cultures can intersect to shape strong personal and community identities. Although Deloria's indictment of the Western tradition is well taken, his tribal alternative is too limited in its envisioning of cultural hermeneutics. The next section turns to a political theory that can uncover and develop the relational quality of multiculturism.

Multicultural Relations through Unity-in-Diversity

Instead of setting both community and individuality, on the one hand, and assimilation and separatism, on the other, in opposition to each other, we need to articulate a pluralism in which the common good is not simply the net outcome of competing interest-group preferences, but a set of normative practices continually being recast through the interactions among the diverse cultural groups of the United States. Rather than just focusing on procedural access of interest groups to the political system and on the degree to which fair and equitable rules serve such groups in the competition for government attention, I am arguing that a substantive sense of community can emerge through a democratic integration—not assimilation or separation—of diverse cultures. This substantive pluralism articulates a unity-in-diversity in which (1) a democratic community is constituted and reinvigorated through—not in spite of—the intersections of diverse cultures and (2) the distinctiveness of each culture is accented through—not apart from—this nexus of cultures.

THE PRIMACY OF INTERSUBJECTIVITY
IN HUMAN RELATIONS

My articulation of unity-in-diversity is heavily indebted to the rendering of reality in phenomenology and hermeneutics. Phenomenology moves beyond the dichotomy between the subject and the object established in modern philosophy by Descartes. Instead of identifying reality either as the projection of a subjective *cogito* (ego) or conversely as "the outside world" separate from the subject, phenomenology accents one's 'consciousness-of' the world: reality is constituted through the entwining of subject and object.

This emphasis on the 'consciousness-of' things leads to the centrality of interpretation in terms of understanding reality. Hermeneutics, especially as articulated by Hans-Georg Gadamer, focuses on the "dialogical encounter" between the interpreter and the text.[42] One engages a text through one's 'consciousness-of' it. In the act of interpretation, one not only becomes open to the tradition informing a text, but one also realizes the "prejudices" that inform one's 'consciousness-of' the text. These "prejudices" are not to be understood in the conventional sense of stubborn outlooks that lead people to discriminate against others—especially in terms of ethnic, racial, and religious identities—but, according to Gadamer, as "fore-projects" and "fore-conceptions" of one's outlook that are challenged by the freshness of the text: "interpretation begins with fore-conceptions that are replaced by more suitable ones."[43] Hermeneutics is not a matter of revealing past original meanings, but, as Gary Madison puts it, a depiction of "the possible senses that a text has for us today, what it says to us, here and now."[44]

Moving beyond texts to human encounters, Gadamer stresses that hermeneutical interpretation and understanding entail remaining "open to the meaning of the other person."[45] Consequently, the encounter with the 'other' entails a "fusion of horizons" between the present and the past as well as between the prejudices that inform one's 'consciousness-of' the world as well as the historical background informing the outlook of the 'other.'[46] As Paul Thiele explains, this hermeneutical fusion enables a "sufficient level of understanding such that meaningful conversations can take place" between distinct persons or outlooks.[47] One does not achieve complete understanding between diverse perspectives nor is one fated to utter incomprehensibility of other outlooks, but a common ground of understanding continues to grow as one persistently tests one's prejudices against those of others. This intersubjective character of the world—the intersecting of our 'consciousnesses-of' the world through language—simultaneously discloses what diverse persons share in common as well as their personal distinctiveness: "Being a *linguistic* affair, understanding is perforce a cultural, public, intersubjective sort of thing."[48]

Hannah Arendt's political theory especially communicates the inter-subjective and public character of understanding, as rendered by phenomenology and hermeneutics. In particular she urges the primacy of a public life that moves beyond either/ors such as the individual *v.* community or assimilation *v.* separatism. Arendt stresses both the plurality and equality that characterizes the political world. By *plurality* Arendt means that our personal distinctiveness emerges through our speeches and deeds in the company of other people.[49] By *equality* she means that despite our differences we all share in the capacity for mutual communication.

As opposed to a master who rules slaves in a household, for Arendt political interaction is characterized by the absence of sovereign relationships; domination in any form is antithetical to the freedom constituted between citizens in the public realm. As opposed to political theories that stress solely the pursuit of private interests or, conversely, the imposition of a collective good, for Arendt the mutual engagement between citizens discloses the public space simultaneously binding us together and distinguishing us one from another.[50] This intangible "in-between" renders politics as a mutual, intersubjective activity instead of as a conflict between disembodied isolated egos.[51] Consequently, political power is not a possession to be superimposed on others but rather is a consensus established through lateral, not hierarchical, relationships. Indeed, the distinct identity of each person and that of the community itself are realized through the interaction of citizens in the public realm. Ultimately, this pursuit of a public, not private, happiness is the basis for both human freedom and responsibility.[52]

Arendt's political theory is quite relevant to articulating unity-in-diversity. Her elucidation of the human condition of plurality fits congenially with the critique, made in the "politics of difference," of so-called "objectivities" that in a hegemonic fashion superimpose one view of reality over all others. By the same token, Arendt's stress on the intersubjective character of politics provides a heterogeneous articulation of community in contrast to those critics—from a gender, racial/ethnic, or sexual-preference standpoint—whose conclusions culminate in separatism and prove no more inclusive than the previous hegemonies masquerading as communities. Consequently, in our public actions and discourses, we can pursue and realize a heterogeneous community in which differences are engaged and embraced rather than extinguished.

Applying Arendt's articulation of plurality and equality to the relationship between diverse cultures, especially in terms of realizing a substantive sense of community, presents two difficulties. First, Arendt focuses on the intersubjective ties between diverse persons, not diverse cultures. That fact alone would lead Geyer, for instance, to invoke Arendt in a defense of political citizenship and community consonant with Geyer's radical individualism, in which the person transcends the fetters of creed and clan through liberal democracy.

Second, and more crucially, Arendt takes for granted that the citizens engaging one another in the public space are actually equal. Indeed, Arendt is notorious for relegating economics to pre-political phenomena, when in fact economic status, educational achievement, and related forms of socialization are integral to determining who has preexisting advantages in public debate. Further, she presumes that equality reigns among the interlocutors, when in fact factors may exist that undemocratically enable some of the interlocutors to dominate others.[53] Rather than to presume such equality, the challenge is to rid the "web of human relationships"[54] of forms of domination preventing a genuine democratic interchange between equals from ensuing. In this context the challenges posed to the U.S. political consensus by marginalized cultural groups over the past four decades have merit. Contrary to Geyer's fear that we are "Americans No More," these challenges make clear that we still need to realize a genuine democratic discourse of citizens.

THE LATERAL BASIS OF MULTICULTURAL INTERACTION

Other insights from phenomenology and hermeneutics offer direction on how to recast Arendt's articulation of the intersubjective "web of human relationships" in the context of multiculturalism. After all, diverse cultures and languages ensue through the same hermeneutical medium of communication and understanding described above in disparate ways by Gadamer and Arendt. Rather than being a limit on communication or a fragmentation of reason, such diversity gives us access to "the infinite realm of possible expression."[55] In particular a hermeneutical phenomenology stresses that the ontological plurality that characterizes multicultural relations rejects both philosophical absolutism and relativism and, by extension, assimilation and separatism.[56] Six principal points amplify this substantive pluralism.

First, in contrast to the assimilationist's claim that culture is an objective package identifiable from a distance and fully accessible to anyone choosing to be part of it, culture is a set of shared meanings whose content is revisited and revised daily through the interactions of human beings. In contrast to the positivist's disposition to analyzing cultures from an 'objective' distance, we should engage culture as a "system of symbols."[57] This engagement enables us to speak of "totalities or articulated wholes of varying richness" in which one is not superior to the other.[58] Society or culture, thereby, is "a many-faceted reality amenable to more than one interpretation."[59]

Second, in contrast to separatism's claim that particular cultures are so unique that they are inaccessible to other cultures, let alone to a universal social science, understanding can successfully ensue between distinct cultures, as long as we do not expect perfect translation. A semiotic concept of culture, as Clifford Geertz puts it, brings "us into touch with the lives of strangers."[60] Even if a universal standard of culture proves elusive, we can still make sense of the webs of human experience that are shared across cultures. Such an interpretive anthropology thinks not *"about"* 'others,' but *"with* them."[61] As Geertz puts it, the interchange with the 'other' makes "available to us the answers that others, guarding other sheep in other valleys, have given, and thus to include them in the consultable record of what man has said."[62]

Third, the pursuit of hermeneutical understanding offers a basis for encountering one's self and culture through the engagement with the 'other.' Rather than contending like separatists that the identity of a particular culture is so unique that it cannot possibly be shared or translated to another, engaging the 'other' enables one to recognize one's own identity: "By means of the dialogical encounter with the other, [a self] comes to a greater realization (in the concrete sense of the term) of itself."[63] This creative interchange does not culminate in assimilation; rather, one finds previously undiscovered riches in one's own perspective.[64]

Fourth, hermeneutical understanding between cultures realizes the *lateral* dimension of truth in contrast to the abstract, univocal truth of assimilation or the particular truth scripted by each culture in separatism.[65] Geertz, for instance, seeks within cultural patterns "the defining elements of a human existence which although not constant in expression, are yet distinctive in character."[66] He adds that what we should be looking for, then, is the "systematic relationships among diverse phenomena, not for substantive identities among similar ones."[67] Continuing this hermeneutical exposition, he concludes: "It is thus not truth that varies with social, psychological, and cultural contexts but the symbols we construct in our unequally effective attempts to grasp it."[68] Truth cannot be imposed universally, nor can particular cultures be so distinct as to preclude the pursuit of truth. Engagement and mutual transformation between cultures ensues in a lateral fashion.

Fifth, once truth is viewed not in a universal or particular but in a lateral fashion, then it is possible, according to Merleau-Ponty, to have a cultural interchange in which cultural frontiers are erased and a world civilization emerges.[69] This articulation of lateral truth cuts between, on the one hand, the conception of modern rationality as uniform idea and, on the other hand, deconstructions of rationality that lead to relativism and undecidability.[70] Whatever universality culture may contain, it is only realized and sustained through what Paul Ricoeur terms an authentic dialogue, not through "some vague and inconsistent syncretism."[71]

Sixth and finally, contingency, ambiguity, and uncertainty remain integral parts of the human condition. Quite in contradiction to the assimilationist's assumption of "one best way" for pursuing cultural relations that newcomers or outsiders to the community must adopt, multiple characterizations of the same human experience abound: "Reality itself is thoroughly pluralistic."[72] This does not mean that everything is relative and that therefore no common ground can be defined between distinct cultures. To contend that each culture should remain autonomous is to abandon reason for nihilism. To the contrary, not only can cultures be translated into each other, but this fertile interchange transforms and sustains each participating culture.

Thus, in contrast to the overbearing uniformity of assimilation and the divisive parochialism of separatism, hermeneutical phenomenology's articulation of unity-in-diversity suggests that fruitful multicultural relations will never culminate in either complete unanimity or an utter breakdown of interchange. At the same time, communication is possible and grows with attentiveness to what Gadamer terms "the inner infinity of the dialogue that is in progress between every speaker and his partner."[73] Through recognizing the pluralistic character of human interaction, this unity-in-diversity offers the hope that a manifold set of possibilities lies ahead for multicultural relations.[74] Precisely because we are "inescapably acting and narrating beings,"[75] we have the wherewithal to find in our respective cultures the resources for dealing with other cultures.

THE POSTMODERN JUXTAPOSITION OF MULTIPLE IDENTITIES

Many of the possibilities of articulating an ontological plurality when dealing with multicultural relations have also been advanced in postmodern, poststructuralist, and deconstructionist renderings of personal identity. Although there may be as many postmodernisms as there are postmodernists, the principal figures of this disparate movement, Derrida and Foucault, have made social science and political theory, in particular, come to grips with "the social construction of identity."[76]

In contrast to the highly autonomous and resolute self of modernism, postmodern perspectives articulate that our "selves" are a constellation of social influences apart from whether economic, political, or social institutions are dominating us in an external sense. In contrast to the tyrant who lords over us, postmodern theorists focus on how our personal identities are inscribed by the "systematized groups of mores, that permeate society and channel its activities."[77] In particular, postmodern thinkers are particularly critical of metanarratives—the especially modern endeavor to construct universal philosophies of history in which society is seen "as a coherent totality with a fixed or stable 'subject.'"[78] Although postmodern thinkers debunk the autonomous power and agency of the modern self, they contend that the creative power of the mores and social structures that inscribe personal identity provides a basis for resistance to particular hegemonies of domination. Power is thus not just a matter of one person or group subduing another, as in the master-slave relationship, but a capacity to act in concert together as Arendt would phrase it.

Postmodern resistance to metanarratives makes clear that individuals, groups, and cultures are characterized by a multiplicity of identities. Consequently, personal and group identity has a fluid, not static, character—a persistent combining and coping with multiple outlooks. As opposed to the static universalism of assimilation and the static particularism of separatism, postmodernism's articulation of the relational character of identity provokes us to grope with the agonal tension between unity—what we share in common with others—and difference—the wide chasms thwarting mutual understanding. To rush too quickly to a possessive scripting of multiculturalism, either as superimposed common identity or as regimented preservation of particular identities, denies how complex and variegated are the relations within and between cultures. At the very least, post-modernism provides a language useful when wrestling with the simultaneous identities that define individuals and cultural groups.

There are many ties between a hermeneutical phenomenology and postmodernism. Both stand in opposition to the objectivist rendering of the world by modern scientific rationality, which dates back to Descartes. Both, consequently, challenge the autonomous sense of self accented in modern philosophy. Phenomenology's stress on the intersubjective character of reality also has some parallels to the juxtaposition of multiple identities and the contest between domination and resistance within power relationships accented by postmodernism.

If there is a difference between hermeneutical phenomenology and postmodernism, it is that phenomenology has a great deal more confidence in the capacity of human beings, in view of their differences, to realize a sense of universality through rational dialogue. According to Merleau-Ponty, as Gary Madison points out, "Human beings are rational . . . because of the fact that, despite all the differences which set them apart, they can still, if they make the effort, communicate with and understand one another."[79] Phenomenology, for Merleau-Ponty, may challenge the Cartesian rendering of reality and in turn be suspicious of metanarratives, but it does not entail the rejection of reason per se nor the reduction of reason to the mere cultural bias of the Western European tradition.[80]

In moving beyond Descartes, phenomenology does not abandon the significance of the self in interpretation and understanding to the degree we see in postmodernism—another crucial distinction. In contrast to Derrida's stress on "free-floating" antimetaphysical interpretations, Gary Madison maintains, for Gadamer, that "understanding is inseparable from *application*, i.e., from the reading's subject reaction to and appropriation of the text."[81] In its critique of metanarratives, phenomenology stresses the particular context that particular interpreters encounter in engaging texts; understanding is not just an anchor-less form of play.[82] Rather than concluding that the desubjectivized subject leads understanding to culminate in undecidability, phenomenology's recognition of the situated self emphasizes the inexhaustible character of understanding: "In contrast to deconstruction," says Madison, "hermeneutics maintains that there is always the possibility of meaning, but in contrast to logocentrism, it maintains that it is never possible to arrive at a final meeting."[83] Between both transcendental reductionism and deconstructive relativism, phenomenology's articulation of the intersubjective character of the relationship of the subject and the world reveals a knowledge "sure and stable enough to allow for a viable and enduring *human* community."[84]

Even though distinguishing between postmodernism's emphasis on undecidability versus phenomenology's accent on inexhaustibility puts distance between Derrida and Gadamer, Fred Dallmayr suggests that this chasm is overstated. Subsequent to Gadamer's *Truth and Method* (1960), the influence of the later work of Martin Heidegger, French poststucturalism, and the poetry of Paul Celan lead Gadamer to articulate hermeneutics in a way coming closer to Derrida's articulation of interpretation.[85] Conversely, Dallmayr illustrates how Derrida's position has come closer to phenomenology's stress on understanding's inexhaustibility.

Derrida had long criticized Gadamer's hermeneutics for containing an idealist or metaphysical notion of correctness, especially in the latter's articulation of understanding as a fusion of horizons. Conceding the value of Derrida's articulation of *différance,* the difference within identity, Gadamer clarifies that the fusion of horizons is not "an abiding or identifiable 'oneness,'" but rather a persistent interrogation in the manner of the Socratic dialogue that wrestles with the reality that "difference exists within identity; otherwise, identity would not be identity."[86] By the same token, Derrida in *The Other Heading: Reflection on Today's Europe* articulates understanding, according to Dallmayr, as a "reciprocal happening or disclosure."[87] The nexus of identity and difference is, in Derrida's terms "to be able to take the form of a subject only in the non-identity to itself or, if you prefer, only in the difference *with itself (avec soi)*."[88]

Hwa Yol Jung's critique of Foucault from the standpoint of Merleau-Ponty's phenomenology has some parallels to Madison's earlier critique of Derrida from the standpoint of Gadamer's hermeneutics. If Gadamer's hermeneutics supposedly had idealist tendencies, Foucault, especially in *The Archaeology of Knowledge,* insists that the sovereignty of consciousness is intrinsically linked to the notion of historical continuity. Postmodernism, for Foucault, is to move beyond the trappings of subjectivity in the articulation of power and resistance.[89]

However, Merleau-Ponty's articulation of the "instituting subject" as opposed to "constituting subject" suggests a self whose persona is not one of sovereignty but is continually being mediated in the complex ambiguity of identity and difference, self and others, and interpreter and text underscored by Gadamer and Derrida:

> If the subject were taken not as a constituting but as an instituting subject, it might be understood that the subject does not exist instantaneously and that the other person does not exist simply as a negative of myself. What I have begun at certain decisive moments would exist neither far off in the past as an objective memory nor be present like a memory revived, but really between the two as a field of my becoming during that period. Likewise my relation to another person would not be reducible to a disjunction: an instituting subject could co-exist with another because the one instituted is not the immediate reflection of the activity of the former and can be regained by himself or by others without involving anything like a total recreation. Thus the instituted subject exists between others and myself, between me and myself, like a hinge, the consequence and guarantee of our belonging to a common world.[90]

As elaborated by Jung, this articulation of the "instituting" as opposed to the "constituting subject" amplifies phenomenology's articulation of the primacy of intersubjectivity in three ways:

- It neither over-determines nor under-determines the relation between the self and the other.

- It offers a prudent balance between the relationship of innovation and tradition.
- It offers an articulation of plurality as a simultaneous presence of distinction and equality.[91]

If Gadamer offers "the hermeneutical notion of *inexhaustibility*" in contrast to deconstruction's emphasis on "undecidability,"[92] Merleau-Ponty's elucidation of the instituting subject stands in contrast to Foucault's inability to come to grips with the dynamic of power and resistance in terms of intersubjectivity. Rather than articulating the subject as a possessive entity apart from a phenomenal world of objects, phenomenology constructs a "social ontology" in which the subject is fundamentally relational.[93]

One might wonder what this debate between phenomenology, on the one hand, and Foucault's poststructuralism and Derrida's postmodernism, on the other, has to do with multiculturalism. But as Dallmayr points out, Gadamer's and Derrida's respective reflections on particularity and plurality ultimately address both the multiple cultures that comprise Europe and the relationship between Europe and other regions of the world in the postcolonial era. The crux of such encounters, according to Gadamer,

> is the future of Europe and the significance of the humanities for the future role of Europe in the world. The central issue is no longer Europe alone, but the cultural framework produced by the global economy and the world-wide network of communications—and thus the prospect of cultural multiplicity or diversity as emblem of the emerging civilization on our planet.[94]

In consonant fashion, Derrida emphasizes:

> It is necessary *(il faut)* to make ourselves the guardians of an idea of Europe, of a difference of Europe, *but* of a Europe that consists precisely in not closing itself off in its own identity and in advancing itself in an exemplary way toward what is not, toward the other heading or the heading of the other, indeed—and this is perhaps something else altogether—toward the other *of* the heading, which would be the beyond of this modern tradition, another border structure, another shore.[95]

In their respective passages, both Gadamer and Derrida articulate the mutual engagement of cultures as a set of intersubjective relations that eschews the objectivist and relativist alternatives of assimilation and separatism. Moreover, Gadamer's reflections, as Dallmayr points out, also capture the tension between economic global development and the values and traditions of particular life-worlds, reminiscent of Barber's distinction between McWorld and jihad. But unlike Barber's rendering of this tension, Gadamer and Derrida show how any articulation of civil societies and political communities, both national and international, in the postmodern world, can only ensue through the ongoing crossing of borders both within and between cultures.

In this section I have reviewed phenomenology's connection to many of the key themes of postmodernism. As an alternative to the impasse of *unum* v. *pluribus*, postmodernism insists that individuals, groups, and cultures are comprised of multiple identities and that the locus of intersection between these identities is constantly shifting. However, when the postmodern critique of foundations gets mired in interpretative indeterminacy or looks askance on the intersubjective basis of reality, then phenomenology, as articulated by Arendt, Gadamer, and Merleau-Ponty, provides the more cogent expression of the notion of unity-in-diversity. In Gadamer's eloquent words:

> The human solidarity that I envision is not a global uniformity but unity in diversity. We must learn to appreciate and tolerate pluralities, multiplicities, cultural differences. . . . Unity in diversity, and *not* uniformity or hegemony—that is the heritage of Europe. Such unity-in-diversity has to be extended to the whole world—to include Japan, China, India, and also Muslim cultures. Every culture, every people has something distinctive to offer for the solidarity and welfare of humanity.[96]

At the same time, to realize genuinely what Merleau-Ponty has stressed as a lateral truth across cultures, we have to move beyond the Eurocentrism that even characterizes Gadamer's vision.

Phenomenology's exegesis of intersubjectivity and lateral communication articulates a relational basis for cross-cultural engagement, in contrast to the possessive character of both the universal civic identity of assimilation or the particular cultural identities of separatism. In both of the latter cases, identity is too tightly scripted. National identity and political citizenship, as conveyed by Geyer, disavow the relevance of cultural traditions and risk inflation of a particular cultural tradition—in her case the European Reformation/Enlightenment tradition—into a prescribed universal. Conversely, when cultural groups motivated by separatism reduce civil rights initiatives from opportunities for engaging in constructive discourse with other cultures to opportunities for seizing what is "rightfully theirs," then politics becomes a cacophony of atomized cultural groups. In the end the assimilationist and separatist renderings of identity are reverse reflections of each other: if assimilationists draw too narrow a portrait of national identity, the rising reflection of separatist cultural enclaves contemptuous of a national identity that excludes them should surprise no one.

Instead, the relational characterization of cultural identity drawn by phenomenology and hermeneutics insists that the fulfillment of each person and the "public happiness" of the community are both served by enabling all cultural groups to engage each other in a lateral—albeit sometime tempestuous—democratic set of relations. Indeed, the benefits of pursuing unity-in-diversity accrue not just to previously excluded groups, but to the previously dominant group(s) as well as to the common good. The dismantling of obstacles that deter full political participation enables a much wider diversity of gifts to enrich the community.

Consequently, pursuing a unity-in-diversity is not just a matter of guaranteeing civil rights or overcoming discrimination for the sake of the individuals or groups wronged, but a commitment to realizing a substantive democratic community. Ensuring that diverse cultural communities have equal access to decision-making forums should be pursued, not just for each group's interests in a possessive and procedural sense but for the sake of the public interest that sustains political life.

Effecting Unity-in-Diversity in the U.S. Cultural Context

But how does one effect this inclusive yet agonal engagement of unity-in-diversity in the cultural context of the United States? The rising voices of previously marginalized groups and new migrant and immigrant groups in the United States speak to issues that go deeper than the surface level of public policies affecting their communities. They contend that if the discourse shaping the U.S. political consensus is to be genuinely democratic, then all represented by those rising voices need to be equal partners at the table, not having to abandon their heritages as a condition of gaining a seat.

REEXAMINING THE "PREMISES" OF U.S. AMERICAN POLITICAL CULTURE

Indeed, too many scholarly commentaries on multiculturalism, even if sympathetic, still speak of non-European cultural heritages as geographically distant to the United States. In turn, commentators such as Geyer or Schlesinger take the more hostile posture that such alternative cultures constitute a threat to the U.S. identity. To the contrary, these so-called alien cultures are part and parcel of the U.S. experience. As Susan Wolf argues, to recognize multiple cultures in U.S. cultural, educational, and political discourses is not just a matter of putting the great works of African and Asian culture on a par with European and European American works but to acknowledge that the United States is a multicultural country; African, Asian, and Native American cultures are not somewhere out there to be discovered and incorporated but rather are an unrecognized "part of our culture."[97]

U.S. culture is an ongoing, open-ended set of practices forever being renegotiated between its long-standing and nascent members. As Bharati Mukherjee puts the matter, immigrants "are creating American culture, daily. It is not something static. But through our art, and through the dangerous, improvised lives that we have to lead, we are creating a new American culture."[98] In the same vein, even Schlesinger acknowledges that "the American identity will never be fixed and final; it will always be in the making."[99]

No doubt Mukherjee's and Schlesinger's sentiments could be interpreted as mere restatements of Geyer's radical individualist casting of citizenship. Still, when we, any of us, try to shed our cultural pasts in their entirety, these heritages continue to resurface in how we deal with other people or things. Conversely, our ongoing engagement with other cultures transforms how we will proceed in the future. In light of phenomenology's rendering of culture—outlined in the previous section—U.S. culture is not a tabula rasa but is constituted through the hermeneutical interchange of its cultures. Being U.S. American is neither to adopt a uniform static identity nor to script one's identity according to the dictates of any single unamalgamated group. Instead, it is to grasp how the values and standards of one's perspective and that of the political consensus are continually recast through the contributions of past, present, and future cultural groups.

What U.S. political discourses might lead us past Eurocentrism to realize a democratic unity-in-diversity? Although many scholars turn to critical theory and postmodern perspectives, Robert Bellah and his consociates in *Habits of the Heart* and *The Good Society* draw upon alternative U.S. discourses to Lockean individualism—the civic republican and Biblical covenant traditions—to rekindle communitarianism.[100] To his credit Bellah grasps that political change and transformation by peaceful means occur through terms congenial to and heartfelt by the members of the body politic; therefore, any successful, peaceful recasting of U.S. political culture must ensue from symbols and ideals indigenous to U.S. history and politics.

However, apart from recognizing via Murray that the U.S. political consensus can no longer be centered in the white Anglo-Saxon Protestant heritage, Bellah's alternative discourses are not broad enough to capture Wolf's insight that non-European heritages are not from some distant foreign land but part and parcel of the U.S. experience. Bellah's civic-republican and Biblical-covenant alternatives to Lockean individualism still do not challenge the conventional rendering of the U.S. experience as an east-coast to west-coast expansion—the spread of primarily European Americans across the continent. Although the roots of the civic-republican and Biblical-covenant traditions clearly reach back beyond the Reformation/Enlightenment period, their strongest growth is firmly embedded in the ideals of that period, as Geyer successfully shows. Even though Bellah recognizes the ongoing transformation of U.S. political culture by multiculturalism, the compass of U.S. cultural traditions in his communitarian discourses is much too narrow to effect a unity-in-diversity.

The United States is not just the result of a westward expansion of European Americans across the countryside from Jamestown and Plymouth Rock to Silicon Valley. First, there are also the tribal cultures of the indigenous peoples who previously populated these lands. Second, there is the blight of slavery and the consequent subordination but not obliteration of African traditions in African American history. Third, there are the eastward migrations from Asian and Pacific Rim counties to the United States, starting in the nineteenth century, but especially accelerating since 1965. Finally, since 1492 but especially since 1848, there are the multiple waves of Latinos who moved northward into what is now the United States. Bellah's discourses do not engage these other U.S. legacies.

Those voices that have articulated the political symbols and practices leading to the European American casting of U.S. political culture are "the premise keepers."[101] To deal effectively and democratically with the multiple cultures comprising the United States, one needs to recast U.S. political culture along alternative directions that have been unfolding in some cases for at least five centuries. Following the cue, rather than the content of Bellah's work, we can effectively draw upon other symbols and ideals that are intrinsic to the U.S. heritage to move beyond the *unum-pluribus* divide.

PROJECTING A MESTIZO DEMOCRACY

In particular, the experience of mestizaje in the U.S. Southwest—the lateral mixing of especially European American, indigenous, and Latino cultures in a way distinct from "the melting pot"—offers a vivid alternative to Bellah's Eurocentric political discourses. Like Bellah's discourses, the cultural values of mestizaje are concrete and "heartfelt"—no need for abstract deliberations on justice or consensus in the manner of John Rawls or Jürgen Habermas. But unlike Bellah's discourses, mestizaje is much more inclusive of the non-European heritages that Wolf rightly argues are integral to the U.S. experience. Indeed, mestizaje combines Deloria's concern for the dignity of indigenous cultures with Geyer's and Schlesinger's emphasis on the European American heritage, without leading either to separatism or assimilation.

Therefore, beyond its experiential legacy in U.S. history, mestizaje conceptually moves multicultural relations in the United States beyond the *unum-pluribus* divide by asserting that multiple cultures can intersect and transform one another in a way that does not culminate in the privileging of one culture over all others. Even though, for instance, African American and Asian American cultures have historically been on the periphery of the mestizaje of the U.S. Southwest, the inclusive conceptual ethos of mestizaje envisions a genuine unity-in-diversity composed of the increasing contributions of U.S. Americans, not just from Latin America, but from Asia, Africa, and every imaginable region of the globe. To petrify mestizaje as *only* a Latino experience not only betrays its ethos, but retrogressively renders cultural identity as a possession, the fatal flaw of both assimilation and separatism.

A final reason to draw upon the legacy of mestizaje in the U.S. Southwest for effecting unity-in-diversity in the twenty-first century is that it also accents the critical need for equal access of all peoples to political, social, and economic opportunity. In the United States most people of indigenous, dark-skinned, or mixed racial background have been cast to the margins of society. Even in Mexico, the locale of the original mestizaje, indigenous peoples for the past five centuries have been relegated to the bottom of Mexican society, as re-announced so clearly by the Zapatista indigenous-rights campaign of the past decade. Articulating how mestizaje charts a constructive path beyond the *unum-pluribus* divide, therefore, is not just a chic engagement of multiculturalism, but entails a forceful pursuit of social justice principles.

Indeed, the population of the United States under twenty-five is rapidly becoming Latino, overwhelmingly so in California and Texas, and the job force nationwide is increasingly made up of people of color. A mestizo democracy entails the realization of political, social, and economic networks that enable diverse cultural groups to engage and transform each other in mutual, lateral relations. The alternative vision is of a twenty-first-century United States split by an ever-widening gap between the haves and the have-nots and, worse, of an ugly cultural overlay in which a growing servant class, largely constituted of people of color, will attend to the needs of the elite of primarily European Americans—a neocolonialism at home instead of abroad.

Ultimately, the grist of U.S. political ideals lies neither in "speaking English only" nor in guaranteeing every cultural group its identity, but rather in the intersubjective interaction among the varied peoples who have come to this country for political freedom and economic opportunity. The challenge to U.S. Americans of long standing is not to petrify the success that their families or their cultural group has accomplished, but to recognize that this legacy will be carried on by persons who in all likelihood will be distinct from their cultural background.[102] In effecting this transition, the key question remains whether these 'others' will carry forth this legacy starting from a position of subordination or of equality to their successful predecessors.

Though multiculturalism in the United States poses more of a challenge to national unity today than at any time in the past century, confronting this reality does not have to lead to solutions that sacrifice diversity for the sake of unity, or vice versa. Unity-in-diversity urges a sense of community through heterogeneity, each culture contributing both to the community and to one another without any one culture necessarily becoming hegemonic. The more we grasp that the United States is at its heart a "multicolored marble"[103] the colors of which never fully blend nor remain utterly distinct, the more we can engage the challenges that presently lie before us precisely through the combinations of our diverse cultural legacies.

For the historical, conceptual, and ethical reasons reviewed above, a mestizo democracy offers a realistic alternative to the prevailing models of assimilation and separatism when it comes to realizing unity-in-diversity in the United States. In the next chapter, I trace the intellectual heritage that informs the idea of a mestizo democracy, from José Vasconcelos's aesthetic yet moral recasting of a mestizaje in early twentieth century Mexican philosophy to the updating of Vasconcelos's vision by contemporary Mexican American scholars, such as Virgil Elizondo and Gloria Anzaldúa, in light of the Latino experience in the United States.

CHAPTER 2

Mestizaje as Holistic Engagement
of Multiple Cultures

*H*istorically, *mestizaje* refers to the commingling of the races and cultures of the African, European, and indigenous peoples in the Spanish and Portuguese conquest of the Americas. In contrast to the English decimation of the indigenous tribes in North America, the Spanish conquistadors, especially through the rape and subjugation of indigenous women, begat a new culture and race, particularly in Mexico: "*En 1521 nació una nueva raza* [in 1521 a new race was born], *el mestizo, el mexicano* (people of mixed Indian and Spanish blood), a race that had never existed before."[1]

Geographic, historical, and cultural differences in the Spanish and English conquests of the Americas resulted in much more cultural and racial mixing in Latin America than occurred in English North America. Whereas the English conquerors encountered indigenous nomadic tribes that lived off the land, the Spanish encountered rich, densely populated, and highly developed civilizations like the Aztecs and the Incas. In English North America, the colonists brought their families intact to the New World to establish farms in a climate similar to England's and were motivated by the principles of modern liberal individualism emerging in seventeenth century England. In contrast, the Spanish brought few women with them, and marriages with indigenous women thus became commonplace.[2] Indeed, the highly established civilizations of Mesoamerica in many ways reflected the aristocratic, authoritarian order of late medieval Spain, a theme I explore at greater length in chapter 4.[3]

Even though more racial and cultural mixing occurred in the Spanish than in the English conquest of the Americas, the Spanish, like the English, nevertheless decimated many indigenous tribes through both war and the spread of diseases against which the indigenous peoples had no resistance. Gloria Anzaldúa estimates that prior to the arrival of the conquistadors, 25 million indigenous people lived in Mexico, but that shortly after Cortés's triumph this number decreased to less than 7 million and that by 1650 "only one-and-a-half-million pure-blooded Indians remained."[4] Any rendering of the original mestizaje in Mexico or elsewhere in Latin America has to take into account the immense suffering endured by the indigenous peoples at the hands of the Spaniards and that the Spaniards were the dominant party in the "mixing." Without denying these harsh realities, in the Mesoamerican experience there remains a heritage of combining multiple identities not replicated in the English expansion across North America.[5]

Over the past century Mexican, Mexican American, and Latino scholars have been recasting this historical mestizaje among African, European, and indigenous peoples into an aesthetic moral rationality mutually critical of both the assimilation and separatist models of multicultural relations. To capture this recasting of mestizaje, I turn initially to the great Mexican educator José Vasconcelos and his articulation of *una raza cósmica* (a cosmic race)—an integration of the world's races that is antithetical to advocates of racial purity or materialist uniformity. In the ensuing section I then empirically pinpoint how the rapidly expanding Latino presence in the U.S. Southwest and other parts of the United States is actually even more emblematic of the cultural mixing Vasconcelos had attributed to Mexico and Latin America. In the final section, I then address the optimistic and agonal renderings of *el mestizaje nuevo,* presented respectively by the Mexican American theologian Virgil Elizondo and the Mexican American poet Gloria Anzaldúa. By synthesizing Elizondo's and Anzaldúa's perspectives, we can envision a mestizo democracy whose lateral, egalitarian, and nonmaterialist rendering of multicultural relations (1) overcomes the lingering sense of European superiority that undermines Vasconcelos's otherwise noteworthy outlook and (2) moves us beyond the *unum-pluribus* divide.

Vasconcelos: Mestizaje As Holistic, Aesthetic Rationality

In the twentieth century José Vasconcelos, the great Mexican philosopher and educator, moved beyond the literal description of the mixing of the

African, European, and indigenous races in Mexico by painting an aesthetic vision of why the Latin American experience offers a basis for *la raza cósmica*—a race integrating the world's races. Vasconcelos's concern is to synthesize heterogeneous cultures, but in a way that does not culminate in one culture dominating all others.

Vasconcelos originally wrote his essay, *La raza cósmica*, in 1925 in an atmosphere abounding with theories of racial superiority. Many advocated the Darwinian notion of natural selection, especially as they understood the theory through Herbert Spencer's recasting as "survival of the fittest," and the Nazi notion of the superiority of the Aryan race was about to make its nefarious impact upon the globe. Vasconcelos's essay sought to counter the prevalence of positivism and materialism in late nineteenth and early twentieth century Mexican thought. Positivist ideas of progress lay at the heart of Mexican dictator Porfirio Díaz's regime during the years 1876–1910. Díaz's modernization of Mexico through industrialization principally financed by foreign investors led to the disparity of wealth and the restlessness of the poorer classes that eventually incited the Mexican Revolution in 1910.

At the outset of his essay, Vasconcelos clearly states his primary thesis "that the various races of the earth tend to intermix at a gradually increasing pace, and eventually will give rise to a new human type, composed of selections from each of the races already in existence."[6] He identifies the four basic races as "the Black, the Indian, the Mongol and the White" and envisions "a fifth universal race" that will synthesize the previous four.[7]

To this point Vasconcelos has simply anticipated that advances in transportation and in what today is referred to as economic globalization will lead to an integration of the world's races. But for Vasconcelos it is pivotal that this integration be guided by a spiritual, aesthetic vision that counters the materialism of the modern economic system and its spread in an imperialistic fashion by the white race.[8]

Conventionally, within the Western tradition, aesthetics is an important branch of philosophy but not a form of knowledge central to either morals or politics. In contrast to logical, analytical types of ethics, art and aesthetics, for Vasconcelos, are at the core of moral and spiritual expression.[9] In the age of the universal cosmic race, he states, "Life, founded on love, will come to be expressed in forms of beauty."[10]

In Hegelian-like fashion, Vasconcelos contends that three principal stages comprise the evolution of human relationships: "the material or warlike, the intellectual or political, and the spiritual or aesthetic."[11] In the first stage, material and violent combat by tribal groups prevails; whatever mixing of the races ensues is through domination and submission, not by choice. In the second stage, Vasconcelos argues that reason prevails, but it is a reason whose sole focus is to contain the violence and chaos characteristic of the previous period. Hence, abstract treaties, contracts, and formulas prevail: "This period does nothing but gives norms to intelligence, limits to action, boundaries to the nation, and reins to the emotions."[12] The condemnation of racial mixing in the eugenics of this period is based on shallow logic and incomplete information. In the third period life will be engaged with "creative feeling and convincing beauty."[13] The rules and duties characteristic of the previous period will be surpassed, according to Vasconcelos, by an "aesthetic *pathos*" that is "beyond good and evil" and moved by beauty, joy, and love.[14] In turn, these "laws of emotion, beauty, and happiness" will supposedly orient the mixing of the races in a creative, not scientific, fashion, and marriage "will become a work of art."[15]

Instead of a cold, logical rationality, Vasconcelos envisions a poetic, evocative, lyrical rationality that will enable "the first truly universal, truly cosmic culture."[16] Instead of one race being able to dominate all others in the manner of the social Darwinist or Nazi visions, *la raza cósmica* will engage life through an aesthetic taste and a spiritual reflection oriented by "the mystery of divine beauty."[17] For Vasconcelos, the Hegelian concrete universal is achieved through art and music; in this aesthetic rationality, "creative imagination and fantasy" prevail.[18]

As much as Vasconcelos's articulation of *la raza cósmica* envisions a mixing of the world's races through the pursuit of the above aesthetic rationality, he unfortunately characterizes this mixing as civilizing inferior and mediocre peoples—especially blacks and the indigenous peoples of the Americas:

> The lower types of the species will be absorbed by the superior type. In this manner, for examples, the Black could be redeemed, and step by step, by voluntary extinction, the uglier stocks would give way to the more handsome. Inferior races, upon being educated, would become less prolific, and the better specimens would go on ascending a scale of ethnic improvement, whose maximum type is not precisely the White, but the new race to which the White himself will have to aspire with the object of conquering the synthesis. The Indian, by grafting onto the related race, would take the jump of millions of years that separate Atlantis from our times,

and in a few decades of aesthetic eugenics, the Black may disappear, together with the types that a free instinct of beauty may go on signaling as fundamentally recessive and undeserving, for that reason, of perpetuation. In this manner, a selection of taste would take effect, much more efficiently than the brutal Darwinist selection, which is valid, if at all, only for the inferior species, but no longer for man.[19]

Although Vasconcelos takes exception to the social Darwinist and Nazi vision of just one race dominating all others, his *raza cósmica* still pursues a fusion of peoples: an integration, not an elimination, of races will develop through his ascending aesthetic rationality, and this integration supposedly will lead to a more civilized people. A Darwinian eugenics is replaced by a Mendelian one stressing "racial hybridization."[20] In fact across Latin America prior to World War II, Vasconcelos-like articulations of mestizaje steeped in eugenics abounded.[21]

Vasconcelos's portrait of *la raza cósmica* also frequently exhibits an Iberian chauvinism and a rather idyllic portrait of the Spanish conquest of the Americas:

The advantage of our tradition is that it has greater facility of sympathy toward strangers. This implies that our civilization, with all of its defects, may be the chosen one to assimilate and to transform mankind into a new type; that within our civilization, the warp, the multiple and rich plasma of future humanity is thus being prepared. This mandate from History is first noticed in that abundance of love that allowed the Spaniard to create a new race with the Indian and the Black, profusely spreading white ancestry through the soldier who begat a native family, and Occidental culture through the doctrine and example of the missionaries who placed the Indians in condition to enter into the new stage, the stage of world One. Spanish colonization created mixed races; this signals its character, fixes its responsibility, and defines its future.[22]

In the same vein of superiority, he adds subsequently, "Only the Iberian part of the continent possesses the spiritual factors, the race, and the territory necessary for the great enterprise of initiating the new universal era of Humanity."[23] Contrary to Vasconcelos, the mestizaje that ensued in the conquest of the Americas was not out of any great superordinate or compassionate love, but was due first and foremost to the rape and subordination of the natives by the Spaniards.

The accent Vasconcelos places on the Spanish "spiritual mission" to the Americas runs throughout his presentation of *la raza cósmica*. This dimension of his argument combined with his emphasis on Christianity as a universal civilizing force does nothing to lessen the charge that his aesthetic moral rationality is simply an "aestheticization" of the "cross and sword" evangelization manifested by the conquistadors: "A religion such as Christianity made the American Indians advance, in a few centuries, from cannibalism to a relative degree of civilization."[24] His rendering of Christianity entails no syncretic commingling with other traditions nor even any inkling of the notion that universal truth is realized in the context of particular cultures, as stressed in contemporary inculturation studies.

The greatest drawback to his argument remains the apolitical character of the aesthetic rationality of *la raza cósmica*. In attempting to transcend the "intellectual or political" stage of human development, Vasconcelos ignores the ethical, political, and economic dimensions of aesthetic action. As suggested by Roberto Goizueta, true fusion between persons, in the manner Vasconcelos seeks, can only ensue when both parties engage each other as equals, not as conquerors vis-à-vis the conquered or as civilizers vis-à-vis the supposed uncivilized: "True empathy is rooted and issues in ethical-political action, which must, in turn, be expressed through a transformation of unjust relationships of production."[25]

Vasconcelos is so preoccupied with countering the materialist and positivist articulation of politics of the Mexico of his day that he insufficiently explains how an aesthetic rationality, rather than transcending ethics through a rather evanescent emphasis on spirit and love, suggests an alternative politics and economics in which people can mutually engage one another with dignity and realize relationships of equality. Although *la raza cósmica* pursues the issue of the mixing of races beyond the domination motif of social Darwinism, Vasconcelos is more focused on generating unity than on explaining how cultural, linguistic, racial, and religious clashes relate to the distribution of power in political, social, and economic structures. As long as significant differences remain in the relative access distinct peoples have to these decision-making networks, the aesthetic pursuit of *la raza cósmica* will remain a quixotic quest, not a practical possibility.

Despite all these drawbacks to Vasconcelos's argument—especially the tones of missionary zeal and sense of responsibility to civilize the 'other'—positive aspects of his argument emerge that can be culled and developed for articulating an aesthetic yet ethical rationality steeped in mestizaje. First, he criticizes European and especially European American notions—then common across North, Central, and South America—regarding the inferiority of blacks, indigenous peoples, and mestizos: "Even we have come to believe in the inferiority of the mestizo, in the unredemption of the Indian, in the damnation and the irreparable decadence of the Black."[26] Even if his own vision privileges unity over diversity, his countering of materialism with spirituality and his Mendelian, rather than Darwinian, articulation of racial mixing broach the possibility that multiple cultural and racial identities are in fact juxtaposed in each of us and in presumably homogeneous cultures. This juxtaposition becomes even more pronounced through the intersection of diverse peoples in the growing global economy. To his credit, Vasconcelos saw there would be the need to articulate a universal normative vision to temper the capitalist and consumerist ethos encircling the planet, the very issue at the heart of Benjamin Barber's deliberations on the deleterious and interrelated consequences of jihad and McWorld, as presented in chapter 1.

Second, Vasconcelos argues successfully that there has been a greater openness to cultural and racial mixing historically in Latin America than in the melting-pot vision of the United States. In contrast to the U.S. tradition that one drop of black blood made a person black, the widespread existence of mestizos in Latin America, especially in Mexico, attests to the vast experience Latin America has had in cultural and racial mixing. Especially in Mesoamerica, the juxtaposition of multiple cultures has been a fact of everyday life for at least five centuries. If Vasconcelos overstates his position by arguing that the destiny of Latin Americans is to lead the way when it comes to articulating a universal notion of racial or cultural mixing, he nevertheless correctly shows that across Latin America, including the U.S. Southwest, there thrives a heritage of the mixing of African, European, and indigenous peoples that neither assimilation nor separatism can impart.

Vasconcelos unfortunately retains the "civilizing" and "purifying" motives in his articulation of *la raza cósmica,* rather than simply recognizing that the indigenous and black cultures survive and persist as well as the European cultures, albeit in new form, in mestizaje. The Latin American experience with mestizaje illustrates that peoples can coexist and integrate without getting into the "either/or" syndrome of multicultural relations discussed in chapter 1.

As much as Vasconcelos's aesthetic articulation of *la raza cósmica* is seemingly apolitical, his evocation of a Latin American spiritual vision did engage the prevailing political winds of his age and in many respects anticipated many of the issues that preoccupy our attention at the outset of the twenty-first century. First, for Vasconcelos, the idealism of the Mexican Revolution offered an alternative to the competing *material* economic systems of capitalism and communism.[27] His defeat in the Mexican presidential election in 1929, combined with the institutional rigidification of the Revolution into the Institutional Revolutionary Party, the PRI, soon dashed his ideals. This setback, though, did not diminish his quest to articulate a vision of human community, which would not only mix the races in an equal, integral fashion but would also promote human relationships that can foster the dignity of the whole human person and do not reduce human beings to their material or utilitarian value.

For Vasconcelos, though, and other Latin American visionaries of a century ago—the Cuban José Martí (1853–1895) and the Uruguayan José Enrique Rodó (1871–1917)—the principal exponent of materialism vis-à-vis Latin America was the growing imperialism of the United States.[28] The military expansion of the U.S. through the 1846–1848 war with Mexico and then the 1898 Spanish American War was fresh in the memory of these writers. U.S. business interests were deeply entangled with the Díaz regime prior to the Mexican Revolution, and the U.S. government ultimately lent support to the more professional classes and to those representing the establishment in the Mexican Revolution—to Carranza, for instance, enabling him to defeat the more volatile Villa. These Latin American writers' association of materialism and utilitarianism with the United States and the Anglo-Saxon world has an eerie contemporary resonance, given the expansion of McWorld across Mexico and Latin America through free trade agreements.[29]

Despite what may be the official pronouncements of the recent Mexican governments about the need for neoliberalism and the merits of the global economy, a clear awareness persists on the level of cultural understanding that Mexico has been the front line between this historic tension between the Anglo-Saxon and Latin American cultures in the Americas for especially the past two centuries. As Carlos Fuentes has pointedly said:

> This is a border [U.S.-Mexico] unique in the world. It's the only border between the industrialized world and the emerging, developing, nonindustrialized world. It is the border between the northern, Protestant, capitalistic culture of the United States, and the southern, Mediterranean Catholic culture of Latin America. We're conscious in Mexico, that Latin America begins with the border—not only Mexico, but the whole of Latin America.[30]

Even though the ongoing rebellion by the Zapatistas in Chiapas is much more a protest motivated by indigenous rights than by an aesthetic, spiritual vision of Latin American culture, its commencement simultaneously with the North American Free Trade Agreement (NAFTA) and its clear critique of U.S. economic imperialism makes it consonant with the countercultural dimension of Vasconcelos's writings.

Furthermore, this Latin American vision articulated by writers such as Vasconcelos, Martí, and Rodó is equally a critique of the nationalisms that have persisted across Latin America since the wars of independence from Spain in the early nineteenth century. Vasconcelos shows that the inability of Latin Americans to realize a pan-Latin American political entity is precisely what has made it so vulnerable to U.S. and Anglo-Saxon domination:

> The greatest battle was lost on the day that each one of the Iberian republics went forth alone, to live her own life apart from her sisters, concerting treaties and receiving false benefits, without tending to the common interests of the race. The founders of our new nationalism were, without knowing it, the best allies of the Anglo-Saxons, our rivals in the possession of the continent. . . . We ignore the contrast presented by Anglo-Saxon unity in opposition to the anarchy and solitude of the Ibero American emblems. We keep ourselves jealously independent from each other, yet one way or another we submit to, or ally ourselves with, the Anglo-Saxon union.[31]

Therefore, though Vasconcelos is adamantly opposed to U.S. domination of Latin America (McWorld), he is equally critical of the Latin American penchant for forming petty separatist states, a nation-state equivalent of jihad. These Latin American nation-states have predominantly been led by rich elites more aligned with the business leaders of U.S. and multinational corporations than with their own people.

Conceptually, Vasconcelos's aesthetic, spiritual articulation of *la raza cósmica* entails a transnational vision that is critical of the political relations engendered by the global economy. Vasconcelos seeks a transnationalism that is not an imperialism, especially not a transnationalism centered in the United States, but is, rather, a form of transnationalism anchored in the belief that the Latin American experience with the mixing of races offers a deep experiential basis for realizing an international politics oriented by mutuality, not dominance. Although Vasconcelos's attempt to transcend politics and ethics through spirituality and aesthetics may seem void of political and economic savvy, on another level his evocation of a transnationalism driven not only by economic values but also by an ethical, egalitarian intersection of races, cultures, and tradition cuts to the heart of contemporary debates regarding multiculturalism.

As discussed earlier, Vasconcelos's critique of U.S. imperialism through materialism converges somewhat with Barber's critique of McWorld. The critical difference between Barber and Vasconcelos, however, remains that Barber's constructive alternative to McWorld is a reaffimation of the importance of nation-states with the hope that we might begin developing transnational ties and associations among peoples in a way that can counter the excessive displacements and impacts of a global economy. For Vasconcelos, the detrimental legacy of nation-states in Latin America explains why this region is so vulnerable to domination by the economically developed regions of the world. Instead, Vasconcelos turns to this alternative-rich tradition of the mixing of races and cultures in Latin America to offer a vision of transnationalism in which ethics and values would be articulated and practiced through an aesthetic spirit of inclusion, not materialist domination.

Because of the drawbacks of jihad Barber shies away from articulating a transnationalism rooted in a deep sense of cultural traditions. Vasconcelos, on the other hand, recognizes that one can counter the oppressiveness of uniformity, be it imposed by global materialism or local parochialisms, by cultivating the Latin American heritage of juxtaposed cultural, linguistic, racial, religious identities, that is, by moving beyond either/ors to both-ands. Though writing almost a century ago, and perhaps still too infused by notions of unity rather than diversity in his own presentation, Vasconcelos anticipates the twenty-first century reality that each of us is "crossing borders" daily in many aspects of our lives.

Finally, Vasconcelos's articulation of *la raza cósmica* as a racial mixing that transcends the limitations of the nation-state system and offers an aesthetic yet ethical alternative to schemes of domination—be it neocolonial economic imperialism or social Darwinist assimilation—appeals to groups who have been marginalized by modernity and the prevailing nation-state framework. Vasconcelos's popularity among Chicano writers is not coincidental, for as Joseba Gabilondo observes, Chicano "writers articulate their position from an awareness of not belonging to the formation of the nation-state; they come after modernity."[32] The Chicano movement, in both its artistic and political dimensions, articulates the experience of a people whose identity, though shaped by both U.S. and Mexican national identities, transcends the fetters of such narrow nationalist scripting.

In this regard, it is wrong to reduce Vasconcelos's perspective to merely representing pre–World War II Latin American populist nationalisms "stressing genetic or biological factors, much as articulated by the Italian philosopher Benedetto Croce."[33] Actually, Latin American political elites in the 1930s water down Vasconcelos's vision into being "a liberal version of 'racial harmony'" that sustains their nationalist power.[34] Certainly the connection between genetics and culture that Vasconcelos draws is to play "with fire,"[35] but it is even more perilous to ignore how motifs of ethnic and racial superiority have been inscribed in the European and European American domination of the world during modernity. An ethical transnationalism, as depicted by Vasconcelos, must overcome this domination by *affectively* envisioning and realizing a mixing of cultures and races in which no one heritage becomes hegemonic. Writing a half-century before the onset of postmodernism and its emphasis on multiple identities and shifting boundaries, Vasconcelos anticipates notions such as Homi Bhabha's hybridity that I expand upon in chapter 5.

Overall, Vasconcelos's depiction of *la raza cósmica* suffers from (1) an overemphasis on unity as opposed to diversity, (2) a retention of the notion of purifying and civilizing peoples of color in racial mixing, and (3) an excessive reliance on an aesthetic, spiritual vision at the expense of realizing this vision in terms of concrete, political realities. Nevertheless, his recognition (1) of the grave shortcomings of modern philosophy, especially in its positivist and materialist dimensions, (2) of the impact of imperialism on Latin America long before NAFTA, (3) and of the fact that any meaningful moral transnationalism cannot ensue without a genuine collaborative mixing of races and cultures makes him a seminal figure for articulating a mestizo democracy. Contrary to contemporary appeals for homogeneous assimilation or to the opposing view that racial and cultural differences are so vast and deep that separatism is preferable to irreconcilable conflict, Vasconcelos articulates a concrete universal through the aesthetic engagement and integration of difference.

El Nuevo Mestizaje in the U.S. Southwest

The above-mentioned connection between Vasconcelos and Chicano writers is hardly accidental, for Mexican Americans have in concrete terms been wrestling with the political, economic, and cultural impact of "border crossings" since Stephen F. Austin and his European American compatriots settled in Texas in the 1820s at the invitation of the Mexican government. The history of this region offers a cultural hermeneutical basis for envisioning a politics, based on mestizaje, that moves beyond the nation-state system yet tempers the imperialist and materialist excesses of the global economy. In the 1920s Vasconcelos predicted the mixing of the African, Asian, European, and Latin American races in terms of *la raza cósmica,* and the U.S. Southwest offers an excellent example of these multiple intersections.

These political, economic, and especially cultural interchanges between the United States and Mexico find their origins in the U.S. American colonization of Texas and the subsequent war between the U.S. and Mexico between 1846 and 1848, which culminated in Mexico's loss of much of its territory. Instead of politically being part of the northern *frontera* of Mexico, Mexican Americans overnight found themselves in the nascent U.S. Southwest, without ever having moved. It is inaccurate to label many Mexican Americans as immigrants because they did not come to the United States; the United States came to them. Subsequent waves of migrants from Mexico are coming to a geographic region which, to the Mexican consciousness, has a deep familial tie to Mexico: "Mexican workers who cross the border are not crossing a frontier, they're crossing a scar into a land that they consider theirs. . . . This is my land."[36]

Consequently, post-1848, Mexican Americans and other Latinos have been caught between their ancestral ties to Mesoamerica, on the one hand, and primarily the European American culture of the United States, on the other. Although the United States is clearly the sovereign power of California, Arizona, New Mexico, Colorado, and Texas, there remains in this region a strong cultural bond to Mexico and Latin America. Nevertheless, the African American, Asian American, and European American imprint on Mexican American and Latino culture distinguishes it from Mexican and other Latin American cultures. Vasconcelos evokes the vision of *la raza cósmica,* but it is the peoples of the U.S. Southwest who have been experiencing *un mestizaje nuevo.*

"WE DIDN'T CROSS THE BORDER; THE BORDER CROSSED US"

Although some Spanish settlements in what is now New Mexico date back to 1598, Spanish colonization of what is now the U.S. Southwest occurred primarily from 1680 until the end of the eighteenth century: Ysleta (El Paso, 1682), San Antonio (1751), Tucson (1775), San Diego (1769), San Francisco (1776), and Los Angeles (1781). Under both Spain and then Mexico as of 1821 these frontier outposts were as detached from each other as they were from the rest of Mexico.[37] "Tejanos," "Hispanos" (New Mexico), and "Californios" were separate groups, a distinctiveness that will also come into play when their descendants distinguish themselves from later migrants from Mexico into the U.S. Southwest.[38] There was no uniform Mexican culture across *la frontera* before the arrival of U.S. American colonists; rather, each settlement distilled its unique version of Mexican culture, a practice that persists today throughout the U.S. Southwest. This legacy of diversity also anticipates some of the problems besetting attempts today to form a Latino coalition among Mexican Americans, Puerto Rican Americans, Cuban Americans, and other Latino nationalities in the United States. Still, early nineteenth-century Texas was the most accessible state in this northern region of Mexico and was strongly affected by the Mexican political turmoil generated by the fight for Mexican independence and then by Santa Anna's rise to dictatorial power.

The defeat of Santa Anna's forces by Sam Houston's Texan army at the Battle of San Jacinto in 1836 enabled the independent Republic of Texas to secede from Mexico. However, the southern region of Texas between the Rio Nueces, to the north, and the Rio Grande, to the south, was comprised primarily of Mexican towns and ranches and remained disputed territory until the 1848 Treaty of Guadalupe-Hidalgo, concluding the U.S.-Mexico War of 1846–1848 and moving the boundary southward to the Rio Grande. Nevertheless, the Mexican settlements in South Texas persist, and to this day Spanish remains a principal language in this region. Indeed, Mexicans and Mexican Americans frequently refer to the other side of the U.S.-Mexico border as *el otro lado* (the other side), suggesting a cultural bond irreverent to political sovereignty. Although the legal boundary shifted, the Mexican cultural legacy remained. After the 1846–1848 war, however, the new political authorities in collusion with wealthy Mexicans, especially in New Mexico, were able to obtain many of the preceding private land grants and in turn to undermine the communal land system that was the locus of life for poor Mexicans.[39]

Subsequent to 1848 several vital waves of Latino migration from Mexico, and eventually from Central America, have had a great impact on the U.S. Southwest:

- Between 1880–1920 the Mexican population in the United States increased nine times as job opportunities became plentiful during the U.S. expansion into an industrial power.[40]
- In the 1910s many Mexicans fled northward from the turmoil of the Mexican Revolution.

- In the 1940s, 1950s, and 1960s many Mexicans were brought into the United States to work for agribusinesses through the U.S. Government's bracero programs.
- In the 1980s and 1990s many migrants crossed the Rio Grande to escape economic hard times or civil wars, especially in El Salvador, Guatemala, and Nicaragua.

Such waves of migration manifest a green-light–red-light pattern: when U.S.-based businesses need cheap labor, then the doors are pushed open for these migrants, but when the economy declines or when migrants seemingly put undue pressure on government resources, these migrants become the scapegoats for hard times. During the Depression, for instance, Mexican Americans (U.S. citizens) were deported deep into Mexico through an arrangement between the United States and Mexican governments.

In sum, leaving aside South Texas, it is difficult to claim an extensive Mexican presence in the U.S. Southwest prior to 1848 or that a great deal of communication and transit developed between the settlements in California, New Mexico, and Texas. Nevertheless, from the late seventeenth century forward an indigenous-Spanish-Mexican presence preceded the westward expansion of U.S. Americans into this region and persisted after 1848 despite European American political and economic domination. Consequently, subsequent Latino migrants came to cities such as Albuquerque and San Antonio quite accustomed to integrating multiple cultural identities.

This long-standing Latino heritage, in all its variety, is revitalized and transformed by each new wave of Latino migration from Mexico, Central America, and elsewhere. The U.S. Southwest, thus, is the intersection of two different directions of migration: not just a westward progression of especially African Americans and European Americans, but also a northward Latin American movement whose presence precedes the arrival of U.S. settlers by over a century in some places and is still ensuing. In cultural, not legal terms, Latinos are hardly "aliens" in the U.S. Southwest. More importantly, denying this long-standing Latino legacy leads to a myopic outlook on the future direction of this region, as extensive waves of Latino migration persist.[41]

THE IMPACT OF ADVANCES IN TELECOMMUNICATIONS AND TRANSPORTATION

In addition to the historical heritage, other evidence suggests an unfolding *mestizaje nuevo,* not just assimilation, in the U.S. Southwest and other parts of the United States. According to the U.S. Census Bureau, there are currently 35.3 million Latinos in the U.S., or 12.5 percent of the overall population.[42] Mexican Americans constitute 20.6 million out of this population—an increase of 53 percent in just the past decade.[43] In Miami, El Paso, and Santa Ana, California, Latinos constitute an absolute majority of the population. In Los Angeles and Houston, Latinos are now the largest ethnic/racial group in those cities, though not an absolute majority. In Phoenix and New York, Latinos are the largest minority group.[44] Most importantly, this growing Latino population is predominantly young—35 percent of Latinos are under the age of eighteen, as opposed to 26 percent of the U.S. population.[45]

Moreover, beyond the traditional concentration of Latinos in the U.S. Southwest, Florida, and the New York City and Chicago metropolitan areas, the Latino population is rising significantly in other regions of the country—Arkansas, Georgia, and North Carolina among other places—principally because of the rise of manufacturing and meat-packing businesses in these locales. In North Carolina, for instance, the Mexican American population has increased by 655 percent in the past decade.[46]

The demographics of language are also telling. The United States is now the world's fifth largest Spanish-speaking country, with over 17.3 million speakers, and the Strategy Research Corporation contends that by 2025 the United States will be second only to Mexico in this regard.[47] Like the past experience of other immigrant groups, many Latinos speak only English by the third generation. However, unlike the situation of most immigrant groups, new waves of Spanish speakers continue to come into the United States. So unfading is the presence of their mother tongue that the U.S. telecommunications industry is increasingly reinforcing the retention of Spanish. AT&T, MCI, and other telecommunication networks are engaged in fierce competition for the long-distance phone-call market from the United States to Mexico, Central America, and other parts of Latin America. *Univision* and *Telemundo* are the only major U.S. commercial television networks coast to coast that broadcast in a language other than English. The nightly news broadcasts of both networks, in addition to covering major events in the United States, focus much more on Latin American events than their English-speaking counterparts at ABC, CBS, and NBC. Advertisers are increasingly using Spanish phrases and Latino cultural symbols to market their products; Spanish billboards increasingly dot the landscape. Such commercial examples perhaps sully the integrity of Latino culture, but they pointedly indicate that Spanish will remain one of the two principal languages of the United States. In cities such as Houston, Miami, and Los Angeles, a working knowledge of both English and Spanish is becoming vital for professional advancement.

Indeed, these major communication markets include numerous Spanish commercial radio stations; in terms of mestizaje, many of these stations' announcers throughout the broadcasts move naturally back and forth, along with their listeners, between English and Spanish, frequently within the same sentence. This multilingualism is not an effort to provide simultaneous translation but rather an indication of a large audience that speaks "Spanglish," a mixing of Spanish and English. Along the same lines Tejano music, which developed in Texas in the early decades of the twentieth century, integrates Mexican, German, and Czech dance music. Even if Tejano singers primarily speak English, they sing in a "Tex-Mex" Spanish.

Advances in transportation systems mirror the advances in telecommunications. The opening of a new highway from Nuevo Laredo to Monterrey in 1994 makes it much easier for Mexican Americans and Latinos to return south to visit relatives. The proposed Interstate 69 in Texas will further reduce travel time between Houston and Monterrey. Major U.S. airlines have been expanding their service across Latin America and especially to Mexico. As a result of these transportation changes, it is not unusual for many Mexican Americans and Latinos to board buses and planes at Christmas time destined for Mexico and other parts of Latin America to visit families and friends. The period especially between the feast of Our Lady of Guadalupe (December 12) and the feast of the Three Kings (January 6) is characterized by caravans of travelers moving back and forth across "the border" to visit friends and family. Setting aside the historical and geographic ties between the U.S. Southwest and Mexico, the advances in communications and transportation systems over the past century make it much easier for Latinos to maintain an umbilical cord to Mexico and Latin America. Retaining their linguistic and cultural ties is far easier for them than it was for the nineteenth- and early twentieth-century immigrants to the United States from Europe and elsewhere.

"WE MAY NOT OVERCOME, BUT WE WILL OVERWHELM"

By the year 2020 the U.S. Census Bureau projects that Latinos nationwide will constitute 15.7 percent of the population or 51.2 million persons. In at least four states they will constitute at least 30 percent of the population, and in New Mexico they will constitute an absolute majority of the population.[48] According to the 2000 U.S. Census report, whites already constitute only 52.4 percent of the Texas population, and a Texas A&M University study projects that by the year 2030, assuming zero future migration—a very conservative estimate—Latinos will be the largest group in Texas at 45.9 percent.[49] Presently in Texas, Latinos represent the largest group (37.5 percent) of the state's population under the age of eighteen. In every scenario in the Texas A&M study, figuring for different levels of future migration into Texas, this plurality will remain the case. Indeed, the study projects that through the year 2030 the median age of all Latinos will remain lower in Texas than that of white, black, and other U.S. Americans.[50]

Using the data from the U.S. Census Bureau and even the most conservative projections in the Texas A&M study, one gets a graphic representation of the spreading Latino presence across Texas, county by county. Even in 1990 the vast majority of counties south of Interstate Highway 10 between El Paso and San Antonio and west of Interstate Highway 37 between San Antonio and Corpus Christi had a Latino population of at least 40 percent. Such data reinforces the fact that South Texas has been Mexican or Mexican American in orientation for the past two centuries.

But if one considers the projected Latino population across Texas for the year 2030, the "cultural border" will be moving well north of Interstate Highway 10 and east of Interstate Highway 27. It will stretch from the intersection of Interstate Highway 40 and Interstate Highway 27 in Amarillo south to Lubbock and then in a southeastward direction through Abilene, Brownwood, Austin, and ultimately Victoria. West of this "border" there will lie seventy-one counties with a Latino population of 40 percent or more, compared to only forty-seven counties in 1990. Already according to the 2002 U.S. census, the cities of Dallas and Houston, respectively, have Latino populations of 36 percent and 37 percent. Over the next three decades a Latino population wave will move steadily across the state in a northeast direction into regions that historically were not extensively settled either by Spain or Mexico.[51]

Indeed, Houston provides a fascinating case of this growing Latino presence. The largest city in Texas was founded after the establishment of the Republic of Texas and is certainly not associated as strongly in the popular mind with Mexican culture as is San Antonio. Nevertheless, Houston is rapidly becoming Latino. In the 1980 U.S. census, Houston's ethnic/racial demographic breakdown was 52 percent white, 27 percent black, 18 percent Latino, and 2 percent Asian. By the 1990 census Latinos had drawn even with blacks while the percentage of whites had diminished: 41 percent white,

28 percent Latino, 28 percent black, and 4 percent Asian. In the recent 2000 U.S. census, Latinos have emerged as the largest group at 37 percent, followed by whites at 31 percent, blacks at 25 percent, and Asians at 6 percent.[52]

The degree to which this increasing Latino presence in Texas and the U.S. Southwest will turn into political and socioeconomic power is uncertain. For instance, the 2000 census does not specify how many of the nation's 35.3 million Latinos are noncitizens who cannot vote. In the Houston case many Latinos are migrants from Mexico and Central America as opposed to South Texas, where family roots in some instances extend back before the siege of the Alamo. The contour and character of future political participation will depend upon a number of factors:

- the level and quality of grassroots mobilization of Latino communities,
- the degree and manner to which non-Latino political leaders and both major political parties anticipate and respond to the growing Latino presence,
- the differences in political outlook between different generations and diverse communities among Latinos,
- the impact that intermarriage and mutual socialization between Latinos and non-Latinos will have on political identification and outlook.

Furthermore, the Texas A&M study projects that although Latinos and non-European Americans will increasingly comprise the majority of persons in Texas, growth in the private economic sector will diminish while demands for government services will increase if the present lack of access to educational and socioeconomic opportunities for minorities persists. Essentially, the new majority of non-European groups will still be subservient to what will be a primarily European American "minority" control of state resources. The study concludes that if Texas is to remain economically viable, changes that enable non–European Americans to gain the education and the skills necessary for competing in the global economy are imperative. Otherwise, we will also face the undemocratic reality of a rich ethnic/racial minority prevailing at the expense of the majority of the people.[53]

If Mexicans experienced a border crossing in the U.S. Southwest in the nineteenth century, in demographic terms it is primarily European Americans who are now experiencing a border crossing in Texas and the U.S. Southwest, despite initiatives such as California's Propositions 187, 209, or 227, which desperately strive to stem the immigration tide. Moreover, NAFTA has accelerated this interrelationship of the politics, economics, and cultures of the United States and Mexico. Indeed, the U.S.-Mexico border is the front line of the emerging North-South encounter between the developed and developing nations of at least the Western Hemisphere. The repercussions of this agreement will strongly influence whether the global politics and economics of the twenty-first century will be genuinely multipolar or simply a network of multinational corporations replacing the governments of the developed world as the principal power brokers in transnational politics.

As pointed out earlier, Vasconcelos's holistic aesthetic rationality had at its heart a critique of what he considered to be the materialistic, legalistic, and scientific fixation of Anglo-Saxon civilization and its growing dominance in the Western Hemisphere. NAFTA certainly accelerates the potential for expanding such domination, making the need for a countervailing consciousness even more urgent. At the same time, NAFTA is just the latest instance of border crossings that have characterized the history of the U.S. Southwest. The peoples of this region have been wrestling with the confluence of indigenous, Latin American, and U.S. American cultures, politics, and economics for most of the past two centuries. To give Vasconcelos's aesthetic rationality practical import, we need to recast it in terms that capture the cultural ambiance of *la frontera* in which one's being is neither solely Latin American nor solely U.S. American yet is inscribed with both of these identities. As observed by Virgil Elizondo:

> Real change is taking place. Efforts are being made, coalitions are being formed, and new leadership is emerging everywhere. The Mexican American Southwest is being Anglocized at much the same pace that the Anglo Southwest of the U.S.A. is being Mexicanized. Neither group is simply allowing the other in; rather both are forming a new human space wherein all feel more at home. Some see it as scandalous while others see it as welcome, but regardless of how it is viewed, it is taking place. Culturally, a new human group is in the making.[54]

In this recasting of what it means to lie between cultures in these "borderlands," Vasconcelos's holistic, aesthetic rationality is juxtaposed with the democratic pluralistic orientation of the United States. This juxtaposition offers not just an articulation of unity-in-diversity, but a twenty-first century experiential basis for realizing Vasconcelos's vision of a counter-materialist civilization.

The Ecstatic and Agonal Dimensions of Mestizaje

The preceding historical legacies and empirical developments in the U.S. Southwest support the notion that the growing Latino presence in the United States is the culmination of a northward migration that has been underway for almost five centuries and has been integral to U.S. history for most of the past two centuries. What does it mean to live in the borderlands between European American, Latino, and Native American cultures (and increasingly Asian American and African American cultures too)? In what way does the Mexican American experience of marginalization actually offer hope for articulating a set of multicultural relations that moves beyond the assimilation-separatism impasse? How does the mestizaje ensuing in the U.S. Southwest enable us to celebrate difference while still being able to articulate a substantive common good? On the one hand, Virgil Elizondo's exegesis of mestizaje provides hopeful answers to these pivotal questions. On the other hand, Gloria Anzaldúa's emphasis on the painful side of mestizaje imposes a sober realism on assessing mestizaje's import for dealing with contemporary multicultural relations.

VIRGIL ELIZONDO'S HOPEFUL PORTRAIT OF MESTIZAJE

Elizondo, a Mexican American, is the "dean" of Latino Catholic theologians. For the past two decades his scholarly projects and his grassroots initiatives, such as establishing the Mexican American Cultural Center (MACC) in San Antonio, have paved the way for the work of most subsequent Latino theologians. Elizondo reinterprets mestizaje in light of both the Christian tradition and his Mexican American experience. His exegesis of Christian theology via Mexican American culture has made mestizaje the lodestone of Latino theology.

The plight of the Mexican American is emblematic of *el mestizaje nuevo* in the U.S. Southwest. To be Mexican American, Elizondo contends, is to be caught between Mexican and U.S. American traditions. Reflecting on growing up in San Antonio, Elizondo relates how he "was *not just* U.S.-American and *not just* Mexican but fully both and exclusively neither."[55] The ambiance of the barrios, especially the centrality of life around the churches, was essentially that of little Mexico: "We [Mexican Americans] might be living outside the political boundaries of Mexico, but Mexico was not outside of us."[56] Still, when his family visited Mexico, his relatives were quick to remind him that he was a *pocho*—an American of Mexican descent. Finally, discrimination at the hands of European Americans, even during his seminary studies, made it painfully clear that to them he was a "Greaser"—a Mexican.[57]

Rather than seeing this "half-breed" identity as a drawback, Elizondo contends that a positive dynamism emerges from such integration of cultures: "Racial and cultural mixture does not have to be destructive of cultural identity, but . . . can even strengthen it."[58] Those who live on the margin between cultures, he suggests, have little to fear from engaging new cultures because the combination of cultures is their very existence.

To substantiate his position, Elizondo turns to the cultural context and significance of both Jesus of Nazareth and Our Lady of Guadalupe. In the case of Jesus, Elizondo contends that he was a mestizo. Galilee, he argues, was an economic and cultural crossroads in the ancient Middle East. As a Jewish Galilean, Jesus was too Jewish to be acceptable to Gentiles, and, conversely, was too tainted by Gentile mores to be acceptable to the Jews of Jerusalem. Moreover, he adds, Jesus' ministry engaged the scandalous— "outcasts, public sinners, rejects, women."[59] In addition to how Jesus' identity parallels the negative branding of Mexican Americans as "half-breeds," Elizondo emphasizes that Jesus' illegitimacy as a mestizo suggests that it is through the outcasts of society—those on the margin–that a new universality emerges.

Our Lady of Guadalupe is a figure whose significance permeates not just Mexican spirituality but many Mexican and Mexican American political and social movements, especially that of César Chávez's United Farm Workers of America. Elizondo's exegesis of Guadalupe, though, pinpoints that Guadalupe brings people together in a way distinct from the notion of synthesis in European and European American philosophy or in the assimilationist's "melting pot." Prior to the appearance of Guadalupe in December 1531 at Mount Tepeyac, the Spaniards had had little success in evangelizing the indigenous peoples to Christianity. Elizondo discusses at great length the Nahuatl symbolism conveyed in Guadalupe's appearance, as the indigenous goddess Tonantzin, before the indigenous peasant Juan Diego. The blooming of roses and flowers out-of-season, the exquisite singing of birds, and the beautiful combination of colors adorning her attire do not simply highlight the event but communicate the aesthetic orientation of the indigenous grasp of reality and knowledge. Though she appears as a native, according to Elizondo, Guadalupe also sheds Tonatzin's malicious side.

Juan Diego becomes an empowered person, Elizondo continues, through Guadalupe's engagement of him as a dignified human being, in contrast to the derogatory way he and other indigenous people had been treated by the Spaniards. The conversion to Christianity among the indigenous could not ensue until this spirituality was grasped and embraced in indigenous terms. As opposed to the presumption that the indigenous had to become European in culture in order to convert to Christianity, Elizondo contends that the Guadalupe event offers

- a lateral, not hierarchical, combination of cultures which is stronger than the original separate cultures;
- a relational, concrete, aesthetic portrait of truth;
- a universal respect for others in their differences.

Each of these themes, especially the intensely aesthetic character of the Guadalupe event, echoes the aesthetic rationality of Vasconcelos's *la raza cósmica* minus the "civilizing" and Eurocentric motifs that mar Vasconcelos's presentation.

Our Lady of Guadalupe and Jesus of Nazareth, in Elizondo's exposition, are concrete universals through which particular peoples can integrate their differences and the most oppressed can overcome their suppression. Although borders remain part and parcel of human existence, "they don't have to divide or separate. They can be privileged meeting places."[60] Christianity, in Elizondo's presentation, envisions the gifts of the 'other' as something that can enrich family and community well-being. Since God enters our lives through the stranger, Elizondo suggests, hospitality and welcoming, rather than just tolerance, is essential for community life.[61]

Although Elizondo's claim that "Guadalupe is the most prodigious event since the coming of our Lord and Savior, Jesus Christ" is hyperbolic,[62] his exegesis of Guadalupe as a mestiza illustrates that cultures can combine without one culture necessarily becoming hegemonic if the inculturation of a universal truth ensues through the particular contexts of each contributing culture. Elizondo amplifies the moral dimension of Vasconcelos's aesthetic rationality by concretely illustrating that cultures can transform each other without culminating in assimilation. Beyond just describing the relevance of mestizaje for theology, Elizondo's work teaches us that vibrant communities can manifest openness to the hermeneutical intersection of cultures.

Elizondo's theological exegesis of mestizaje has several implications for political theory. First, his focus on the concrete experience and history of Mexican Americans uncovers a long-standing case within the United States of a people who, from the start, have had to wrestle with unity-in-diversity. Political transformations are more easily effected through long-standing and vivid substantive traditions; the Mexican American and Latino experience of combining multiple cultural identities is a vital resource for realizing a democratic, multicultural politics.

Second, contrary to many postmodern philosophers, Elizondo is able to reconcile a vision of the transcendent with his reflections on the negotiation of difference. Recall that even for Vasconcelos, the ethic of *la raza cósmica* is deeply informed by Christianity, especially its accent on unity. In Elizondo's case, though, the Christian transcendent is inculturated in *particular* cultures: the accent shifts from preoccupation with unity to combinations of diverse cultures. Elizondo's portrait of Christianity, in contrast to Vasconcelos's, has a much stronger indigenous hue: African, European, and indigenous perspectives are on equal terms. Rethinking the relationship of the universal to the particular in this manner enables one to engage in a public discourse regarding a substantive common good and the role of transcendent truth without rejecting difference.

Third, the virtues of cultural mixing and openness toward the stranger, as reflective of Mexican American spirituality, suggest an experiential basis for recasting John Courtney Murray's Judeo-Christian moral consensus. As discussed in chapter 1, the shortcoming of Murray's discussion of the truths enabling civil political discourse in the United States is not his endeavor to discuss universals or a common good in a supposed age of relativism, but his much too limited compass of the moral traditions of the United States. Murray simply focuses on the Catholic, Jewish, and Protestant traditions when in fact the spiritual landscape today in the United States includes Islam, Buddhism, Hinduism, and an array of other traditions coming largely from outside the Western world. The mestizo and indigenous recasting of Christianity by Elizondo suggests a more inclusive and hospitable engagement of the plurality of spiritual traditions when it comes to articulating values in political and public-policy debates. Elizondo's theology moves us past the static Reformation–Counter Reformation debate to the rapidly ensuing encounter among world religions in the United States.

Fourth and finally, by dwelling on the marginalized and outcast status of mestizos, Elizondo will not let us forget that a political community informed by justice has to be concerned with economic inequality. In this regard Elizondo's theology builds upon Vasconcelos's critique of Anglo-Saxon imperialism and its impact on the developing worlds. Given the growing gaps between rich and poor, both within the United States and also between the developed and the developing world, a mestizo democracy is not just a pleasant interchange of cultures; rather, it entails a genuine solidarity of mixed peoples that cannot tolerate inequality of political, economic, and social opportunities, especially if such inequality has a cultural, linguistic, racial, or religious hue.

GLORIA ANZALDÚA'S AGONAL AFFIRMATION OF MESTIZAJE

Elizondo's characterization of mestizaje is extremely hopeful. However, before becoming too optimistic, one also has to acknowledge the great degree to which strife and struggle are also endemic to the intersections of cultures. The original mestizaje in Mexico and Central America initiated by the Spanish conquest led to the decimation of much of the indigenous population and to the subsequent domination of the ensuing political, social, and economic structures by the Spaniards. Contrary to Vasconcelos's elegy of the Spanish embrace of the indigenous peoples, many of the original mestizos in Mexico were begotten through coerced sexual submissions.[63] Mestizos or ladinos, as they are called in Guatemala, have in turn been persecutors of indigenous peoples.[64]

In analogous fashion, across Latin America the more light-skinned a person is and the more one's complexion retains European features—light hair and blue eyes for example—the greater that person's potential for professional success and high social status. There remains a hierarchy of race and skin color from light to dark in these supposedly mixed cultures.[65] In the U.S. Southwest European Americans, by and large, remain dominant in the political and economic decision-making structures while most Latinos remain poor.

Without dismissing the salience of all these realities, the agonal dimension of mestizaje still lies primarily in the *process* of cultures transforming each other. Gloria Anzaldúa, the Mexican American poet, vividly captures in her work the stress and strain of those who "cross borders"—be it the U.S.-Mexico territorial border, the European indigenous-Latino cultural border, or the male-female or straight-gay symbolic borders.

Anzaldúa especially traces the subordination of indigenous peoples and women to the Spanish Conquest of Mexico. On the one hand, Mexican and Mexican American culture, with its emphasis on extended family and person-to-person relationships, has much to offer a world in which each of us feels pressured by time and cut off from one another. On the other hand, Anzaldúa contends that these cultural traits have not traditionally allowed individuality or deviance. If a woman does not marry and have any children, for instance, then she is considered a failure.[66] Most importantly she emphasizes that the bottom line in gender relationships is "men make the rules and laws, women transmit them."[67]

Although she acknowledges the symbolic importance of Our Lady of Guadalupe, especially for poor Mexicans and Mexican Americans in their struggles for political and economic justice, Anzaldúa also traces how Guadalupe has been manipulated by political and religious authorities to make people subservient. Anzaldúa interprets Guadalupe as the Aztec goddess Tonantzin. She argues that even prior to the Spanish conquest, the Aztecs split this goddess into "light" or good and "dark" or bad sides: Tonantzin emerges as the Good Mother while Coatlicue, her serpent/sexual dimension, is removed. The Spaniards and the Roman Catholic Church, she continues, recast this dichotomy into Guadalupe/Virgin María, the pure virgin, and Coatlicue, the *puta* or whore.[68] The powerful symbolism of Our Lady of Guadalupe "as the virgin mother who has not abandoned us," she concludes, has been used by the Church to make Mexicans "docile and enduring."[69]

In like fashion the two other pivotal Mexican feminine symbolic figures, la Chingada (Malinche) and la Llorona, Anzaldúa continues, have been used symbolically to pacify "Indians and *mexicanos* and Chicanos." La Chingada, "the raped mother whom we have abandoned," has made "us ashamed of our Indian side." La Llorona, "the mother who seeks her lost children," has "made us long suffering people."[70] Anzaldúa takes comfort in the fact that some indigenous persons and mestizos remain who "worship the original indigenous spirit entities (including Guadalupe) and their supernatural power, under the guise of Christian saints" and thus do not propagate the virgin/*puta* dichotomy.[71]

Much more so than Elizondo, Anzaldúa emphasizes that in mestizaje "the coming of two self-consistent but habitually incompatible frames of reference causes *un choque,* a cultural collision."[72] Still, she maintains that it is precisely the Mexican American experience of such collisions that provides a basis for combining opposites. For instance, she describes at least eight different languages spoken in the borderlands between the United States and Mexico. She insists that Mexican Americans, rather than feeling ashamed of their use of Spanish and English as being inferior to that of Mexicans or to that of European Americans, should engage these 'others' on both sides of the border from a position of dignity in being mestizos.[73]

Fully acknowledging that the original mestizaje in Mexico was "the product of conqueror and conquered,"[74] Anzaldúa nevertheless elicits an inclusive consciousness that intrinsically deals with contradictions, ambiguity, and the combination of opposites. Ultimately, in Anzaldúa's work, Mexican and Mexican American identity emerges as a way of being that transcends borders: "Being Mexican is a state of soul—not one of mind, not one of citizenship. Neither eagle nor serpent, but both. And like the ocean, neither animal respects borders."[75]

More so than Vasconcelos and Elizondo, Anzaldúa is quite incisive regarding the long-standing repression of those who are different within Mexican and Mexican American culture. She understands that the crossing of borders is a variegated undertaking, full of tensions and contradictions. Although Mexican culture, according to her rendering, has been repressive to supposed misfits and outcasts—especially with regard to gender and sexual preference, she amplifies Vasconcelos's theme that in Mexico and Latin America this wrestling with difference has been at the heart of the culture for the past five centuries. In the end, Anzaldúa's sober account of the plight of those on the margin, both literally and symbolically, tempers both Elizondo's sanguine rendering of mestizaje and the predisposition to unity and fusion in Vasconcelos's account of *la raza cósmica*.

ANZALDÚA-ELIZONDO NEXUS

Despite the differences in tone in their renderings of mestizaje, Anzaldúa and Elizondo mutually develop the ethical dimension of Vasconcelos's notion of *la raza cósmica*. In Vasconcelos the Latin American experience with mixing races and cultures cultivates a humanity that combines multiple peoples in lateral, collaborative relationships and elicits an aesthetic vision capable of countering the growing materialism and economic preponderance of his day. This ethical concern is even more salient today in terms of the global economy than it was for Vasconcelos almost a century ago.

In terms of Vasconcelos's emphasis on racial mixing, both Anzaldúa's and Elizondo's articulations of mestizaje stress much more than Vasconcelos the contributions made by the cultures of peoples of color, especially the indigenous peoples of the Americas. The Eurocentric accent on "civilizing peoples" found in Vasconcelos's presentation does not appear in Anzaldúa's and Elizondo's accounts. Anzaldúa recognizes that the presence of multiple identities in the Mexican American experience has never resulted in a cozy unity and instead has acknowledged the multiple levels of tensions and strains in racial and cultural mixing, contrary to what Vasconcelos would have us believe.

Nevertheless, even though Anzaldúa provides a much more agonal, conflict-ridden depiction of mestizaje than Elizondo, her presentation suffers from the same shortcoming seen in Vasconcelos, except in reverse: she dwells on the indigenous side of the Mexican American experience at the expense of the Catholic, European American, and Spanish sides. In this regard her outlook resembles the radical breach Deloria makes between particular local indigenous spiritualities and universal "placeless" Christianity. If the "civilizing" ethos undermines the ethical import of Vasconcelos's *la raza cósmica*, an articulation of mestizaje that clearly distances indigenous spiritualities from Christianity, other philosophies, and potentially other world religions raises the question of how genuinely lateral and authentic the mixing of cultures being proffered really is.

Anzaldúa's critique of Catholic Christianity focuses on the hierarchical institutional church that traditionally supported the ruling elites throughout Latin America from the time of the conquest through the 1960s, not the "popular church" stressed in the notion of Christian-base communities since the Second Meeting of the Latin American Episcopal (Catholic) Conference in Medellín, Colombia, in 1968 and more importantly in the notion of popular religion currently being advanced by contemporary Latino theologians. Popular religion involves the historical mixing of African, European, and indigenous spiritual practices in Mexico, the Caribbean region, and other parts of Latin America. This intriguing combination of Christianity with antecedent folk rituals—a practice that has served as a counterculture for the "popular church" against political, economic, and even ecclesiastical elites in Latin America and the U.S. Southwest—I explore at greater length in chapter 3. Suffice it to say here that popular religion illustrates that it is possible for diverse spiritualities to encounter each other without one being assimilated or exterminated by the 'other.' Deloria and Anzaldúa never envisage such an authentic mixing of spiritual traditions.

By contrast, Elizondo's rendering of mestizaje elicits a space for dynamic interaction between diverse religions and spiritualities. He reminds us that most of the great Christian shrines in Europe are at locations venerated by the pre-Christian peoples. Just as the appearance of Our Lady of

Guadalupe bridged Catholic and indigenous spiritualities in Mexico, Elizondo contends, "What the world needs today is a Guadalupe-event, an eruption in an unsuspected region of the world through the mediation of an unimagined person who offers the masses a new source of unity and hope."[76] Ironically, the mixing of spiritual traditions, contained in popular religion and Elizondo's version of mestizaje, illustrates Anzaldúa's accentuation of contradictions and contending opposites even more clearly than her articulation of indigenous spirituality.

Influenced by post-Vatican II studies of inculturation—the dynamic between the universal Christian message and its expression in particular cultures—Elizondo adds that "it is in opening up to others, with all the risks and possibilities involved, that the particular, without ceasing to be particular, now becomes universal."[77] Through the interchange of diverse particulars, he continues, the exclusivity of each particular is left behind and mutual enrichment ensues. As suggested previously, Elizondo's post-Eurocentric articulation of Christianity, with its emphases on hospitality and engagement of the 'other,' suggests how to move beyond the Reformation–Counter Reformation debate to a genuine dialogue among world religions. This is especially crucial for articulating a moral consensus in countries such as the United States that are no longer, in religious terms, just Judeo-Christian nations.

Elizondo revitalizes Vasconcelos's aesthetic critique of what he saw as Anglo-Saxon economic imperialism and especially the materialistic bent of that civilization. The global economy of today, though, transcends any one nation or civilization, even though Elizondo tags it as the "U.S. way of life."[78] Elizondo insists that the Mexican American experience of combining cultures amid extensive economic marginalization offers a positive counterculture to the universalization through uniformity, spread by McWorld. Amid the rapid spread of consumer goods and ideals, he suggests that regional groups nevertheless exist that are revitalizing their cultures in a deep, legitimate way without leading to the xenophobia of jihad: "They want to participate in the universal culture that is emerging without being consumed by it."[79]

As opposed to Barber's polar opposition of McWorld and jihad and to his recourse to the acultural nation-state as an alternative, Elizondo elicits through the Mexican American experience of mestizaje a dynamic relationship of the universal and the particular in which one does not overwhelm the other. Instead of "unity through uniformity" or "sheer diversity," Elizondo articulates a vision of unity-in-diversity. Congruent with

Vasconcelos's vision of *la raza cósmica,* but without its "civilizing" motif, he contends that a mestizo "U.S.-Americanism is radiating a new image and experiencing a new soul—no longer the face and voice of a soloist, but the countenance and heart of an entire symphony."[80]

In contrast to Elizondo, Anzaldúa's critique of European and European American civilization is much more biting. She emphasizes the indigenous legacy in the Mexican American experience through her portrait of the subtle but long-standing resistance of Mexican Americans to the dominant European American civilization of especially the past two centuries:

> *Los Chicanos,* how patient we seem, how very patient. There is the quiet of the Indian about us. When other races have given up their tongue, we've kept ours. We know what it is to live under the hammer blow of the dominant *norteamericano* culture. But more than we count the blows, we count the days the weeks the years the centuries the eons until the white laws and commerce and customs will rot in the deserts they've created, lie bleached. *Humildes* yet proud, *quietos* yet wild, *nosotros los mexicanos*—Chicanos will walk by the crumbling ashes as we go about our business.[81]

Although the tones of Anzaldúa's and Elizondo's presentations are quite different, they both nevertheless depict a culture that has not only crossed borders without losing a sense of its identity, but through this extensive experience with crossing borders has found a resourcefulness to resist, and in some instances counter, the prevailing motifs of assimilation, homogenization, and uniformity in the rapid spread of universal consumerism.

Both Anzaldúa's and Elizondo's arguments criticize any philosophy, theory, or perspective that ascribes to the notion that there is "one best way" of doing things, a phrase made famous by Frederick Taylor in his notion of scientific management a century ago.[82] In fact, it is precisely the positivist and engineering orientation of theories such as Taylor's that motivates Vasconcelos to articulate his holistic, aesthetic notion of *la raza cósmica.* He seeks to cultivate instead a qualitative approach to pluralism, ambiguity, and difference that avoids the sterility of uniformity without leading to the anarchy of relativism. Anzaldúa and Elizondo, despite differences in tone and style, seek this same end.

Even given her more agonal portrait of mestizaje, Anzaldúa still acknowledges that crossing borders genuinely means that all sides have to be willing to engage in a mutual, lateral transformation: "At some point, on our way to a new consciousness, we will have to leave the opposite bank, the split between the two mortal combatants somehow healed so that we are on both shores at once and, at once, see through serpent and eagle eyes."[83] Elizondo, in like fashion, shows that ethically mestizaje entails synthesizing cultures and traditions in a way that does not lead to dominance by any of the intersecting parties:

> *Mestizos* may struggle to become one or the other of the great traditions out of which they are born, but even if they were to succeed, that would be a mere return to the previous divisions of society. We usher in new life for the betterment of everyone when we consciously assume the great traditions flowing through our veins, not by denying them but by synthesizing them into something new.[84]

Mestizaje, as a moral praxis, illustrates the possibility of traversing contradictions, combining opposites, and engaging opposites in an intersubjective, lateral, nonviolent fashion. This is not to suggest that disagreement, conflict, and even repression will not be experienced in crossing borders; to the contrary, moving beyond either/ors—whether in terms of culture, language, race, or religion—is taxing. Nor does this ethos of crossing borders deny the marginalization and impoverishment that Mexican Americans and other Latinos have frequently endured in being caught between cultures. Actually, the domination of one culture or group over other cultures and groups is usually endemic to either/ors, such as in Barber's jihad *v.* McWorld. Therefore, the path of mestizaje is not a matter of scripting things this way or that way, but of opening oneself to experiencing both, fully, without having to come to a cozy, superficial consensus.[85] This heritage, as recast in moral terms by Vasconcelos and Elizondo, suggests that personal and community well-being can be fostered through multicultural encounters.

To recapitulate, in the U.S. Southwest, there has been a mestizaje of European American, Latino, Native American, and other cultures ensuing since at least the 1820s. Subsequent waves of migration especially from Mexico and Central America combined with advances in telecommunications have made the present spread of the "Latino presence" in the U.S. Southwest and other areas of the country a distinctly different development from the immigration of especially European groups to the United States in the nineteenth and early twentieth century. Moreover, attempts to mitigate this presence through public policy—such as Propositions 187, 209, and 227 in California—are only further tesitmony to how pervasive the "Latino presence" has become.

Rather than rendering this presence as a negative, Anzaldúa and Elizondo, building upon Vasconcelos's recasting of mestizaje as a holistic, aesthetic rationality, in disparate ways suggest that mestizaje provides both an experiential and intellectual basis for engaging in multicultural relations in a *democratic* fashion, not just in the U.S. Southwest but throughout the country. Almost a century ago Vasconcelos sought to counter the racial assimilation promoted by social Darwinism and Nazi ideology and aimed to counter the burgeoning materialism of what he termed Anglo-Saxon civilization. However, his privileging of unity over diversity and his retention of a Eurocentric motif of "civilizing" other cultures ultimately undermines his articulation of *la raza cósmica* as an aesthetic reconciliation of the universal and the particular.

The struggles that Mexican Americans and Latinos have had crossing borders between U.S. American and Latin American cultures over the past two centuries, however, provide an effective experiential basis for (1) moving beyond the assimilation and separatist models of multicultural relations and (2) realizing the aesthetic, counter-materialist politics projected by Vasconcelos. Anzaldúa's and Elizondo's respective agonal and ecstatic depictions of mestizaje shed the latent Eurocentric bent to Vasconcelos's *la raza cósmica* while revitalizing his dynamic reconciliation between the universal and the particular. In the next chapter, I discuss and develop specific attributes of a mestizo democracy, as intimated in contemporary Latino theology.

CHAPTER 3

Attributes
of a Mestizo Democracy

nzaldúa's and Elizondo's depictions of mestizaje provide the
basis for realizing a unity-in-diversity that culminates neither
in assimilation nor separatism. In this chapter, I put forward
and discuss the following attributes of a mestizo democracy
that I find embedded in the works of Latino theologians and
scholars:

- an engagement of reality as both/and, not either/or;
- the permeability of borders in contrast to the inelasticity of
  frontiers;
- the political countercultural implications of popular religion;
- an affective, aesthetic rendering of rationality and epistemology;
- a relational as opposed to a possessive rendering of morality and
  community;
- the transformation of relations of domination into relations of
  empowerment;
- the engendering of hope in the struggle for justice for all peoples.

To develop each attribute at length, I draw specifically upon the work
of María Pilar Aquino Vargas, Ana María Díaz-Stevens, Allan Figueroa Deck,
Virgil Elizondo, Orlando Espín, Ismael García, Sixto García, Roberto
Goizueta, Justo González, Ada María Isasi-Díaz, Ana María Pineda, Harold
Recinos, Jeanette Rodriguez, Fernando Segovia, Samuel Solitán-Román,
Anthony Stevens-Arroyo, and Eldín Villafañe, in addition to other scholars

writing in this rapidly expanding discipline. In particular my exegesis emphasizes, on the one hand, the process and manner of inclusion (the affective dimensions) and, on the other hand, the realization of just political, social, and economic arrangements (the effective dimensions) of this alternative politics. Engaging the above seven normative attributes in combination will suggest why a mestizo democracy is crucial for realizing an inclusive and just politics of crossing borders.

The Primacy of the Latino Experience as Both/And, not Either/Or

Even though Latino theology is indebted to the work of Gustavo Gutiérrez and other Latin America liberation theologians over the past four decades, mestizaje as either theology or political theory is not just a northward projection of liberation theology. In contemporary political theory, philosophy, and theology informed by cultural hermeneutics, being sensitive to the particularities of context, place, and situation is very important. Both Anzaldúa and Elizondo, as shown in the previous chapter, capture the experience of being caught between worlds: being neither Mexican nor U.S. American, yet simultaneously both/and. As also reviewed in the previous chapter, the attraction of the Chicano movement to Vasconcelos's notion of *la raza cósmica* is provoked by this predicament of being situated in a nexus of cultures. As suggested by the title of Fernando Segovia's essay, Latinos find themselves between "Two Places and No Place on Which to Stand."[1]

Thus, a mestizo democracy is a challenge to frameworks that squeeze the multicultural reality of the United States into either a European American orientation, on the one hand, or a Latin American framework, on the other.[2] Instead, Goizueta suggests we engage in a "critical appropriation" of these diverse theological traditions in the light of Latino experience: "Such a task requires that we approach and critique traditional theological sources and methods, whether European or Latin American, from the perspective of U.S. Hispanics in order to be able to articulate the significance of that perspective for the life of our communities, the church, and society."[3]

Taking Goizueta's insight a step further, my critique of both Bellah's and Geyer's articulation of community in the first chapter is not that their emphasis on cultivating heartfelt mores is unimportant to the health of U.S. democracy, but rather that their renderings of these mores and values are too exclusively rooted in the European American experience. In a country increasingly characterized by the vital contributions of African Americans, Asian Americans, Latinos, and Native Americans—and as dealing with the 'other' becomes, increasingly, a daily experience—our core community values need to be rooted in the concrete experience of simultaneously engaging multiple traditions, a long-standing reality for Latinos.

Displacing the Frontier with the Border

The Latino experience with crossing borders, both literal and figurative, is vital for dealing with multiculturalism in a constructive fashion. As Segovia suggests, the Latino experience is "a radical sense of mixture and otherness, *mezcolanza* and *otredad*, both unsettling and liberating at the same time."[4] Moreover, this radical dynamic ensues not only when Latinos mix with other U.S. cultural groups, but also when Latino groups intermix. Consequently, "barriers of exclusion" are antithetical to a mestizo democracy.[5]

Conceptually, Justo González's distinction between "borders" and "frontiers," based on the different character of the respective Spanish and English colonizations of the Americas, illustrates in cultural terms the difference between collaborative and heterogeneous "mixing," on the one hand, and oppressive and homogeneous domination, on the other. The English conquest, according to González, manifested a frontier mentality in which peoples deemed alien were pushed back or eliminated as English colonists spread "civilization" westward across the North American continent:

> What the northern colonists wanted was land. The original inhabitants were a hindrance. So instead of subjugating the Indians, they set about to push them off their lands, and eventually to exterminate them. If the myth in the Spanish colonies was that the Indians were like children who needed someone to govern them, the myth in the English colonies was that the Indians were nonpeople; they didn't exist, their lands were a vacuum. In north Georgia, in the middle of Cherokee Country, there is a monument to a white man who was, so the monument says, "the first man to settle in these parts." And this, in a county that is still called "Cherokee!"[6]

Not surprisingly, according to González, it became the "Manifest Destiny" of this "civilization" to enter and give significance to this void.[7]

A "border mentality," by contrast, according to González entails mutual interaction and enrichment. He suggests that the Spanish conquest of the Americas, was illustrative of this mixing, albeit with the Spanish in control of political and economic relations:

> Today in a plaza in Mexico City, which marks the place of the last great armed struggle between the Aztecs and the Spanish, there is a marker that attempts to explain what took place there: "There were neither victors nor vanquished; it was rather the painful birth of the new race which is the Mexican people." . . . This is too rosy a picture, for the Aztecs were indeed vanquished, and for many generations had to pay dearly for it. Nevertheless, it is true that from the moment the true growing edge of Mexican life was not the geographic frontier, but rather the other less discernible though real border at which people of different cultures thrown by history met, clashed, rebelled, intermarried, and eventually produced a new, *mestizo* reality.[8]

Whereas a frontier, he continues, is "unidirectional" and clearly demarcates progress from backwardness, a border is "bidirectional" and growth ensues through "mutual enrichment," not "conquest."[9]

A border, in contrast to a frontier, suggests a lateral interchange of equal cultures and an openness to differences whose intersection does not have to culminate in uniformity. Granting that the Spaniards did conquer Mexico and most of Latin America, González's point is that with mestizaje the engagement of the 'other' is a positive encounter, in contrast to notions of impurity and defilement that characterize the assimilation or annihilation ethos of the frontier. Indeed, this multidirectional ebb and flow of cultures underlies Elizondo's notion of a synthesis that can bring contradictory forces together.

In contrast is the position that views U.S. culture as a possession requiring defense from foreign contamination, as in Geyer's *Americans No More*. "English only" proposals, the militarizing of the U.S.-Mexico border, and a call for increased immigration restrictions are contemporary manifestations of "frontier" thinking. When that frontier reaches its geographic limits, then it will have to be defended at all costs from "inferior" races and cultures that threaten its hegemony.

Envisioning cultural relations as borders to be crossed rather than as frontiers to be defended, suggests the possibility that diverse cultures can interact in a lateral, egalitarian fashion and that a democratic set of political relationships requires such interaction. For example, rather than insistence on "English only," "Spanish only," or "any-language-only"—all possessive renderings of identity—the emphasis should be on communication. Daily in the U.S. Southwest, many peoples communicate through a combination of English and Spanish. These "border crossings" are not just out of necessity but involve an opportunity for mutual growth, as suggested by Carlos Fuentes:

> There are different systems in the world. There are different nation-alities, different cultures, different personalities. There are many people that are not like me in the streets, but that doesn't mean I can't communicate with them. On the contrary, it's a wonderful challenge to be able to communicate with what is not like you. What is terrible is when a nation with power says that what is not like me should be exterminated—Nazi Germany or Stalinist Russia, for example. But as long as you say, "I am what I am, but that doesn't mean I'm better than anybody else, it means I am different, and the other one is different too, and we can understand each other, we can talk, we can communicate"—that is the basic attitude that makes life civilized and communication possible.[10]

Indeed, contrary to those who have turned to the Bible to defend slavery, segregation, and "religious and cultural purity," González points out that many stories in the book of Joshua, for instance, actually convey "fluid identity boundaries."[11] In these narratives, mestizos employ a wily subversion rather than a direct confrontation of the frontier mentality. Moreover, González, from the standpoint of the border, views the exile or alien as a blessing for the dominant society, just as Joseph's gifts ultimately benefited Pharaoh and Egypt. Thus, counter to contemporary nativism that would exclude the alien or the foreigner, the contemporary waves of new "Americans" coming to the U.S. from Latin America, Asia, Africa, and other places enrich our cultural, political, and social networks. Ultimately, from the standpoint of borders, not frontiers, González concludes that by excluding others, "we exclude ourselves."[12]

But before waxing too romantic over this Latino crossing borders experience, we should recall from our previous examination of Anzaldúa that women and 'others' considered different have frequently been marginalized in Mexico. Similarly, machismo and other forms of domination are hardly foreign to the Latino experience. González emphasizes that part of the marginalization experienced by Protestant Latino Americans comes from the dominant Roman Catholic Latino culture in their communities. Each of these barriers must be confronted, and the notion and experience of crossing borders provide a vital, lived basis for doing so.

Another merit of the ethos of crossing borders rather than "expanding or preserving frontiers" is that it is applicable not just to relationships between diverse cultures, linguistic groups, and races, but to other categorizations too quick to separate people into "this group" and "that group," with one group being dominant. *Mujerista* theology, especially as presented by Ada María Isasi-Díaz integrates González's articulation of crossing borders with the feminist dimensions of Anzaldúa's work. Isasi-Díaz, in particular, cautions that feminists, who struggle against patriarchalism within both Christian communities and society at-large, must ensure that they in turn do not dominate other women. For example, she takes to task European American feminists who do not treat women of color as co-participants in articulating feminism:

> Somewhat naively I had thought that together we would decide not only how to garden but what the garden was to look like, what it would be. But the European American feminists, being part of the dominant culture, deal with Hispanic women—and other racial/ethnic women—differently from the way they deal with each other. They take for granted that feminism in the USA is *their* garden, and therefore they will decide what manner of work racial/ethnic women will do there.[13]

Instead, Isasi-Díaz stresses that mutual border crossings involve not just respecting what 'others' are saying, but giving those perspectives substantial consideration in articulating "what is normative for all feminists."[14] Thus, a genuine sharing of diverse perspectives in a lateral, collaborative fashion entails not just including previously excluded perspectives, but recasting the terms of the conversation to enable all interlocutors to carry on the dialogue.

Ultimately, the Latino experience and ethos of crossing borders is what Elizondo terms a mestizo anthropology. As opposed to the frontier mentality's insistence on either assimilation or annihilation of 'others,' a mestizo anthropology involves an inclusive and progressive synthesis of different ideas and cultures that is not a melting pot. At the same time, this anthropology entails a universal respect for the differences of 'others' and exemplifies the Christian act of hospitality to the stranger.[15] In a world in which heterogeneous, not homogeneous, identities are proliferating and continually shifting, crossing borders as a concrete engagement and combination of opposites moves beyond either uniformity or incommensurability.

The Portent of Popular Religion

The substantive basis of the capacity for crossing borders lies rooted in the extensive historical legacy of popular religion in Latino and Latin American culture. It is one thing to articulate a unity-in-diversity in the abstract, but truly heartfelt attachments and experiences are essential for such a notion to be realized as a concrete political culture. Popular religion provides such a concrete legacy and orientation.

Popular religion involves long-standing spiritual rituals performed by ordinary people: for instance, home altars, *el Día de los Muertos* (the Day of the Dead) celebrations, personal devotions to saints, and *las posadas* (a house-to-house pilgrimage held the nine nights before Christmas in which pilgrims join Mary and Joseph in their search for shelter at Jesus' birth). In the Caribbean the pursuit of Santeria—a commingling of Christian and especially African rituals—is widespread. Popular religion as a people's spirituality is also a descendant of "the medieval fascination with saints, shrines, relics, images, miracles, and religious storytelling."[16]

Within mainstream institutional Christian churches in the United States, Mexico, and other parts of Latin America, these popular practices have been disparaged as unsophisticated, if not uncivilized, supposedly needing purification and modernization. Such "civilizing" myopia does not grasp the profound way in which popular religion synthesizes supposedly distinct religious traditions into a mestizo spirituality. The inclusiveness, the people-centeredness, and the constructive embrace of the marginalized that all characterize popular religion also offer a more democratic vision of politics that can effectively engage unjust economic and social disparities.

The normative and historical sources for Latino popular religion are a combination of African, European, and indigenous practices. Espín contends that popular religion is a combination of the "sacral worldviews" of "pre-Tridentine Christianity" and "Amerindian and African religions" in the Americas.[17] The originality of Espín's scholarship lies in his claim that this "sacral worldview of the village" derived in part from Spanish medieval Catholic practices that predate the Council of Trent.[18] The Catholicism that comes to the Americas with the Spaniards, he maintains, is one that relies a great deal on "lay leadership at the local level" and "catechizing through symbols, stories, and dramas."[19] It is not until Trent, he adds, that rigidification of Catholic practices in the institutional church, in response to the Reformation, takes hold.

The sacral worldviews of pre-Tridentine Christianity, Amerindian spirituality, and African spirituality, Espín emphasizes, share a holistic and heterogeneous orientation that engages the distinction between the sacred and the profane as a border, not as a frontier, and does so through the aestheticism of *flor y canto* (flower and song). For instance, one cannot understand the deep meaning of the appearance of Our Lady of Guadalupe at Tepeyac without appreciating the symbolism of flowers blooming out of season, the song of the birds enveloping her presence, and the specific colors adorning her visage. As Elizondo and others have shown, the recasting of the Aztec goddess Tonantzin as Guadalupe inculturates Christian revelation in a way perceptible in Nahuatl (indigenous) terms and incomprehensible to cold, linear rationalities. Consequently, Espín argues, Hellenistic Christian concepts like the Trinity become recast in the Americas in terms more akin to African or indigenous outlooks.

Several vital implications of this holistic and heterogeneous sacral worldview disclose the import of mestizaje for pastoral theology, political theology, and especially political theory. First, popular religion prompts a rethinking of what we understand to be Catholic Christianity, as it has existed over the past five centuries in the Americas. Historically in Latin America, at least until the 1960s, the institutional Roman Catholic Church had been aligned with the political and economic elites of the region. The reforms of Vatican II and the key meetings of the Latin American bishops in Medellín, Colombia, in 1968 and in Puebla, Mexico, in 1979 reoriented the formal church to "the preferential option for the poor" and to other central themes of liberation theology. Over the past two decades this radicalization of the church has been tempered by the appointment of more conservative bishops to the region by John Paul II. Catholicism in Latin America has simultaneously sustained a hierarchical institutional church and a "popular church" associated with Christian-base communities and the practices of popular religion.

The legacy of popular religion among the laity, and especially the poor, as an amalgam of African, European, and indigenous practices suggests that there have always been simulaneous Catholic churches in post-conquest Latin America. The poor—especially the indigenous—church has practiced popular religion alongside the institutional church and in some cases in lieu of it. As noted by González, it was the Franciscans, Dominicans, Jesuits, and Mercedarians, not diocesan clergy, who evangelized the indigenous peoples of the Americas; the diocesan clergy were content to minister to the Spanish colonizers and their indigenous servants in the towns and cities.[20]

After the conquest, popular religion emerged as the heart of the poor peoples' spirituality. This orientation, especially, has identified with the suffering, crucified Christ, who is seen as being in solidarity with those who endure poverty, rejection, oppression, and marginalization.

Nor has Catholicism in what is now the United States been spared the Latin American heritage of the hierarchical-popular church split. When New Mexico became part of the United States subsequent to the U.S.-Mexican War of 1846–1848, Antontio José Martínez, the pastor of Taos, came into conflict with Jean Baptiste Lamy, the new bishop appointed by the U.S. hierarchy. Martínez defended his parishioners, accustomed to closer collaboration between the pastor and the people, against the attempts of Lamy to "Americanize" them. As a result of this impasse, Martínez ultimately formed an alternative Catholic Church in northern New Mexico that became legendary among the long-standing Spanish-speaking families, who, as González points out, understood Catholicism "as the faith of the people and not as the monopoly of the hierarchy."[21] González also points out in this context that the Spanish phrase "*soy católico, pero no creo en los curas* (I am a Catholic, but I don't believe in priests)" should not be construed as anti-clerical but rather as the conviction that "only those priests who live up to their vocation . . . are believable priests."[22]

Second, both the heterogeneous and counterinstitutional church orientation of popular religion, especially as elucidated in Espín's studies, suggests that the growing "conversion" of many Latinos from Catholicism to Pentecostalism, both in the U.S. and across Latin America, is more a change of label than one of spiritual worldview. The Catholic Charismatic movement and Protestant Pentecostalism, as practiced by Latinos, are the latest vestiges of the affective and aesthetic character of popular religion. In this regard González relates the story of how a seminary professor, a Mexican Protestant, responded to the negative remarks about Our Lady of Guadalupe made by one of his students: "Young man, in this class you are free to say anything you please. You may say anything about me. You certainly are welcome to say anything you wish about the pope and the priests. But don't you touch my little Virgin!"[23]

At the same time, González does acknowledge that Latin American Pentecostals have historically envisioned their faith as liberating them from a "backward and anti-democratic" Catholic culture, as they look to the Protestant United States as a paragon of modernity and progress.[24] Still, this optimistic assessment subsequently has been revised by some Pentecostals who have come to realize the deleterious materialism and consumerism of

North American culture. The anticultural stance previously directed at Catholic Latin America is now being directed by some Latin American Pentecostals at Protestant and secular North America.[25]

Third, the heritage of popular religion both as "the people's church" and as a mixture of spiritualities constitutes a dynamic response to both Deloria's critique of Christianity raised previously in chaper 1 and Anzaldúa's critique of the same in chapter 2. Recall that Deloria contends that Christianity is an abstract universal religion that violates the sense of geography and place so sacred to indigenous religions in the Americas. Popular religion, as depicted by Latino theologians, suggests, to the contrary, that African, indigenous, and European practices have been mixing in the Americas in popular religion over the past five centuries without losing the sense of place, community, and nature so dear to Deloria. Contrary to Deloria's contentions, Christianity and indigenous spiritualities can intersect and transform each other in a way that does not vitiate the vitality and integrity of either.

Anzaldúa's charge that Spanish Catholicism fosters servility on the part of the indigenous peoples is cogent primarily in terms of the historic institutional church, but not the popular church. As discussed above, the popular church, both in its Catholic and Pentecostal varieties, has always been in critical engagement with repressive political, social, economic, and religious structures. As González points out, this countercultural legacy is leading especially to "a new ecumenism" in the United States in which Catholics and Protestants mobilize together on civil rights issues such as the state of migrant workers, community organizing, and access to political participation.[26] Finally, Anzaldúa's vivid critique of the subordination of women in Latino and Latin American cultures is also being addressed by *mujerista* and *feminista* theologies.

Fourth, a well-known thesis in the field of sociology of religion in the United States, originally made by Will Herberg and Ruby Kennedy, is that as immigrant groups assimilate in the United States they are less likely to lose the religion of their native culture than its ethnicity and language. Hence, Italian, Irish, and Polish Catholics, supposedly within three generations, lose their distinctive ethnic identities but continue to remain Catholic as opposed to becoming Protestant or Jewish.[27] Latino popular religion, however, especially as captured in this "new ecumenism," suggests that for Latinos the dividing lines between Catholic and Protestant, Charismatic and Pentecostal, and indigenous and Christian spirituality are not especially salient. If anything, the sacral worldview of popular religion manifests a capacity to engage and eventually combine diverse spiritualities in a lateral, not hierarchical, fashion. This capacity for combining opposites is a valuable orientation for a twenty-first century United States in which Islam and non-Western religions are becoming more visible parts of the religious scene.

Similarly, Latino popular religion also reshapes David Tracy's and Andrew Greeley's delineation between the analogical and dialectical spiritual imaginations. On the one hand, according to Greeley, Protestants manifest the dialectical imagination, a point of view that sees "human society as 'God-forsaken'"; thus, believers can only be redeemed as individuals through their relationship with a sovereign, transcendent God. On the other hand, Catholics manifest the analogical imagination, which sees "society as a 'sacrament' of God and therefore social relationships reveal, however imperfectly, the presence of God."[28] Greeley, in turn, demonstrates through sociological surveys that these different spiritual imaginations lead Protestants and Catholics to have different social and political outlooks: Protestants tend to focus on individual rights and see social and governmental bodies as hostile, whereas Catholics tend to focus on the importance and goodness of familial and social networks.[29]

However, a fault line is emerging in U.S. spirituality as a consequence of popular religion, as suggested by Espín's work. On one side stand primarily European American Catholics and Protestants, whose spiritual imagination is rooted in the Reformation-Counter Reformation debate and is closer to Tracy's dialectical outlook. On the other side stand Catholics, Protestants, and practitioners of indigenous rites, primarily Latinos, whose sacral worldview is closer to Tracy's analogical outlook. European American Catholics, despite their heritage of the analogical imagination, have had to contend with the extensive influence of the Reformation on the history of the United States and have had to accommodate themselves to subsequent Protestant ideals—John Winthrop's "city-on-a-hill," for example—that have played a powerful role in shaping U.S. cultural identity. In a sense, as Mark Massa contends, as liberal Catholics gained access to the social mainstream of United States in the 1940s, 1950s, and 1960s, many became more zealous defenders of the U.S. way of life than their Protestant counterparts.[30]

By contrast, up until the recent proliferation of Pentecostal evangelism, the religious divide in Latin America has not been between Protestant and Catholic or between Reformation and Counter-Reformation, but between the popular church informed by a holistic and heterogeneous spirituality and the hierarchical church oriented by the more elitist and formally rigid framework set in place after the Council of Trent. As Ana María Díaz-Stevens and Anthony M. Stevens-Arroyo point out, before the Reformation Christianity provided a "buffer zone between the officially sacred and the daily experience of the mundane," or what they term "a com-munitarian spirituality."[31] The Reformation, they continue, has had a "corrosive" effect on the Catholic sacramental rendering of this spirituality across northern Europe. By contrast, the isolation of "the Latino homelands," has insulated Latin America from some of these developments.[32]

Therefore, when Deck refers to the ongoing migration of Latin Americans into the United States, especially from Mexico and Central America, as "the second wave," he intends more than just a historic and geographic discrimination from the "first wave" of primarily European immigrants to the United States.[33] Two very different substantive movements are meeting and clashing in the U.S. Southwest. The first wave—primarily European migration east-to-west across the continental U.S.—was driven by the frontier mentality whose intellectual origins lie in the Reformation and then the Enlightenment. The second wave—primarily Latino migration south-to-north—is keenly oriented by the "border mentality" whose intellectual origins lie in the heterogeneous and holistic worldview of popular religion.

The ability of popular religion to endure—for at least five centuries in the Latin American instance—all the while remaining open to other outlooks and other spiritualities, provides a formidable alternative to the prevailing frontier mentality in the U.S., whose benign name is the "melting pot." Although historically most immigrants to the United States have assimilated according to past U.S. norms within three generations, the deep cultural hermeneutical roots of popular religion in Latin America and its long-standing resiliency in the face of oppression by religious, political, and economic elites suggest that endeavors to "Americanize" Latinos may prove futile. Moreover, the historical presence of Latinos in the U.S. Southwest, the geographic proximity of this region to the rest of Latin America, and the dynamic ethos of integrating, not assimilating, traditions in popular religions combine to form a border ethos that could very well challenge the hegemony of the frontier ethos.

At the very least the intensity and depth of popular religion calls into question the Herberg/Kennedy typology reviewed above. In addition the spiritual imagination of popular religion will have an impact on U.S. political and social attitudes. We need more studies similar to Greeley's to assess the content and contour of this impact. At a minimum, popular religion's concrete integration of spiritual traditions provides a basis for:

- moving beyond the Christian-centric discussion of religion in the United States,
- engaging Islam and non-Western religions in a more inviting way,
- and realizing an "affective" politics of unity-in-diversity.

An Affective, Aesthetic Rationality

Popular religion captures in practice the affective, aesthetic rationality emphasized by Vasconcelos in the previous chapter. Vasconcelos's work, however, remains that of an educator and a philosopher, whereas popular religion is steeped in concrete experience. Anyone who is active in Christian churches in the U.S. Southwest knows firsthand of the enormous turnout of Latinos on Ash Wednesday, Good Friday, and the feast of Our Lady of Guadalupe. The heartfelt fervor expressed by Latinos on *el Día de los Muertos* (All Souls' Day) and even on Mother's Day is likewise striking. The vivid raw reenactments on Good Friday of Christ's suffering and resurrection in Latino communities illustrate that in the Latino worldview ideas and concepts must be realized and communicated first and foremost through the sensory realm.

Popular religion also overcomes one of the Eurocentric biases in Vasconcelos's work. Although Vasconcelos elicits the notion of *la raza cósmica,* his presentation retains a notion of "civilizing" the indigenous peoples. This preponderance of Eurocentric thinking is even a problem in the early articulations of liberation theology of the 1960s and 1970s, the frameworks of which are still indebted to the Hegelian/Marxist project. The affective, aesthetic rationality communicated by popular religion and the mestizo experience of Latinos combine African, European, and indigenous outlooks in a lateral way that does not privilege any one tradition. Conversely, if Vasconcelos's shortcoming is his Eurocentric inclinations, this heterogeneous juxtaposition of traditions also challenges Deloria's or Anzaldúa's privileging of the indigenous worldview over those stemming from Europe.

The affective, aesthetic rationality conveyed in the Latino worldview addresses the following pivotal question, as phrased by Elizondo: "How to reconcile the western world of individualism, materialism, and rational thought . . . with the ancient Mexican world of *divina providencia* (which appears as magical ideas to the outsider), mystery, and myth which are the

effective cause of our communion with God and God's effective interven-
tion in our lives?"[34] Indeed, the concrete pursuit of this question is especially consonant with contemporary philosophical debates regarding how
to move beyond Eurocentric modernity to realize a lateral truth between
cultures without slipping into an anarchic cultural relativism or, conversely,
into a tyrannically imposed communitarianism having little or no respect
for differences.

In this affective, aesthetic rationality, truth is not something disconnected
in an abstract way from the world but, as Elizondo conveys, something that
"exists in the relational, the interconnected, the beautiful, and the melodic.
. . ."[35] As opposed to the Cartesian separation of the thinking ego from the
world of experience, Latino rationality makes use of "all the avenues of
knowing: the senses, the mind, and the heart."[36] This affective, aesthetic
rationality is steeped in intuition and a great deal of mysticism. Indeed, poets and other authors are integral to the expression of this rationality; the
work of Anzaldúa, among others, comes to mind. In the words of Sixto García,
poets capture "the ineffable mystery of the graced encounter."[37] The rumina-
tions of Latino theology, in turn, are often poetic in character.

In simple terms, the affective, aesthetic rationality available in popular
religion and in Latino theology has the following orientations. First, it manifests a relational, concrete, aesthetic portrait of truth akin to the analogical,
sacramental imagination articulated by Tracy and Greeley earlier. Second,
it emphasizes a lateral not hierarchical integration of cultures; the heterogeneous character of this rationality engages in both/and, not either/or,
thinking. Third, it accents a universal respect of 'others' in their "differences";
indeed, such differences are not utterly separate from community life, nor
are they to be subsumed under some convenient unity. Fourth, it emphasizes the revelatory character of concrete particulars. Truth realized "in the
totality of events"[38] springs from the dynamism between subjective particular events and so-called objective universals—"the intrinsic connection
between particular meaning and universal truth."[39]

There are at least four immediate applications of this affective, aesthetic
rationality for ongoing conceptual debates. First, this rationality, especially
as realized in the popular church, looks askance at so-called objective perspectives and professional "credentialism"; as put by Isasi-Díaz, exercise of
this rationality is "to be suspicious about what we have not participated in
defining."[40] Specifically, Isasi-Díaz is referring to the exclusion of women
from the definition of the spiritual and conceptual frameworks that affect
their lives.

Nevertheless, the "suspicion" she raises is also relevant to the questions that the Latino affective, aesthetic rationality put to prevailing canons. More often than not, those who have power are those that *define* the standards of recruitment and advancement in workplaces and decision-making structures. This aesthetic rationality calls into question the legitimacy of precise, almost scientific compartmentalization of standards whose formulation occurs without the contributions of the people they will affect. So as to move beyond objectivity lorded over others, this rationality suggests that a much larger group of people must be included in substantive deliberations and that the contours of the deliberation must not be restricted to narrow scientific, technological, materialist, or especially "means-end" approaches. This affective, aesthetic rationality engages the ambiguous and contradictory dimensions of reality that escape instrumentalist rationalities.

Second, this affective, aesthetic rationality is highly critical of the individualism, materialism, and hedonism of the consumer culture that has come to characterize the United States and, increasingly, much of the world through the global economy. The globally constructed economy's reduction of life's values to quantitative terms, and the concomitant diminution of people to consumers, is the logical extension of the objective inclination of modernity. Recall that Vasconcelos's articulation of *la raza cósmica* was as much intended to counter the spreading commercialism of what he termed Anglo-Saxon civilization as to celebrate the valuable mixing of cultures and races in the Latin American heritage. Indeed, it is precisely the virtues of heterogeneity and juxtaposing differences that enable an affective, aesthetic rationality to be a subversive yet constructive counterculture to the modernist, homogenizing model of McWorld.[41]

Third, in view of the prevailing modernization and secularization and the failure of this "civilizing project,"[42] the affective, aesthetic rationality in popular religion and Latino theology offers an alternative to premodern, modern, or postmodern solutions. Like premodern perspectives, this rationality affirms a sense of the sacred and the transcendent but, unlike premodernity, rejects political, social, and economic arrangements that stress inequality and elitism. Like postmodern perspectives, this rationality affirms the importance of embracing differences and "distributing opportunities, resources, and benefits in an inclusive way"[43] but is more confident than most postmodern schemes in the capacity of opposites to combine in a heterogeneous sense of community. The fluid intersection of cultures in crossing borders moves beyond simply celebrating difference and incommensurability to effect a substantive mutual engagement of perspectives in pursuit of the truth.

Langdon Gilkey, the famous Protestant theologian, has gone as far as to claim that Catholicism is better situated than liberal Protestantism to contend with the pernicious dimensions of modernization and secularization because of its focus on "ritual, symbol, and myth."[44] If that is the case, Latino popular spirituality—with its aesthetic rationality and its sacral worldview of multicolored hues drawn from the African, indigenous, and medieval European worlds—is even better situated to grapple with the corrosive aspects of modernism, especially since this spirituality is steeped in the lives of the people.[45]

Fourth, in view of Greeley's insight that one's spiritual imagination has a vital influence on one's political and social actions, the affective, aesthetic rationality evoked in Latino popular spirituality can potentially grow into a counterculture more effectively opposing modernity than abstract ethical, philosophical, or theological schemes. It is unlikely that a unity-in-diversity is going to be realized by people studying Lawrence Kohlberg's levels of moral development, engaging in Jürgen Habermas's communicative practices, or wrestling with John Rawls's exegesis on justice. These "ideas," however admirable and modern in their own "right," are too abstract and removed from the concrete lives of people and communities.

Instead, inscribed in Latino popular spirituality is a sense of community amid multiple identities—what Díaz-Stevens and Stevens-Arroyo have termed a "cultural citizenship."[46] This citizenship is not just a nostalgic turn to the past or a mere claim "that somehow the language, values, customs, or traditions of Hispanics can be preserved from the inexorable forces of Americanization."[47] Instead, it provides a basis for effecting a concrete unity-in-diversity that *realistically* overcomes the negative aspects of modernity, while simultaneously and critically sustaining its liberating dimensions.

The Relational Character of Morality and Community

Given the above experiential and intellectual bases of the Latino sacral worldview, it should not be surprising that the accompanying conception of human relationships and community emphasizes a great deal of inter-subjective interaction. Ismael García offers three key characteristics of the ethics of Latino culture. First, in contrast to the long-standing tradition of individualism in U.S. culture, Latinos stress the social and relational character of morality: personal relationships are more important than abstract rules. Consequently, Latinos "give priority to care, responsibilities, and connectedness over separation, individual achievement, and individual rights."[48] Finally and most importantly in terms of politics, Latinos' emphasis on "the interdependent nature of social reality" leads to an awareness of how their actions affect others, especially in terms of social justice.[49]

During a political science discourse, I once referred to the political theory oriented by mestizaje as a "politics of relations," to which a critic sneered, "How could it be otherwise?" Such cynicism ignores the Latino in-depth alternative to the Cartesian conception of reality—autonomous subjects examining and manipulating a world of objects—and to the ethic of possessive and aesthetic individualism, which, as pointed out by Bellah and others, is so inscribed in U.S. culture.

As Goizueta stresses, in Latino culture the community, not the individual, has "ontological priority."[50] Because of the Latino experience and emphasis on the heterogeneous quality of life, this sense of community is not suffocating or coercive. Yes, relationships not rules are the priority, but this does not mean that community is forced upon individual Latinos. Instead, one learns to articulate one's persona within the context of one's place in a concrete sense of community.

Moreover, the Latino emphasis on community life does not imply simply a "chosen" community. In the liberal-communitarian debate over the past two decades in the United States, a subject I examine at greater length in the chapter 5, one salient notion is that of the individual choosing his or her community or "lifestyle." For instance, Bellah, in a critical vein, depicts the spread of lifestyle enclaves in the United States—groups of people who choose to come together in the same neighborhood or locale around a common hobby or activity. As much as this is a liberal or individualist way of trying to articulate a community supposedly void of repression and censorship, it is not the Latino "border" sense of relationships.

Much of the difficulty in discussing community is the objective, possessive way we conceive of it. Either community is imposed upon others—Barber's jihad—or it is something chosen by the individual—Bellah's lifestyle enclaves. Note again the "either/or." For Latinos, community is not an either/or but a both/and; it is a set of relationships into which one is born but that one can subsequently transform. Community life consists of interpretive relationships that precede one in time and to a certain degree shape one's character yet, at the same time, extend beyond one's life into the future upon which one's actions will have a decisive impact. A community is not just a set of tribal practices to be "pickled." For instance, I have always been struck by the fact that one of the first questions a Latino will ask when he or she sees you is, "How is your family?" This is not just perfunctory courtesy but to ask, "How are the relationships that have fostered you, and are you being attentive to these relationships?"

Over the past two decades, especially with the rise of the religious right, a lot of platitudes have sprung up surrounding "family values." In the Latino worldview, families are not warm, friendly havens in the midst of a competitive hostile world, but the building blocks—both lateral and mutual in orientation—for a sense of extended *relationships* in the world. Ironically, politicians who beat the family-values drum the loudest also push for economic practices, especially through the global economy, which disrupt the livelihood and close-knit character of families and neighborhoods.

The emphasis on *la familia* in Latino culture is just the first dimension of the complex network of relationships that form the basis of the Latino community. Families are "extended" not just by blood but by substantive relationship, especially by the roles of *madrinas/padrinos* (godmothers/godfathers). By becoming a godparent, one is literally joining another family; the commitment is in-depth, not just ceremonial. As opposed to the nuclear family stressed in mainstream U.S. culture, Latino culture emphasizes interdependent extended family networks.

This intersubjective mutuality is not restricted to families in Latino culture. The success of the *Encuentros* (encounters) movement in U.S. Catholic communities is rooted in such politics. Since the 1970s the U.S. Catholic Church has used small group meetings in predominantly Spanish-speaking parishes and communities to foster pastoral priorities and to develop leaders from within such communities. These *encuentros* or meetings start at the grassroots level and then continue through regional and national meetings to coalesce the substance of these discussions. The Catholic Hispanic Pastoral Plan of the 1980s and 1990s was generated through such a process. The most recent prominent example of this process was "*Encuentro* 2000: Many Faces in God's House," held in Los Angeles in July 2000 and whose participants were not only Latinos but members from the African American, Asian American, European American, Native American, and Pacific-Islander American Catholic communities.[51]

Ultimately, the mutual collaborative character of such encounters has the potential for transforming politics at large. This *pastoral de conjunto*, another name for the encuentro process, is not just an effort to empower Latinos through decision-making structures from which they were previously excluded or simply to make such structures more efficient, but to transform these structures in order to realize a politics of mutuality, not of domination: "Pastoral planning is viewed as a method of praxis ultimately concerned with bringing about serious, if not radical, change in conformity with a vision, a utopia. . . . Pastoral planning leads us to *historical praxis*—action geared to the transformation of society."[52] This *conjunto/ encuentro* process seeks to move beyond competitive "zero-sum" political institutions and processes.

A striking example of this alternative political vision is the *mujerista* theology articulated by Isasi-Díaz. Isasi-Díaz conducts interviews and collaborative retreats with Latinas at the grassroots level. In particular these retreats try to elicit spiritual perspectives from *lo cotidiano* (lived daily experience). Given that both indigenous women and mestizas for at least five centuries have been subjugated by the double barrel of cultural and patriarchal domination, this lived experience has been the struggle for survival or, as Isasi-Díaz puts it, *"¡La vida es la lucha!"*[53] Consequently, this spiritual encounter comes "from within" and "from below" and accents *"permítanme hablar"* (permit me to speak), especially against long-standing oppression and marginalization.[54]

These spiritual engagements among Latinas enable us to see the encuentro process with different eyes. Whereas traditional mores relegated Latinas to responsibilities within the home, Isasi-Díaz's exegesis of Latina experiences and values suggests that the experience of the Latina with developing strong interdependent networks that value personal worth through family life prepares them for leadership roles in greater society. Moreover, they bring to these roles a vision that is highly critical of hegemonic relationships; they seek "win-win" as opposed to "win-lose" strategies. This vision seeks to effect an inclusive, nonelitist pluralism: "The coming of the kin-dom of God has to do with a coming together of peoples, with no one being excluded and at the expense of no one."[55]

Another example of the collaborative praxis of mutuality from within the Latino experience is the work done in poor churches and communities in San Antonio by COPS, Communities Organized For Public Service, founded by Ernesto Cortes. COPS and its parallel organizations in Los Angeles—L.A. Metropolitan Organization—and in Houston—TMO (The Metropolitan Organization)—work with primarily poor church and religious communities to cultivate leaders and strategies that enable those communities to become active participants in political forums that determine the distribution of public resources and services, especially public school districts, city governments, county governments, and special districts. As opposed to being mere advocates for poor people, COPS activists seek to train church community members how to organize, first, by clarifying what the church community hopes to accomplish and, second, by developing the skills and strategies necessary for realizing their goals. Similar to the conjunto/encuentro process, COPS stresses the importance of members of a community coming together in a lateral and collaborative fashion to initiate a transformation of political, social, and economic forums—a method guided by a Christian vision of hope, empowerment, and justice.

Much of the success achieved by Cortes and COPS has involved taking the ethos of the traditional familial networks in Latino culture and making it a basis for collaborative organization and mobilization outside the home. As articulated by Cortes, the institutions and forums in which poor people participate become a basis for mobilizing for access to public forums and resources denied them previously: "You take institutions—the family, the church—and you use them as a source of power, of confidence, of authority. If you get people to talk about what's in the interest of their families, what are the threats to their families, what are the threats to the churches and community, they're willing to look at things like zoning, and they're willing to look at things like the school."[56]

The COPS orientation is very much a recasting of de Tocqueville's stress on the importance of intermediate institutions that connect people to government as well as to private-sector organizations. Ironically, at a time when scholars such as Bellah and Robert Putnam are bemoaning the loss of civic virtues and a sense of public community, examples such as COPS and the conjunto/encuentro process in Latino communities are revitalizing civic engagement and the cultivation of political judgment.

However, even though Cortes acknowledges the indebtedness of his vision of organizing to Saul Alinsky and the Industrial Areas Foundation (IAF), to de Tocqueville, and to Arendt—especially her notion of a citizenship focused on public happiness—COPS and related IAF organizations have tapped successfully into the Latino emphasis on extended families and relational networks. If freedom for Latinos, as Goizueta suggests, is "grounded in community,"[57] this ontological priority on collaborative relationships provides a fertile basis for successful organizing by groups like COPS. The organizers may bring the technical experience necessary for effective mobilizing, but the values of mutual interdependence and commitment to "staying the course," essential to sustaining mobilization, are deeply rooted in the relational ethos of Latino communities.

As highlighted by Ismael García, authentic moral agency for Latinos entails a loyalty given to a community's values after careful moral deliberation by each person.[58] This commitment to collaborative decision making in community, as suggested by Pineda, provides a constructive counterculture to the excesses of U.S. individualism: "In a society fragmented by individualism, competition, consumerism, violence, and blatant disregard for human dignity, the concept and methodology of *pastoral de conjunto* is a contribution that Hispanics make to the church and society."[59] At the same time, this ontological sense of community is not repressive or suffocating, especially in terms of dealing with differences. As opposed to tightly-scripted communities in the manner of Barber's jihad, the border consciousness of mestizaje emphasizes how multiple identities intersect and transform one another against this backdrop of community.

Thus, in contrast to modernity's accent on the freedom of the self, postmodernism's preoccupation with difference, and conservatism's reduction of the self to the larger community, this mestizo sense of community asserts the realization of personal and community identity through concrete, lateral, intersubjective relations between persons and between cultures. Beyond just recognizing that personal and community identities are entwined, this outlook elicits fluid identities that are neither too self-driven nor too scripted by social relations and institutions.

Moreover, the spirituality that informs the Latino sense of extended family and community stresses the importance of "hospitality to the stranger."[60] As most Latino theologians stress, Jesus' ministry was especially to the marginalized—those in prison, those suffering from disease, those suffering from social discrimination and stigma, and those in poverty. As Goizueta makes clear, Jesus' basic political action is "transgressing boundaries, the act of walking and living with the outcast where he or she walks and lives."[61]

Consequently, the Latino practice of conjunto/encuentro relationships combined with the sensitivity of border consciousness is to engender a community that will be open "to everyone without exception."[62] As Elizondo emphasizes, "compassion, understanding, tenderness, and healing" characterize such community and recapture the "original heart and face of Christianity."[63] The visage of Guadalupe especially, he continues, generates a feeling of inclusion and respect for the 'other': "In her eyes, we find recognition, acceptance, respect, and confidence."[64]

Contrary to the either/or of individualism *v.* communitarianism, the Latino stress on a mestizo community imbued with the above Christian

ethic seeks extended political relationships that extirpate "racial segregation, classism, racism, sexism, enslavement, and exploitation."[65] In contrast
to the age-old paradigm of power politics characterized by conflict and strife,
which is rooted in an Augustinian portrait of human affairs, a mestizo democracy projects the realization of an egalitarian, lateral multicultural
politics.

Seeking Justice: Transforming Relations of Domination into Relations of Empowerment

The exegesis of this affective, aesthetic rationality can take on romantic hues
if it becomes detached from the emphasis in Latino political theology on
the poor challenging and overcoming economic, political, and social
marginalization. Without the backdrop of long-standing injustice experienced by indigenous peoples in the Americas, poor mestizos in Latin
America, and many Latinos in the United States, the preceding concerns
with crossing borders and mestizo community life quickly degenerate into
a quaint idyllic retreat from the dominant culture. If the cultural focus on
flor y canto (flower and song) in Latino theology becomes separated from a
critique of political and economic realities, this affective ambiance becomes
a fascinating but apolitical diversion from the harsh economic realities engendered by neoliberal economics.

Consequently, Latino theology repeatedly ties the realization of genuine community to the overcoming of onerous economic, political, and social practices. As captured by Ismael García, the essence of Latino theology
identifies the Christian God with the poor and vanquished and calls for
Christian communities to practice justice as solidarity, thereby welcoming
and empowering "those kept silent and made passive."[66]

First and foremost, as Arturo Bañuelas points out, one has to grasp
the impact of the "double conquests" in the Latino experience.[67] The first
conquest was the colonization of the indigenous peoples of Mexico and
Central America by the Spaniards. Then, three centuries later, the U.S.
Southwest and Puerto Rico were conquered by the United States, respectively, through the U.S.-Mexican War of 1846–1848 and then the Spanish-
American War of 1898. Indeed, Puerto Rican nationalists consider
themselves members of a "conquered and colonized people."[68] Among
Mexican Americans, the feeling is more that of being strangers in one's
own land.

Therefore, as rendered by Segovia, Latino theology "cannot but be a theology of struggle, liberation, and self-determination."[69] As much as the Latino experience is characterized by mixture and otherness (*mezcolanza* and *otredad*), Segovia insists that theology steeped in this experience strives to overcome cultural and social marginalization: "from exclusion to inclusion, from passivity to action, from silence to speech, from marginalization as an inferior other to an autochthonous, self-conscious, and critical irruption of an other that does not regard or present itself as superior . . . but rather as an equal."[70]

In this context of liberation, the two Christian figures that repeatedly come to the fore are Jesus Christ and Guadalupe. The crucified Christ as a "tortured, suffering human being" in Spanish, Latin American, and Latino iconography, as Espín points out, literally and graphically evokes solidarity and compassion.[71] Goizueta, in turn, provides an arresting account of the literal identification by San Antonio Latinos with the suffering Christ on his road to Calvary, as reenacted in downtown San Antonio every Good Friday.[72] Guadalupe, as discussed more extensively in the preceding chapter, appears not to the Spaniards, or even to the clergy, but to the downtrodden, indigenous peasant Juan Diego in symbolism that transforms but does not reject Nahuatl mythology. Indeed, Juan Diego is transformed from his downtrodden status into being an emancipated new person: "The old, defeated, victimized, 'inferior,' humiliated, 'worthless' self ceases to exist, and a new, confident, noble, self-assured, joyful human being arises."[73] As Elizondo suggests, such transformation continually recurs as poor Latinos through their spirituality "defy the controlling and limiting rules and regulations of the dominant culture."[74]

The situation of Latinos caught between the North American and Latin American worlds adds a dimension to the standard "option for the poor" stressed by Catholic social thought and in liberation theology. In the Latin American context, of course, there has been an institutional tie between the Roman Catholic church and the prevailing governments dating back to *los conquistadores*, a link between "Cross and Crown" that has only been challenged from within the institutional Church in the past four decades. The challenge before Latinos is how to reject this heritage of colonial paternalism and hierarchical relationships that prevent the realization of collaborative forums of decision making. The affective and relational dimensions of Latino culture unfortunately can lead to networks that are dependent on powerful leaders, as Deck illustrates in his review of different Latino church organizations.[75] Corporatist or organic schemes of politics do not advance justice for the poor. By the same token, the movement of industries and job opportunities to places far afield in neoliberal economic development also disrupts extensively the familial and neighborhood networks crucial for sustaining both personal and community well-being. This shifting of resources, and of people in particular, often culminates in greater accumulation of wealth in the hands of the rich at the expense of a growing number of poor people.

González's discussion of the changing outlook of Latin American Protestants defines the drawbacks of both the corporatist and neoliberal models. Traditionally, Protestants in Latin America blamed the region's "backwardness" on the long-standing medieval and paternalistic Catholic culture. They looked instead to the North American emphasis on freedom of thought and religion, education for everyone, an economy that rewarded personal effort, and a government and society of merit rather than patronage as the path to progress.[76] Indeed, some Latin American Protestants went so far as to defend both the U.S.-Mexican War and the Spanish-American War on the basis that "Protestantism and the United States were seen by some as the forces of liberation from obscurantism and medievalism."[77]

In contrast, González points out that once Latin American Protestants migrate to the United States, the supposed "land of milk and honey" proves disillusioning. Economic, social, and political discrimination against Latinos leads them to question the veracity of the above modernist "manifest destiny" outlook. González, in particular, is leery of enlightened liberals who welcome the marginalized "so long as there are not too many of them and they do not threaten the privileges of the center."[78]

As a result, the countercultural critique of Latino Protestants has come to focus as well on the drawbacks of liberal society. This change of place and heart, combined with disillusionment generated by the fact that the U.S. civil rights movement pitted Protestants against Protestants, has led to "A New Ecumenism" between Latino Protestants and Catholics.[79] This has especially ensued in the context of Latino community organizing and political mobilization.

Thus, Latinos, regardless of religious denomination, have experienced both the best and the worst of both "worlds." Through political theology, however, they seek to bridge the gap between the U.S. emphasis on human rights and the modern values of liberty, equality, and democracy, on the one hand, and, on the other, the emphasis on human dignity, the vital importance of caring, and personal relationships in the indigenous and Latin American traditions. Whereas Latinos are a minority, albeit the largest minority, within the United States, Latinos and Latin Americans are a majority of the people of the Western Hemisphere. If genuine democracy is to prevail in this hemisphere in this century, neither premodern corporatism nor modern neoliberalism is the answer.

Realistically though, the growing global paradigm, even in Latin America, is neoliberalism. According to Aquino Vargas, Latino theology, especially in its *feminista* variety, challenges not just the outcomes but the underlying anthropology of neoliberalism. Specifically, the competitive individualism at the heart of neoliberalism dismisses as "inefficient, illusory, and irrational"[80] the attempt to recast human relations in terms of social justice and in solidarity with all of creation.

At the very least, the experience and vision evoked by Latino theology leads to an empowerment contrary to this prevailing neoliberal paradigm. As González stresses, the Bible gives Latinos "a new sense of worth and of hope" despite their experience of marginalization.[81] In contrast to the poverty, exile, and worthlessness Hispanics experience in society, he adds, "The Bible tells us, no matter whether we have green cards or not, that we are citizens of the New Jerusalem."[82] Although this revelation seemingly has quietist implications, González maintains that the Gospel of Jesus Christ focuses on "bringing the marginalized to the very center of God's love and God's community."[83]

This empowerment rooted in Latino theology challenges repressive societal norms and practices. The alien, the half-breed, and the outcast thus become a blessing rather than a detriment to society. As Aquino Vargas poignantly argues, the communitarian basis of the Latino worldview projects "new ways of living" in which the measurement of human worth would no longer be reduced to the profits one has earned or the material goods one has consumed.[84]

Thus, a mestizo democracy not only questions the disparity between European American and Latino access to political, economic, and social decision-making structures and the similar disparity in material wealth between these same groups, but projects an alternative politics characterized by people as genuinely equal partners in dialogue—Isasi-Díaz's "kindom of God." In contrast to the dominant "white, male, Euro-American culture," according to Aquino Vargas, "Latina communities in the midst of their oppression continue to envision a world in which we all can live."[85]

Ultimately, Guadalupe's appearance to the conquered, marginalized peoples of Mexico does not merely accent a "preferential option for the poor" or a just distribution of resources in a Rawlsian sense. As Elizondo expresses the matter, the Guadalupe event brings forth an "understanding of truth, beauty, and goodness that will overcome the multiple limitations, divisions, distortions, and oppositions by which men and women are made opponents, enemies, and slaves of one another."[86] The Juan Diegos, marginalized by a politics of materialism and conquest, find in Guadalupe's vision a sense of "recognition, acceptance, respect, and confidence."[87] A mestizo democracy transforms political, economic, and social relations of domination into relations of empowerment.

Hope in the Struggle

Finally, the pursuit of this alternative collaborative politics, informed by an affective, aesthetic rationality and rooted in the relational character of Latino communities, projects and realizes hope, especially for those on the "underside of history."[88] As insisted by Segovia, Latino theology entails "an unwavering commitment to the world with a driving vision of a different and better world, and a profound sense of joy in the midst of anguish."[89]

One of the principal practices within Latino popular religion is the reenactment of suffering, especially in terms of Christ's path to Cavalry. Rather than merely encouraging a sense of mortification, the reenactment of this event is precisely to recognize that suffering does not have "the last word."[90] The preoccupation with both the Crucified Jesus and the Virgin Mary in Latino popular religion, as Goizueta points out, arises because both manifest the message of hope. Elizondo, in the context of his exegesis of Guadalupe, puts the matter thus: "While others crucify us, she resurrects us."[91]

Although Latino theologians stress that God cannot "be known apart from the practice of love and justice" for the poor and oppressed,[92] equal emphasis should be placed also on the importance of empowering the poor through community activism. The hopefulness in Latino spirituality emphasizes not only the pursuit of equal representation in political forums and a narrowing of the gap in income and wealth between haves and have-nots, but also the belief that previously downtrodden people can discover their own power in civic participation.

A pivotal principle for radical mobilization, as accented by Alinsky and Cortes, is "never, ever do for people what they can do for themselves."[93] Consequently, the community mobilizing done by the IAF has pointedly avoided focusing on organizers as paternalistic advocates for the poor and, instead, has always focused on enabling people to realize their own gifts and their potential power in common with others. This "enabling" has been cultivated primarily by showing potential leaders how to network with other such persons in their respective religious and political communities.

Among Latino theologians, Goizueta best captures this concrete, personal sense of empowerment when he distinguishes between the Aristotelian as opposed to the Marxist notion of praxis—the former stressing political activity as an "end in itself" as opposed to achieving particular ends outside the person. This notion of praxis as realizing an end in itself is also a cognate of Arendt's "public happiness" reviewed in chapter 1. Although the Marxist notion of praxis engages the political, economic, and social marginalization experienced by Latinos, Goizueta contends that it too readily degenerates into an instrumentalist *techne*. Conversely, the Aristotelian end-in-itself praxis too easily ignores the impact that political, economic, and social structures have on realizing mutual collaborative relations: "Before there can be a genuine dialogue or conversation among different social groups (racial, cultural, gender, class, etc.), these must be recognized as equal partners in the dialogue."[94]

This and the preceding sections in this chapter have therefore focused on two distinct but integral dimensions of a mestizo democracy. On the one hand, the relational character of Latino ethics and extended family structures bears a sense of the Aristotelian praxis articulated by Goizueta: a relational sense that has proved valuable to community organizations aligned with Alinsky's IAF, especially in poor Latino neighborhoods. On the other hand, the Marxist heritage of praxis with its focus especially on overcoming economic disparity and oppression is reflected in the preceding section's emphasis on realizing relationships of collaboration, not domination. To reiterate an earlier theme from this chapter, it is not a matter of either/or but of both/and; that is, both types of praxis are integral to realizing a political community in which specific peoples, especially on the basis of culture, race, and religion, do not constitute a permanent underclass. Emphasizing solely one type of praxis leads either to a romantic aesthetic politics that never critically engages market and political hegemonies or, conversely, to a technical materialist politics, which, in spite of its grasp of exploitation, has no concrete presence in the lives of poor people through which to effect significant change.

Ultimately, however, this exegesis of different types of praxis remains pedantic apart from the affective sense of hope and liberation manifested in a mestizo democracy. As Bañuelas points out, fiesta in Latino culture is not merely a party but a festive anticipation of a new universalism in which all peoples can engage each other as equals: "It [fiesta] proclaims who we are as *mestizos* and offers the possibility of a new universalism already beginning in a people who through rejection and struggles continue to proclaim *que la vida es la lucha, pero con victoria* (that life is a struggle, but with victory)."[95]

In contrast to past universalisms scripted by political, economic, and social *conquistadores,* the universalism of "the *pueblo mestizo,*" as delineated by Aquino Vargas, mutually draws upon the creativity of its diverse cultural and, especially, indigenous heritages.[96] As Elizondo concludes, Guadalupe's synthesis of cultural contradiction and her critical engagement of oppressive power structures pursues "a common home for all the inhabitants of the Americas and the world."[97]

Synthesis

The preceding seven parameters of a mestizo democracy project a unity-in-diversity that in a lateral fashion synthesizes diverse cultures without privileging any one culture or, conversely, exterminating contributing cultures. The relational focus on "both/and" and "border" not "frontier" consciousness acknowledges cultural and racial mixing as an intrinsic part of human history. Such mixing, in contradiction to philosophies that value purity and homogeneity, has a positive value, especially for the multicultural reality of the United States of the twenty-first century. If we treasure democracy as the access of each person to fundamental decision-making forums and processes, then this relational, community-centered orientation from the Latino tradition is an invaluable resource.

At the same time, as stressed by the latter sections of this chapter, this articulation of unity-in-diversity through mestizaje is not just a romantic appreciation of cultural differences and their creative potential. An essential part of a mestizo democracy is a genuine lateral mixing of peoples and cultures that obviates unjust distribution of economic resources and, especially, opportunities. As painfully reiterated over and over again by Latino and Latin American theologians, the majority of Western-Hemisphere people of indigenous, African, and Latino backgrounds are poor. Without apology, a mestizo democracy challenges this long-standing injustice and projects the vision of a genuinely integrated democracy in which "segregation and discrimination will have no place. . . ."[98]

Indeed, the concrete, lived character of unity-in-diversity in the Latino experience, especially as conveyed in the preceding sections on popular religion and the relational character of community, is vital for articulating and realizing a mestizo democracy. As discussed earlier, the call for increased community in the United States made by figures like Bellah and Putnam is not wrong per se, but it does not provide a concrete discourse relevant to the multicultural United States of the twenty-first century. Mestizaje, as an affective, heart-felt U.S. cultural and normative tradition, offers such a discourse.

By the same token, the indebtedness to the indigenous and African heritages of the Americas also distinguishes a mestizo democracy from the Hegelian/Marxist paradigm, which was so important to the gestation of Latin American liberation theology, a theme I address further in chapter 4. Recall too that although Vasconcelos's articulation of *la raza cósmica* recognizes the indigenous presence in Mexico, his vision still underscores the notion of purification by European ideals. The interpenetration of African, indigenous, and European traditions in popular religion, the corpus of lived Latino experience, and the intellectual framework articulated by Latino theologians not only compensate for this Eurocentric hangover in past calls for community and/or liberation, but also provide a basis for democratic engagement with the growing presence of non–Judeo-Christian cultures and religions, especially those from Asia.

To those previously uninitiated to Latino culture and spirituality, my characterization of a mestizo democracy as a constructive counterculture to the rapacious dimensions of neoliberal economics, assimilation schemes of multicultural relations, and zero-sum politics might seem impractically wishful. Contrary to such cynicism, Latino theology's extensive deliberation on cultural hermeneutics, popular religion, and a mestizo recasting of Tracy's and Greeley's analogical spiritual imagination elicits a concrete and tangible politics of unity-in-diversity.

Given the rising numbers of Latinos across the United States, a mestizo democracy has the potential to transform the normative bearings of U.S. politics. In particular, popular religion's capacity for synthesizing both Christian and non-Christian outlooks as well as African, European, and indigenous perspectives offers the possibility of engendering a substantive "rainbow coalition" between poor and minority groups in the United States, vis-à-vis public policy debates on every level of politics.

At the same time, the import of mestizaje is not just for minority or poverty politics. In the global economy more and more people are literally and figuratively crossing borders daily through intercontinental transportation and telecommunications networks to previously foreign locales.

Isolating oneself from the 'other' will grow increasingly difficult in the twenty-first century. Especially in the United States, most people have to contend with multiple cultures and juxtaposed identities on a daily basis.

The preceding discussion of the attributes of a mestizo democracy suggests that diverse cultures and groups can mix in ways that do not culminate in the ascendancy of one way of being over all others. Engaging reality as both/and, not either/or, displacing the frontier mentality with the border mentality, acknowledging the heterogeneous yet concrete temperament of Latino popular religion, and pursuing an affective, aesthetic practical rationality enable us to see the nexus of diverse cultures not as a locus of inherent conflict but as a web of intersubjective relationships that can effect unity precisely through diversity. Further, acknowledging the relational character of community, seeking a politics of collaboration rather than domination, and projecting a spirit of hope in political, economic, and social undertakings mutually underscore the vigilant pursuit of just political, economic, and social opportunities and resources intrinsic to a mestizo democracy.

Once in a church in Houston, Texas, I was struck by the ironic symbolism of portraits that faced each other from opposite walls. On the east wall was the victorious Christ the King, all too often misappropriated by the frontier mentality to justify military or economic conquest in spiritual terms. On the west wall was Our Lady of Guadalupe in her effulgent colorful countenance, symbolic of the border mentality in which the combination of differences need not conclude in assimilation. This "interface" captures the contesting paradigms increasingly encountered at every level and type of human association in the U.S. Southwest, if not the Western Hemisphere. Mestizaje as a political theory of crossing borders elicits a concrete yet vivid vision for dealing with *este futuro* in a just, democratic fashion. In the next two chapters I examine how a mestizo democracy connects to the modern-postmodern and liberal-communitarian debates over multiculturalism in contemporary philosophy and political theory.

Part II

The Politics of Multiculturalism

CHAPTER 4

A *Post*-liberation Philosophy and Theology

*I*n this chapter I consider the relevance of Enrique Dussel's liberation philosophy to the realization of a mestizo democracy. Although I am sympathetic to Dussel's critique of Eurocentric modernity and his articulation of transmodernity, I contend— principally through the work of Octavio Paz—that Dussel's arguments ironically manifest a Eurocentric "hangover." By contrast, the mixing of heritages on a lateral and equal basis intrinsic to a mestizo democracy emerges as a vital resource for moving beyond Eurocentrism in the twenty-first century.

The merit of Dussel's project is that he recognizes the limitations (and the graphic ramifications) of modernity without opting for a type of postmodernity that deems universal communication among peoples impossible. Therefore, his elucidation of a transmodernity provides for a critique of both neo-Kantian schemes of universal communication—in particular, Habermas and Rawls—and postmodern arguments that dwell on local and particular discourses. I amplify this latter critique of postmodernity through the work of Roberto Goizueta. If in chapter 1 I suggested that a mestizo democracy moves between assimilation and separatism when it comes to multicultural relations, in this chapter I chart a path between the contemporary contending poles of modern and postmodern rationalities.

In turn, engaging Dussel's liberation philosophy in a critical fashion also provides a basis for reevaluating liberation theology. Two decades ago liberation theology was the lodestone of radicalism in Latin America. Most observers are well aware of the controversy it has engendered within the institutional Roman Catholic Church. Formal critiques made by the Vatican and the appointment of conservative bishops to posts across Latin America have indeed diminished its practical impact. But in terms of Dussel's focus on the import of modernity, the more critical evaluations of liberation theology have not come from the right but from the left—particularly those radical theologies stressing indigenous cultures, the environment, and gender concerns. In other words, the limitations of Dussel's argument—defined especially by the degree to which a Hegelian/Marxist paradigm still drives his thinking—are also relevant to the prospect of liberation theology. A critical engagement of Dussel provides the opportunity to project a *post*-liberation theology consonant with mestizaje.

Engaging the Critique of Eurocentric Modernity

THE MYTH OF MODERNITY

Dussel's thesis in *The Invention of the Americas* is that the rise of so-called modern civilization in Europe over the past five centuries is intrinsically connected to the European colonization of the Americas and, then, most of the rest of the non-European world. Prior to 1492, Dussel contends, Europe was a backwater in terms of international relations and power. Blocked to the east by the Islamic world, the center of Mediterranean civilization at the time—Spain and Portugal, followed by France, Holland, and England—expand to the west to chart a new route to the riches of the Indies. These European ventures instead encounter and conquer the so-called "New World," whose vast resources in turn enable the European nation-states to emerge as the preeminent powers of the modern era: "In my opinion, western Europe's bursting the bounds within which Islam had confined it, gave *birth* to *modernity*."[1]

The *myth* of modernity, according to Dussel, is the projection of European superiority onto the rest of the world, simultaneous with the conquest and colonization of the world by the European powers. He cites numerous excerpts from Hegel that suggest this superiority complex, for instance: "Universal history goes from East to West. Europe is absolutely the *end of universal history*. Asia is the beginning."[2]

Specifically, Dussel examines the notion of a linear development, according to which some cultures are less mature than others; they are, therefore, supposedly still in need of development, and he traces this "development" back to Kant's rendering of enlightenment as "the exit of humanity by itself from a state of culpable immaturity."[3] Therefore, intrinsic to modern

European philosophy, in Dussel's analysis, is this notion of Europe as the center of civilization with the rest of world on the periphery in a developing stage, not just economically but intellectually and emotionally speaking: "*European* modernity constitutes all other cultures as its *periphery.*"[4]

Dussel focuses primarily on the conquest of the Americas because it is the first region on the so called periphery to feel the wrath of European "civilization." Obviously, the very fact that the peoples of the Americas were conquered by European military superiority, as well as by devastating plagues spread by *los conquistadores,* contradicts the notion of a so-called "civilizing" people. In essence European modernity espouses universal rights while denying them to indigenous peoples.[5]

Dussel's major concern, though, is not to dwell on this empirical contradiction but rather to argue that it lies at the heart of the norms of modernity. Although the conquest of the Americas by the Spanish *conquistadores* predates Cartesian philosophy by over a century, Dussel contends that the notion of subjectivity vis-à-vis the 'other' at the heart of Descartes's work is actually projected and realized in the conquest. The notions of "discovery" and "conquest" are at the core of the modern subjectivity "that takes itself to be the center or end of history."[6] He adds, from the standpoint of the modern ego, that the peoples who represented the lands to be colonized were not seen as a different "Other, but as the possessions of the Same to be conquered, colonized, modernized, civilized, as if they were the modern ego's *material.*"[7]

Therefore, the very notion of America, according to Dussel, was the projection by the European conquerors of their own vision of themselves. This Eurocentric outlook never perceived or recognized the distinctiveness of the indigenous civilizations prior to the conquest as anything other than an "*empty,* uncivilized, or barbaric world."[8] In this light, Cortés's Conquest of Mexico was a vivid projection of the modern ego over the 'other': "The 'I-conquistador' forms the protohistory of Cartesian *ego cogito* and constitutes its own subjectivity as will-to-power."[9] Indeed, building on Dussel's theme, Leslie Paul Thiele points out that Cortés was well aware that the Aztecs initially considered *los conquistadores* gods and that he manipulated this misunderstanding to facilitate his Conquest of Mexico.[10]

Apart from the defense of the indigenous peoples made by the Spanish missionaries such as Bartolomé de Las Casas, the Spanish political and spiritual leaders did not try, in rational terms, to persuade the Aztec, the Maya, the Inca, or any other indigenous peoples to Christianity and Spanish "civilization." Instead, salvation through the sword was the dominant motif. As

Pineda amplifies, only after *los conquistadores* had eliminated the principal spiritual leaders among the Aztecs did they engage the remaining leaders in a rhetorical effort at spiritual conversion, and that "dialogue" clearly favored the Spanish missionaries.[11] When indigenous leaders did make substantive counterarguments, the missionaries, as Dussel records, became dogmatic and simply imposed their positions by force.

Against this backdrop of the "I-conquistador" school of evangelization, Dussel observes that the notions of the *meeting* or the *encounter* "between two worlds" made fashionable in commemorations of the five hundredth anniversary of Columbus's voyage occlude "how the European ego subjugated the world of the Other."[12] There was no serious attempt, apart from that of Las Casas, to engage in a lateral equal discourse between diverse peoples and cultures; one culture was in a position of dominance and simply imposed its positions on the other. One could counter, in Thucydidean fashion, that cultures and peoples have been conquering one another from the predawn of history. However, Dussel defines the Spanish conquest—and anticipates subsequent conquests by the English, French, and other European powers—not just as a triumph of superior technology and military might, but as the weaving of a myth of modernity to justify the accompanying violence: "Modernity elaborated a myth of its own goodness, rationalized its violence as civilizing, and finally declared itself innocent of the assassination of the Other."[13] Instead of seeing 1492 as the *meeting* between diverse worlds, Dussel insists that instead we must understand it as an *encubierto,* a covering over of the world of indigenous peoples—the 'other.'[14]

To expand further on what Dussel means by "the possessions of the Same" and "the occlusion of the Other" in the conquest of the Americas, it is helpful to consider Graciela Limón's novel *The Song of the Hummingbird.* The protagonist, Huitzitzilin, an Aztec princess prior to the conquest, recounts—six decades after the fact—the fall of the Aztec capital city, Tenochtitlán (now Mexico City) to the Spaniards. Huitzitzilin is a Malinche figure—the indigenous woman who became Cortés's consort and begat mestizo progeny. This figure captures the ambiguity and contradictions of the conquest. Is la Malinche a traitor to her indigenous people, or is she the quintessential example of both the physical and symbolic rape of indigenous and then mestiza women by European and European American conquerors from Cortés to the present? In *Hummingbird* Huitzitzilin indeed becomes the partner of a conquistador, but mistreatment at his hands eventually leads her to trap him in a cave, a circumstance culminating in his death.

The genius of the novel is that Huitzitzilin retells the conquest through the device of confession. Her confessor is a young, recently ordained priest from Spain. The reader can almost smell the odor of holy water on his hands as he eagerly and diligently assumes his duties in "New Spain." Hearing Huitzitzilin's confession proves to be a tumultuous experience for Father Benito, for she graphically recounts the destruction of the magnificence and beauty of the Aztec civilization by the Spaniards, as well as her own notorious "sins"—from the missionary's Christian perspective—committed both before and after the conquest. Ultimately though, Huitzitzilin's intention is not to seek penance but to deconstruct Father Benito's sense of Spanish and Christian superiority. This deconstruction enables him to understand the conquest as something wholly different from what he had learned in seminary. Huitzitzilin's "confession" itself is imbued with references to the spirits that inhabit the birds and the surrounding flora—the aesthetic rationality and spirituality of the indigenous people discussed in previous chapters. On Huitzitzilin's death at the climax of the novel, Father Benito finally realizes her intent:

> His mind went deeper into his spirit until it became clear to him that it was not absolution or even mercy that she had expected of him, but understanding of her life, of her people, and of their beliefs. . . .
> The monk sighed as the silence wrapped itself around him, and he abandoned himself to his thoughts. . . . Dejection clung to him until he understood that she was now with those people who had been part of her life, those who had seen the world as she had seen it, those who had lived as she had lived.[15]

But, to recast this denouement in Dussel's terms, *los conquistadores* unfortunately precluded such an alternative understanding by introducing the modernist projection of the 'same' over the 'other': "The modern *ego* was born in its self-constitution over against regions it dominated."[16] Rather than seeing the 'other' in its own terms or striving for at least an imperfect exchange of worldviews, *los conquistadores* saw the 'other' as simply a barbarian to be civilized by European culture.

In contrast to this characterization of indigenous spirituality and culture as barbarian, Dussel's depiction is of the richness of the intellectual world of Mexico prior to the conquest. The "*tlamatinime*," or Aztec wise figures, attended rigorous education programs comparable to Plato's academy or

Aristotle's lyceum, especially with respect to rhetoric.[17] The content and character of this worldview were hardly Cartesian, for they manifested the aesthetic rationality of *flor y canto*—comprehension and communication with the divinities through flower and song. In fact, this preconquest orientation was in conflict with the "sacrificial myth of *Tlacaélel*"—the leader of the Aztec empire a century before the conquest.[18] Tlacaélel stressed motifs of militaristic domination, not unlike, as Dussel notes, the myth of modernity that would replace them. Dussel adds that it is this militaristic myth that sustained the length of "the fifth sun" in Aztec mythology prior to the conquest.

Given this hermeneutical backdrop, Dussel contends Moctezuma acted quite rationally when confronted by Cortés. Specifically, Dussel suggests that Moctezuma had three options in terms of comprehending the significance of *los conquistadores:*

(1) They were human beings bent on invasion, which Dussel maintains Moctezuma could have only known based on subsequent data.

(2) They were gods and Cortés was the god Quetzalcóatl, who had left a long time ago to the east and now seemingly had returned to temper the excesses of the Tlacaélel myth.

(3) The presumed return of Quetzalcóatl was actually the "divine principle *Ometeótl*" and thus the end of the fifth sun in Nahuatl mythology.[19]

Tragically, Moctezuma chose option two, hoping to appease Quetzalcóatl (Cortés) by giving up his throne. By the time Moctezuma realized that these so-called gods were humans and invasion was underway, according to Dussel, it was too late for the militaristic Aztec faction to repel the invaders. Indeed, in this light the fifth sun—"the *tlamatinime* vision of the world" had come to an end.[20]

Even though indigenous resistance movements persisted after Cortés's triumph, for all intents and purposes the mythological world of the Aztec and Maya had ceased. The rise of the "sixth sun," according to Dussel's exposition of the myth of modernity, did not accent the *flor y canto* of the tlamatinime nor the sacrificial myth of Tlacaélel but, rather, the new god of capital in mercantilism that would in turn evolve into capitalism. Instead of the human sacrifices that characterized Aztec worship just prior to the conquest, this new world order's sacrificial myth, according to Dussel, exploits the labor and resources of the Americas and ultimately other non-Western regions of the world to bring about and sustain European dominance post-1492. Essentially, the genesis of the contemporary global economy is rooted in the Spanish and Portuguese colonial money system that transfers wealth and value from what we now term the developing to the developed world: "Money facilitated the transference of value and eventually the domination of North over South and the center over the periphery."[21]

It would be a mistake, however, to restrict the import of Dussel's argument just to economics, for on a normative level he stresses that the *myth* of modernity has been the concoction of a Eurocentric superiority to justify the economic pillaging of what becomes the colonial world. As Elizondo points out, when one pre-Columbian civilization triumphed over another in the Americas, the conquering group always attempted to incorporate the gods and mythologies of the conquered civilization with their own gods and mythologies.[22] However, *los conquistadores*—at least prior to the apparition of Guadalupe—simply imposed a European "civilization" that had no room, at least initially, for indigenous superstitions and mysticisms. Although modernity supposedly promises liberation from tyranny and "cultural immaturity," it simultaneously enslaves the developing world economically and politically, according to Dussel, as "the necessary price of modernization."[23] Consequently, the challenge before us is to bring about a genuine liberation for all peoples and cultures that does not entail the assimilation of the stranger or the so-called foreigner—the 'other'—into a Eurocentric 'same.'

THE EUROCENTRIC HANGOVER
IN DUSSEL'S CENTER-PERIPHERY DYNAMIC

Several critical concerns need to be put to Dussel's indictment of the rise of modernity and the onset of the prevailing center-periphery international system initiated by the conquest of the Americas. I do so not to vitiate Dussel's arguments but to refine their grist.

Central to Dussel's argument is the claim that Eurocentric modernity arises through the subjugation of the non-European world and that the Americas are the first places to endure this subjugation. The philosophical motif behind this modernity is that the 'self' sees the 'other' not as something distinctive in its own right but as a projection of the 'same' by the 'self.'

However, this projection of the 'same' over the 'other' is rooted in Descartes's philosophy: the subjective cogito in a detached fashion observes, analyzes, and organizes reality as a collection of objects. Dussel's depiction of "the invention of the Americas" and "the myth of modernity" is an incisive critique of the reason of modernity. Indeed, modern reason has a hard time dealing with "the difference" which characterizes other peoples, lands, and cultures. In turn, engagement of the world as a collection of objects leads to a technological manipulation and domination of reality: the 'other' is not a distinctive entity in its own right, but simply a means toward realizing the supposed civilizing project of modernity.

Unfortunately, Descartes is a seventeenth-century philosopher born a full century after Columbus's first expedition reaches the Americas. Although some dimensions of the Conquest of Mexico anticipate the Cartesian subject-object dichotomy and its genesis of modern scientific and technological thinking—for instance, the mythological contrast between "civilized Europeans" versus "barbaric heathens"—it is dubious that the philosophical mind-set of *los conquistadores* was primarily rooted in modernity.

As Octavio Paz incisively points out in *The Labyrinth of Solitude,* the outlook and accompanying hierarchical institutions of the conquering Spaniards were as much medieval as they were modern in inspiration. Dussel looks to the Enlightenment's stress on emancipating people from oppressive political and social structures as a key motif for his liberation philosophy, but the Spanish conquest of the Americas was actually about petrifying the organic order of the medieval period. Rather than being informed by the Protestant Reformation and then modernity's ensuing emphases on individualism, scientific objectivity, and faith in the notion of progress in human affairs, at the core of the conquest lies the Counter-Reformation and its resistance to fresh ideas and critical thinking:

> The modern world began with the Reformation, which was the religious criticism of religion and the necessary antecedent of the Enlightenment; with the Counter-Reformation and Neo-Thomism, Spain and her possessions closed themselves to the modern world. They had no Enlightenment, because they had neither a Reformation nor an intellectual movement like Jansenism. And so, though Spanish-American civilization is to be admired on many counts, it reminds one of a structure of great solidity—at once convent, fortress, and palace—built to last, not to change. In the long run, that construction became a confine, a prison.[24]

The hierarchical, if not caste, structure of the Spanish colonial period was a throwback to the political, social, and economic structures of Europe prior to modernity and, if anything, petrified an order whose vitality had long passed. In turn, this perpetuation of a premodern political, social-economic order, animated more by inequality of station than equality of opportunity and censorship rather than freedom of thought and belief, has hampered Latin America's ability to achieve genuine liberal democracies and to become an equal player in global markets. Essentially, the Reformation never took hold in Latin America. As reviewed in the previous chapter, the rise of Pentecostal and Catholic charismatic spiritualities in recent decades should be seen as a third wave of Christianity distinct from the Reformation–Counter Reformation debate.

By contrast, it is the English colonization of North America that mirrors much more closely the characteristics of modernity as depicted critically by Dussel. As Paz points out, the Reformation and then the Enlightenment's emphasis on freedom, change, and progress is much more concretely realized in the United States than anywhere in Latin America:

> The United States was born of the Reformation and the Enlightenment. It came into being under the sign of criticism and self-criticism. Now, when one talks of criticism one is talking of change. The transformation of critical philosophy into progressive ideology came about and reached its peak in the nineteenth century. The broom of rationalist criticism swept the ideological sky clean of myths and beliefs; the ideology of progress, in its turn, displaced the timeless values of Christianity and transplanted them to the earthly and linear time of history. Christian eternity became the future of liberal evolutionism.[25]

Paz argues further that whereas evangelization was crucial to the Spanish Conquest of the Americas as a way of legitimating the conquest, "the idea of evangelization occupied a secondary place in England's colonial expansion."[26] As a consequence, the Spanish conquest manifests an inclusive attitude toward the 'other,' whereas the English conquest manifests an exclusive attitude: "New Spain committed many horrors, but at least it did not commit the gravest of all: that of denying a place, even at the foot of the social scale, to the people who composed it."[27]

Paz's discrimination between the character of the respective conquests is reminiscent both of Vasconcelos's distinction between the Anglo-Saxon and Iberian ways of dealing with diversity and González's distinction between frontier and border mentalities. However, Paz's depiction of Spanish "inclusion" is not one that stresses equality. To the contrary, Paz stresses that the Spanish colonial combination of domination and conversion led to a society that was "hierarchical, centralist, and respectful of the individual characteristics of each group."[28] In other words each community knew its place within the social hierarchy, but the universal community was held together by the same religion and political power structure. In contrast, the English conquest, according to Paz, stressed exclusion, if not elimination, of the conquered, for the latter were uncivilized heathen; principles of freedom and equality were only to be practiced among the political communities constituted by the conquerers. The Reformation theme of pure communities of believers reinforced this irony of extirpation for others outside the community, but freedom and equality for like-minded folk within the community.[29]

At a minimum Paz qualifies Dussel's association of the Spanish conquest of the Americas with the genesis of modernity. The roots of Spanish consciousness informing the conquest extend well back into medieval culture. The Catholicism of the Counter-Reformation is hardly a basis for engendering the philosophy of modernity: "The decadence of European Catholicism coincided with its apogee in Spanish America: it spread out over new lands at the very moment it had ceased to be creative."[30] Essentially, what Dussel sees as the negative side of modernity and in turn what will become the Enlightenment—the eclipse of the 'other' and the manipulation of the world as a set of objects—is much more closely realized in the English conquest a century later.

An honest appraisal of the Aztec legacy in Spanish colonial and Mexican political and cultural life is another factor that should be taken into consideration when assessing Dussel's argument. When reading Dussel's account, or for that matter other commentators who defend the dignity of the indigenous perspective, one almost gathers the impression that the indigenous peoples of the Americas were innocents prior to the arrival of *los conquistadores*—Spanish, English, or otherwise. In fact, the Aztecs were the prevailing empire—not a democracy—prior to the arrival of the Spaniards, and indeed, some of the tribes they had subjugated joined forces with Cortés in the hope of liberating their peoples.

Paz points out that the hierarchical framework prevailing after the conquest was as much Aztec as it was Spanish in origin: "If Mexico was born in the sixteenth century, we must agree that it was a child of a double violence, imperial and unifying: that of the Aztecs and that of the Spaniards."[31] Indeed, Paz points out that the Aztec state was characterized by militarism and theocracy.[32] Although subsequent postconquest ruling structures in Mexico from the Spanish colonial period to the present may not have engaged in the specific rituals of the Aztecs, Paz notes that the ancient Aztec symbols of the pyramid and the sacrifice are still mythically present in Mexican political structures stressing hierarchy and domination.

As opposed to Dussel's rendering of the conquest in which the 'other' was assimilated to models of the 'same' without much regard to the religion, philosophy, or culture of the 'other,' Cortés and subsequent Spanish rulers in Mexico essentially supplanted Moctezuma and the Aztec elite at the top of the pyramid. Catholicism, in turn, replaced Aztec spirituality as a vital way for indigenous peoples to sustain a connection with the cosmos: it reconstituted "their social, human and religious relationships with the surrounding world and with the divine."[33] In this light, the Spaniards become "the heirs of México-Tenochtitlán."[34]

Over the next five centuries what Paz terms "the centralist, authoritarian, Aztec-Spanish tradition" recasts itself repeatedly.[35] Colonial Mexico is the quintessence of an organic, heirarchical order. The early nineteenth century fight for independence, incited initially by Father Hidalgo as a populist peasant uprising, quickly became co-opted by the criollo elites (those of pure Spanish descent) as a way to protect their privileged past and to ward off the liberal and modern reforms that were beginning to take hold in Spain. Indeed, in contrast to positivism's use of scientific reason to critique European society and supposedly engender progress in the latter half of the nineteenth century, positivism in Mexico was simply a set of empty ideals to which Mexican leaders like Porfirio Díaz rhetorically appealed but that were never used to challenge the prevailing social hierarchies: "Mexico changed its laws, not its social, economic, and cultural realities."[36]

Similarly, in the Mexican Revolution in the second decade of the twentieth century, despite the rallying cries for justice for the people, especially by the Villista and Zapatista revolutionary factions, the faction under the leadership of Carranza ultimately prevailed and declaimed once again, in no less triumphal a fashion, the shallow, empty liberal and positivist ideals of the Díaz regime.[37] In fact, as Paz observes, the twentieth century Mexican state proved to be "a hybrid of the Spanish patrimonialist state of the seventeenth century and the modern bureaucracies of the West."[38] Although Paz does not make the point, the logical conclusion of this pseudo-positivism was the transition to freer markets under the "neoliberal" Mexican presidencies of de la Madrid, Salinas, and Zedillo in the 1980s and 1990s, the impact of which has only magnified the historical economic and social hierarchical disparities of Mexico. The election of Fox in 2000 as the first non-PRI President of Mexico since 1929 offers just a glimmer of hope for a transformation of the pyramid archetype. Therefore, as opposed to Dussel's contention that the domination inherent in Latin American political and economic structures stems from the onset of modernity, as propagated by European *conquistadores,* just as crucial to this domination are the historical antecedents that lie in the indigenous political and social heritage: "There is a bridge that reaches from *tlatoani* to viceroy, viceroy to president."[39]

Although the Aztec political structure was indeed reshaped, not supplanted, by *los conquistadores,* another dimension of the indigenous heritage in Mexican culture provides a basis for resistance to the imposition of modernity. Paz notes that despite the triumph of the Spaniards, the indigenous heritage is vital to understanding Mexico: "Though the language and religion, the political institutions and the culture are Western, there is one aspect of Mexico that faces another direction—the Indian direction."[40] In contrast to the United States, he continues, whose "historical memory" has been primarily European—again the frontier mentality—one cannot grasp Mexican cultural identity without coming to grips with its Mesoamerican past.[41]

Reminiscent of Elizondo, Paz portrays Guadalupe as emblematic of a Mexican culture that is a hybrid of indigenous and Spanish culture. Paz's Guadalupe, however, manifests an edge of indigenous resistance: "The Virgin unites the religious sensibilities of the Mediterranean and Mesoamerican, both of them regions that fostered ancient cults of feminist divinities, Guadalupe-Tonantzin is the mother of all Mexicans—Indians, mestizos, whites—but she is also a warrior virgin whose image has often appeared on the banners of peasant uprisings."[42] In the context of indigenous rebellion Paz notes that the Zapata faction of the Mexican rebellion was an attempt to return to a past in which indigenous communal landholdings—*los ejidos*—were the norm, not "hierarchies, classes and property."[43] One should add that although the recent Zapatista revolt in Chiapas took advantage of modern telecommunications to broadcast its cause, at the same time, like Zapata's "radically subversive" movement, it has reawakened a primordial tie to an indigenous past.[44]

In turn, Paz argues that another key feature of the Mexican heritage, which has both indigenous and Catholic roots, is the focus on festive communal celebrations: "Any occasion for getting together will serve, any pretext to stop the flow of time and commemorate men and events with festivals and ceremonies."[45] Specifically, such festivity defies one of the hallmarks of modernity—the rationalization of "chronometric time" and enables human beings "to emerge from . . . solitude and become one with creation."[46] In fact, one of the reasons the above-mentioned philosophy of positivism never developed deep roots in Mexico over a century ago, though espoused superficially by the ruling elites, is that it could not provide a sense of communion for the people. Despite the Westernization of Mexico that comes from the incursions first by Spain, later France and the United States, Mexican culture remains "a plurality of pasts," among which the pervasive heritage of resistance and communion lurks just under the surface.[47]

Against this cultural backdrop of resistance and communion, the studies by Espín and other Latino theologians of popular religion that I reviewed in the previous chapter take on a new import. Although, as Paz emphasizes, the ruling power structure of Mexico is a hierarchical pyramid whose antecedents lie in both preconquest Aztec society and medieval Spain, there remains simultaneously among the people this mythic spirituality—what Espín terms the "sacral worldview"—that has always provided a vibrant sense of community and a political alternative to the prevailing elites of the day, be they Aztec, Spanish, or Mexican. This spirituality, over time, becomes a mixture of African, indigenous, and Spanish Catholic practices and manifests a sense of community marked by inclusiveness and diversity, which stands in stark contrast to the Puritan model of New England, in which the community was only open to the members of that tightly scripted faith. Admittedly, this "sacral" popular religion has never been the formal basis for the ruling structure of Mexico or other parts of Latin America over the past five centuries. However, popular religion has the potential for transforming the long-standing hierarchical politics of the region without succumbing to the problems posed by the frontier mentality in the pursuit of liberal democracy in the United States.

Essentially, with respect to "myth of modernity," Dussel's tendency is to emphasize the European contribution to the problem or to the solution. First, the repression and domination ensuing through the Spanish conquest of the Americas is not just a consequence of modernity because, as I have already shown, both Aztec and Spanish medieval antecedents for hierarchical ruling structures are just as crucial to this outcome. Aspects of both European and indigenous cultures have been integral to the structures of domination that have prevailed in Mexico as well as across Latin America.

Second, the Mexican indigenous heritage and its ensuing mestizaje with the African and European spiritual heritages that came to the Americas also provide a basis for resistance to such hierarchical repression and domination.

Dussel's project to move beyond modernity to a transmodernity relies too heavily just on the articulation of liberation in the European Enlightenment, the very same philosophical tradition whose ideas ironically contribute to the frontier mentality that characterizes the English colonization of the Americas. Just as Dussel does not discuss the Aztec contribution to the pyramid archetype in Mexican history and politics, he also does not sufficiently grapple with how popular religion can be integral to any project of liberation. Although he thoroughly indicates how the perspective of the 'other' is reduced to the 'same' in the outlook of the European conquerors, he insufficiently develops how indigenous and mixed cultural heritages can challenge the myth of modernity.

Conversely, acknowledging how indigenous spirituality can contribute to an alternative politics that manifests an inclusive unity-in-diversity does not entail a rejection of the liberation ethos in the European Enlightenment tradition. Little is accomplished by reversing the myth of modernity in a way that puts aside European thought as tainted in deference to a concocted idyllic portrait of indigenous life in the Americas, pre- or post-conquest. Consonant with the ethos of crossing borders, we need to acknowledge how European and indigenous heritages both contribute to the long-standing structures of domination in Latin America and, in turn, how both heritages project ideas that can engage and overcome such domination.

A PAZ-DUSSEL RAPPROCHEMENT

In fairness to Dussel, however, he does focus and elaborate on the cultural diversity of Latin America. He specifically refers to six cultural visages whose perspectives have been dominated or marginalized by modernity: indigenous peoples, African slaves in the Americas, mestizos, criollos, peasants, and workers. At first glance the choice of criollos—the Spaniards and Portuguese born in the Americas—seems curious, since they historically have been part of the dominant elites of Latin America. Dussel's point, though, is that it was this group that initiated a project of emancipation by waging the wars for independence across Latin America.[48] However, as reviewed earlier, this project of liberation—Bolívar's dream of a unified Latin America—falls short in that these criollo elites, postindependence, do not include the indigenous peoples, the slave descendants, and the mestizos into collaborative and egalitarian decision-making structures.[49]

In his exegesis of the plight of the mestizos, Dussel does accent very strongly the indigenous presence that must be integral to any authentic project of liberation in the Americas. Dussel takes Elizondo's rendering of mestizaje and casts it in terms of being caught between the modern and traditional worlds: "Mestizos live in their own flesh the contradictory tension of modernity as both emancipation and sacrificial myth."[50] On the one hand, from their European side, they inherit the rationality of modernity as expressed in eighteenth century colonial Enlightenment thought, nineteenth century positivism, and twentieth century economic-development theory. On the other hand, Dussel contends that the mestizos' true emancipation is impossible unless they reclaim their 'other' side—la Malinche—the indigenous side violated by the conquest.[51]

On this score, Dussel's and Paz's arguments are in accord. Paz is particularly critical of partisans on either side of the European-indigenous divide who emphasize one side's perspective to the exclusion of the 'other's':

> The Hispanic thesis, which would have us descend from Cortés to the exclusion of La Malinche, is the patrimony of a few extremists who are not even pure whites. The same can be said of indigenous propaganda, which is also supported by fanatical *criollos* and *mestizos,* while the Indians have never paid it the slightest attention. The Mexican does not want to be either an Indian or a Spaniard.[52]

The culture of Mexico, thus, is an enmeshing of traditions, and any attempt to sort or categorize them neatly cannot do justice to the complexity of the challenge in effecting transcultural dialogue. Indeed, Dussel renders Guadalupe in paradoxical terms. Like Elizondo's rendering of Guadalupe, Dussel accents the indigenous casting of Guadalupe's appearance before Juan Diego, "the Indian par excellence"; like Paz's rendering, Dussel acknowledges how her countenance has been the basis for an indigenous refuge from, if not resistance to, the conquest.[53] However, Dussel adds how this powerful symbolism has been appropriated over time by both mestizos and criollos as a way of asserting independence from Europe. He concludes that Guadalupe coalesces the indigenous, mestizo, and criollo facets of Mexican and Latin American culture into "a unity at once dispersed and contradictory."[54]

When Dussel examines these cultural intersections and intricacies, he strengthens his indictment regarding the myth of modernity. Unfortunately, his exegesis of these issues is so limited in *The Invention of the Americas* that it leaves the reader wanting more. His passages regarding the plight of the indigenous and African peoples in the Americas focus more on what was done to them by the conquering Europeans than on the mythological sense of community and resistance presented by Paz. Although his accent on the mestizo heritage is vital for his overall project of effecting genuine dialogues among diverse cultures, he still focuses too narrowly on the historical record of mestizos in Latin America. He fails to develop why the ethos of mestizaje—creation of a new culture, via cultural mixing, that simultaneously reflects and is distinct from the contributing cultures—is so crucial for realizing the liberation of those exploited and dominated by the myth of modernity.

Finally, long before terms like the "global economy" were in vogue and well before Dussel's indictment of modernity, Paz, at the height of the Cold War, recognized that the so-called modern world is increasingly the only world, that the past "plurality of cultures . . . has been replaced by a single civiliza-tion and a single future."[55] Reminiscent of Dussel, Paz maintains that the global triumph of modernity has put an end to the immense differences that existed between civilizations of the past, such as those that distinguished the Aztecs and Spaniards on their first encounter. Ironically, he continues, as Mexico has been on the margin of world developments for the past five cen-turies, this triumph of modernity has led to a situation where all cultures, including those of Europe, Canada, and the United States, find themselves on this same margin: "We Mexicans have always lived on the periphery of his-tory. Now the center or nucleus of world society has disintegrated and every-one—including the European and the North American—is a peripheral be-ing. We are all living on the margin because there is no longer any center."[56]

Given the chronology of events, Paz's contention is startling, for clearly the global economy has become "the center." However, the implications of Paz's observation, when placed alongside Barber's distinction between McWorld and jihad and Geyer's despair at how moguls of multinational corporations have little sense of national citizenship, become even clearer. In the global economy in which entire communities, be they in the devel-oped or developing worlds, can be created or erased almost overnight by the shifting vagaries of supply and demand, all extant cultures are moved to the margin. Even the distinction between developed and developing worlds makes sense only in economic terms; the moral traditions of Western and non-Western civilizations alike have to contend with the growing utilitar-ian measurement of well-being.

Considered another way, marginalization of all civilizations, Western and non-Western, by the global economy is the logical outcome of Dussel's myth of modernity. Modernity has become so successful at projecting an objectivist notion of reality that even the European colonial powers that perpetrated this myth now find much of their cultural heritages to be just a list of commodities in the global economy. Against this backdrop, Dussel's project of effecting lateral and democratic dialogue between diverse rationalities and cultures is not just a way of overcoming past Eurocentric colonialism and U.S. neocolonialism, but of generating a normative discourse that can serve as a counterculture to the cold quantitative ethos of global economics.

Indeed, rather than signaling retreat or resignation, Paz transforms this notion of marginality from subordination and disgrace into a locus from which to pursue a more lateral, empowering unity across cultures. The multiple cultural struggles and contradictions that Mexicans have grappled with over the past five centuries—especially vis-à-vis Europe and then the United States—have become a common plight for most peoples around the globe: "Ever since World War II we have been aware that the self-creation demanded of us by our national realities is no different from that which similar realities are demanding of others. The past has left us orphans, as it has the rest of the planet, and we must join together in inventing our common future."[57] The consequent challenge, therefore, is moral, not just socioeconomic, in character: to effect a transnational vision of humanity that does not just project materialism and hedonism, but instead cultivates collaborative, not hegemonic, multicultural relations.[58]

In the case of the United States, Paz concludes, such a vision entails a return to the country's "origins," not in the sense of reliving the past but of revitalizing its political practices in a manner that liberates minorities both within this country and in so-called developing nations from the margins of political discourse: "If the United States is to recover its fortitude and lucidity, it must recover itself, and to recover itself it must recover the 'others'—the outcasts of the Western World."[59] Ultimately, despite the differences I have drawn between Paz's and Dussel's analyses, this denouement of Paz's argument is very Dussel-like: achieving the liberation valued in the Enlightenment tradition means engaging the 'others,' who more often than not have been displaced in modernity's pursuit of civilization or progress.

I have drawn extensively upon Paz's exhaustive review of the evolution of Mexican culture in *The Labyrinth of Solitude* in the hope of strengthening, not enervating, Dussel's critique of the myth of modernity and his project of effecting rational discourse among diverse peoples. Dussel's principal fault, at least in *The Invention of the Americas,* is that he oversimplifies the relationship between the conquerors and the conquered as reflective of the rise of modernity and insufficiently develops the normative resources, especially from indigenous cultures, for realizing an alternate, more inclusive democratic politics. These drawbacks, though, are easily remedied by imbuing his argument with both the positive and negative legacies of indigenous and mestizo cultural traditions in Mexico and Latin America. Still, Dussel's overall project—a dialogue between nations and cultures in a world that has moved beyond modernity—as Paz concludes above, remains one of the fundamental tasks of our age.

Beyond Modernity and Postmodernity toward Transmodernity

THE CRITIQUE OF ENLIGHTENMENT RATIONALISM

Even if, as Paz contends, we are all at present on "the margin" and that as "orphans . . . we must join together in inventing our common future,"[60] how do we go about pursuing this dialogue, especially if the only contemporary "center" is seemingly the global economy? What conditions must be in place to facilitate a fair if not perfect conversation among disparate cultures and worldviews, a conversation that raises, simultaneously, uncomfortable questions regarding distributive justice? After all, one can easily imagine token dialogues in which the interlocutors engage each other in a civil fashion but at the conclusion maintain their relative positions of privilege. This is precisely the predictable conclusion upon which some Latin American scholars have based objection to the repeated calls for North-South dialogue over the past two decades; it is not really a dialogue if the terms of the conversation are weighted to one side. But by engaging Dussel's exegesis of multicultural discourse, we can bring to bear terms consonant with a mestizo democracy and, at the same time, show why such terms are preferable to those put forth by the principal modern and postmodern alternatives in contemporary philosophy and political theory.

A major component of Dussel's critique of the myth of modernity and its accompanying "invention of the Americas" is that in the conquest of the Americas, the Europeans—initially the Spanish and Portuguese, later the Dutch, English, and French—set terms of debate precluding "the excluded or dominated one ever being able to intervene *effectively* in dialogue."[61] In the initial discussions between Spanish missionaries and indigenous religious leaders, as noted previously, the Spanish gave no quarter to the indigenous perspective: "They treated the *tlamatinime* in the same way that cat-echists treated children when imparting doctrine to them in Seville, Toledo, or Santiago de Compostela."[62] In broader terms, Dussel stresses that "the indigenous, Afro-Latin American, and colonial past" has always been de-nied by "modernity's Eurocentric, developmentalist, sacrificial myth."[63]

Dussel, instead, hopes to overcome this hegemony of the center over the periphery by effecting a dialogue in which all parties to the conversation are equal interlocutors. "I want to develop a philosophy of dialogue as part of a philosophy of liberation of the oppressed, the excommunicated, the excluded, the Other."[64] This is not just a superficial North-South diplomatic interchange, for once again terms like *meeting* or *encounter* conceal that one side actually retains the balance of power in the discussion. No, includ-ing perspectives previously consigned to the periphery means recasting the prevailing consensus so as to enable these contributions to be brought forth and, in turn, understood. Providing for understanding of contributions, as Dussel sees it, exemplifies "an amplified rationality which makes room for the reason of the Other within a community of communication among equal participants, as envisaged by Bartolomé de las Casas in the 1550 Valladolid debate."[65]

Las Casas, as already mentioned, is the one notable exception to the "I-conquistador" mentality of the early Spanish colonizers. Arriving in the "new world" in 1502, he was initially the manager of an *encomienda*—a large es-tate through which the Spanish controlled the indigenous people in slave-like fashion. However, as early as 1514, as a missionary priest he began to speak out for the human dignity of the indigenous peoples of the Americas and criticized the atrocities committed against them by *los conquistadores* in the name of Christianity. Eventually becoming bishop of Chiapas in 1543, Las Casas spent most of his life justifying the perspective of the indigenous peoples through Scholastic debate, both oral and written, with the leading Spanish theologians of the day.

In the 1550 Valladolid debate in Spain regarding the status of the indig-enous peoples vis-à-vis Christianity, Las Casas's principal antagonist was the theologian Juan Ginés de Sepúlveda. Sepúlveda's position was that the indigenous peoples were less than human—they worshipped pagan gods and committed human sacrifice. Therefore, conversion to Christianity, even brought about by the sword, would bring eternal happiness otherwise de-nied indigenous people, given their pagan ways. The Spanish leaders and missionaries were supposedly bringing civilization and salvation to these creatures, regardless of evangelistic excesses.

Las Casas, in opposition, contended that the indigenous peoples were equals with the Spaniards in God's eyes. In his interchanges with Sepúlveda and the other theologians he communicated the advances made by the Aztec and Mayan civilizations prior to the conquest. While not denying the practice of human sacrifice in Aztec rituals, Las Casas argued that the coercive, militant process of evangelization and the conquistadors' preoccupation with gold and material wealth were contradictory to Christianity.

Indeed, Las Casas urged the Spanish leadership, both political and theological, to consider the indigenous peoples from the indigenous point of view, rather than just imposing a Spanish or European outlook. Specifically, he remonstrated against the contention that the indigenous peoples were incapable of intellectual discourse. He challenged the other theologians to consider how they would have felt as participants in a debate conducted in a foreign language and within an equally foreign conceptual framework—the plight of the indigenous peoples. As emphasized previously by Dussel, imposition of doctrine rather than real, substantive interchange by and large characterized the "meetings" of Spanish and indigenous leaders. Las Casas, in contrast to Sepúlveda, uncovered the complex hermeneutical challenges intrinsic to engaging the 'other' in a way that does not lead them to being subsumed under the 'same.'

The Sepúlveda–Las Casas debate foreshadows González's distinction between the frontier and border mentalities. On the one hand, Sepúlveda's insensitivity to the intricacies of the inculturation of Christianity in diverse places leads him to adopt the frontier mentality of bringing civilization to the so-called barbarians. This rationale justifies Spanish domination of Mexico and much of the Americas in the process. Las Casas, on the other hand, evoked the border mentality, in which diverse cultures and civilizations can intersect without having to culminate in uniformity or with one culture/civilization being subordinate to the other.

Contrary to the perspective of Eurocentric modernity, Las Casas, according to Dussel, struggled to bring about the conditions under which the Spanish and the indigenous could begin a dialogue between equals. According to Dussel this entails coming to terms with and respecting the culture and "alterity" of the other and being willing to engage the 'other' in "free, creative, collaboration."[66] In an age when the intellectual contributions of the indigenous world were not taken seriously, Las Casas was able to critique the Eurocentrism of the Spanish conquest and to query concerning terms and conditions that could provide for a genuine conversation between diverse peoples.

Of course, Dussel's intention is not just to address what might have worked five hundred years ago, but to describe the conditions for a genuine dialogue between cultures here and now. His accent on the *myth* of modernity argues that the rise of European civilization over the past five centuries was achieved through the instrumental and violent subjection of the 'other' in colonialism. Consequently, to realize a genuine dialogue between cultures as equals—the vision of Las Casas—Dussel contends that reforms merely within the Eurocentric intellectual heritage are insufficient. Reminiscent of Paz, he insists that such reforms in the history of Latin America have only worked to the advantage of the criollo elites. In the nineteenth century "the *criollos* transformed themselves from being dominated to dominating the neocolonial, peripheral order. Their class mediated the domination externally imposed by the centers of industrial capitalism, England and France in the nineteenth century and the United States beginning with the end of the second so-called world war."[67]

Dussel extends his critique of the European intellectual tradition even to Habermas's project of communicative praxis, which at first glance seems congenial to Dussel's insistence on discussing the terms on which substantive discourse between diverse entities can ensue. Habermas, over the past three decades, has been the principal figure within the modern tradition insisting that the rational justification of principles of justice and morality have to be worked out continually in public discourse. Indeed, Simone Chambers in her exegesis on Habermas's discourse ethics has shown how such an approach has proved useful in mediating the conflict between the English-speaking and French-speaking populations in Quebec, a conflict I examine more closely in chapter 5.[68]

Dussel contends that Habermas's discourse ethics does not grasp how radical a shift in orientations is involved in overcoming the hegemony of modernity and the relegation of the 'other' to the periphery: "Modern humanist Ginés de Sepúlveda shared the conquistador framework, as do contemporary rationalists who anticipate too easy a dialogue or as does Jürgen Habermas who has yet to develop a theory of the conditions of the possibility of dialogue."[69] Building upon Dussel's insight, we can see that the difficulty with the neo-Kantian approach—as in Habermas or Rawls—to dealing with diversity is that it privileges abstract rational procedures as the vehicle for testing and validating moral intuitions, rather than what Susan Bickford—through Merleau-Ponty's phenomenological rendering of embodiment—depicts as an active listening and deliberative courage that can engage "a world that has multiple meanings, but whose ambiguity is not equivalent to nonsense."[70] The challenge before us is to effect a dialogue among *diverse* rationalities. This is more easily achieved through a border mentality, in which there is a reciprocal interpenetration of cultures that does not culminate in uniformity, instead of a frontier mentality, in which "one size fits all" and the intrinsic plurality of community life is simply ignored or, worse, extirpated.

In some ways, Rawls's neo-Kantian approach to issues of justice and political discourse is even more vulnerable than Habermas's to Dussel's critique. The "veil of ignorance" in Rawls's early *Theory of Justice* is a classic example of a neo-Kantian mechanism for effecting a deliberation on what would be principles of justice, without getting into particulars and the embodied quality of people's lives. The later Rawls does try to ameliorate this abstract, logical hue of argument by recasting his notion of "justice as fairness" as "political, not metaphysical."[71] Even though Rawls's argument becomes much more engaging as it becomes more practical in orientation, his emphasis on an "overlapping consensus" in public life among diverse cultural, moral, and religious perspectives still retains the Kantian preoccupation with deontological principles. Rawls does not engage the agonal dimension of diverse interlocutors trying just to understand each other, to arrive at some sort of consensus.[72] To transcend the hegemonic legacy of modernity, Dussel insists that all parties in dialogue "ought to be welcomed in their alterity, in that otherness which needs to be painstakingly guaranteed at every level, whether in Habermas' *ideal speech situation* or Karl-Otto Apel's *community of ideal and transcendental communication*."[73] Effecting dialogue between diverse cultures and worldviews is thus a much more daunting undertaking than many rationalists admit.

THE MYTH OF POSTMODERNITY

If the rationalists are too confident that dialogue between diverse cultural interlocutors culminating in transparent consensus can be accomplished, postmodernists, by Dussel's reckoning, too easily deny the possibility of such discourse because of the supposed incommensurability of diverse cultures and creeds. At the same time, aspects of the postmodern critique of modernity are consonant with Dussel's project. First, Dussel does acknowledge "[postmodernism's] critique of reason as dominating, victimizing, and violent."[74] In turn, postmodernism's insistence on scrutinizing decision-making philosophies and structures in order to reveal the particular set of motivations enabling some people to dominate others—frequently based on class, race, ethnicity, gender, and sexual preference, among other cat-egories—is certainly consonant with Dussel's indictment of Eurocentric hegemony. Finally, the antipathy of postmodernism toward universals and foundations is certainly connected to Dussel's critical portrait of the center-periphery dynamic of modernity.

Still, in contrast to postmodern perspectives such as that of Richard Rorty, Dussel contends that cultural perspectives are not so incommensu-rable that genuine understanding or communication is impossible.[75] Dussel renders postmodernism as the flip-side of modernism: if modernism fo-cuses on the assimilation of all other outlooks to that of the self or 'same,' postmodernism's preoccupation with distinct 'others' precludes that there may be nonhegemonic ways to engender dialogue between diverse ratio-nalities and perspectives. Contrary to many postmodern perspectives, Dussel does not want to abandon "the Emancipative tendencies of the Enlighten-ment and modernity" but "the irrationality of the violence of the modern myth."[76] If we are to move beyond this violence, on the one hand, and, on the other, the irrationality of postmodernism, he submits that we must "affirm the reason of the Other as a step toward a transmodern *worldhood*."[77] Dussel wants to develop the hopeful, liberating aspect of modernity while extirpating from modernity its past projection of such hegemonies as "the invention of the Americas."

Dussel's caution regarding postmodernism is expanded by the Cuban American theologian Roberto Goizueta. Similar to Dussel, Goizueta ac-knowledges that postmodernism's celebration of "ambiguity, diversity, and fluidity" counters the tendency in modernism of superimposing models—especially technological in character—over reality.[78] The Cartesian casting of modern reason leads to a theoretical orientation that "distorts reality, turning it into an abstract concept or idea that can be controlled, analyzed, molded."[79] In this light, postmodernism's critique of the hegemonic quality of modernity is worthwhile.

Further echoing Dussel's concerns, Goizueta suggests that post-modernism's quite valid critique of the abstract and instrumental quality of modern reason unfortunately ends up rejecting reason in favor of arbitrari-ness and "random irruption."[80] Specifically, counter to the affective, aesthetic rationality articulated through Latino theology in the previous chapter, rea-son in the modern framework is separated from emotion, and aesthetics is reduced to the domain of the emotions. Postmodernism, according to Goizueta, inasmuch as it maintains that "lived experience . . . can only be 'known' through the irrational, ambiguous feelings," still validates the modern dichotomy between reason and emotion; postmodernism becomes identified with irrationalism.[81] Even though modernity instrumentalizes reason at the expense of (1) human intersubjectivity, (2) the aesthetic dimension of human relationships and (3) the relationship between human beings and nature, the incoherence that all too often typifies postmodern perspectives likewise proves antithetical to articulating a rationality that integrates these three crucial dimensions of human experience.

There are at least three pernicious consequences resulting from the dichotomies of modernity *v.* postmodernity, on the one hand, and reason *v.* emotion, on the other, especially for Latino concerns, according to Goizueta. First, the reason *v.* emotion dichotomy leads to the stereotype that Latinos, as "emotional, passionate persons," are acceptable as entertainers— Jennifer Lopez or Ricky Martin, but not as "rational" professionals—doctors, lawyers, or scholars.[82] Second, Goizueta raises the curious, if not cruel, irony that at the very moment the poor, the disadvantaged, and racial/ethnic minorities begin to question modernity's "rationality" through their new found access to decision-making structures, relativism and absurdity suddenly become chic in educational and political establishments.[83] Raising the banner of relativism can become a convenient way for people in positions of power to avoid addressing issues of fairness and merit, thereby retaining their places in their "academies."

Third and most important in terms of the ethos of a mestizo democracy, to accept the postmodern stress on (1) irrationality as opposed to modern rationality and (2) particular experiences as opposed to any sort of universal or transcendent rendering of reality is to see Latino experience as just one of many particular worlds that have no intrinsic value beyond their own distinct domains: "For U.S. Hispanic theologians to enter and promote pluralism, as thus construed by the dominant groups, would necessarily reinforce our continued marginalization by isolating us as but one 'social location' among many others of equal validity."[84] A pluralism that eschews the possibility of mutual, lateral, intersubjective engagement among cultures can never effect a unity-in-diversity between diverse cultures and essentially reinforces the prevailing political and economic power structures. The above emphasis on irrationality and particularity essentially represents a "myth of postmodernity."

Recall that Dussel insists that modernity establishes its "superiority" through subordinating the 'other': military conquest, not deliberative interchange was the modus operandi of the European colonizers. In the case of postmodernism, the 'other' is so utterly unique that incommensurability of perspectives becomes the norm. Short shrift is given to the rational contributions the 'other' can make to a genuine pluralism that strives, however imperfectly, for communication and interchange across cultures and challenges hegemonic power structures that privilege some cultures over others. In Goizueta's rendering of postmodernity, the *particular* value of the 'other' is not seen as having any *universal* merit for community deliberations over the common good or philosophical deliberations over truth.

Whereas the myth of modernity clearly distinguishes between the conquerors as "civilized" and the conquered as "uncivilized," what I am terming the "myth of postmodernity" more subtly acknowledges the presence of the 'other' without threatening the power of the privileged in society. Moreover, whereas the European colonizers rationalized their acts of violence through the framework of modernity, Goizueta adds that once postmodernism permits the abrogation of criteria for rational argumentation, violence unfortunately becomes the only alternative remaining for those on the margin who otherwise want to articulate "the *rational validity* of [their] experience and values."[85]

A TRANSMODERN QUEST FOR LIBERATION

As opposed to either the well-intended but abstract neo-Kantian recastings of modern reason in Habermas or Rawls or the rejection of both modern reason and universal communication in some postmodern thought, Dussel's notion of transmodernity therefore strives to engage the particularity of the 'other' without abandoning rational intercultural dialogue that "endeavors to construct not an abstract universality, but an analogic and concrete world in which all cultures, philosophies, and theologies will make their contribution toward a future pluralist humanity."[86]

In particular, Dussel revitalizes the theme of liberation so pivotal to the Enlightenment and especially accented in the Hegelian/Marxist political theoretical tradition, but he wants to shed the Eurocentric trappings of that project. At a minimum, he stresses that a transmodern rationality "makes room for the reason of the Other within a community of communication among equal participants."[87] In light of Goizueta's scathing critique of postmodern thought that validates unique particular cultures without striving to engender multiple, mutual interchanges between cultures, Dussel's transmodern project pursues a conversation among distinct cultures in which the terms of the dialogue are not weighted to the advantage of any side.

Once again, Dussel returns to Las Casas's debate with Sepúlveda at Valladolid to exemplify this substantive ethos. For Las Casas, according to Dussel, modernity could be engaged constructively as long as the alterity of the indigenous peoples was not eliminated in the process.[88] Rather than conversion by the sword, Las Casas contended that "a single, same method for teaching the true religion [is] the persuasion of the understanding through reasoning, inviting, and gently moving."[89] Sepúlveda, by contrast, advocated using violence to coerce the indigenous peoples into the conversation, then relying on persuasion in the subsequent conversation. For Las Casas, compulsion could never be a basis for rational interchange; he focused first and foremost "on how the Other should *enter* the [deliberative] community and begin to *participate* in it."[90]

At the same time, Dussel's transmodern pursuit of liberation unequivocally entails social justice and a broadening of the scope of democracy: "As a practical-political program, liberation surpasses both capitalism and modernity in search of a new transmodernity characterized by ecological civilization, popular democracy, and economic justice."[91] Modernity at its core promised liberation from government and social tyranny—specifically medieval hierarchical elites—so as to advance individual rights and popular sovereignty in terms of politics. However, as Dussel has pointed out, this so-called modernization and emancipation as projected by the European powers entailed in a contradictory fashion the irrational sacrifice of the peoples of Latin America, Africa, and Asia: progress was achieved through subjugation of the 'other.' In turn, as postmodernists have emphasized, modernity's emphasis on realizing personal freedom from the domination of political and social institutions does not go far enough in terms of recognizing that practically every system of power has inscribed in it practices of domination. By articulating a transmodernity, Dussel hopes to rid modernity of its "irrational sacrificial myth" and thereby resuscitate and project modernity's noble aims of liberation.[92] In so doing, he acknowledges the critiques of modernity put forth by postmodernists without accepting the relativist conclusions of many of their analyses.

Unfortunately, Dussel's articulation of liberation philosophy remains intensely abstract; although he shares Las Casas's focus on how to engender lateral, nonhegemonic dialogue between diverse parties, Dussel does not develop the affective dimension of how to effect transmodernity. Ironically, as critical as Dussel is of Kant's and Hegel's Eurocentric casting of modernity, at least in *The Invention of the Americas*, Dussel's presentation is still typical of many political and philosophical discourses currently prevailing in both Europe and the United States. Apart from the use of Las Casas, Dussel takes issue with Habermas, Apel, or Rorty in a fashion that is quite familiar to those who follow academic journals and attend academic conferences. Dussel does not consider as extensively, as do the Latino theologians covered in the previous chapter, the substantive contributions that indigenous orientations and mythologies offer for a genuine mestizaje between cultures. In Dussel's presentation, such contributions are implicit not explicit.

Goizueta's critique of postmodernism, building upon Dussel's emphasis on liberation, makes explicit the indigenous and Latino contributions toward effecting a transmodernity. Contrary to both the instrumental dimension of reason in modernity and the isolation of emotion and feeling from reason by postmodernism, Goizueta emphasizes that the Latino worldview as "organic and relational" engages reason as an intersubjective and contextual experience.[93] In contrast to the dichotomy between objective impersonal reason and subjective irrational emotion, he asserts that reason is embodied in "an aesthetic, affective, and active intersubjectivity."[94]

In contrast to prevailing individualisms and pluralisms that inherently separate people and cultures because they do not allow for the possibility of an intersubjective sense of community, Goizueta and other Latino theologians depict an aesthetic practical reason rooted in the deep sense of Latino extended networks. Indigenous and Latino scholars articulate this aesthetic practical reason not just to legitimate their orientation but to critique both the relentless competition and superficial multiculturalism that characterizes the prevailing society. This *ethos* of a mestizo democracy offers a constructive counterpoint to the global economy's reduction of human relations to market objectives and consumer preferences.

Nevertheless, Goizueta does acknowledge the indebtedness of Latino and Latin American theologies to the Enlightenment tradition: "We are thus products of the Enlightenment. Indeed, the very notions of human rights and liberation at the heart of Third World theologies are notions inherent in the Enlightenment tradition itself—even if not always practiced . . . If we critique U.S. society, it is precisely to insist that our adopted country live up to its noble ideals."[95] Indeed, like Dussel, Goizueta accents a *"liberating* reason . . . grounded in intersubjective praxis."[96]

Still, the contribution of Goizueta and the other Latino theologians reviewed in chapter 3 is their insistence that this project of liberation will be more effective if guided by the aesthetic practical rationality that has emerged from the crucible of the intersections of African, European, and indigenous cultures in the Americas. In this fashion the pursuit of transmodernity moves beyond the impasse between modernity's accent on objectivity and postmodernity's accent on incommensurability to realize *affectively* Las Casas's articulation of a just substantive multicultural discourse.

A *POST-LIBERATION* THEOLOGY

Recasting Dussel's liberation philosophy in an affective way through the work of Goizueta and other contemporary Latino theologians also has implications in turn for liberation theology in the twenty-first century. Two or three decades ago, liberation theology was the radical edge of any discussion regarding religion and politics, and especially social justice, in Latin America. Its articulation of the preferential option for the poor incited passionate debate between its proponents and detractors. Indeed, most of the Latino theologians reviewed in chapter 3 are very much descendants of this heritage.

At least three factors over the past two decades have diminished the centrality of liberation theology in the Latin American context:

- the democratization of most Latin American countries from the 1980s to the present,
- the growing conservatism of the Vatican in the 1980s, especially in terms of episcopal appointments to Latin America,
- and the end of the Cold War in the early 1990s and its consequent impact on the cogency of Marxist perspectives.

In terms of the first and third factors, liberation theology is a victim of its own success. The coalition forged by the institutional church, liberation theologians, and Christian base communities from the 1960s into the 1980s in places like Brazil proved effective in bringing an end to military dictatorship and forging a democratization of society and government. However, now that liberal democracies are in place, it has become more difficult for liberation theology to bring about a more radical transformation of society. Indeed, the collapse of the Berlin Wall and the demise of the Soviet Union has made the articulation and realization of participatory democratic alternatives to liberal democracy that much more challenging.[97]

But just as crucial to the transformation of liberation theology over the past two decades is the fact that other radical perspectives—specifically those whose focus is on ethnic and racial cultures, the environment, and gender concerns—have challenged liberation theology's tack when it comes to mobilizing political participation, decentering decision-making networks, and redistributing wealth. The overreliance on a Hegelian/Marxist paradigm combined with an emphasis on dependency theory makes it difficult for liberation theology to deal with the critique of Eurocentrism made by postmodern thinkers. Liberation theology certainly engages the 'other' as the poor, but is it capable of engaging the 'other' in terms of gender, nature, or indigenous cultures?

Such challenges to liberation theology, not from the right but from the left, parallel many of the concerns of my friendly critique of Dussel. Dussel's articulation of transmodernity and liberation theology's pursuit of the preferential option of the poor need to be imbued by the affective, aesthetic rationality communicated by Latino theologians. The articulation of this rationality by Elizondo, Goizueta, and others is deeply steeped in indigenous perspectives while still engaging both the positive and negative dimensions of the European intellectual tradition. Latino theologians place strong emphasis on cultural traditions, especially popular religion, as a vehicle for challenging political, economic, and social injustice. Even Gustavo Gutiérrez, one of the key founders of liberation theology, in his dense exegesis of Las Casas's defense of the indigenous peoples moves in this cultural hermeneutical direction.[98]

When liberation theology and Dussel's liberation philosophy become mired in the language of dependency and exploitation, their respective characterizations of the 'other' as a counterculture to the dominant mainstream culture are just radical versions of Augustine's pilgrims who in pursuit of the City of God have to endure the power politics of domination of the City of Man. In contrast, when such "liberation" perspectives develop the implications of Latino rationality and spirituality for the transformation of public and civic life, they manifest a concrete, lived sense of unity-in-diversity. This vivid concreteness is in stark contrast to either abstract neo-Kantian configurations of democratic dialogue—Kant and Habermas—or nostalgic calls for community in the United States—Bellah—which insufficiently engage the growing range of cultural traditions integral to the U.S. political and cultural tapestry.

Just as Dussel renders transmodernity as the recapturing of the Enlightenment's project of liberation through a critical engagement of how modernity has occluded the 'other' through colonialism and neocolonialism, we need to pursue a *post-* liberation theology that recasts this theology's project of liberation through the frameworks provided by feminism, environmentalism, and indigenous thought. Significantly, both Dussel and

Gutiérrez turn to Las Casas's engagement of the dialogue between the indigenous peoples and *los conquistadores* as a locus from which to foster liberation and egalitarian, collaborative dialogue.

In this light I think it is much too soon to consign liberation theology to the obituary page of dated theologies. A postliberation theology that distills its long-standing concern with class through the 'other' perspectives of ethnicity, gender, language, nature, and race can concretely pursue the terms of rational discourse raised by Las Casas and amplified by Dussel. Both liberation philosophy and theology need to follow the example being set by Latino theologians of cultivating the affective contributions of indigenous cultural perspectives and popular religion for the transmodern pursuit of justice.

By suggesting a postliberation theology, I am not suggesting that we leave behind the basic ethos of social justice and the preferential option for the poor that has animated liberation theology since its inception. Given the spread of the global economy, the fundamental themes of liberation theology are even more relevant today than they were in the 1960s. Still, the hangover of a predominantly Eurocentric narrative should be excised from liberation theology. To engage effectively in the project of liberation with the sense of transmodernity evoked by Dussel means taking seriously both the manner and content of the aesthetic, practical rationality raised by Latino theology. Otherwise, liberation theology will be too easily typecast as a utopian City of God that can never be practically realized on this earth.

In turn, this mestizo recasting of both liberation philosophy and theology has enormous implications for the twenty-first century intersection of multiple philosophies and spiritualities. The days of the Reformation–Counter Reformation debate and of the strict dichotomy between religious and secular philosophies are over. Especially in the United States, the coming century of interreligious dialogue will not be only among Catholics, Jews, and Protestants but between the Judeo-Christian tradition and other world religions—Buddhism, Hinduism, and especially Islam. This plurality of religious perspectives will also engage in agonal debate with a variety of secular ethical traditions. A postliberation theology imbued with the ethos of a mestizo democracy can be a key contributor to resolving "culture wars" in a just and caring fashion.

In conclusion the concrete practices of Latino community life as conveyed through the aesthetic yet practical rationality articulated by Latino theologians offer a more plausible vision of unity-in-diversity than abstract liberal or communitarian constructions or postmodern deconstructions.

In turn, these concrete practices and rationality provide a more *affective* way of pursuing transmodernity than does either Dussel's discourse in *The Invention of the Americas* or a liberation theology that has not effected a cultural hermeneutical "turn." Rather than rejecting Dussel's contributions toward the project of liberation, we need to amplify how they are being hermeneutically recast by Goizueta and other Latino theologians. This recasting suggests a postliberation theology in which overcoming occlusion of the 'other' in terms of ethnicity, gender, language, nature, race, and religion is intrinsic to overcoming very real disparities of class.

CHAPTER 5

Reconciling Multiculturalism
with Democracy

*M*y recasting of mestizaje as a political theory that brings about a just unity-in-diversity is by no means the only perspective that aims beyond the *unum-pluribus* divide in contemporary democratic theory. In this chapter I compare and contrast a mestizo democracy with cognate undertakings in mainstream political theory. I use the term "mainstream" advisedly, for part of the import of a mestizo democracy is that heritages and resources previously marginalized—such as the affective, aesthetic rationality intrinsic to Latino culture—are integral, not marginal, to the future direction of democracy, in the United States and elsewhere.

At the outset, I review how the challenge of multiculturalism for democracy is being engaged in the liberal-communitarian debate. Communitarian theory, with its focus on the substantive values and traditions constituting communities, might seem the more congenial approach to this issue, but a new generation of liberal theorists—including William Galston, Will Kymlicka, and Joseph Raz—has sought to move beyond the neutral liberalism of Bruce Ackerman, Ronald Dworkin, and John Rawls to explore "liberal purposes."[1] Conversely, theorists generally considered communitarian such as Charles Taylor and Michael Walzer have moved beyond the politics of homogeneous cultural communities to deal with the politics of nation-states with multiple cultures.[2]

After reviewing Kymlicka's exhaustive recasting of liberalism in terms of cultural rights and Taylor/Walzer's striking articulations of a "'deep' diversity" and an "asymmetrical federalism,"[3] I argue that both sides, in contrast to mestizaje, insufficiently address how cultures intersect and transform one another without necessarily culminating in assimilation. To bolster this critique, I discuss the concordance between mestizaje and Jeremy Waldron's cosmopolitanism, Iris Marion Young's relational group theory, and Homi Bhabha's hybridity. Though there are differences among these four perspectives, together they make clear that the conventional demarcation between majority and minority groups overlooks how cultural groups become hermeneutically entwined through political and socioeconomic interchange.

Moreover, I argue that Young's and Bhabha's approaches, reminiscent of Dussel, also challenge the prevailing Eurocentrism of liberal democratic engagements of multiculturalism: dealing with multiculturalism means resolving the division between haves and have-nots engendered by colonialism, neocolonialism, and now the global economy. Due to globalization and migration, the diverse peoples of the developing world are now part and parcel of the developed world. Kymlicka and Taylor indeed illustrate that the Canadian government has much more explicitly fostered cultural rights through law than has the United States. However, the other U.S. border—between the United States and Mexico—is the front line for articulating a just multicultural democracy in the twenty-first century.

Finally, bringing this scrutiny of the liberal-communitarian debate over multiculturalism together with my previous considerations of democratic schemes for dealing with diversity, I compare and contrast mestizaje as a political theory with liberalism, communitarianism, postmodernism, and tribalism. Such comparisons not only capture the conceptual differences among these four "isms" but underscore why a mestizo democracy, with its hermeneutical claim that cultural intersections are intrinsic to engendering a substantive political community, needs to be a vital interlocutor in so-called "mainstream" discourse.

Kymlicka: Liberalism with a Cultural Heart

One might think that liberalism, with its strong emphasis on individual rights, cannot provide grounds for ensuring cultural communities. It would seem that the norms of such communities preclude the range of available choices and in some instances endorse illiberal practices—for instance, the subordination of women to men. Will Kymlicka, though, makes an ingenious argument for "differential citizenship rights" within liberalism.[4]

Kymlicka maintains that the case of the indigenous tribes of Canada illustrates both the need for justifying cultural rights on liberal grounds and the capacity of liberalism for dealing with political communities that contain heterogeneous cultural communities.

CULTURAL SOCIALIZATION AS A PROPAEDEUTIC FOR THE LIBERAL SELF

Instead of emphasizing culture as antagonistic to the liberal self, Kymlicka renders culture as essential to the development of self-respect: "It's only through having a rich and secure cultural structure that people can become aware, in a vivid way, of the options available to them, and intelligently examine their value."[5] Socialization through a stable culture enables individuals to develop their capacity for self-reflection and personal choice.

The dilemma faced by the indigenous tribes in Canada is that unless legal precautions are adopted, the cultures of these tribes could be overwhelmed by the weight of the national culture brought by outsiders. Kymlicka maintains that if one's upbringing is "a constitutive part of who that person is," then "special political rights" can ensure "that aboriginal communities are as secure as non-aboriginal ones."[6] Consequently, measures such as "denying non-Indians the right to purchase or reside on Indian lands," mandating residency requirements for voting and running for public office (to minimize the impact of nonindigenous transient workers in regions with extensive natural resource industries), or maintaining the "non-alienability of land" (so that individual members of tribes cannot take title to the land and sell it) have been proposed or adopted.[7]

Traditionally for liberals, such proposals to ensure collective rights violate individual liberty: for instance, why should the freedom of nonindigenous individuals to obtain indigenous lands be restricted? Kymlicka's genius lies in employing cultural rights toward a liberal end—ensuring that all individuals have an equal opportunity to come to full moral and personal development through which they can direct their lives.

Kymlicka makes two important distinctions to bolster his position. First, he distinguishes between political and cultural membership. The former provides for pursuit of "the rights and responsibilities entailed by the framework of liberal justice"; the latter provides for sharing with others "a culture, a language and history."[8] A heterogeneous nation-state will be comprised of multiple cultural communities. Kymlicka focuses not on the cultural norms of these communities, for they could conceivably challenge those of the liberal political community, but rather on ensuring that these communities remain intact to develop individuals who can take full advantage of their political membership.

Second, Kymlicka distinguishes the circumstances and contexts of choices from the choices themselves: "The primary good . . . is the cultural community as a context of choice, not the character of the community or its traditional ways of life."[9] His argument is not to justify on liberal grounds "the shared ends which characterize the culture at any given moment," but simply to guarantee that each individual will come to maturity in a stable cultural environment that will enable him or her eventually to make meaningful choices.[10] Eventually, individuals might choose to leave the tribe to follow their own autonomous paths; the key remains to preserve the indigenous culture not for the sake of its traditions, but as a context of choice for its members.

By distinguishing between political and cultural membership and seeing the latter primarily as a context of choice, Kymlicka contends that he avoids the communitarian temptation to confuse cultural membership with the shared meanings of a culture. In conclusion, Kymlicka insists that the political community needs to guarantee through law the claims of cultural communities but in so doing not endorse "systems of racial or cultural oppression."[11]

RECASTING LIBERALISM WITH CULTURAL AFFECTION

Kymlicka articulates a highly sophisticated liberalism vis-à-vis the issue of rights for cultural communities. First, in contrast to the communitarian claim that liberalism inaccurately assumes an atomized self, Kymlicka illustrates how important cultural membership is for developing the capacity for self-reflection and individual choice. Second, in contrast to Rawls and Dworkin who assume a homogeneous cultural community for their liberal presentations, he demonstrates how liberalism can deal with heterogeneous political communities. Third, by moving beyond neutral liberalism to deal with cultural rights, Kymlicka reinvigorates a strain in liberalism—evident in the work of Mill, Green, Hobhouse, and Dewey—which never disassociates the importance of individual choices from cultural membership:

> Mill, Green, Hobhouse, and Dewey were concerned with community, but were not thereby communitarians. . . . They were as much concerned with the value of individual liberty as anyone before or

since. Yet they recognized the importance of our cultural membership to the proper functioning of a well-ordered and just society,
and hence they had a different view of the legitimacy of special
measures for cultural minorities.[12]

In the same spirit, Kymlicka points out that liberal theorists between
World Wars I and II "considered [it] a victory and virtue of liberalism that
the League [of Nations] managed to secure special political status for minority cultural groups in the multinational countries of Europe."[13] It is hardly
the case then that public policy based on ethnic, racial, or cultural considerations is a departure from liberalism. Kymlicka draws upon rich resources
within liberalism to make the case that *neutral* liberalism is inadequate for
dealing with cultural rights.

Finally, his extensive review of Canadian jurisprudence concerning its
indigenous tribes offers an alternative liberal vision of race and cultural
relations to that contained in the seminal American desegregation case, *Brown
v. Board of Education*.[14] *Brown* strikes down legal segregation because it inherently puts a badge of inferiority on the targeted race. But based on the
experience of the indigenous tribes of Canada, Kymlicka responds that forced
assimilation is no better in terms of fostering human self-development. If
African Americans were forcibly excluded by "separate but equal" public
policies, the indigenous tribes are forcibly included unless their cultural
communities are legally guaranteed: "The crucial difference between blacks
and the aboriginal peoples of North America is, of course, that the latter
value their separation from the mainstream life and culture of North
America."[15] For African Americans, segregation impeded the context of individual choice and development; in the case of the Canadian indigenous
peoples, separation sustains that context.

WHITHER THE GOOD?

Though Kymlicka articulates "the need for an integral and undamaged
cultural language with which one can define and pursue his or her own
conception of the good life," Taylor contends that he focuses on ensuring
individual choices, not the survival of the cultures—the French Canadian
accent on "*survivance*."[16] Although Kymlicka moves liberalism beyond a
neutral stance toward the consideration of cultural rights, Taylor emphasizes
that Kymlicka's concern is procedural individual socialization, not the substantive content of a culture. Kymlicka admits as much by distinguishing

between culture as a context of choice, on the one hand, and, on the other, the given set of values of a culture at any one time. Ultimately culture simply seems preparatory to the moment when individual members can transcend their past and direct their own lives. In Kymlicka's approach, no discussion of a substantive good shared by a heterogeneous community can ensue.

Nevertheless, Kymlicka has demonstrated the strength and limitations of liberalism vis-à-vis cultural rights. More like Dewey and Mill than Rawls or Dworkin, Kymlicka acknowledges the vital role cultural socialization plays in the development of individuals who can make mature and meaningful choices. Yet true to the liberal tradition, he argues that the pursuit of cultural rights cannot displace either the need for individual liberties and rights or the need for a critical citizenry.

Taylor/Walzer: "Deep Diversity" or a Federation of Liberalisms

Charles Taylor and Michael Walzer offer a perspective on cultural rights more rooted in the substantive concerns of the cultures. Though both thinkers are more communitarian in disposition than Kymlicka, they term their respective outlooks as liberal. Although I will focus primarily on Taylor's arguments, I incorporate Walzer's commentary on Taylor's approach because it clarifies the key issues distinguishing their articulation of liberalism from the neutral (Rawls and Dworkin) as well as from the purposive (Kymlicka) types. Thus, I will employ the shorthand term "Taylor/Walzer" to distinguish their approach from other liberalisms.

THE UNIVERSAL-PARTICULAR BIND

Taylor, in broad philosophical terms, notes that the concern raised by minority cultural groups is a variation of the universal-particular nexus. Liberalism invokes universal rights that apply to each individual as an individual, whereas cultural groups want to affirm their particular identity. Kymlicka's effort to move beyond a "difference-blind" liberalism still focuses on culture as a means to facilitate each individual's realization of universal rights.[17]

According to Taylor, cultural groups contend that so-called difference-blind standards are actually particulars masquerading as a universal to which all other cultures must conform: "The claim is that the supposedly neutral set of difference-blind principles of the politics of equal dignity is in fact a reflection of one hegemonic culture."[18] One cannot, thus, dismiss discussion of shared values, traditions, and norms in a liberal democracy, for these issues are intrinsically tied up with the political community. How then does one reconcile the values of diverse cultures in a heterogeneous nation-state?

DUAL LIBERALISMS IN CANADA

Specifically, Taylor and, in turn, Walzer distinguish between two liberalisms in Canada. Canada, as a whole, through the 1982 Canadian Charter of Rights, has adopted essentially Dworkin's neutral, universal-rights, "procedural" liberalism, or what Walzer terms "Liberalism 1."[19] This charter lists a set of individual rights and provides for equal protection of individuals under the law. No particular substantive outlook on the good life is put forth. The state cannot engage, as Walzer puts it, in any "cultural or religious projects or, indeed, any sort of collective goals beyond the personal freedom and the physical security, welfare, and safety of its citizens."[20]

Therefore, any attempt by any minority or cultural group to promote collective goals, Taylor argues, not only violates the charter but is seen as "inherently discriminatory."[21] Specifically, Taylor describes "English Canada" as leery of laws in Quebec that seek to preserve French Canadian culture by

- determining who can send their children to English-language schools,
- stipulating that businesses with more than fifty employees be conducted in French,
- prohibiting commercial signs in any language other than French— (in fact struck down by the Supreme Court of Canada).[22]

Indeed, this basic distrust of collective goals, Taylor contends, led to the failure of the Meech Lake accords—an attempt nationwide "to recognize Quebec as a 'distinct society.'"[23]

The other liberalism, according to Taylor, is Quebec's endeavor to constitute a community "around a definition of the good life, without this being seen as a depreciation of those who do not share this definition."[24] Once again, French Canadians seek *survivance:* "It is axiomatic for Quebec governments that the survival and flourishing of French culture in Quebec is a good."[25] Walzer terms this approach "Liberalism 2," whereby "a particular nation, culture, or religion" is promoted while simultaneously guaranteeing the civil rights of everyone, regardless of their backgrounds.[26]

Consequently, a difference-blind liberalism cannot meet the substantive concerns of French Canadians. As Taylor argues, French Canadians "do not see themselves as being in the same historical position as immigrants."[27] They consider repulsive any endeavor to reduce them to being just one of many hyphenated ethnic/racial groups. In the same vein, merely ensuring that they have the option to speak French is insufficient because at stake is the perpetuation of a substantive culture, "a community of people here in the future that will want to avail itself of the opportunity to use the French language."[28]

Taylor's defense of French Canadians makes present and future cultural integrity a central feature of public policy: "They are willing to weigh the importance of certain forms of uniform treatment against the importance of cultural survival, and opt sometimes in favor of the latter."[29] But how does this recasting of liberalism guarantee the civil rights of non-French Canadians in Quebec? In response, Taylor argues that only privileges and immunities such as "commercial signage in the language of one's choice" can be restricted through public policy, not inalienable liberties.[30] Quebec's adherence to liberalism, he adds, should be measured by how it treats its minorities.[31]

"DEEP DIVERSITY"

Even if *"la nation canadienne-française"* guarantees the inalienable rights of non-French Canadians in Quebec, how does one then reconcile the Liberalism 1 of English Canada with the Liberalism 2 of French Canada?[32] Taylor proposes a "deep diversity." Institutionally, this would involve an "asymmetrical federalism" where the present distribution of powers between the federal and provincial governments would remain intact except for Quebec. Quebec, in addition to its present powers, would also assume responsibility for labor, communication, agricultural, and fishing policy, among other areas; the federal government would be relegated to overseeing defense, foreign affairs, and currency.[33] Taylor adds that an "asymmetrical federalism" is already in place insofar as "Quebec is the only province that raises its own taxes, has its own pension plans, is active in immigration, and so on."[34] This reality, he continues, need only be reconciled with Canada's "constitutional texts."[35]

The most salient consequence of this asymmetrical arrangement is that the Quebec provincial government could sustain through public policy a substantive sense of cultural practices distinct from the rest of Canada.

Taylor proposes that Canada institute multiple types of citizenship: most of English Canada would articulate a mosaic understanding of national identity in which individuals would stress a common Canadian identity while still taking pride in their various ethnicities, whereas French and indigenous Canadians would stress their particular ethnicities while still remaining Canadians.[36] These plural models of citizenship, he contends, would mediate the present impasse in which the English Canadians stress national allegiance to Canada and relegate French Canadians to being just one ethnicity among many, while the French Canadians insist that Canada is "a pact between 'two nations.'"[37]

Through a deep diversity, Taylor wants to move between the universal and particular, procedural and substantive, unitary and separatist poles of the cultural-rights debate in the context of liberalism. He finds the simple guarantee that every citizen in Canada will be given equal protection under the law, which has led to the protection of the French language, insufficient to guarantee French culture. By the same token, he opposes any Quebec separatism that would reject the historic and economic ties of Quebec to the rest of Canada. Instead, he urges "a national life founded on diversity," in which the determination of Canada's identity would be debated politically "without definitive closure, between a plurality of legitimate options."[38] Such a unity without uniformity would allow "one group to breathe without imposing its model on the other" and simultaneously offer a basis for constructive dialogue.[39]

In larger terms, Taylor adds that deep diversity is not just relevant to the peculiarities of Canada, for "in many parts of the world today the degree and nature of the differences resemble those of Canada rather than the United States."[40] Essentially, the "uniform model of citizenship," of Liberalism 1, has had its day; the new century belongs to versions of deep diversity yet to be articulated, as more and more countries due to international migration are becoming comprised of multiple substantive ethnic communities.[41]

MUTUAL ACCOMMODATION RATHER THAN PENETRATION

Walzer moves Taylor's recasting of liberalism in terms of deep diversity beyond the Canadian situation. Walzer points out that a liberalism stressing a particular substantive culture yet ensuring the civil liberties and rights of non-cultural members—Liberalism 2—is actually closer to the past and present practices of European nation-states than is Liberalism 1. On the other hand, he maintains that Liberalism 1 is appropriate for the United

States because it is a "nation of nationalities" in which "there is no privileged majority and there are no exceptional majorities."[42] Governmental guarantees of cultural group survival in the United States, he argues, would entail much more extensive violation of individual rights than any such policies presently undertaken in Quebec.[43] Walzer insists that by choosing Liberalism 1 from within Liberalism 2 one moves beyond a universal or "absolute commitment to state neutrality and individual rights" as well as beyond any "deep dislike of particularist identities. . . ."[44]

Like Kymlicka, the Taylor/Walzer argument moves liberalism beyond its past neutral, procedural, or difference-blind trappings. In contrast to Kymlicka, Taylor/Walzer places much more importance on the substantive distinctiveness of cultures: cultural sensitivity is not just reduced to being concerned about the context of choice that enables each person to realize universal rights. Second, unlike Kymlicka's separation of political and cultural membership, Taylor/Walzer renders liberal democracy as being constituted through cultural norms, not apart from them. Whereas Kymlicka replaces neutral liberalism with a liberalism sensitive to cultural rights for individuals, Taylor/Walzer proposes a more radical plurality of liberalisms to sustain substantive cultures.

If Kymlicka's stance still leans toward universalism or assimilation, Taylor/Walzer's solution leans toward particularism or separatism. Taylor establishes the possibility of formats of Canadian citizenship other than the mosaic model (a subtle variation of the universalist model) but does not seriously pursue how different citizens and cultures transform one another, consonant with the emphasis on intersubjectivity in his philosophical works. He simply seeks a mutual accommodation between two or more distinct ways of being Canadian.

Nor does Walzer's notion of choosing Liberalism 1 from Liberalism 2 salvage matters: either a nation-state cultivates a principal culture while ensuring the liberties and rights of nonmembers, or, when too many diverse cultures make that impossible, it opts for a liberalism that focuses on a procedural rather than on the hermeneutical interaction between diverse citizens. Though Kymlicka merely focuses on an individual's context of choice, one can project from his approach how an individual's outlook could come to reflect a combination of indigenous and other Canadian cultures. As much as the Taylor/Walzer approach provides a more substantive articulation of culture in the context of liberalism than does Kymlicka, it does not engage the entwining of cultures, other than in assimilationist (mosaic) or separatist (French or indigenous) terms.

Mestizaje and Related Approaches to Multiculturalism

In contrast to Kymlicka's purposive liberalism or Taylor/Walzer's deep diversity, mestizaje as a political theory renders the interaction between cultures as a politics of intersubjective relations. Rather than rendering cultures in terms of "us *v.* them"—a politics of possessive identity—a mestizo democracy accents how cultures dynamically interpenetrate and transform each other—a hermeneutical unity-in-diversity. Indeed, mestizaje contends that a full and rich sense of community is realized through the border crossings between diverse cultures; cultures can transform each other without the outcome being assimilation to the dominant culture or extermination of minority cultures. In contrast to focusing on cultural rights (Kymlicka) or cultural survival (Taylor/Walzer), mestizaje accents empowerment and participation: a genuine democratic community is only realized to the degree that each of its diverse cultural traditions is able to contribute actively to the political, economic, and social life of the community.

Kymlicka makes a powerful case, for instance, for justifying cultural rights, in liberal terms, for the indigenous tribes of Canada. By recognizing the importance of cultural membership to developing political citizenship, he advances liberalism beyond the neutral approaches of Rawls and Dworkin and resuscitates the liberalism of Mill and Dewey, insofar as they argued that individual well-being is entangled with community and culture. However, Kymlicka merely recognizes that cultural socialization is essential to individual development; Taylor is quite right that Kymlicka cannot guarantee the survival of the indigenous tribes because Kymlicka stresses cultural membership, not shared cultural meanings. Kymlicka's liberalism may be purposive, but it still eschews the substantive sense of community experienced by a cultural group and leaves no room for the mutual transformation of cultures as in mestizaje.

Taylor is much more sensitive to why shared cultural meanings are integral to political participation. He demonstrates that neutral liberalism, or Kymlicka's purposive alternative, cannot guarantee the French Canadian insistence on cultural *survivance.* Rejecting separatism, Taylor seeks a deep diversity that would enable Quebec, within a Canadian federation, to articulate public policies that would affirm French Canadian mores. Taylor envisions a unity without uniformity and a pluralism that culminates neither in neutral liberalism nor separatism. Walzer's amplification of Taylor emphasizes that most liberalisms are actually those of Liberalism 2, whereby cultural norms are guaranteed without violation of the liberties and rights of the members of other groups.

Though Taylor and Walzer recognize more than Kymlicka the role cultural norms play in liberal democracies, they do not advance the notion that diverse cultures can transform each other to engender a community that both reflects and is distinct from the contributing cultures. They are simply more willing than Kymlicka to justify predominant cultural norms in liberal democratic terms and opt for a federal scheme when this cultural community is a part of a larger country—Quebec vis-à-vis Canada. Kymlicka is actually more sensitive to how individuals can change their belief systems, but he does not engage this dynamic in terms of cultures. Neither Kymlicka nor Taylor/Walzer moves the discussion of engendering community while recognizing difference in heterogeneous liberal democracies beyond the majority/minority divide.

In addition Taylor and, especially, Walzer invoke the stereotype of the United States as a melting pot of hyphenated Americans whose ethnic/cultural loyalties lack the depth or intensity of French Canadians or European national identities and thus provide a suitable terrain for Liberalism 1. The long-standing development of mestizaje in the U.S. Southwest, though, suggests that cultural diversity in the United States is much more multilayered and complex. The Taylor/Walzer portrait of multicultural relations in the United States is colored too much by what Dussel terms the Eurocentric cast of modernity. By contrast, mestizaje offers direction on how to generate a sense of community through intersecting cultures in a world in which the North-South contest between haves and have-nots is rapidly displacing the dated Cold War framework of East-West global relations.

Both Kymlicka's and Taylor/Walzer's approaches need to engage the implications of a mestizo democracy if they are to have more plausibility. That is more difficult for Kymlicka, despite the significance he places on the cultural socialization of individuals, because of the primacy of the liberal self in his framework. Taylor, on the other hand, would find such engagement easier because of the centrality of intersubjectivity in his general philosophy. Rather than an "asymmetrical federalism," Taylor needs to develop a "multifaceted federalism" that places less emphasis on territorial units and more emphasis on political participation procedures, deliberative legislative forums, and public policy outcomes that enable the contest and transformation between cultures to ensue in a democratic, not hegemonic way. Examining and transforming the power relationships between the cultures that infuse our political communities is a major and necessary step toward realizing genuine democratic dialogue between equal citizens.

REJOINDERS TO MESTIZAJE

Although I have taken both Kymlicka's and Taylor/Walzer's approaches to task, at least two objections to my articulation of a mestizo democracy require serious consideration. First, even though mestizaje has been part and parcel of the U.S. Southwest, European Americans remain the dominant economic players in relation to Latinos. There is hardly parity between the two cultures in the United States; if anything, the consumer culture of the United States is rapidly spreading worldwide: the "Wal-Martization" of Mexico since the North American Free Trade Agreement is just one example. Second, regardless of the cogency of mestizaje, French Canadians, other nationalist groups, and indigenous peoples throughout the world will still insist upon separatist schemes that pursue cultural *survivance* rather than the cultural mixing of mestizaje.

On the one hand, in terms of the first objection, the consumer culture of the United States is undoubtedly becoming pervasive across the globe. In turn, many Latinos do assimilate to the dominant culture, just as have previous immigrants to the United States within three generations. In terms of wielding power, Latinos indeed are subordinate players in the United States economy, and glaring underrepresentation of Latinos persists in political assemblies across the country.

On the other hand, there is the growing Latino presence as a counterculture. Mexican traditions such as *posadas* at Christmas time and *quinceañeras* when young ladies turn fifteen are flourishing, not disappearing in the United States. As reviewed in chapter 2, when Mexicans and other Latin Americans cross the territorial boundary between the United States and Mexico, they enter as migrants, not as immigrants—a consciousness highlighted by the Chicano movement's insistence that Mexican Americans are "from here," not from some faraway place. Over the past one hundred fifty years, Spanish has remained a primary language in many counties in South Texas. As reviewed in chapter 2, based on projected birth rates not migration, a Texas A&M University study shows that by the year 2030 close to two-thirds of the counties in Texas will have a Latino population of at least 40 percent, and that is a conservative projection.[45] Finally, and most importantly, the share of Latino businesses in the U.S. economy is growing, as is the impact of consumer spending by Latinos. All of the above information cannot promise political and economic parity between European Americans and Latinos, but it does suggest a set of conditions that will enable Latinos to penetrate and transform both economic trends and the overall culture of the country.

In terms of the second objection and in contrast to the French Canadians, Mexican Americans, with some exceptions among Chicano activists, are not fearful of losing their culture but, rather, pursue their cultural mores in the face of domination by European Americans and others. This quiet strength through persistence is nothing new: just as Mexicans outlasted the colonialism of the Spanish and then the French (during the reign of Maximilian in the 1860s), Mexican Americans have been enduring the predominance of the European Americans for the past century and a half. In all three instances the unstated tactic is not to confront the dominant culture in a direct fashion but to engage it in a steady but subversive fashion, as water currents over time wear down a rock in a stream.[46]

Actually, the dominant cultural group seems to be the more fearful, given the rash of propositions in California in the 1990s against state support of undocumented aliens (187), affirmative action (209), and bilingual education (227). These initiatives endeavor to marginalize Latino and other non–European American cultures in the name of an assimilated U.S. identity in which European American culture remains hegemonic. Moreover, these propositions actually testify to the pervasiveness of mestizaje in the U.S. Southwest: "When you get a proposition in California to vote the English language as the official language of the State of California, this only means one thing—that English is no longer the official language of the State of California."[47] The irony of these initiatives is that since 1994 they have incited extensive voter registration and increased political mobilization by Latinos in California.

The xenophobia of some European Americans, not the subversive engagement by Latinos, resembles the defensive nationalism of the French Canadians. Even if we acknowledge Simone Chambers's conclusion that members from both sides in the Quebec divide have been constructively engaging in a Habermasian politics of discourse,[48] French Canadians, if Taylor is to be our guide, fear their culture would not survive in the cultural blurring of mestizaje. Those preoccupied with the *survivance* of French Canadian culture manifest in a separatist mode what many European Americans project in an assimilationist mode—cultural identity as a possession to be preserved, not as a dynamic engagement of difference.

Indigenous tribes in the Americas, Australia, as well as other places, constitute the best case for solutions such as Kymlicka's cultural rights or Taylor's asymmetrical federalism because they are the long-standing peoples whose lands and ways of life were conquered by European colonizers. Granting this concession, Native American activists such as Vine Deloria go too far when they insist on the wide chasm between the spiritual and cultural practices of indigenous peoples and the mores of the Europeans and European Americans. As reviewed in chapter 3, Latino popular religion illustrates how the spiritual and cultural practices of Latinos have roots in the practices of African, European, and indigenous peoples and have served as a counter-culture to the religious and cultural norms of the well to do. Mestizaje cannot preserve indigenous, or for that matter, any culture in a pristine sense, but for five centuries it has enabled indigenous cultures to have a transformative, albeit surreptitious, impact on presumably dominant cultures.

KINDRED SPIRITS OF MESTIZAJE: COSMOPOLITANISM, RELATIONAL GROUP THEORY, AND HYBRIDITY

Mestizaje is hardly the only notion that acknowledges the ongoing blurring of cultures. A similar theme is captured in Jeremy Waldron's cosmopolitanism, Iris Marion Young's relational concept of group difference, and Homi Bhabha's sense of hybridity. These outlooks refuse to make strict separations between majority/dominant cultures and minority/subordinate cultures, unlike Kymlicka's and Taylor's approaches. Moreover, Young's and Bhabha's approaches, like mestizaje, make clear that to engage multiculturalism is to pursue political and economic justice.

Instead of Kymlicka's focus on reconciling cultural rights with the liberal accent on individual autonomy or communitarianism's attempt to ensure that a person's identity is grounded in a stable set of social practices, Waldron's "cosmopolitan" consciously fashions an identity that is a combination of cultures:

> The cosmopolitan may live all his life in one city and maintain the same citizenship throughout. But he refuses to think of himself as *defined* by his location or his ancestry or his citizenship or his language. Though he may live in San Francisco and be of Irish ancestry, he does not take his identity to be compromised when he learns Spanish, eats Chinese, wears clothes made in Korea, listens to arias by Verdi sung by a Maori princess on Japanese equipment, follows Ukrainian politics, and practices Buddhist meditation techniques. He is a creature of modernity, conscious of living in a mixed-up world and having a mixed-up self.[49]

Waldron's cosmopolitan combines the substance of culture stressed by the communitarianism with the autonomy praised by liberals.

Young, in contrast to Waldron, does not only focus on how individuals mix and match diverse cultures, but on how cultures are in relationship to each other through "a more fluid, explicitly relational conception of difference."[50] Similar to Anzaldúa, she emphasizes how borders are basically undefinable; in contrast to either the homogeneous public that eliminates difference or the separatist public that protects difference, Young articulates "the heterogeneous public."[51]

Even though groups and cultures may be distinct, Young argues that they have a political and economic impact on each other in the contemporary world. Rather then replicate the cultural strife that has enveloped Bosnia-Herzegovina or mitigate it by an abstract liberal individualism, Young contends that we must acknowledge and validate the notion of "heterogeneous publics that guarantee respect for the cultural specificity and needs of different groups."[52] In these heterogeneous publics, it is perfectly appropriate to provide for representation of such groups in political decision-making processes, especially if those groups are "oppressed or disadvantaged."[53] As an example, Young discusses how the two principal cultures of New Zealand—Maori and Pakeha (European)—have formally ensured access by both groups to the state's political structures. As a result of this formal policy of "biculturalism," the Maori have received legislative protection of their land and have gained greater control over government agencies.[54] Although equal distribution of political and economic power is more a goal pursued rather than a reality effected by "biculturalism," Young notes that proportional-representation discussions have given the Maori greater access to the country's decision-making networks.[55]

Homi Bhabha's articulation of hybridity and transculturation is closely akin to the multifaceted juxtaposition of cultural boundaries in mestizaje. According to Bhabha, what constitutes a nation is not a clearly identifiable authoritarian set of cultural mores and practices, but contesting perspectives characterized by constantly shifting boundaries and by the transformative impact they have on one another. National memory is thus a hybrid of histories communicated through agonal incommensurability rather than through cozy consensus.[56]

Three points amplify Bhabha's position. First, rather than seeing nations or large cultural systems as homogeneous units, we need to recognize them as being ambivalent creations composed of many cultures that daily engage and transform each other. What it means to be a nation, therefore, is always undergoing composition. Second, according to Bhabha, once we acknowledge the multiple and shifting cultures comprising nations, we

can comprehend marginal cultures as interventions that unsettle "the justifications of modernity—progress, homogeneity, cultural organicism, the
deep nation, the long past—that rationalize the authoritarian, 'normalizing'
tendencies within culture."[57] Third, once we admit that national identities
are fluid, "discontinuous," and "interruptive," we uncover a modus vivendi
for engaging other nations and peoples: "The anti-nationalist, ambivalent
nation-space, becomes the crossroads to a new transnational culture."[58]

There are differences between mestizaje on the one hand and Waldron's,
Young's, and Bhabha's respective perspectives. At first glance, mestizaje resembles cosmopolitanism because both stress that individual identity can
be a combination of cultures. Waldron's cosmopolitan, though, chooses
and combines the myriad of cultural artifacts that comprise its makeup;
personal identity is a kaleidoscope of cultures, but one directed by egocen-
trism. By contrast, in mestizaje, the self can only be understood against the
horizon of the community's combination of cultural practices. Mestizaje
is not a matter of creating one's identity from among many possibilities,
like food items on a cafeteria line, but of dealing with the fact that one's
identity is simultaneously enmeshed in multiple cultural backgrounds.
Mestizaje articulates a multifaceted person, culture, or community as not
just a matter of choice but as an entwining of intricate, hermeneutical
histories.

Young, more so than Waldron comes closer to mestizaje's emphasis on
how cultures and communities are in interrelationship with each other. Still,
Young's New Zealand case study focuses more on the access of the Maori to
the economic and political decision-making process than on how the Maori
and Pakeha cultures transform each other in the manner of mestizaje. Certainly, mestizaje does not necessarily lead, for instance, to proportional
representation in decision-making bodies because that would petrify each
culture in a corporatist fashion. Instead, mestizaje would pursue reforms
that do not segregate cultures into geographic enclaves and do not prevent
individuals from crossing cultural boundaries. Young's perspective shows
how cultures are linked politically and economically but does not accent
their hermeneutical nexus.

Bhabha's narrative of nationhood is the most closely linked to the substantive mutual transformation of cultures in mestizaje. Still, Bhabha's
articulation of this process is very much in the postmodern vein, wherein
practically any construction of nationhood simultaneously begets counter-
practices that engender open-endedness. In some respects Bhabha's articulation of nationhood bears some similarity to Waldron's cosmopolitanism

in that both accent the dynamic melange of cultures that constitutes narratives. Whereas Waldron's cosmopolitan self directs the composition of national identity, in Bhabha's hybridity national identity is so variegated and ambivalent that these border crossings disrupt any clear definition of community: the narrative is always in process.

Mestizaje shares hybridity's accent on multiple cultures and their mutual interpenetration, but the former has a much stronger sense of a specific history and tradition that informs border crossings—the original mixing of the African, indigenous, and Spanish peoples to form the Mexican and other Latin American peoples and, in turn, the more recent engagement between European American, Latino, and other cultures in the U.S. Southwest. In contrast to hybridity, the hermeneutics of mestizaje, especially as articulated in Latino theology, never abandons comprehensive notions of a transcendent God, universal reason, or even a political common good, and it insists that the realization of any of these ends is through a composite of cultural, philosophical, and spiritual heritages. Mestizaje's pursuit of concrete universals through both/and rather than either/or takes place against the horizon of a vivid and tangible cultural heritage from over the past five centuries that remains in process.

To become preoccupied with the differences among cosmopolitanism, relational-groups theory, hybridity, and mestizaje, however, is to miss their mutual insight that contrary to Kymlicka's and Taylor/Walzer's outlooks, multiple transformations of cultures are the course of community or national life. Rather than becoming mired in "us *v.* them" frameworks, we need to acknowledge that it is the degree of blurring that is at stake in public debates regarding the interaction between cultures, not the fact of blurring itself. Consequently, we need to pursue a political theory that reflects the reality that juxtaposed cultures are more intrinsic than extrinsic to each other.

Waldron's cosmopolitanism, Young's relational group theory, and Bhabha's hybridity, similar to mestizaje and in contrast to Kymlicka's and Taylor/Walzer's respective frameworks, provide a more complicated but realistic account of how diverse cultures are entwined in personal, group, and community life. Whereas Kymlicka and Taylor/Walzer accept the communitarian stress on the importance of culture to personal identity and try to recast this outlook in a liberal fashion, Waldron's, Young's, and Bhabha's perspectives provide a much more incisive challenge to both the "thin," neutral, atomized liberal self and the "thick," constituted, communitarian self. Cosmopolitanism, relational-group theory, hybridity, and mestizaje render cultural identity not as a possession to be preserved but as a kaleidoscopic intersubjective relationship among 'others.'

In addition, Young's and Bhabha's frameworks, consonant with mestizaje, point out that the examination of the dynamic intersections of multiple cultures in twenty-first century democracies must come to grips with the legacy of colonialism and neocolonialism. If we are to realize the Enlightenment's project of liberation, following Dussel, we need to move beyond center-periphery frameworks, especially those that mistakenly project, in the manner of the frontier mentality, the superiority of one civilization over another. As most clearly argued by Bhabha, center-periphery frameworks unsuccessfully mask how so-called marginal and peripheral cultures inherently subvert the "normalizing" practices of the "center."

In this context of subversive engagement, the Latino experience of mestizaje, even with its many historic warts and drawbacks, offers some valuable direction for a world moving beyond Eurocentrism and, especially, the East-West contour of international relations of the past century. Indeed, the U.S.-Mexico border, as the longest-standing divide between the developed and developing worlds, redirects the compass of international and intranational politics in a North-South direction and, in addition, graphically calls attention to the hegemonies of the frontier mentality and the consumer-oriented McWorld, both challenged by Bhabha's notion of transnational culture and by Dussel's project of transmodernity.

Even if heterogeneity, not homogeneity, were the more appropriate rendering of cultural identity, the objection would still be raised that French Canadians or the cultural antagonists in Bosnia, Cypress, and Ulster, among other places, would still defend their cultural monism at all costs. Perhaps that is true, but after a certain point such steadfast possessive preoccupation with cultural integrity becomes a mask hiding racism or its ugly ethnic or religious cognates. The prevalence of hegemonic cultures claiming to be homogeneous and universal is why the counter-insights of cosmopolitanism, relational-group theory, hybridity, and mestizaje have ethical and not just empirical implications for democracy. These "counter-frameworks" offer hopeful, open-ended relational portraits of multiculturalism that move beyond the possessive rendering of cultural identity still lingering in both Kymlicka's and Taylor/Walzer's views. As much as Kymlicka's articulation of a purposive liberalism and Taylor/Walzer's cultural recasting of federalism advance the liberal-communitarian debate in terms of reconciling multiculturalism with democracy, both insufficiently incorporate how integral heterogeneity is to cultural identity.

Liberal, Communitarian, Postmodern, and Tribal Critiques

Where, then, does a mestizo democracy stand vis-à vis other approaches dealing with multiculturalism in democratic communities? When combined with the issues and concerns of the previous four chapters, the preceding discussion suggests some distinct schools of thought. In terms of liberalism, I have reviewed Kymlicka's purposive approach and neo-Kantian approaches—Rawls and Habermas. In terms of communitarianism, I have considered the work of Bellah, Geyer, Barber, and, now, Taylor and Walzer (although the last two contend that their approaches are a form of liberalism). In chapter 3 I critiqued postmodernism, and in chapter 1 I differentiated between the outlooks of Gadamer, Merleau-Ponty, Derrida, and Foucault on the subject. Finally, especially through the work of Deloria, I have articulated and critiqued what I would like to term "tribalism." Even though this term has a pejorative tone in popular discussions of multiculturalism, it does communicate the perspective of cultural groups who intentionally pursue either geographic or psychological separatism vis-à-vis other cultural groups.

So as to synthesize these discussions in the ensuing section, I project the critiques that I believe each of these four camps—liberalism, communitarianism, postmodernism, and tribalism—would make of my recasting of mestizaje as a political theory and then respond to each of these critiques. Besides clarifying the differences between each camp and mestizaje, the ensuing discussion will pinpoint the salient differences between the camps themselves. Throughout this text I have been stressing that we need to move from a possessive to a relational rendering of cultural identity; Kymlicka's and Taylor/Walzer's limited engagements with heterogeneity exemplify again the pitfalls of the former. Comparing mestizaje with these other four schools of thought clarifies why mestizaje cogently presents a relational approach to multiculturalism consistent with democracy.

THE LIBERAL CRITIQUE: SCRIPTING "BADGES OF SERVITUDE"

Two objections have been made of my work from a liberal perspective. First, I am supposedly suggesting that the United States should turn its back on its individualist roots, and, second, my articulation of a substantive pluralism, along the lines of mestizaje, supposedly "institutionalizes social fragmentation along group lines."[59]

I am hardly calling for the abandonment of American individualism, though I prefer to recast it in what Catholic political and social thought terms personalism. I have no doubt that prevailing interest-group pluralism is linked to a Lockean materialist individualism, but I do not reject other possibilities of nonmaterialist individualism, even potentially rooted in Locke.[60] Akin to Bellah's argument that Biblical thought and civic republicanism are long-standing U.S. political languages alternative to the prevailing one of individualism, I think we can identify alternative outlooks within the U.S. heritage that link personal development with civic participation and render the common good as being constituted substantively through citizen interaction. The Latino experience and the articulation of mestizaje make a vital contribution toward articulating these ends in multicultural terms.

Even if we can specify, as Kymlicka suggests, a purposive liberalism rather than a materialistic liberalism, the latter has prevailed, with no better example being the disintegration of U.S. communities wrought by the economic and political practices of some corporate and political elites over the past three decades. As Bellah stresses, an alarming number of Americans cannot justify their conduct in terms of any moral tradition, even those of Mill or Dewey, emphasizing instead materialistic motives or psychological feelings. "Public happiness" basically takes a back seat to "private happiness"—the pursuit of material self-interest through the market and through welfare-state programs and services.[61] Materialism may not be at the core of Kymlicka's purposive liberalism, but it prevails in political and economic practice.

Furthermore, a mestizo democracy does not institutionalize racial-ethnic-religious-linguistic group fragmentation. I do not make "cultural identity a prerequisite to political activity" or "a badge" to "be worn when engaging in the public sphere."[62] Both the stifling uniformity of the melting pot and the divisiveness of separatist cultural enclaves are rooted in a possessive politics of identity in which either a prefigured U.S. American character is impressed upon everyone or, conversely, a characteristic of one's background utterly separates one from anyone not possessing that same characteristic. By contrast, mestizaje, as a political theory, accents a politics of relations in which personal, cultural, and community development are intersubjectively entwined, and cultures permeate each other in the manner of crossing borders, not extending frontiers.

Admittedly, I have advocated "representation of multiple cultures on city councils and other legislative forums" but never in terms of proportional representation or corporatism.[63] For instance, although the Voting Rights Act of 1965 seeks to change election systems that have diminished the capacity of members of particular ethnicities or races, the act does not establish legislative bodies whose seats would be allocated in a corporatist fashion by ethnicity or race. Such corporatism would advocate and reinforce a possessive understanding of cultural identity to the detriment of the political community and all of its members. Instead, in terms of engendering a relational unity-in-diversity, we need to implement measures that engender multicultural interchange in the political community for the well-being of the community as much as for the particular interests of any cultural group. As opposed to gerrymandering, a scheme that can culminate in racial and ethnic enclaves, other electoral alternatives such as cumulative voting need to be tried—an option I explore at greater length in chapter 7.

I approach the role of culture for political community in dynamic, not static, terms. As I argued in chapter 1, being a U.S. American affords the opportunity to create a new life that is not determined by one's cultural past. Indeed, U.S. American identity is constantly being renegotiated between old and new U.S. Americans—*unum* is not a given. At the same time, I maintain that cultural heritages, even granting their multivocal character, still influence one's decisions and direction, even if one consciously tries to reject one's past. Consequently, I am leery of Waldron's cosmopolitanism if it means only that one's culture is simply a matter of individual choice and has very little to do with one's ties to others in the political community. A mestizo democracy in personal terms is not just a matter of choosing a lifestyle option.

Given the practical imperative that in California, Florida, and Texas, among other places in the United States, multiculturalism is a reality and not just a cause, fad, or trend, we must articulate a democratic community oriented by multicultural *relations*. Even though purposive liberals, such as Galston and Kymlicka, acknowledge the role culture plays in the formation of the liberal self, they still reject the role culture plays in the formation of community norms. In the name of autonomy, they render any substantive sense of community as coercive collectivization: "The liberal citizen is not the same as the civic-republican citizen. In a liberal polity, there is no duty to participate actively in politics, no requirement to place the public over the private and to systematically subordinate personal interests to the common good, no commitment to accept collective determination of personal choices."[64]

Although purposive liberals emphasize how essential cultures are for enabling individuals to make free, autonomous choices, culture, for them, seems to be a prolegomenon to the moment when the individual can transcend the past and direct his or her own life. This liberalism still places secondary importance on how one's own culture and those of others shape but do not determine one's self. The key difference between purposive liberals such as Galston or Kymlicka and myself is that I focus on intersubjectivity, not on subjectivity, as the basis for a democratic engagement between diverse cultures.[65]

THE COMMUNITARIAN CRITIQUE: MESTIZAJE AS LEADING TO BABEL

Responding to a mestizo democracy, the communitarian would argue that mestizaje places too much stress on diversity at the expense of the specific substantive norms that should guide a democracy. Supposedly, unless an overarching set of shared values informs and tempers political deliberation between diverse cultural groups, dissonance and discord will tear apart the body politic.

However, the long-standing drawback of communitarianism has been that its emphasis on established moral principles, reinforced by educational institutions and public policy, leads too easily to political repression of dissident views and violation of civil liberties in the name of community mores. *Anti*-federalism and *con*-federalism are simply out-of-date because they would still envision a politics of small regional communities where there would be what James Madison described as natural majorities.[66] At its best, communitarianism can only cope with diverse cultural groups in terms of assimilation—for example, the infamous Christian schools experiment, which sought to "civilize" and "Americanize" Native Americans. At its worst, communitarianism becomes a sophisticated cover for race-supremacy politics. Indeed, a "thick" communitarianism in an age where multiple cultures are a given is a recipe for genocide.

A mestizo democracy, like communitarianism, emphasizes that the common good is a qualitative undertaking irreducible to any quantitative, incremental summation of preferences. However, a mestizo democracy, with its accent on juxtaposing multiple perspectives, also insists that public discussion of the common good should include as many perspectives as possible and should not rush too quickly to closure. For instance, being Mexican American, as conveyed by Anzaldúa and Elizondo in chapter 2, implies a combination of Mexican and U.S. American mores that could not have been predicted in an a-priori fashion, nor could it be replicated as on an assem-

bly line. With mestizaje, both personal and community identities lie somewhere between the autonomous sense of liberalism and the deterministic
sense of communitarianism. In a unity-in-diversity the substantive common good is not static but, rather, persistently contested and reconfigured
through democratic engagement among diverse persons and cultures in
public life.

THE POSTMODERN CRITIQUE: MESTIZAJE
AS CONSTRUCTING HEGEMONY

The postmodern response to a mestizo democracy would be at least two-
fold. First, mestizaje understates how vast and deep the differences are that
separate cultures, languages, races, genders, religions, and moralities and
thus overstates the degree of communicability and convergence that can
ensue between cultures. Second, the accent on a substantive common good
in a mestizo democracy, albeit one less "thick" or "scripted" than that of
communitarianism, still ends up being a sermon, reminiscent of "neo-
Tocquevillians" such as Bellah.[67]

Admittedly, engendering a lateral intersection of diverse cultures that
retains some sense of substantive community is a complex matter. In chapter 6 I illustrate the difficulties that just one church congregation has had
with such an intersection. One should not naively expect that a multicultural
nexus can ensue without a lot of painful disagreement, misinterpretation,
and disillusionment. Precisely because there will rarely be complete agreement or understanding, the ethos of crossing borders entails keeping discourse open, civil, and attentive to the mutual permeation of perspectives.

Nevertheless, if sermonizing means to be committed to generating political discourses that enable a panorama of cultural perspectives to engage
one another on equal terms, then I plead guilty. Indeed, if one contends
that Dussel is fantasizing in his quest for a dialogue in which multiple cultures can genuinely address one another in a nonviolent, nonhegemonic
fashion, then one consigns politics to endless violent struggles, symbolic or
literal, among incommensurable cultural groups. On this score I concur
with Goizueta's conclusion that those postmodern approaches that absolutely insist upon such radical incommensurability abandon reason.

In contrast to such incommensurability, I am suggesting, reminiscent
of Murray, that multiple cultures and moralities can seek a substantive consensus by peacefully yet rigorously contesting one another's perspectives.[68]
To its credit, postmodernism—and Bhabha's deliberation on hybridity is

most helpful in this regard—cautions that such consensus building can only ensue once we have grasped how heterogeneity is intrinsic to the life of political communities.

THE TRIBAL CRITIQUE: MESTIZAJE AS "SUGAR-COATED" ASSIMILATION

The most serious critique of a mestizo democracy issues from Native American and Chicano scholarship. Mestizaje from the Conquest of Mexico by the Spaniards to the present, the argument goes, has simply been a clever way for those in power to subdue the conquered indigenous peoples by offering the pretense of cultural and racial mixing while, actually, assimilating these peoples. A long-standing critique of the story of Our Lady of Guadalupe argues that the story was created by the Catholic missionaries in Mexico, long after her supposed appearance in 1531, as a means of converting the indigenous people to Christianity. In fact, as previously reviewed, though Mexico officially proclaims itself to be a mestizo people, in reality the descendants of the Spanish conquerors—*los criollos*—historically have had greater access to positions of political, social, and economic power. As previously reviewed in chapter 4, this criollo outlook is continually recast and revitalized through pivotal historical events such as the nineteenth-century war for independence in Mexico and the twentieth-century Mexican revolution.

Worse yet, as I have pinpointed previously in chapter 2, even in Vasconcelos there is the Eurocentric motif that the indigenous peoples of the Americas became purified through the mestizaje with *los conquistadores*. The charm and allure of mixing cultures and races can easily be manipulated into a subtle form of the Nazi motif of racial superiority. Díaz-Stevens and Stevens-Arroyo rightfully caution that the ethnic, genetic, and racial dimensions of the intellectual heritage of mestizaje can have disastrous implications for the political and social sciences.[69]

Racist manipulation of mestizaje should be condemned. Covert assimilation, though, is neither the intent nor the outcome in Latino theologians' rearticulation of mestizaje. A mestizo democracy, instead, highlights how heterogeneity is intrinsic to personal and community life and, in turn, projects an ethos of non-hegemonic mixing of cultures. Perhaps another term for this undertaking would avoid the connotations of genetic engineering—for instance, Díaz-Stevens and Stevens-Arroyo's *transculturation*—but for the moment mestizaje remains the most widespread term for the ethos that I have elicited from Latino theology. In this vein, mestizaje as a lateral, mutual mixing of cultures is the antithesis of Aryan-type racisms.

Nevertheless, when arguments are made, such as that by Geoffrey Fox, that the rising Latino identity in the United States is just another ethnicity being added to a U.S. mosaic, then the previous charge that Latino cultural icons are fostering assimilation has some validity: "They [Latinos] are beginning to embrace the new and less precise categories of Hispanic or Latino so that they can be part of a larger and more influential group and thereby negotiate better terms of assimilation. When they call themselves Hispanics or Latinos, they are not declaring allegiance to any foreign place, but just the opposite. Declaring oneself "Hispanic" is a step back from allegiance to Mexico, Cuba, Puerto Rico, the Dominican Republic, or some other land and a step toward joining America."[70]

Fox correctly argues that a Latino identity is emerging that transcends divisions based on cultural origins from Mexico or Cuba or Puerto Rico, but he misconstrues the import of this mixing of Latino nationalities. To be Latino is not just to embrace an umbrella identity in the way that Irish Americans embrace being "Irish" rather than identifying themselves with a particular county in Ireland, or Italian Americans embrace being "Italian" rather than being from a particular region of Italy. Rather, the unfolding of the Latino identity in the United States is just the latest chapter of the intersection and transformation of cultures that has been ensuing for several centuries in Latin America. As opposed to a petrified articulation of cultural identity that clearly distinguishes one heritage from another, Latino culture thrives in the inclusive mixing of multiple cultures. Indeed, the ethos of mestizaje is that one can cross symbolic borders in a way that recognizes how essential variety and plurality are to the integration of cultures.

Therefore, a mestizo democracy is not restricted to the above combination of Latino groups in the United States, but entails the pursuit of a democratic unity-in-diversity among Latinos, African Americans, Asian Americans, European Americans, Native Americans, and 'other' Americans, without privileging any of these contributing groups. As opposed to the melting pot, which still strives for a uniform communal identity under the guise of distinctly labeled ethnic identities—such as Polish American or Korean American—mestizaje, as a political theory, offers the possibility of a political community whose unity is forever being reconfigured without being forsaken through the democratic interchanges of its contributing cultural groups.

```
                        Assimilation
                             |
                             |
                             |
                             |
     liberalism              |        communitarianism
                             |
                             |
                             |
Individuality ───────────────┼─────────────── Community
                             |
                             |
                             |
   postmodernism             |            tribalism
                             |
                             |
                             |
                        Separation
```

CUTTING ACROSS FOUR QUADRANTS

The preceding distinct perspectives of liberalism, communitarianism, postmodernism, and tribalism comprise four different solutions to these two issues intrinsic to dealing with multiculturalism in a democracy: (1) the individual-community dynamic and (2) the assimilation-separatism contrast vis-à-vis cultural diversity. In terms of the above graph, the horizontal x-axis represents a continuum that runs from individuality on the left to community on the right and the vertical y-axis is a continuum that runs from assimilation on the top to separation on the bottom.

Liberalism, the upper left quadrant of this graph, places a strong emphasis on individual autonomy. Contractual rules, accordingly, provide unity for the political community—a thin assimilation. The legal guarantee of individual autonomy, according to the liberal, deters the repression of individual liberty posed potentially by separatist traditional cultures—one of Kymlicka's key concerns.

Communitarianism, the upper right quadrant, shares liberalism's concern for a foundational consensus but considers the liberal accent on autonomy insufficient for sustaining unity. Instead, communitarianism insists that members of a political community need to share a substantive set of norms—a "thick" assimilation. Therefore, for the communitarian, the multiple sets of substantive norms manifested by separatist cultural enclaves simply rend apart the overall political community.

Postmodernism, the lower left quadrant, shares liberalism's concern for freedom and autonomy, but counters that liberalism's scripting of these values does not recognize that government and economic institutions are not the only power structures that threaten individual freedom. If, as the postmodernists argue, both individual and group identities are shaped by a multiplicity of social forces, then indeed, for the sake of freedom, we need to investigate the power structures intrinsic to particular social practices and acknowledge, if not celebrate, the heterogeneous character of identity. Postmodernists are particularly wary of practices that claim to eliminate oppression or difference, whether in the name of the liberal self or communitarian mores.

Tribalism, the lower right hand quadrant, shares postmodernism's contention that given the incommensurability of cultural worldviews, one should necessarily be suspicious of the "thin" and "thick" unity, proclaimed, respectively, by liberalism and communitarianism. Such "unities" accordingly entail the imposition of a particular outlook on every other worldview. At the same time, tribalism is leery of characterizing individuals and groups in terms of multiple identities. Instead, like communitarianism, tribalism stresses the socialization of the individual in terms of clear-cut tribal customs and normative practices. However, unlike communitarianism, tribalism contends that worldviews are specific to particular locales and have no business in proselytizing other locales. Indeed, *tribalism* denotes the belief that only "thick," particular communities that believe in "live and let live" can survive and that such communities should not be assimilated into some comprehensive politi cal community.

Missing in all four quadrants, however, is a willingness to recognize plurality as intrinsic to the identities of personal, cultural, *and* political communities. Communitarianism is preoccupied with homogeneity and is wary of the threat that individual and cultural group autonomy puts to the overall political community. Liberalism accents individual plurality and tolerates the plurality of cultural groups, as long as they remain in the private sphere and do not try to infect the public sphere with their substantive claims. Conversely, in tribalism, there can be many different substantive communities, each informed by a particular worldview, but individual identities must be oriented by the substantive norms of each tribe; any aspirations for a political community combining tribes must be eschewed. Finally, postmodernism is preoccupied with heterogeneity, especially with the hybrid identities of individuals and cultural groups; yet postmodernism has a hard time envisioning a political community that does not deny multiple identities in its pursuit of a substantive unity.

Where would a mestizo democracy be located on this graph? Although it is tempting to place it at the intersection of the axes, especially since mestizaje depicts the relationships of individual and community and political communities vis-à-vis constituent cultural groups in dialectical terms, such a placement would seem to render mestizaje as static. Moreover, critics, especially of the postmodern vein, would be quick to accuse me of perpetrating a centered, foundational perspective in contradication to mestizaje's presumed sensitivity to the agonal and ecstatic dimensions of heterogeneity.

Instead, I submit that a mestizo democracy is on a different plane from each of the four perspectives because it projects a relational, not possessive, affiliation of individuals with groups and of political communities with cultures. The shortcoming of the graph, ultimately, is that it is still constituted of two either/or, not both/and, formulations: (1) individual autonomy *v.* the conformity of social groups and (2) political communities and substantive universal political communities *v.* substantive particular cultural groups. By contrast, a mestizo democracy suggests that individual identity is incomprehensible apart from the impact of social and community forces and that individuals in turn transform these same forces, both alone and in concert with one another. Consequently, cultural groups can intersect and engender a new culture in which the contributing groups mutually transform each other—offering hope for pursuing a substantive common good in multicultural democracies.

A mestizo democracy moves beyond either/ors to focus on the pluralistic yet interconnected identities of persons, cultures, and political communities. The Mesoamerican experience—of balancing unity and diversity in spite of Eurocentric domination over the past five centuries—is an invaluable resource for ethically and constructively dealing with the hemispheric integrations and dislocations being engendered by the global economy:

> Exploring such alternative approaches to the world as maintained by indigenous Mesoamericans and studying the Mesoamerican cultures allows people of Mexican descent everywhere to share common ground, and to also respect differences, "in different valleys." There is much to recommend in this perspective, in the face of continued racism and xenophobia, as a way of a new understanding in the present based on a renewed examination of the past, and a deep appreciation for the civilizations of this continent and their tremendous ability to be tolerant of difference.[71]

Ultimately, the merit of mestizaje is its long experience with mixing cultures in a way that does not culminate in assimilation, that respects autonomy and difference, and, consequently, that enables the building of bridges to 'others.' Given that the cultures of Africa, Asia, Europe, and indigenous peoples have been intersecting in the Americas for at least five centuries, this Mesoamerican heritage of wrestling with cultural mixing and of confronting the economic domination by haves over have-nots is invaluable for realizing a heterogeneous, mutual democracy through a chiasma of cultures. In the next two chapters I pursue practical applications of a mestizo democracy: a case study of a faith-based community's engagement of multicultural relations and an exegesis of public policies consonant with bringing about a mestizo democracy.

Part III

Practical Applications

CHAPTER 6

Fostering Unity-in-Diversity

*T*hroughout the United States, religious communities, like their political counterparts, face increasing racial and ethnic diversity in their memberships. In this chapter I offer and analyze my own experiences during the 1990s while cultivating multicultural relations at a Catholic parish with over thirty-five hundred families in Houston. Specifically, I peruse the philosophical, theological, and political concepts and practices that informed the conduct of a multicultural relations committee, which met on a monthly basis in this parish from 1991–1998, and of a multicultural choir formed in 1994. For purposes of professional distance, I will refer to this congregation as "St. Nessan's" instead of its actual name. In addition, I will give pseudonyms to the members of this faith community—"Arnoldo," "Long," and "Ruth"— whom I quote periodically in my ensuing presentation. Although some readers might find the inclusion of their comments distracting, I used these comments in my original article about the committee published in the *Journal of Pastoral Theology* on the recommendation of that journal's editorial team. They felt that inclusion of these remarks would give poignant, concrete illustrations of the committee's experiences, and I concur. Indeed, this methodology is consonant with Isasi-Diáz's use of interviews and collaborative retreats to elicit spiritual perspectives from concrete experiences, which I reviewed in chapter 3.[1]

This case study provides a limited application of my articulation of mestizaje as a political theory in the previous five chapters. I have always been inspired by Emmanuel Mounier and the French personalists of the journal *Esprit*, who in the 1930s and 1940s insisted upon *engagement:* it is not enough to reflect upon the political and socioeconomic worlds; one must strive in collaboration with others to transform these worlds. The ensuing reflections thus dwell not just on the affective, aesthetic rationality accented by Latino theology but on the degree to which this orientation can generate community in a church congregation, through, not in spite of, its diverse racial, ethnic, and linguistic groups.

Pastoral theology, the most germane academic discipline to this study, is a two-way street: not only did the import of mestizo affect my participation in the experiences of this case study, but, conversely, those experiences have also influenced my articulation of a mestizo democracy throughout this text. If indeed, pastoral theology, as Jernigan claims, is an integrative, relational, inductive, and transcultural discipline, then this case study offers insight for anyone wrestling with the challenge of multiculturalism in the fields of pastoral theology, political theory, and public administration.[2] Moreover, even though psychology is of crucial importance for much of pastoral theology, this case study also reveals the additional relevance of many concepts of political theory and public administration.

Admittedly, there are serious limitations to applying any findings from this case study to secular politics, since a church community operates on a stronger substantive foundational consensus than a political community. However, the emphasis on the *processes* of inclusion in the ensuing case study is consonant with Las Casas's deliberation on the conditions necessary for a rational dialogue between diverse perspectives and Dussel's attempts to engender rational discourse that moves beyond the Eurocentrism of modernity. In less lofty tones, this case study's focus on the procedural engagement of multiculturalism is also consistent with management studies of the past decade that espouse collaborative, "win-win" strategies rather than divisive, "win-lose" strategies. For instance, Donna Markham's groundbreaking text *Spiritlinking Leadership,* which discusses how to create synergy through creative conflict, is an excellent example of how dispositions traditionally associated with theology can bring about organizational change. As much as one should differentiate among the private, public, and nonprofit sectors, effective principles of leadership transcend these categories. My observations in the ensuing case study also have relevance for fostering unity-in-diversity for secular workplaces and communities.

Another potential limitation of this case study is that it might be considered too "egocentric": I created and chaired the multicultural relations committee under consideration, and in the case of the choir I served as co-director with my wife, Mary Jane, from its inception until September 2000. Some would critically contend that I am "the hero" of this narrative, a format that is contradictory to the stress on plural voices and alternative, multiple points of view in postmodern perspectives and in mestizaje. No doubt some "white knightism" permeates the ensuing case study. From the standpoint of the above-mentioned personalist ethic of *engagement,* however, the seeming alternative would be to remain mute about these pastoral experiences or, worse yet, to undertake no such multicultural initiatives in the first place. I find either alternative unconscionable. Ultimately, if others choose to deconstruct the ensuing narrative, such deconstruction still furthers the democratic pursuit of imperfect communication between diverse perspectives that is very much at the heart of mestizaje as a political theory.

Background to the Formation of the Multicultural Relations Committee

At a town meeting at St. Nessan's early in 1991 the pastor bemoaned the fact that the parish was so segregated in terms of linguistic constituencies—English-speaking, Spanish-speaking, and Vietnamese-speaking. Though we claimed to be "one Church," realistically we had been what Deck terms a divided parish in which "three or more parallel parishes [function] physically at the same place."[3] Arnoldo, a Mexican immigrant and one of the original members of the Multicultural Relations Committee, observed in this regard: "It is common to find parishioners, in many of these 70 organizations that actually function in the parish, say: 'The Hispanics are organizing their Guadalupana celebration,' 'The Anglos are having their annual Christmas dinner,' 'The Vietnamese are celebrating their New Year.' It is very sad to see how as Catholics we divide among ourselves."

The leadership structure and ongoing practices reflected primarily the concerns of European Americans in the parish, largely because they had more education and had been the founders and financial base of the parish. However, those receiving baptism, receiving First Communion, and being confirmed in the early 1990s were increasingly Latino, Vietnamese American, and other non-European American parish members. Indeed, there were as many, if not more, Latinos as European Americans in the parish. The pastoral challenge became to effect a dialogue through which the English-speaking community would begin to see its destiny in the other linguistic communities, and the newer, growing communities would begin to carry forth the legacy built over three decades by the long-standing community.

Inspired by the pastor's reflections at the town meeting, I met with him on Ash Wednesday in 1991 to propose that we create a multicultural relations committee, comprised of representatives of the different linguistic communities. This committee would explore how we could break down the barriers separating these communities in the parish and build bridges in their place. I emphasized that I had a strong background in race relations and civil rights, both in my scholarly life as a political scientist and in my spiritual life; for instance, Mary Jane and I in 1988 had helped initiate Spanish liturgies for migrant worker families in the Mississippi Delta. The pastor was very enthusiastic but rightly cautioned that this initiative would require discussion and approval by the parish council.

Catholic Sources for Pursuing Unity-in-Diversity

I presented the justification for a multicultural relations committee to the parish council in April 1991. In brief and simple terms I contended that the Catholic insistence that human persons realize their spirituality in networks of communities called us to break down the barriers—be they intentional or unintentional—between the cultural/linguistic communities in our parish. Without using the term *mestizaje,* I suggested that we needed to move beyond the assimilationist and separatist models of multicultural relations to envision how each of the long-standing cultural communities of our parish could contribute toward the building of a substantive sense of community in the parish as a whole and, at the same time, retain its own core of cultural traditions. Specifically, I suggested (1) that such a unity-in-diversity could only be realized through this lateral interchange of cultures, as trying as this endeavor might prove to be and (2) that creating the committee would be a constructive first step toward effecting such engagement.

Fortunately, the Catholic heritage has a rich set of documents and intellectual traditions that support and sustain such a vision of unity-in-diversity. It is much easier to move people toward change if one can justify the change in terms of values they consider authoritative. In preparing my presentation, I drew from the following scholarly sources:

- Jacques Maritain's discussion of integral humanism and a "practical consensus,"
- John Courtney Murray's notions of building consensus and a "growing end,"

- papal documents, especially "Octogesima Adveniens" and "Evangelii Nuntiandi,"
- the documents of Vatican II, especially "Gaudium et Spes,"
- U.S. Catholic bishops' documents, especially "Cultural Pluralism in the United States,"
- Andrew Greeley's and David Tracy's portrait of the analogical or sacramental spiritual imagination,
- and inculturation studies.[4]

I will review some of these sources briefly for those who may be unfamiliar with them.

Greeley, building upon David Tracy's exegesis of the analogical or sacramental imagination, contends (and proves this contention through sociological surveys) that Catholics accept diversity because they envision human affairs as basically good and imperfectly disclosing "the presence of God."[5] Though Catholics give the transcendental relationship with God its just due, just as important are the human relationships among human beings in this life, especially socioeconomic and political matters. Consequently, Catholics place great emphasis on the dense intertwined networks that comprise this life: family, neighbors, church activities, and political and social groups. Diversity, therefore, is integral to the expression of Catholic faith.

Greeley, however, articulates diversity without specific reference to cultural or linguistic differences. Church documents provide more specificity. Paul VI in "Octogesima Adveniens" contends that worldwide diversity makes it "difficult for us to utter a unified message and to put forward a solution that has universal validity. Such is not our ambition, nor is it our mission."[6] Instead, Paul VI looks to "cultural and religious groupings ... to develop in the social body, disinterestedly and in their own ways· those ultimate convictions on the nature, origin, and end of man and society."[7]

Toward this end, the U.S. Catholic bishops in "Cultural Pluralism in the United States" characterize America as a "multicolored marble ... of many hues and patterns; in their joining and confluence they contribute their own element of beauty to the Church and the land we love."[8] Unlike the prevailing alternatives of assimilation or separatism, the "multicolored marble" captures how cultures influence one another while remaining distinct—once again the Catholic accent on the networks of group relations. The bishops of the Diocese of Galveston-Houston, in their document "Many Members, One Body: A Pastoral Letter on the Cultural and

Ethnic Diversity of the Church of Galveston-Houston," explicitly pinpoint that seeking unity-in-diversity entails interacting with the 'other' in a lateral, nonhegemonic way:

> Embracing cultural diversity is not simply a matter of being tolerant of others, nor is it merely a matter of accommodation, accepting a temporary difference in the practice of the faith until others are ready to embrace *our* expression of the faith. Each person must come to see a positive engagement with other cultures as a means of enriching one's own faith. . . . To put the matter more strongly, we cannot be content with diverse cultures simply co-existing at a respective distance. The catholicity of the Church demands that these diverse cultures engage one another in conversation and extended social and liturgical interaction.[9]

This pastoral letter rejects both cultural uniformity and sheer diversity in favor of a dynamic in which each contributing culture as well as the overall church community are mutually enriched and transformed.

Finally, studies dealing with inculturation—how the Christian faith simultaneously transforms and is realized through the concrete experience of particular cultures—are helpful in the pursuit of unity-in-diversity in parishes such as St. Nessan's. In particular, the exegesis of mestizaje and popular religion by Latino theologians, as previously reviewed in chapters 2 and 3, provides concrete spiritual illustrations of how cultures can combine without one culture becoming dominant or all cultures being reduced to a bland, generic blend. Elizondo's recasting of mestizaje in terms of the growing nexus of Latino and European American cultures is of direct and special relevance to parishes such as St. Nessan's that are at the front line of such encounters.

Although I drew upon such sources for my presentation before the parish council—excepting the bishops' "Many Members, One Body," which was not published until 1994—I did not deliver a scholarly lecture, nor did I expect that most of the council members had previously studied these sources. Nevertheless, I suspected that the language and normative mores conveyed in these scholarly and pastoral resources were authoritative for many of those members and would help me capture their attention, concern, and commitment.

Vision and Charge

Ultimately, building on the above authoritative values, I stressed the practical fact that given the changing demographics of the parish and its surrounding neighborhoods, the question was not whether or not our future was to be multicultural, but whether we responded with a long-term vision dealing with this reality rather than just letting fate takes its course. Arnoldo, in this context, observed, "There are two types of Catholics, those that seeing these situations decide to leave and look for another parish to feel better or abandon their religion altogether. The second type, quite rare, decides to be part of the change and works to improve the situation."[10]

Whether we liked it or not, the parish and its environs were in fact going to become more multicultural and diverse. Instead of *reacting* to these developments at some future point, I challenged the council to engage these developments *proactively* in a way that would improve not only the overall well-being of St. Nessan's, but would serve as a model for other faith communities wrestling with these challenges. Rather than seeing this challenge as a burden, I insisted we envision the moral growth of the parish ensuing through, not in spite of, its diverse cultures.[11]

To realize this vision, I proposed that the Multicultural Relations Committee be advisory, not administrative, in its orientation and fluid in its scope—all topics and concerns to be considered. Were the committee to assume administrative responsibilities, it would quickly become just another "turf conscious" entity. A fluid scope, however, would give the committee free rein to uncover the obstacles preventing greater interaction among the parish's cultural communities. The committee, thus, would be both a clearinghouse of ideas and experiments that other parts of the parish could draw upon, and a forum, in the manner of an ombudsman, for those who felt they "were not being heard" or lacked access to existing parish communication channels.

The parish council ultimately approved the creation of the committee in terms of the above vision and charge. The committee met for the first time in May 1991 and continued meeting on a monthly basis through 1998.

Recruitment and Representation

At the committee's inception, four members from each of the linguistic communities in which we regularly held liturgies—English, Spanish, and

Vietnamese—made up the committee's membership. We quite consciously made sure the representation from the three linguistic communities was equal. The pastor, the pastoral council chair, and I chose the initial members. I recruited individuals I thought would be congenial to the notion of unity-in-diversity, would contribute a great deal based upon their professional background or my previous dealings with them, and would not use this opportunity just to advance personal agendas.

In selecting committee members we also thought it crucial to take into account the diversity within two of the principal linguistic communities. The English-speaking community at this church has been comprised of a wide variety of subcultures: European American ethnicities, African Americans, non-Vietnamese Asian Americans—especially Filipino Americans—Mexican Americans who primarily speak English, and a number of other cultural groups whose primary language is not Spanish or Vietnamese. The Spanish-speaking community, though predominantly Mexican in heritage, has varied widely in how long its members have been in the United States and, for those born in Mexico, according to their state of origin. In turn, the Spanish-speaking community has been made up of members from all over Latin America, especially El Salvador.[12]

I knew three of the original Spanish-speaking members through a monthly bilingual healing service; the fourth representative was suggested by one of them. In the Vietnamese case, I simply started with the one Vietnamese person I knew through the Cursillo prayer movement. He happened to be an officer of the Vietnamese council in the parish, and I relied on his choices for the other representatives. Those representing the English-speaking community were people with whom I knew I could work, who shared the vision of unity-in-diversity, and who reflected the diversity of the English-speaking community: two of the original members were African Americans, and another member, born in Europe, spoke several languages.

By 1998 none of the original Latino members remained on the committee, and over a dozen members from that community had at different times served. We found it challenging to find representatives who saw themselves as representing the views of their communities as opposed to just voicing their own perspectives—a distinction political scientists label "delegate" (representing the views of one's group) as opposed to "trustee" (representing a personal view).

The Vietnamese community participated formally on the committee until 1996; since then, most of this community has built and moved into a separate church. When the Vietnamese participated on the committee, rarely did as many as four representatives attend. The Vietnamese representatives were indeed delegates chosen by their leadership council. However, their insistence on unanimity among themselves and on not embarrassing others in public at times obscured the differences of opinion within their community.

The most continuous representation proved to be from the English-speaking community, which suggests that the conduct and orientation of the committee still reflected primarily the cultures and backgrounds of those individuals. Still, most of the English-speaking committee members represented the perspective of those who wanted the parish to move in a multicultural direction, as opposed to those who maintained that the forums were already in place, albeit European American in disposition, for anyone who wanted to get involved in the parish.

Format

The atmosphere at the meeting was crucial for cultivating dialogue. The stress on the dignity of the human person in Catholic social thought was essential for having good meetings. I have often attended secular and church meetings in which a "free-for-all" ensues in which the interlocutors persistently cut each other off, the loudest personalities dominating the discourse. In such situations one never grasps what the demure members of the meeting think. As Arnoldo noted, "One of the greatest problems that I have encountered is [the need some feel] to see who has most power in the parish and to demonstrate it. We forget that one who does not live to serve leads a life not worth living." If a group is making its decisions by consensus, especially when there are multiple cultures represented, it is imperative for all members to have genuine access to the discourse if the "consensus" is to have any legitimacy.

I tried to conduct the committee meetings in a way that did not privilege any one community yet brought out the gifts of each committee member. To set an inclusive tone, at the outset of the meetings, we would usually begin by praying and singing in multiple languages. Second, although we primarily conducted our meetings in English, if anyone attending spoke primarily Spanish, Vietnamese, or another language, then we translated back and forth as much as possible.

To thwart domination of the discourse by strong personalities, as chair I monitored who had the floor and ensured that the discourse remained focused on the agenda. To deter interruptions and simultaneous speakers, some small-faith communities give a small seashell to the person who wishes to speak: the speaker holds it only as long as it takes to make the point, then gives the shell to the next person who wishes to respond. In this fashion everyone is made to feel a part of the group, people learn how to disagree without being personally critical, and each individual learns how to make a point but also how to yield control to the next speaker.[13] Although as a committee we did not employ this tactic per se, we emulated these principles of caring, effective discourse.

My endeavor to ensure an atmosphere that did not privilege any one culture or language also prompted the committee to deal with subtle and hidden forms of discrimination, matters having to do with cultural habits, level of education, and style of speech and clothing, among others. Such often unconscious prejudices by which we distinguish ourselves from others are very difficult to bring into the open but nevertheless obstruct understanding and cooperation. Still, in spite of discomforts committee members felt, getting them to talk with each other in an atmosphere of dignity, openness, and trust over time led to friendships that begot much more cooperation among the communities on subsequent parish-wide events like confirmation liturgies.

Open Agenda

At the outset, I had hoped that the committee would undertake certain specific issues—especially regarding liturgy, youth ministry, continuing education, and social activities. At the same time, I felt it was crucial that the committee set their own agenda. Indeed, because the committee operated in an open fashion, not according to a blueprint formulated by me or an outside expert, it maintained its authority and credibility to address any particular issue regarding multicultural relations that committee members and parishioners deemed unaddressed in the parish.

By gathering members from the different communities to talk with each other, we strove to clear the air of mutual misperceptions. For a long time a rumor had circulated in the parish that the Vietnamese intended to build their own church. Was that in fact true, for knowing this would be important for the parish's future plans? Indeed, the Vietnamese community eventually built a separate church. Was the Latino community content with Spanish masses only at peripheral times—Saturday evening, Sunday afternoon, or Sunday evening, even though they were rapidly becoming the majority in the parish? The answer to this question was obviously crucial if we were to have leadership practices in the parish that were faithful to Christian precepts, not just to the power of money.

In practice, the initial pastor during the committee's tenure suggested several committee projects. For instance, the committee coordinated the discernment process for parish council members for several years. Prior to the committee's involvement the pastoral council was comprised almost entirely of members from the English-speaking community. Spanish- and Vietnamese-speaking parishioners were not intentionally prevented from serving, but the structure of the process and the way in which it was advertised were reflective of the mores of the English-speaking community. By taking advantage of alternative channels of communication and mores, the committee enabled more Latinos and Vietnamese not only to participate in the discernment process but ultimately to serve on the parish council. During some years of the committee's tenure the pastoral council was evenly divided between English-speaking and Spanish-speaking members.

The committee by and large did not discuss gender issues, other than with regard to the need for child care during liturgies and other church activities. But the committee's membership, over time, included varying combinations of women and men. Certainly much of the feminist scholarship in philosophy, theology, and the social sciences dovetails with ethnic/racial critiques in terms of acknowledging and overcoming the processes and structures that promote hegemonic rather than egalitarian decision making. The parish has no doubt experienced hegemonic practices in the channels and mores of communication that have obstructed the discussion of gender issues. However, because of the subordinate role of women in the institutional Catholic church, any attempt to change this status at the local level alone is nearly futile. In hindsight, we of the committee could have shown more courage in this matter. At the same time, we did try to model the lateral, holistic collaborative style of decision making articulated by some feminists.[14]

Measuring Progress "in Process"

The committee did not plot its course or measure its success in the conventional goals-and-objectives format. Even if the operationalization of such a method can generate useful outcomes, the claim that a goal can be clearly established and that the steps to realizing that goal neatly compartmentalized and measured was contrary to the committee's collaborative format. Instead, the direction of the committee unfolded in an inductive, holistic fashion—what Elizondo terms in the context of Latino culture, "living in process":

> The Latino is one who accepts the totality of life. He is realistic in
> this sense and idealistic in the striving for something beyond, in
> reaching for what ought to be. He aims in this direction which he
> may or may not reach. He is constantly striving for the ideal, though
> often he does not know how he will get there. If it is God's will, it
> will work out. If not, why worry? In this combination of idealism
> and realism, the Latino will not hesitate to begin a project for which
> he does not have a plan, a time schedule, or a completion date
> projected. He sees the ideal vaguely and begins, knowing that the
> plan will emerge in the process and that someone, some day, will
> finish the job. The Latino is very comfortable living in process, and a
> quick termination of the process is not part of his objective.[15]

Arnoldo's evaluation of the committee's accomplishments, in turn, captures this perspective:

> The results of the Multicultural Committee are not easily seen. The
> challenge is to think that everyone can learn from each other
> without regard for where you were born, what language you speak,
> or what culture you have. To succeed in getting everyone to think in
> this manner is not easy. Much of this is sowing the idea, and we
> don't know if this seed will germinate or not; it may take a long time
> or we may possibly not see the fruits. The majority of the results are
> not easily measured. You can only feel for yourself how people are
> changing, and then you begin to glimpse a ray of light from the
> union of members of a parish divided by many problems, but with
> a great future in which God plays the most important role.

Indeed, the way one measures progress—the affect as opposed to the effect—can reveal as much about one's mores and practices as any outright discussion of prejudice or discrimination.

Committee initiatives did challenge the outlook of parish leaders who subscribed to an expertise model of leadership, in which one has to go through intense specialized courses and workshops in a narrowly defined area before gaining access to the decision-making structure—an epistemology dating back to Descartes. Instead, the committee—reflecting norms found in inculturation studies, phenomenology, and Aristotelian practical reason—operated on the basis that there is no "one best way" of doing things, that most people have natural inclinations and worldly experiences, albeit different ones, that prepare them for leadership roles, and that formal training cultivates and hones these capacities.

The Multicultural Choir as a Case of "Living in Process"

In February 1994 the Multicultural Relations Committee sponsored what would be the first of four African American gospel-music concerts to coincide with Black History Month (subsequent concerts occurred in 1995, 1997, and 1998). At each of these concerts two or three choirs from African American Catholic parishes in Houston were kind enough to share their music with us. Subsequent to the first concert, the committee discussed how inspiring it would be to incorporate some of this gospel-music sound and tradition into our, especially English, liturgies. After several painstaking meetings in 1994 with the pastoral team and the parish liturgy committee, the Multicultural Relations Committee successfully created a multicultural choir under Mary Jane's and my direction. Starting in August 1994, this choir led the congregation by singing in multiple languages and in different styles and rhythms, in contrast to the traditional European American organ-centered liturgical approach.

Those of us who started this initiative hoped to combine the tightly structured traditional approach that had previously characterized all our English liturgies with the charismatic style of our Spanish liturgies—a mestizaje of the cultures and spiritualities that comprised our parish. The hymns would be in English primarily, but we would use a lot of bilingual (Spanish-English) hymns. Many of the English hymns would also reflect the African American spiritual tradition, and the sung parts of the liturgy such as the Gospel Acclamation and the Lamb of God would use arrangements featuring the highly rhythmic style of African American, Caribbean, and Latino music. We would "decenter" the organ by relying on piano, guitar, percussion, and other types of instruments for accompaniment. Frankly, we also hoped that making one of our English liturgies more rhythmic and charismatic in character, would make it more attractive to parishioners who otherwise attended our standing-room only, 1:00 P.M., Sunday Spanish liturgy.

Beginning in 1994, the evolution of the choir truly became one of "living in process." First, our principal cantor, an African American gospel singer, left the choir to pursue another spiritual path at a different church. Although we had been able to effect a lively mestizaje of musical styles and had even made a joint trip with our parish's Spanish *coro* (choir) to sing at the internationally televised *Misa de las Américas* (Mass of the Americas) at San Fernando Cathedral in San Antonio in June 1996, the choir's success at that juncture remained too dependent on the musical talents of a few key members. In addition, even though some congregational members had switched from the overcrowded Spanish liturgy to this multicultural liturgy, the number of those switching was not overwhelming.

The turning point came in the summer of 1996, subsequent to the San Antonio trip. Although the choir had several bilingual members and two bicultural couples (Mexican American–European American), that summer a Filipino American–European American couple joined the choir. The ensuing fall, several Filipinos and a Vietnamese parishioner came forth from the congregation to sing with the choir. By the spring of 1997 we were able to sing not only in Spanish and English, but also in Tagalog [Filipino] and Vietnamese. Then, in the summer of 1997, more Filipino families and a few more Vietnamese members joined the choir. In the space of a year the choir had changed from being a predominantly European American and Mexican American choir to being a mixture of U.S. Americans representing an amazing array of cultural and ethnic backgrounds: African, European, Filipino, Jamaican, and Vietnamese, with the Filipinos being the dominant group. In addition most of the new choir members were now of middle- and high-school age, and many of them played instruments: trumpet, trombone, electric bass, clarinet, saxophone, flute, and drums, all of which we used regularly. Whereas in the summer of 1996 a dozen active members made up the choir, from 1997–2000 the choir grew to a membership of from two to three dozen.

Those of us who began the choir in 1994 had hoped that from the outset we would be able to recruit Asian American members, especially given the parish's rich Vietnamese heritage. But nothing that we did specifically brought about the mushrooming of Filipino and Vietnamese members, other than encouraging that initial Filipino-European American couple to join in the summer of 1996. However, as an illustration of Elizondo's insight that "the plan will emerge in the process," the engendering of a holistic multicultural liturgical atmosphere proved very attractive to the Asian American choir members.

Moreover, some of the Filipino adults who joined the choir with their children were accomplished professionals in engineering, law, and nursing, and some of their children were graduates or would soon be graduates of distinguished Texas universities, including Baylor and Texas A&M. Unfortunately, prior to joining the choir, most of these talented, educated persons were not involved in leadership responsibilities in the parish; as one of them admitted to me, they literally kept to the back pews. No one intentionally excluded anybody from participating in parish activities, but the hospitality extended to these parish members prior to the development of the multicultural choir did not motivate them to become more involved in parish activities. The multicultural choir's creation of a different atmosphere within a predominantly English liturgy proved congenial to the spiritual sensibilities of Asian Americans.[16]

Ironically, the choir created by the Multicultural Relations Committee outlasted the committee itself. My wife and I stepped down as coordinators of the choir in September 2000 to pursue other spiritual and professional endeavors. The success of the multicultural choir in bringing forward talented parishioners whose contributions had previously been on the margins of the parish is a testimony to the committee's purpose of examining how parish decision-making and operating structures could be made more culturally inclusive.

The Cessation of the Committee

Just as the choir went through different stages, the Multicultural Relations Committee's role and orientation changed over time. In 1991 it was a major achievement to gather English-speaking, Spanish-speaking, and Vietnamese-speaking leaders around a table to discuss how to forge a common vision for the parish. By 1998 stark *de facto* segregation no longer separated the leaders of the parish's linguistic communities. Challenges to multicultural representation and communication had by no means disappeared, but the parish council, the stewardship committee, and some of the other major deliberative bodies of the parish were much more integrated in terms of English- and Spanish-speaking leadership. At the same time, however, the Spanish-speaking leaders tended to be bilingual, whereas the English-speaking leaders tended to be monolingual. Nevertheless, the parish has had a bilingual pastor since 1994.

At the committee's inception, there were three identifiable linguistic communities in the parish with separate liturgies. After the departure of the Vietnamese community from the parish in the mid-1990s, the diversity within the English-speaking community became much more apparent—as exemplified by the rising Filipino participation in the multicultural choir. Although the English-speaking community at St. Nessan's had been diverse for some time, by 1998 the participation of African Americans, Asian Americans, bilingual Latinos, and English-speaking Mexican Americans was much more visible. Even though European Americans still predominated in leadership roles, the rationale for having the committee had become less urgent than it had been in 1991: the committee was a victim of its own success.

Four specific factors led to the committee's cessation by the end of 1998. First, from 1996–1998 the committee's activity shifted to studying and discussing works on multicultural relations, with mixed results. Second, a change in pastors worked over the long term to the detriment of the committee's original charge. Third, as chair, I put in less and less time on committee activities due to my other parish and professional responsibilities. Fourth, over time the institutional novelty of the committee gave way to a sense of inertia. Each of these factors needs more scrutiny.

In the last two years of the committee's existence, the committee by mutual agreement shifted its attention from bringing leaders of the parish's diverse communities together to educating both ourselves and parish leaders on the intricacies of effecting unity-in-diversity. Principally, we focused on reading texts dealing with issues on cultural diversity, in a study-group fashion, and bringing to the parish speakers and groups on these issues.

This "educational turn" proved ill-fated. Honest discussion of provocative texts and divisive issues can prove very unsettling and entails a commitment to working through conflict—an activity that demands patience and good listening skills when such discussion proves testy. Increasingly, as a committee, we did not want to take the time to work though such flash points. For instance, when the committee read and discussed Elizondo's *The Future is Mestizo*, hardly the most strident text on multiculturalism, one committee member returned the text to me before even finishing it because he felt the tone was too negative. On other occasions, when a committee member argued that certain parish or social practices manifested racial or ethnic discrimination, other committee members retorted that such arguments were dwelling on the past or that European American culture had an integrity that needed to be defended. Unfortunately, instead of exploring further the bases of disagreement in the hope of eventually forging a common direction, we usually ended up "agreeing to disagree." As a consequence, the committee became just a talking forum whose impact on the normative practices of the parish ironically decreased.

The practical result of "agreeing to disagree," however, is that the distribution of power in decision-making structures and processes in communities remains the same; genuine multicultural relations are not realized if one culture still predominates over others. As the Latino presence spreads not only across the U.S. Southwest but across the country, we face the unjust proposition that though Latinos may emerge as the majority in parishes, Spanish liturgies could conceivably still be relegated to less desirable locations and times because Latinos would still be on the margins of parish decision-making forums.

The second specific factor regarding the destiny of the committee was the impact of the respective pastors. Although the reforms of Vatican II, as well as the decline of the number of priests over the past four decades, have led to more lay-centered decision-making in Catholic parishes, the pastor still has a powerful and hierarchical role. During its tenure, the committee worked with two pastors.

The pastor at the time of the committee's creation was quite enthusiastic about the committee's project and participated in the selection of the initial members of the committee. He would assign to the committee creative activities intended to build bridges between the parish's diverse constituencies, such as putting together a Lenten healing service dealing with racism. His successor, by contrast, rarely suggested such projects to the committee, although to his credit he did support and at times participate in activities initiated by the committee—specifically, a series of forums coordinated by the committee to incite constructive engagement between English-speaking and Spanish-speaking parish leaders.

Essentially, the first pastor took an active posture vis-à-vis the committee whereas the second pastor took a passive posture. The second pastor never opposed committee activities; at the same time, in institutional not personal terms, benign indifference can be just as effective as open opposition in minimizing the impact of an advisory group such as the Multicultural Relations Committee. One of the reasons the committee's focus became more explicitly educational in its last two years was that it seemed that the types of projects we had previously undertaken did not match the second pastor's professional concerns.

The third specific factor was that my commitment to being chair of this committee waned over its final two years. The success of committee initiatives all too often came to depend on the energy I was willing to give to them. As the multicultural choir came to demand more and more attention, I found that the energy I once devoted to the committee I was, instead, channeling toward the choir, and rightly so if the choir was to excel at its liturgical responsibilities. In terms of my professional life, in 1997 I switched universities; the very exciting demands of my new academic position also siphoned creative energy that I had formerly given to the committee.

Undoubtedly, this third factor was entirely egocentric and raises again the charge that the inception and sustenance of this committee relied too much on my initiative and concerns. This criticism is well taken, and in hindsight the committee would have been well served to have rotated the position of chair at least every two years. At least in the choir's case, my wife and I were able to create a framework in which other people could assume the responsibility of the choir's direction.

Finally, though the committee's destiny might have been too entwined with my own interests, over time a sense of malaise also came to characterize the committee. At the outset committee members had great enthusiasm and seemed to be making a difference: through our efforts the discernment structure for parish council was amended and the multicultural choir was created, among other examples. Eventually, though, the committee lost its fresh, novel purpose and became too much a part of the parish routines it was supposed to engage and challenge. Although committee members initially pursued their roles with both zeal and commitment, only one committee member besides me remained on the committee for its entire duration. This malaise combined with the "education turn" in focus, the change of pastors, and the committee's dependence on my leadership created a climate that by 1998 pointed to the committee's termination.

The Import of Popular Religion

Beyond these specific reasons for the committee's cessation, the reality remains that the differences among contending viewpoints and spiritualities in a multicultural church community are going to work against any easy, tranquil integration of cultures. Based on the combination of my own concrete experiences during the 1990s at St. Nessan's and the discussion of Latino spirituality—especially popular religion—in chapters 2 and 3, the Houston Catholic bishops' "extended social and liturgical interaction" between diverse cultures is unlikely to ensue unless preceded by full recognition of the deep theological and philosophical differences likely separating such cultures.[17] Fundamental differences in multicultural congregations over such matters as conducting liturgies, raising funds, or making leadership decisions are not simply surface misunderstandings of language or cultural customs, but frequently entail deep-seated differences of perceiving, understanding, and practicing spirituality.

For instance, at St. Nessan's, and for that matter in many other Christian communities, one can experience a stark shift of spiritual worldviews at different Sunday liturgies. An organ-centered English-Catholic liturgy in the United States, in format and atmosphere, is frequently not unlike what one would experience at a neighboring mainline Protestant church. A Spanish-Catholic liturgy, especially one imbued by the Charismatic Movement, is in many respects closer in spirit to that of Pentecostal churches than it is to such English liturgy. The principal divide in U.S. Christianity, in many respects, is no longer between Catholics and Protestants but increasingly between Christians reared in a modern European, individualistic spirituality dating from the Reformation and the Enlightenment, on the one hand, and Christians reared in a more charismatic, holistic spirituality, on the other hand, that is an amalgamation of African, indigenous, and medieval European spiritual practices.

This divide is hardly arbitrary, as I have made clear in my review in chapter 3 of the centrality of popular religion to the affective, aesthetic spirituality and rationality manifested in Latino and Latin American cultures. Most European American Catholics have been affected by the Reformation on at least two levels: the Reformation–Counter-Reformation debate from the Council of Trent to Vatican II and the predominance of Protestant and in particular Calvinist norms in U.S. culture from the days of John Winthrop until today. Therefore, when Vatican II modernized the Catholic Church in the 1960s, European American Catholics were strategically situated to advance these institutional reforms, since for three centuries they had already been accommodating themselves to the predominance of Protestant norms in the United States. Some would even argue that American Catholics of the 1940s, 1950s, and 1960s became even more accommodating to the prevailing national culture than Protestants, who had supposedly engendered it.[18] Without a doubt, the Protestant heritage of the United States has made an indelible imprint on many long-standing U.S. Catholics.

Nevertheless, the spirituality in the Spanish Charismatic liturgy derives from the holistic, sacramental worldview depicted by Espín and predates the Reformation/Counter-Reformation debate. In an affective way this worldview integrates African, medieval European, and indigenous traditions. Although this charismatic spirituality, apart from some parallels in the African American tradition, is a relatively recent and widespread phenomenon in the United States, its roots are as old as, if not older than, the prevailing individualistic Reformation spirituality. In addition, even though Protestant spiritualities have been gaining devotees over the past few decades in Latin America, they have been largely Pentecostal, not mainline, in character.

This distinction between spiritual worldviews is of enormous importance for parishes like St. Nessan's seeking to realize "extended social and liturgical interaction" between diverse cultures. An incisive critique of the prevailing decision-making structures and practices should lead to a structure of conversation, in the manner of Las Casas, that enables members of diverse worldviews—in this case "Reformation Catholics" and "sacral Catholics"—to understand each other on equal terms. As Demetria Martinez points out, simply inviting multiple cultures to the table for discussion is not enough, if the mores that prevail at the meeting are predominantly from one culture: "I've seen time and again how well-intentioned whites invite Latinos to join, say, church task forces—and then never take time to hear our opinions. Because we might enunciate our thoughts, differently, or, God forbid, take longer to do so. So the meetings go on, power wielded yet again by those who brandish English like a sword."[19] Unless this hermeneutical quandary commands the attention of vitally interested groups, like St. Nessan's Multicultural Relations Committee, success at building bridges between diverse communities will be severely limited.

Case in point: in 1996 the Multicultural Relations Committee made a meager effort to get the highly successful Spanish-speaking Charismatic prayer group to create a parallel organization in English because the English-speaking community had had no structured prayer group on the same large scale. In the discussion that ensued at a Multicultural Relations Committee meeting, one of the Spanish prayer-group leaders queried, "Well, how do you [those of us proposing the initiative] feel about the life of the Spirit?" Touché. In a simple and direct fashion this leader had made it plain that expanding the Charismatic prayer group at St. Nessan's to include an English-speaking division involved more than just opening the doors to non-Spanish speakers, for these potential participants would need to undergo a conversion to a more charismatic spiritual outlook.

The deep roots of Latino spirituality in a holistic, aesthetic worldview work against an easy assimilation to U.S. American culture in the manner of the melting pot. If anything, as discussed previously in chapters 2 and 3, this aesthetic spirituality has not only sustained Latino communities within the United States for several generations; it has also been the wellspring for persistent counter-cultural resistance by Latinos to the dominant culture.

At the same time, such resistance can be a double-edged sword. The breadth and depth of Latino spirituality can also reinforce the marginalization and subordination that Latino communities experience vis-à-vis dominant political and socioeconomic decision-making structures. In the case of St. Nessan's the Spanish-speaking community has historically had a separate leadership structure—largely centered in the Charismatic prayer group—distinct from that of the English-speaking community, but it is the latter community's leaders who have largely controlled the overall direction of the parish, especially on financial issues.

Along the same lines, leaders of subordinate communities can be tempted to keep their communities separate from the dominant power structure because such leaders would actually have less power in any genuine integration of the cultural communities. Along distinct but parallel lines, if a prayer-group leader like the one described above were to insist on the kind of conversion his or her question implied, that might prove as exclusionary as the frontier mentality González associates with European American culture.

The success of the multicultural choir at St. Nessan's, however, suggests that through a holistic spirituality one can successfully bring together people of diverse races and cultures in relationships of mutuality and equality. As opposed to church leaders who wield power by either brandishing "English like a sword" or insisting on a "Spirit litmus test," the choir—through an affective, rhythmic mixing of African American, Caribbean, Irish, Filipino, Latino, and Vietnamese musical styles—engendered a joyful atmosphere through which diverse parish members could engage each other as equals.

Consonant with the "border mentality," the choir tried to engender a liturgical atmosphere in which diverse traditions could come together and transform one another in a lateral way without becoming overly preoccupied with liturgical standards or spiritual tests. This example of crossing borders offers the hope that African Americans, Asian Americans, European Americans, and Latinos—reminiscent of Vasconcelos's *la raza cósmica*—can transcend their cultural differences to effect a unity-in-diversity. The growing divide in some church communities between the individualist spirituality stemming from the Reformation and the Enlightenment, on one side, and a more charismatic spirituality especially stemming from the African American and Latino heritages, on the other, is an enormous challenge that ought not to be ignored. In terms of mestizaje, we are not fated to remain on one side or the other of this either/or.

Although there are methodological limitations to projecting the implications of this case study for multicultural relations in the United States, the holistic aesthetic spirituality conveyed by both Latino popular religion and theology should be studied in terms of its political possibilities. Just as Greeley has shown through social science surveys that Tracy's distinctions between the dialogical and analogical spiritual imaginations lead to very different social and political preferences, we need to probe in the same fashion the political preferences of those informed by this affective, aesthetic outlook. In so doing, we can anticipate more accurately the impact of the Latino presence on the political terrain of the twenty-first century.

If crossing borders is indeed intrinsic to this holistic spirituality, can it be the basis for mobilizing powerful multiracial political coalitions in the United States? Given the rising strength of Islam and Asian religions in the United States, will this holistic spirituality's emphasis on mixing traditions be more effective than the Reformation-individualist spirituality at engaging non-Christian religion, and what will be the political import of such engagement? Would such a multi-religious coalition transcend or petrify the spiritual divide suggested in this case study? Each of these questions demands earnest and thorough examination.

Admittedly, the resilience of the frontier mentality that pervades many decision-making forums, from church congregations to national political institutions, is formidable. Given the difficulties experienced by a church community such as St. Nessan's with crossing borders, how much more daunting the task becomes in political communities where the diversity of moralities makes shared universal values even less clear-cut. Still, the limited successes of the multicultural committee and choir at St. Nessan's offer a glimmer of hope for a politics that engages differences and disagreements not as frontiers, in which one side has to triumph over the vanquished 'other,' but as permeable though agonal borders through which cultures can transform each other without extinguishing distinctiveness.

The legacy of the St. Nessan's Multicultural Relations Committee is less a tally of accomplishments than an example of dealing with diversity, not as a problem to be overcome but as opportunity for mutual collaboration, transformation, and growth. As Long, one of the original Vietnamese members of the committee once commented to me, "Our meetings are the way a Christian community should be." Be it in religious or secular forums, the challenge is for diverse cultures to learn how to address each other as equals; on this basis a genuine, substantive consensus can emerge.

Despite setbacks, such as the Vietnamese community's exodus from the parish, Ruth, a committee member, from its inception to cessation, offers that the committee's successes, as minuscule as they were at times, eventually outweighed the setbacks:

> As an African American female, I have been able to appreciate both the disappointments and the accomplishments the committee has encountered. The disappointments have really been nothing new. I've faced them before in my own struggles for recognition and equality. The accomplishments, though many of them small, have seemed like large successes. . . . More Latino and Asian representation is present on the parish council, more dialogue among key members in the different communities has occurred, the MRC has been sought out by some of the Anglo [European American] groups to assist them in their inclusion of the other groups. . . . This has not been an easy ride, I'll be the first to say so. It has been, however, a lesson of individual and communal growth that I hope will continue in the years to come.

In conclusion, seeking unity-in-diversity is neither a "live and let live" tolerance, nor is it an idealistic convergence of cultures in the manner of Esperanto. One cannot bring about harmony overnight between diverse cultures, because the values and perspectives that shape the members of these cultures have been cultivated over generations. In turn, multicultural interchange creates new cultural combinations that defy any sort of tranquil, monistic unity. We will never achieve complete understanding of such matters, nor are we fated to complete misunderstanding.

The Multicultural Relations Committee enriched the well-being of the parish and the lives of its members by treating the principal cultures of the parish not as "possessions" that isolated one from the other, but as "gifts" realized in mutual interchange. In this vein Arnoldo concludes, "The challenge is to continue this task, and at some time in the not so distant future all Catholics and those of other religions will be united without trying to demonstrate who is better or who has more power; as Martin Luther King had a dream, this also is a dream, difficult, but possible." In sum, the committee provoked the parish to engage rather than begrudge its multicultural destiny.

Appendix

The following are the essential principles and concepts that informed and shaped the conduct of the Multicultural Relations Committee at St. Nessan's. Although this list is by no means exhaustive of the norms and practices of effective multicultural relations, I believe they are of use to others interested in effecting unity-in-diversity in both secular and spiritual forums.

ACKNOWLEDGING REALITY AND TRANSFORMING IT INTO VISION

1. recognize that one's future will be multicultural
2. face the future creatively, not fatalistically
3. build upon authoritative values and principles
4. engage the 'other' through one's cultural "gifts"

STRUCTURE AND CHARGE

1. representational—cultures on equal terms
2. advisory, not administrative—no turf building
3. fluid in scope—all topics and obstacles considered
4. tenured in its membership—only as long as necessary

REPRESENTATION

1. members committed to the committee's agenda, not their own
2. intersubjective recruitment requiring time and persistence
3. no substitute for informal interaction with the 'other'
4. members as "delegates" rather than as "trustees"

FORMAT

1. dignity of each person paramount, no "free-for-alls"
2. discourse occurs in multiple languages when needed
3. importance of listening as well as speaking encouraged: inclusion, affection, and relaxation of control
4. stewardship of the floor a key, calling on the reticent
5. necessary to confront "hidden" forms of discrimination
6. openness and trust needed for building collaborative networks

OPEN AGENDA
1. committee is in charge of the agenda, no preset blueprint
2. clearing the air of rumors and misperceptions is a prerequisite
3. necessary to uncover alternative channels of communication
4. committee must function as resource for parish groups to utilize

MEASURING ACCOMPLISHMENTS
1. be inductive and holistic, not deductive and mechanistic
2. let ideas and schedules emerge "in process"
3. emphasize conduct as well as content of interaction
4. reveal each step as measure of the distance yet ahead
5. encourage pluralistic, not monistic, understanding of harmony
6. expect neither complete understanding nor misunderstanding

CHAPTER 7

Crossing Borders as Public Policy

*I*n the previous chapter I focused on the implications of a mestizo democracy for creating forums that enable diverse ethnic, linguistic, racial, and religious cultural groups to engage in constructive dialogue in a lateral and egalitarian fashion. In this chapter I re-examine prevailing public policies from the standpoint of mestizaje. Having considered the process of deliberation, I now suggest how my emphasis on crossing borders and on mixed, juxtaposed identities in a mestizo democracy challenges public policies that have either an assimilationist or separatist orientation. In return, the public policies reviewed in this chapter have an enormous impact on the question of who can or cannot effectively participate in deliberative forums, from neighborhood to international organizations.

Engaging in this review of public policies is not just a pedantic exercise. As reviewed extensively in chapter 2, the United States is becoming more, not less, multicultural, and the Latino presence is becoming pervasive across the country. As noted by Harry Pachon of the Tomás Rivera Policy Institute: "We're going to have to seriously grapple with the issue of moving from a biracial to a multi-ethnic society."[1] As pointed out in the previous chapter, the United States is already a multicultural society; what ethos, therefore, will inform our practical engagement of this reality?

The specific public policies I will examine are multilingualism, political participation, equal education and employment opportunity, housing, migration, and globalization. These issues challenge us to envision a nation, if not a world, in which we can be plural beings who transcend tightly scripted identities and engage community life as a combination of supposedly antithetical identities. As Enrique Trueba argues, Latinos typically manifest such flexibility and a capacity for dealing with ambiguity in the face of economic and cultural domination: "They [Latinos] can code-switch (linguistically and culturally), pass for members of many groups, reproduce interaction styles, and function comfortably across social strata of different ethnic groups in ways that no other immigrants have managed to do. Their accommodation goes beyond their skill in using their phenotypic characteristics and is more about developing flexible, adaptive strategies and the ability to handle stress."[2] In the world of the twenty-first century, these skills that Latinos employ for survival will become increasingly necessary for each of us, as engagement with the 'other' becomes part and parcel of most political, social, and economic situations.

The exegesis of the above-mentioned public policies will not provide detailed prescriptions. Readers seeking fully developed theories of application will need to consider texts devoted to each of these matters. Instead, I will suggest how engaging these issues from the ethos of crossing borders and mixing identities can provide some practical bearings from which to consider a mestizo democracy.

Politics of Language

In response to the reality that Spanish has emerged as one of the two principal languages in the United States, several initiatives have come forward, especially at the state level, to make English the official language. The justifications usually given are to ensure a common language for the transaction of public affairs, either in business or government, and to avoid the counterproductive division and strife among U.S. Americans that might ensue with the use of multiple languages in such transactions. Some commentators have noted that although at the time of the establishment of United States almost as many people in the country spoke German as English, the founders had the good sense to insist upon English as a unifying language.

In the same fashion, there are those today who would contend that to make English the official language simply acknowledges that English is the language of necessity, especially in the global economy, and is not an attempt to prevent people from speaking other languages. Undoubtedly, there is a difference between legislating "official English" and "English only." With the former, English would be the principal language for federal documents and legislative sessions, but other languages still could be used by government when necessary. With the latter, the use of all languages other than English would be illegal.[3]

However, although "official English" on the surface seems more sensible and benign than "English-only," laws inspired by the former still symbolically give English a higher status than other languages. Essentially, "official English" initiatives more cleverly conceal than their "English-only" counterparts the possessive rendering of personal and cultural identity intrinsic to assimilation and separatist schemes—that one's cultural identity is either "this" or "that" as reinforced by a distinct language—and the command of multiple languages and the ability to negotiate multiple identities simultaneously are seen as a threat to the integrity and well-being of the community. In the end, both types of language initiatives, in varying degrees, play to the fear, manifested by many of their defenders, that the security of a monolingual English public discourse is rapidly disappearing.

To the contrary, speaking languages other than English does not mean that one is less patriotic. For instance, in July 1993 a U.S. citizenship ceremony in Tucson, Arizona, which in part was conducted in Spanish instead of English, generated a great deal of furor. These new citizens, though, were simply expressing their heartfelt fidelity to the United States in the most meaningful way possible. In the case of Mexican Americans, patriotism has been a salient characteristic of the culture for a long time: Mexican Americans won more medals of honor in World War II than any other ethnic group. Unfortunately, in situations like the Tucson ceremony, being U.S. American is often equated with speaking English. This identification only undermines the very thing it is supposedly promoting: the cultivation of a substantive national identity.

Equally nefarious are claims that any particular language is superior to others. Anzaldúa, in particular, captures the tendency in any culture not just to prize one's language but to claim that there are, for instance, purer forms of English or Spanish. As she emphasizes, the language of "the borderlands" of the U.S. Southwest is a mixture of tongues; instead of stressing purity and correctness and denigrating hybridization, this open and inclusive language provides a medium through which people can communicate on more equal terms:

> The switching of "codes" in this book from English to Castillian Spanish to the North Mexican dialect to Tex-Mex to a sprinkling of Nahuatl to a mixture of all of these, reflects my language, a new language—the language of the Borderlands. There, at the juncture

of cultures, languages cross-pollinate and are revitalized; they die and are born. Presently this infant Spanish, this bastard language, Chicano Spanish, is not approved by any society. But we Chicanos no longer feel that we need to beg entrance, that we always need to make the first overture—to translate to Anglos, Mexican, and Latinos, apology blurting out of our mouths at every step. Today, we ask to be met halfway.[4]

English, Spanish, or any other language has never been "pure." Therefore, being met halfway in communication is not just a matter of compromise, but of being open to dialogue with the 'other' that is different from us: "Humility is not a matter of self-effacement and self-negation but of being open always to new ways of being responsible and caring."[5] Any conversation involves the struggle of two or more people to communicate with each other; knowledge and use of multiple languages increase the breadth and depth of the understanding that ensues. Indeed, in many instances one can capture an experience better through the terms of another language.

The practical reality remains that speaking only one language—usually English—in decision-making forums in the United States enables English speakers to dominate non-English speakers. If we are committed to democracy as a matter of equal access to discourse, then we must rid our political processes of those elements that artificially enable some to participate more easily than others. In some locales and forums the majority of the people communicate best through languages other than English, yet discussions tend to be only in English because monolingual English speakers serve as leaders or moderators, as a result of economic and educational advantages. The rapid emergence of Spanish as the second principal language, not just in the U.S. Southwest but across the country, particularly accents this predicament.

Consequently, as James Stalker points out, we are disenfranchising those who do not speak English when we insist upon English-only: "We can exclude them from the possibility of taking part in our political system and from our schools, and because they will be uneducated, we can prevent them from benefiting from the economic system. We can ensure a new oppressed minority. If that minority becomes a majority, through immigration (legal or illegal) and through birth, we will live with the consequences of our actions."[6] The issue is not just one of replacing English with Spanish or some other language, but having the flexibility to use as many languages in a decision-making forum as are necessary to generate genuine consensus on issues.

Therefore, we need to use translation in public forums as a means of achieving genuine mutual understanding. Admittedly, there are costs involved in printing ballots in multiple languages and paying for translators and translation equipment. However, there are greater ethical costs to the community when more attention is given to convenience and cost cutting than to ensuring that language is not a barrier to political participation. Without translation measures, we encourage the emergence of a permanent servant class of non-English speakers whose livelihoods are dependent in some places on a *minority* elite of English speakers.

Curiously, at the very moment some are insisting on English-only in our public forums, entrepreneurs and marketers are quite willing to exploit the Spanish-speaking consumer market. Commercial radio and television stations in Spanish and "Spanglish" thrive in many U.S. American cities, and billboards advertising products in Spanish increasingly dot the landscape. Along the same lines, businesses and governments in the United States increasingly recruit bilingual and multilingual individuals, especially for positions that entail oral communication. More and more, the first option on most phone trees in the U.S. Southwest is whether one wishes to communicate in Spanish or English. The private sector is not about to squelch a language community that has demonstrated commercial value and is growing.

This commercial, business-related component moves us closer to one of the motives for the English-only fervor in some sectors. In many U.S. locales bilingual or multilingual education is a prerequisite for future professional success. Monolingual speakers, especially English speakers, will increasingly be at a disadvantage in obtaining professional positions in the public, private, and nonprofit sectors. Insisting on English-only is a political attempt to preserve power and privilege in the professional workplace and in the previously mentioned decision-making forums. Instead, in our educational and professional networks, we need to be promoting an ethos of *multilingualism,* especially given the global economy.

Indeed, a mestizo democracy accents the merit that intersecting languages and cultures place on fostering richer personal and community growth. Rather than restricting the knowledge and use of multiple languages, we should be providing resources and programs designed to enable all of us to learn as many languages as possible. In so doing we cultivate the capacity for "code-switching," the ability to engage in multiple cultures, mediums, and frameworks almost simultaneously.

Toward this end, bilingual and dual-language education programs should be expanded, not contracted or eliminated. Developmental bilingual-education programs are frequently opposed because, it is felt, they impede the assimilation of Spanish-speaking and other non–English-speaking children into the U.S. cultural mainstream. To the contrary, the goals of such programs are:

- maintenance and full development of students' primary language;
- full proficiency in all aspects of English;
- grade-appropriate levels of achievement in all domains of academic study;
- integration into all-English language classrooms;
- positive identification with the culture of the primary language group and with the culture of the majority language group.[7]

Developmental bilingual education suggests that a child who has a solid foundation in the primary language will make a much more successful transition to English than if taught English "cold." The ultimate objective in the bilingual approach is to enable children to make a successful transition into the English-dominant culture, not to position and fortify the student's primary cultural heritage against U.S. American culture. Therefore, the merits and demerits of this endeavor should be based on whether the approach achieves its goals and not by political misrepresentations of its aims.

Dual-language or two-way immersion programs reflect the code-switching ethos of mestizaje even more clearly than developmental bilingual education. Whereas developmental bilingual education focuses ultimately on enabling a classroom of non-English speakers to make a complete transition to English, in dual-language programs the classroom is evenly divided between two language groups—English and non-English speakers (typically Spanish speakers in the U.S. Southwest). The aim in this case is for both groups of students to become bilingual. Moreover, much more explicitly than developmental bilingual education, dual-language education employs cooperative learning techniques to encourage both sets of students over time to develop an understanding and sensitivity for other cultures.[8] Rather than fearing other cultures, students in such programs come to engage other cultures as a natural experience of life.

A mestizo democracy stresses the use of multiple languages, not as a possessive assertion of identity but as a genuine commitment to engaging the 'other' as an equal. Proponents of a common language for the United States are right when they insist that generating mutual understanding between the members of a political community is vital. But it is precisely such striving for mutual understanding that is captured in Anzaldúa's depiction of the cross-pollination of languages. As opposed to imposing one language, fostering the intersection of multiple languages cultivates much more in-depth communication and understanding.

Politics of Voting, Participation, and Representation

In terms of political communication, voting is the principal way in which U.S. Americans participate in the political system. Since the Voting Rights Act of 1965, the federal government has paid a great deal of attention to preventing discrimination against racial and language minorities in voting procedures and practices. Although the Fifteenth Amendment to the U.S. Constitution (1870) guarantees that no one can be denied the right to vote on the basis of race, prior to 1965 numerous tactics and devices were employed especially in the U.S. South to deny African American and other minority populations the right to vote. The Voting Rights Act overcame such practices by (1) deploying federal registrars to these locales to ensure that no one was prevented from registering to vote and (2) mandating that future changes to voting practices in these locales had to be approved by the U.S. Justice Department or the U.S. District Court for the District of Columbia.

Although the Voting Rights Act's initial focus was on ridding the country of discriminatory practices that prevented voter registration and participation, since the 1970s the focus of the Act has shifted to enhancing the impact minority groups can make on election outcomes. For instance, under federal law, voting ballots have to be printed in languages other than English in counties where at least 5 percent of the population does not speak English. This increases the ability of non-English speakers to communicate their views.

A more controversial application of this post-1970s "impact" focus has been the endeavor to enhance the likelihood that members of ethnic and racial minorities can be elected to public office. Even if members of minority groups can register and then vote, the force of their votes can be diluted through the drawing of voting districts so large that it becomes almost impossible for a minority member to be elected if the voting is along racial and ethnic lines. This is especially true in elections for county commissions, city councils, and school boards in which all the candidates have to run in "at-large" districts—a voting district that encompasses an entire county, city, or school district. Hypothetically, if 60 percent of the eligible voters in a district are European American, 20 percent are Latino, and 20 percent are African American, a Latino or African American candidate—unlike a European American candidate—cannot win without putting together a multi-racial/ethnic voting coalition.

Over the past three decades the primary solution to this quandary has been to divide the respective political entity into separate geographic single-member districts. Using the above hypothetical example, a five-member city council would be elected from five separate geographic districts, the boundaries of which would be drawn so as to create three "majority-majority" districts and two "majority-minority" districts. This mechanism would increase the likelihood that the city council would be comprised of members from all three racial/ethnic backgrounds. Gerrymandering of election districts to increase the electoral chances of minority candidates has also been used especially in state legislative and U.S. Congressional contests.

Undoubtedly, gerrymandered single-member "majority-minority" districts have enabled more minority candidates to win public office and have therefore advanced the capacity of members of minority groups not only to vote but to have their perspectives articulated in the political legislative forums across the United States. Without negating the importance of this outcome—a wider contribution by all cultural groups to the constitution of the political consensus—several serious drawbacks to the gerrymandering strategy require examination.

First, gerrymandering "majority-minority" districts lends itself well to communities characterized by "urban blight—suburban flight," where the poorer population, composed predominantly of racial minorities, is concentrated in the inner city and the richer population, predominantly of the racial majority, is concentrated in the suburban areas. In such scenarios of de facto segregation, it is relatively easy to draw boundaries reflecting well-defined geographic ethnic and racial enclaves.

However, some locales do not have such well-defined enclaves. For instance, although Houston has historic African American and Latino neighborhoods, Latinos are increasingly scattered in neighborhoods throughout the city, making the drawing of coherent "majority-minority" Latino districts difficult at best. Consequently, in some instances across the country, the lines of U.S. House districts have been drawn with unusual contortions so as to meet a "majority-minority" goal. The most notorious example occurred in the early 1990s when a U.S. House district was drawn to run all the way across the entire state of North Carolina, to join dense African American populations in the northern and southern regions of the state. In some locations the district was no wider than the interstate highway joining those regions. Although the U.S. Supreme Court in 1993 initially ruled this district unconstitutional because race was too exclusively used as the basis for gerrymandering the district, the Court in 2001 approved a redrawn version, ruling that race can be a factor in redistricting as long as it is not the prevailing factor.[9]

Second, even if one can practically create "majority-minority" districts, there is no guarantee that minority group members will win in such districts. For instance, in 1990, even though Latinos constituted 28 percent of Houston's population, no Latinos were serving as members of the city's U.S. House delegation. After the 1990 U.S. Census the boundaries of the new 29th U.S. Congressional District in Houston were drawn to enhance the chances of a Latino being elected. Even given this gerrymandering, the 29th District has subsequently been won by a European American. Although Latinos in 1990 were the largest group within this district, many were ineligible to vote because of their undocumented status or simply because they were too young. In other instances, many did not register to vote or refused to vote because of alienation from the political system. In turn, factionalism within the Houston Latino community, combined with the incumbent's extensive campaign finance resources, has enabled the incumbent to defeat all challengers.[10] Finally, the initial boundaries of the 29th District have been subsequently rejected by the U.S. Supreme Court for reasons similar to the North Carolina case; the redefined boundaries have further diminished the total number of Latinos in the district.

Third, even if one can conveniently create "majority-minority" districts and, in turn, enable the election of minority-group members, it does not follow that such public officials will necessarily represent the outlooks and views of minority groups. Creating geographic single-member districts whose boundaries are gerrymandered by race—especially for county, city, and school-board electoral districts—can lead to the election of politicians who over time, through the power of incumbency, become "bosses," reminiscent of nineteenth-century machine politics. As Lani Guinier points out, the fact that such leaders only have to win by a simple majority (51 percent of the vote) can actually lead to less political participation on the part of many minority members: "Because only 51 blacks are needed to elect a representative [in a hypothetical district of 100 members], incumbent representatives may be able to control the electorate through political patronage, political contributions, and political control of the district lines. The black voters are not encouraged to participate actively in the political process because a low voter turnout still benefits the incumbent."[11] Such "bosses" can effectively thwart serious challenges, even from members of their own minority. The question becomes whether they truly represent their constituents or are simply concerned with consolidating their political fiefs. Naturally, this same dilemma can be just as characteristic of "majority-majority" districts, but a patronage political outcome in the case of "majority-minority" districts undermines the rationale of utilizing racial gerrymandering.

Finally, taking this "possessive" sense of political identity to a larger scale, gerrymandering electoral districts according to ethnicity or race can beget a divisive interest-group politics rooted in separatist cultural enclaves. As I emphasized in chapter 1, the assimilation and separatist models of multicultural relations share a possessive as opposed to an intersubjective understanding of cultural identity. Whereas in assimilation everyone comes to adopt a uniform cultural identity, in separatism one shields one's particular cultural identity from penetration by all others. Neither model captures the ethos of a mestizo democracy that envisions cultures interacting and transforming each other mutually without culminating in ethnic uniformity or, conversely, in the abandonment of cultural heritages. If electoral practices prior to the Voting Rights Act of 1965 were too reflective of assimilation—in that minorities were simply marginalized if they did not accommodate themselves to the political mores of the dominant majority—gerrymandering districts by race can culminate in "thick" cultural enclaves that are mutually *exclusive* of one another.

The ethos of a mestizo democracy is to move beyond such either/ors. Even though our elected legislative bodies need to have more diverse memberships, the claim by some minority activists that a particular district "belongs to us" reduces the character of political community to being just an agonal contest between cultural enclaves rather than a substantive mixing through crossing borders. Although we need to transform election systems that de facto preclude minority participation, a possessive cultural outlook with regard to electoral districts fatalistically acknowledges the presence of the 'other' without seeking a democratic interchange of perspectives that would edify the political community as a whole. In terms of the 29th U.S. Congressional District, one could argue that the success of the European American who continues to hold the seat has been due, in fact, to his ability to build a multicultural base of support. A mestizo democracy emphasizes that members of diverse cultural groups can engage and come to understand each other as long as this engagement is on lateral, equal terms.

The ultimate danger posed by racially gerrymandered electoral districts is that they could in time lead to a corporatism in which seats for county commissions, city councils, school boards, and other deliberative bodies would literally be divided according to the racial/ethnic breakdown of the population. Indeed, the Voting Rights Act of 1965 does not guarantee proportional representation according to race or ethnicity, but simply aims to increase the likelihood that groups previously discriminated against can make a political impact in elections. A mestizo democracy, in contrast to corporatism, suggests we recast the noble aspirations of the Voting Rights Act to come up with ways for all cultural groups to contribute to the betterment and transformation of the political community. Creating "majority-minority" districts perhaps is better than doing nothing at all, but we need to find creative alternatives for fostering crossing borders in our political communities.

One such alternative to gerrymandering is cumulative voting. In this method, if, say, five seats constitute a county commission, city council, or school board, each voter gets to cast five votes which can all be applied to one candidate or divided up among the candidates. This voting system addresses the problem that plagues single-member districts: a candidate can win with as little as 51 percent of the vote (or with a simple plurality among multiple candidates where there is no provision for runoff elections), leaving close to half the district (or more) without representation in outcome. Communities throughout the country where cumulative voting is being used have seen an increase in the number of minority members serving on county commissions, city councils, and school boards.[12]

Guinier, one of the leading proponents of cumulative voting, suggests six advantages to this approach over racial gerrymandering. First, cumulative voting leads to an increase in voting and overall political participation. With the elimination of geographic districts, voters have a realistic chance of forming, with like-minded voters across the political community, powerful political coalitions that can force both incumbents and challengers to address issues with substantive policy proposals. Second, because cumulative voting emphasizes issues and not the personalities of candidates, incumbents have to stay in touch with the shifting allegiances of voters, lest they be removed from office. Third, cumulative voting rewards grassroots political organization and mobilization, not only for getting a particular set of voters to the polls but for inciting such groups to monitor the legislative record of their representatives. Fourth, cumulative voting overcomes the resentment felt by other minorities in majority-minority/single-member districts—for instance, Latino and Asian American voters in a predominantly African American district. Again, eliminating the geographic boundaries rewards voting groups who galvanize supporters across the political community. Fifth, cumulative voting cultivates consensus building among a wide diversity of interests, as opposed to a simple majority, drawn from "winner-take-all" districts, that can simply impose its set of interests. Consequently, minority constituencies come to see the political process as being fair. Finally, cumulative voting avoids the divisive and polarizing political effects of gerrymandering electoral districts to favor African Americans, Latinos, or some other minority group.[13]

Essentially, cumulative voting addresses the challenge of ensuring minority representation in deliberative forums without leading to the geographic "turf" politics of electoral districts gerrymandered by race. In contrast to the tightly scripted sense of identity connected with racial gerrymandering, cumulative voting provides a way for the intragroup differences within minority communities to gain expression and also encourages multiracial and multiethnic coalition building. By voting according to interests and issues rather than geographic places and racial categories, cumulative voting brings about a more accurate representation of the overlapping constituencies that comprise a political community. For instance, an African American or Latino might find common cause with a European American in support of particular candidates who otherwise could never win in "winner-take-all" electoral districts. Such coalitions reflect what Iris Marion Young terms the "multiple, cross-cutting, fluid" character of groups in complex societies.[14]

This accent on enabling political participation characterized by heterogeneity and multiplicity makes cumulative voting consonant with the ethos of a mestizo democracy. One might argue that such voting on the basis of interest as opposed to race or place is still contrary to the emphasis in a mestizo democracy on generating unity-in-diversity. To the contrary, as Guinier stresses, cumulative voting leads to qualitative deliberation and consensus building in legislative assemblies. Office holders who become insensitive to the diverse constituencies that elected them and their fellow representatives face the real prospect of losing reelection. Reminiscent of Arendt's rendering of the public space as where citizens engage each other as equals, cumulative voting enables a greater diversity of interlocutors to engage each other in legislative assemblies. As opposed to conventional "me-first" interest-group pluralism, such engagement manifests, in Young's terms, "a heterogeneous public" in which "participants discuss the issues before them and come to a decision according to principles of justice."[15]

The Politics of Equal Opportunity

One of the most divisive issues in the United States over the past four decades has been affirmative action. Especially over the past decade and a half, affirmative-action programs have been in retreat nationwide, highlighted by California's Proposition 209 that in 1996 ended "preferential treatment to any individual or group on the basis of race, sex, color, ethnicity, or national origin in the operation of public employment, public education or public contracting" in that state.[16] The 1997 narrow-margin rejection by Houston voters of an initiative to eliminate the city's affirmative-action program has hardly stemmed this negative tide.

The case for affirmative action, in the context of a mestizo democracy, is not to make reparations to peoples who endured injustice due to slavery, segregation, and discrimination but to ensure full and equal access by diverse cultural groups to key economic, social, and political forums and processes. When affirmative action is viewed in terms of possessive terms like quotas, those opposing affirmative action carry the day. Instead, we need to focus on what it is about our business, educational, and political networks that still prevents many minority members and women from having equal access to them. As of 1997 African Americans and Latinos held only 7.3 percent and 5.0 percent of managerial/professional jobs nationwide, respectively.[17] As of 1995 women constituted less than 27 percent of all lawyers, judges, and physicians and less than 14 percent of all dentists, engineers, police officers, and "precision, production, and craft and repair workers."[18] In addition to acknowledging these employment disparities, we also need to ask what contributions minorities and women could indeed bring to these professions, if given the opportunity.

Affirmative-action initiatives enable us to scrutinize the character of the power relationships of our democracy: in particular, to determine whether there remain ongoing education, employment, and personnel practices that deny equal opportunity in substantive, not just procedural, terms. Procedural remedy of such denial is pursued by the nondiscrimination approach to equal employment opportunity (EEO), which ensures that individuals are not discriminated against by employers "on the basis of such factors as race, gender, national origin, and religion."[19] When such violations occur, nondiscrimination EEO turns to the judicial system to remedy the situation. The Equal Pay Act of 1963 and Title 7 of the Civil Rights Act of 1964 are good examples of the procedural, legal approach. By contrast, affirmative-action programs deliberately consider the race, gender, and ethnicity of job candidates in order that women and minorities will comprise a representative share of all lines of work and in all workplace levels. President Lyndon Johnson in a speech at Howard University in 1965 morally justified this approach, which was subsequently put into effect by his Executive Order 11246.[20] Essentially, affirmative-action programs engage the reality that so-called merit systems in education and personnel networks and nondiscrimination EEO policies have not in fact enabled a wide diversity of cultural groups to realize equal educational and professional opportunities.

The other substantive dimension of affirmative action, especially when seen in terms of the hermeneutical relations between cultures, is that integration, not assimilation or separatism, is beneficial both for the individual and the community as a whole. If we find that particular groups are seemingly excluded from community life, we all lose the opportunity to explore how our differences—our plurality—can both positively transform ourselves and enrich the common good. Conversely, facilitating a rich exchange between cultural groups entails integration, not assimilation—the ethos of the border as opposed to the frontier mentality. As argued by W. E. B. DuBois, the elimination of racism "should not require the aesthetic and cultural assimilation of blackness into white values and social norms."[21] Although legal segregation died in the 1950s and 1960s, a color-blind society is still not possible in the United States, as Manning Marable insists, due to institutional racism. Therefore, overcoming discrimination is not just a matter of rooting out instances of conscious discrimination by employers, but of recasting the norms and practices that guide economic, educational, and political institutions so as to realize a democratic polity: "A truly integrated workplace, where people of divergent racial backgrounds, languages, and cultural identities learn to interact and respect each other, is an essential precondition for building a broadly pluralistic movement for radical democracy."[22] The institutions and practices that bind the nation should be inclusive of all cultural groups, but not at the expense of having these groups shed their cultural identities in the process. The task—à la Las Casas—is to engender a conversation in which the nation's diverse peoples and cultures can begin to engage each other on equal terms.

There are five frequent objections made to affirmative action:

(1) Affirmative action supposedly "stigmatizes" its recipients.
(2) Affirmative action constitutes reverse discrimination: it relies on group remedies without ever clearly demonstrating that the benefiting women and minorities were truly subject to discrimination, and it penalizes other individuals who have never committed acts of discrimination.
(3) The attempt of affirmative action to "engineer" balanced workforces in terms of race, ethnicity, and gender assumes that prevailing underrepresentation of certain groups is due to discrimination when many other social factors are involved.
(4) Affirmative action remedies the effects, not the underlying causes of social inequality.
(5) Affirmative action violates the merit system's insistence that the best-qualified candidate for the position or opening should be hired or accepted.[23]

I will assess the validity of each of these objections. Indeed, many critics of affirmative action contend that individuals who benefit from such programs will never know whether they earned the job on merit or on considerations of race, ethnicity, or gender. Unfortunately, individuals in workplaces do get labeled as "affirmative action hires" and are branded as underqualified. Such stereotyping, however, is a case of selective perception. For instance, when European American men succeed professionally, due to privileged access to educational and social networks as much as to abstract achievement, why do we not stigmatize them with the same severity? Barbara Bergmann in her *In Defense of Affirmative Action*, features a picture of a father and four sons—all European American—who proudly stand side by side on a balcony overlooking the bank at which they all serve as executives: "They apparently had little or no fear that they would be disgraced by having their filial relationship to the bank's president revealed to hundreds of thousands of people. Like the alumni children who receive special admissions to Harvard, Yale, and Princeton, they probably had never been anxious that people might make hurtful speculations about whether they deserved the slots they occupied or were competent to fill them."[24]

To overcome such selective stigmatizing, we need to be much more forthright about the combination of achievement and ascriptive criteria associated with education and employment opportunities. More importantly, we need to be able to defend the validity of each criterion if we are to sustain diverse, democratic relations and not just a politics of privilege.

The second criticism of reverse discrimination reduces serious social issues of access to education, employment, and advancement to matters of individual rights. But as reviewed previously in chapter 5, both Kymlicka and Young provide cogent justifications for group rights within liberal democratic theory: minority groups must be able to participate effectively and in an egalitarian fashion in the power structures that affect their lives. From the standpoint of a mestizo democracy, the difficulty with the reverse discrimination argument is that it renders access to educational and employment opportunities strictly in individualist, win-lose terms: attempting to honor the civil rights of one person violates the civil rights of another. Instead, a mestizo democracy emphasizes civil rights in relational win-win terms: detecting and eradicating patterns of discrimination in community life leads to more democratic relations among its members.

The reverse discrimination argument actually has more validity when affirmative action is implemented in a possessive, not a relational, fashion. Although using quotas technically violates the federal government's affirmative-action guidelines, private and public employers informally use them to avoid the daunting tasks of (1) reviewing their personnel policies to ensure that they do not privilege one race, ethnicity, or gender over another, and (2) actually going out into cultural communities to cultivate qualified candidates from every imaginable background. Even goals—the key "monitoring mechanism" of affirmative-action policies—can become a way to avoid changing the underlying causes of social inequality because they at least give the impression employers are making good-faith efforts.[25] Such possessive implementation of goals and quotas proves divisive and certainly does not engender the mutual interchange of diverse cultures intrinsic to a mestizo democracy.

The third charge—that affirmative action constitutes social engineering—contends that other factors besides discrimination account for why minority groups are insufficiently represented in public and private workplaces and educational institutions. Thomas Sowell in particular maintains, for instance, that differences in cultural orientation, socioeconomic status, and type of skills passed from one generation to the next are crucial for explaining lack of minority access.[26] These factors, Sowell argues, should be examined more closely in the fashioning of public policy. But the difficulty remains that although these factors are not the consequence of specific acts of discrimination, they are rooted in the normative type of domination I critiqued through Dussel in chapter 4. Indeed, from the standpoint of a mestizo democracy, affirmative action is not just a legal matter but an ethical means of overcoming deep-rooted forces of domination on the basis of race, culture, and gender in U.S. political, social, and economic networks. If, indeed, affirmative action proves unsuccessful at eradicating these forces of domination, we will need to explore other types of public policy. But not to confront these forces of domination with some type of *public* policy—the import of the social engineering argument—is to advocate a political fatalism inconsistent with the pursuit of democracy.

The fourth criticism's distinction between the causes and effects of discrimination amplifies some of the concerns of the third criticism, principally that differences in class and educational access deter equal employment opportunities; consequently, minorities and women from the middle- and upper-classes are the primary beneficiaries of affirmative-action programs. These points are well taken and in fact make an argument for affirmative action on the basis of class as well as race, ethnicity, or gender. Nevertheless, this newfound concern for class should not vitiate programs that seek to overcome social patterns by which individuals are put at a disadvantage because of race, ethnicity, or gender. Instead of demand-side affirmative action, which aims to force public and private workplaces to diversify, Clarence Page suggests we focus on supply-side affirmative action—"increasing educational and training opportunities and, as a result, the talent pool."[27] Specifically, some companies hire diversity consultants to pinpoint, and then suggest how to overcome, prevailing workplace practices that are racist and sexist. For instance, one option open to higher educational institutions in the wake of California's Proposition 209 is to hold recruitment receptions across the country that suggest to minority students that they are still welcome to apply and enroll. These alternatives constructively respond to the fourth criticism without abandoning the ethos of affirmative action.

The final criticism, that affirmative action is contradictory to merit principles, is the linchpin of the anti–affirmative-action approach. Supposedly, fairness demands that the most qualified applicant, as measured by merit, be hired, making the nondiscrimination approach to equal employment opportunity the preferred system. To the contrary, affirmative action questions the fairness and legitimacy of recruitment and employment practices *so as to realize, not reject, merit systems.* Through affirmative action we can scrutinize and evaluate whether our so-called objective examination and employment standards are truly objective or simply reflective of a set of institutional prejudices that work to the advantage of privileged cultural groups. Where that kind of prejudice is found, we need to replace it with more valid standards, in ways such as those suggested by Page.

In a democratic political community we need to be forever vigilant in our quest to achieve merit standards that do not privilege a particular cultural group over another. Indeed, as previously discussed, when the implementation of affirmative action degenerates into quotas—a possessive instead of a relational approach to educational and employment opportunities —the pursuit of democratic cultural interchange is abandoned. In contrast to evaluation practices that either intentionally or unintentionally favor whites over other races, European Americans over other ethnicities, English speakers over speakers of other languages, and men over women, a mestizo democracy seeks to dismantle such privileges to enable diverse cultural groups to intersect on equal terms and to cultivate richer, inclusive political, social, and economic communities.

The emergence of diversity management, especially in the private sector, is a positive development toward this end. Much along the lines of Page's supply-side affirmative action, diversity management sees diversity as a positive attribute for workplaces and proactively seeks to encourage integration of diverse backgrounds, instead of reacting to ongoing discriminatory practices. In Jonathan Tompkins's analysis, diversity management has three principal dimensions. First, diversity management quite consciously seeks upward mobility in workplaces through training and development. The practical reality remains that although we have more minorities and women in the workplace then ever before, they are not well represented in government and the private sector at high management levels. Targeted training and development attempts to break this "glass ceiling." Second, affirmative action all too often puts the responsibility for cultural change solely on women and minorities placed in a "previously homogenous, all-white, all-Anglo, all-male, all native-born environment."[28] Diversity management, instead, seeks to transform such workplaces into venues that see diversity, creativity, and heterogeneity as leading to the betterment of the organization as a whole. Finally, diversity management addresses the causes of social inequality (1) by implementing multicultural sensitivity programs in workplaces and (2) by training managers in methods of changing their management practices to deal creatively with interpersonal conflicts, language differences, and other challenges generated by diversity.[29] Whereas all too many workplaces still hold assimilation as the preferred organizational ethic, diversity management offers a synergy engendered through the creative conflict of plural perspectives.[30]

Xerox is an example of a corporation that has been practicing diversity management for over two decades before the term became fashionable. Barry Rand, an executive vice president of Xerox, notes that when he initially joined the corporation as a sales trainee in 1968 its institutional culture was more open, flexible, and less regimented than many others of the day. At the same time, it quickly became apparent that African American salespeople were not assigned the most prosperous districts largely because they did not have access to "the informal networks crucial for success in corporate life," such as "living in the same neighborhood, or belonging to the same country club."[31] When discussions within an informal African American support network within the corporation culminated in a legal suit against the way Xerox was dividing these districts, top management started meeting not only with the African American caucus, but also with women and Latinos through their caucuses. As a consequence of these sessions, collaborative strategies were implemented for ensuring excellent performance in each cultural group and for developing the skills of people capable of rising to the top levels in the corporation. Rand concludes that Xerox's legacy of diversity management has enabled the corporation to realize the type of creativity that can flourish in a global market characterized by fluidity and change: "Workers with different backgrounds and perspectives help create this type of workplace, a place where innovative solutions can flourish."[32]

Another success story in terms of enabling minorities to achieve high professional positions has been the U.S. Army. According to Charles Moskos, the U.S. Army has had great success promoting minorities through the ranks by focusing on expanding the pool of qualified African American applicants. This undertaking increases the likelihood that the proportion of African Americans among those promoted will be comparable to their percentage in the initial talent pool—a priori abstract quotas are avoided. If the pool is insufficiently large, the Army commits to providing minorities the education and training that will enable them to enter the talent pool for promotion. It must be said that the Army has an advantage over most workplaces in developing such supply-side affirmative action: from the outset it has a large number of minority recruits whom the Army can cultivate and train for rising within the ranks. Second, Moskos's articulation of the Army's program never considers whether the standards for promotions might be racially skewed. Still, his call for a national civilian youth service modeled after the Army's program remains credible. Such a program would emphasize that affirmative action ends up being just a palliative if it does not address the underlying problems of economic and educational inequalities.[33]

Diversity management is to affirmative action what cumulative voting is to single-member districts and what dual-language education is to bilingual education. The initial programs in each of these comparisons strives to generate ways to effect lateral, democratic multicultural relations between diverse cultures while recognizing that historic political, social, and economic discriminatory practices against minorities must be overcome. In particular, these newer programs—in contrast to affirmative action, single-member districts, and bilingual education—do not convey a "possessive" and "rights-bound" appearance indicating that these initiatives are strictly for minorities. Rather, they cultivate the capacities for crossing the borders that unnecessarily divide us.

As Glenn Loury points out, public policy debates over civil rights at the outset of the twenty-first century, in general, have become rather stale and predictable. On the one hand, liberals focus on "the enemy without"—racism, as especially reflected in discriminatory practices in economic and educational institutions.[34] On the other hand, conservatives are quick to blame the failed policies of the welfare state for minority deprivation. If liberals use racism as their mantra and uncritically turn to government programs as the solution, conservatives are blind, in Loury's words, to "the historical experiences which link, symbolically and sociologically, the current urban underclass to our long, painful legacy of racial trauma."[35] Creative public policy making cannot emerge from this polarity between dated formulas and "benign neglect."[36]

Loury adds critically that the civil rights debate also should focus on "'the enemy within' ... those dysfunctional behaviors of young blacks which perpetuate poverty and dependency."[37] As a remedy he puts forward the communication of moral values, not by government but by family, neighborhood, and religious associations. He adds that it is imperative for African Americans who have benefited from affirmative-action type programs to give back to the minority community in an active way. Although Loury stresses minority self-help as the principal solution to the plague of poverty and dependency, he still sees a role for enforcement of laws against discrimination and for government programs in the areas of employment training and education—especially preschool education.[38]

Even though Loury still tends to focus more on the "enemy within" rather than on the "enemy without," his proposals are an effort to move beyond the ideological either/ors that otherwise have led to a stalemate in the civil rights debate. Picking up on an insight by Rand, Xerox's anticipation of diversity management long before it was fashionable was rooted in a capacity to think creatively "outside the box." The ethos of a mestizo democracy is precisely to envision new, previously thought incompatible combinations that, as discussed earlier, in turn generate a synergistic energy beneficial to all. Dual-language education, cumulative voting, and diversity management may not prove the final cures to our cultural divides, but each creatively moves beyond either/or thinking to raise the questions that must be engaged if we are to realize a democracy characterized by extensive multicultural interchange.

The most troublesome aspect of the backlash against civil rights initiatives over the past couple of decades is the comfortable position that nothing further needs to be done—a disturbing reiteration of the U.S. Supreme Court's toleration of social inequality between the races in *Plessy v. Ferguson*.[39] To the contrary, as emphasized repeatedly by Dubois, one of *Plessy*'s greatest critics, the realization of democracy is at stake in engaging the crucial issues of civic participation—communication, voting, educational achievement, and economic opportunity. As long as political, economic, or social success entails assimilation to the norms and practices of the dominant cultural group, counter-initiatives that manifest the *substantive* pursuit of equal employment opportunity will be essential to realizing what Joan Tronto has termed "the qualities necessary for democratic citizens to live together well in a pluralistic society."[40]

Politics of Housing

A politics concerned with crossing borders has to confront the blatant racial and ethnic segregation in housing that persists in the United States. This segregation is most glaring between blacks and whites. In the following cities, 79 percent or more of the African American population would have to move into other areas of the cities in order to realize full integration: Detroit, Chicago, Cleveland, Milwaukee, Buffalo, St. Louis, Philadelphia, Birmingham, Cincinnati, and Gary, Indiana. Although the percentages are less graphic for Asian Americans and Latinos, these cultural groups nevertheless endure segregation in many areas. In Los Angeles, San Francisco, Stockton, and Vallejo, California, for instance, at least 45 percent of Asian Americans would have to move from their current locations in order to achieve integration with non-Asians. Likewise, in the case of Latinos in

Chicago and San Antonio, respectively, 66 percent and 53 percent of Latinos would have to move to achieve integration with non-Latinos.[41]

To develop further how housing policy in the United States has led to the ghettoization of minorities and the poor, I draw principally upon analysis done by Michael Lemay. Without a doubt the concentration of minorities in inner cities is determined by the economic reality of cheaper rent. Although gentrification has altered this reality in some places, the pattern still holds that minorities occupy the more downtrodden, impoverished areas of cities, while middle-class and upper-class European Americans reside in the suburbs. Unfortunately, the following public policies as well as the practices of the real-estate industry have reinforced the "urban blight—suburban flight" pattern:

- property tax policy that rewards landlords for not attending to their properties,
- assessment of property values in condemnation hearings according to the number of people living in a building,
- capital gains taxes and depreciation policies that work to the advantage of slum owners,
- the centering of public housing projects in inner cities,
- little or no enforcement of housing codes.

In addition, this list does not include illegal conduct such as conspiracy between real-estate agents not to sell to minorities, African Americans in particular.[42]

Federal government policies, in turn, over the past seven decades have also contributed to this urban-suburban divide. From 1930 to 1960 mortgage policies within the Federal Housing Administration, Federal National Mortgage Association, and G.I.-bill programs insisted on fostering "homogeneous neighborhoods."[43] In 1962, for instance, over three times more money was spent by the federal government on housing for middle- and upper-class families, largely in the suburbs, than on housing for the poor: "Although the making of a ghetto was not an intended impact, it was the direct consequence of programs subsidizing white flight to the the suburbs."[44] Undoubtedly, the 1968 Civil Rights Act makes illegal (1) the refusal to sell or rent a residence on the basis of a person's race, color, religion, or national origin and (2) the use of block-busting techniques by real-estate agents so as to prompt the exodus of European Americans to suburban areas. At the same time, federal housing projects in most major U.S. cities remain in the inner core. In turn, Department of Transportation programs that fund urban highways aid and abet the middle-class flight to the suburbs, with commercial concerns soon in tow. Finally, Housing and Urban Development programs that do revitalize urban areas by replacing downtrodden neighborhoods with civic complexes and more upscale residences—the above-mentioned gentrification—ultimately push the poor aside without any genuine attention to their predicament.[45]

Since access to good educational and economic opportunities in the United States frequently relates to the quality of neighborhoods, the above segregation by class, if not by race, runs the real risk of creating a permanent underclass largely relegated to low-pay service-sector or welfare incomes. In view of the fact that a high percentage of minority populations comprises this inner-city underclass, such an economic caste system becomes particularly odious. Given that in some major U.S. cities the so-called minorities collectively are the majority in terms of overall numbers and that current demographic trends suggest a magnification of this development, we face the real possibility that U.S. urban centers will become locales of de facto apartheid. In addition, to the extent that the urban-suburban split is a racial divide, this pattern reinforces "thick" racial and ethnic enclaves rather than creating the opportunities for social interaction between diverse peoples in schools, neighborhood associations, and other civic organizations. Ultimately, we are left with the fatalistic ethos of *Plessy v. Ferguson:* that underlying social inequality cannot be resolved by legal or political means.

In addition to these disturbing forms of discrimination according to class and race, as Goizueta points out, the urban-suburban split presents an ethical divide between the disorderliness of the urban as opposed to the orderliness of the suburban. Goizueta's image turns the frontier mentality on its head: the "civilized" are now those "beyond the pale," in the hinterlands, whose aim it is to shield themselves from the "uncivilized" dwellers in the decaying urban setting:

> The polarization of city and suburbs is the geographic manifestation of the polarization of public and domestic, or private life. Life in the suburbs is perceived as tranquil compared to the "chaos" of the city. Life in the suburbs is private and secluded, as opposed to the publicness and openness of the city. Cities have sidewalks that are open to the general public. Suburbs eliminate sidewalks, replacing their public openness with the private enclosure of cul-de-sacs.

In some suburban neighborhoods, homeowners are even discouraged from placing their address numbers on their houses, under the assumption that anyone who does not already know to which house he or she is going does not belong on the neighborhood streets anyway. The city square is replaced by the suburban mall as the symbol of civic life. The difference is that, in the enclosed mall, everyone looks alike, talks alike, and behaves the same way. The city is dirty and messy, whereas the suburbs are clean and tidy. Life in the suburbs is perceived as human (praxis, "family values"); life in the city as inhuman (poiesis, "the Rat Race").[46]

At the same time, many who reside in the suburbs still make their livelihoods in the cities. The above-mentioned highway system enables suburbanites to endure the vicissitudes of the city, knowing that at the end of the day they can retreat to their well-fortified and highly manicured suburban residences. Indeed, Goizueta notes that we are willing to give assistance to the poor when it is "from a controllable, geographical distance."[47] This mindset essentially engages the poor not as dignified, concrete human beings who aspire for better lives for themselves and their families, but as objects whose needs are best left to public and nonprofit welfare networks and whose plights must not upset the well-being of middle- and upper-class civilization.

Such objectification of human beings through the polarization of public *v.* private life and urban *v.* suburban life is inconsistent with both individuals and groups engaging each other on a mutual, equal basis. Feminists have drawn attention to how the traditional public-private split relegates women to the secondary domain of the home. Goizueta, instead, demonstrates how in the contemporary United States the diverse public realm has become the locale of the poor, giving way to the ascendant private realm available to those who can afford to assimilate to it. De facto discrimination, as manifested in housing practices, is much more difficult to target and remedy than de jure discrimination but just as corrosive of the egalitarian multicultural relations envisioned by a mestizo democracy.

If we are serious about crossing borders, in this instance between rich and poor people, a mestizo democracy offers us the merit of fostering heterogeneous neighborhoods in terms of race, ethnicity, and income. The trouble is that this ideal is easier stated than accomplished. First and foremost, local authorities need to enforce housing codes so as to deter the practices of slum landlords, and state and federal antidiscrimination laws regarding housing must be enforced. However, legal initiatives alone cannot engender the value system essential to moving beyond the tranquility-chaos, tidy-messy, suburban-urban dichotomies: "It is far easier to pass laws of desegregation than to create a desegregated culture."[48]

On an economic front, government, business, and the nonprofit sectors should jointly pursue policies that revitalize urban areas, thereby encouraging local ownership of businesses by minorities and poor people. Many of the current gentrification schemes attract middle and upper classes back into urban areas, but not in a way enabling entrenched poor residents to afford the new residences, restaurants, and entertainment centers.

One class of government initiatives holding some promise is called the "Robin Hood" plans, initiated by many state governments to deal with inequities in the funding of public schools. Since most school districts in the United States are funded through local property taxes, those school districts fortunate enough to be situated in rich neighborhoods have a much easier time funding school programs than districts in poor neighborhoods. Robin Hood plans redistribute money statewide from rich to poor districts to overcome the resource disparities. Even if one chooses to shield one's family in suburban gated communities, the tax resources of these communities are nevertheless shared with needy rural and urban locales.

Since the funding of education is still primarily a state, not a federal, responsibility, Robin Hood plans cannot at present address disparities in property tax revenues between rich and poor states. Therefore, it may eventually be necessary to shift the funding of public education to the national level to address these disparities once and for all. At the same time, to sustain the tradition of local control of schools and to cope with the prospect of increased bureaucracy that would come with more federal involvement, we would need to give local school districts extensive creativity and discretion in terms of spending such education funds.

Without a doubt Robin Hood plans have led to divisive debates in many states. However, contained in these plans is an ethic of solidarity: we are one human family regardless of our racial, ethnic, and economic standing, and we have a responsibility to foster the common good at every level of community life—local, regional, national, and ultimately transnational. From the standpoint of the relational, not possessive, sense of personal and community identity essential to a mestizo democracy, we need to engender political, economic, and social networks that enable diverse 'others' to engage each other on terms they mutually determine, as opposed to accommodating themselves to terms dictated by economically powerful groups who are frequently of a different race or ethnicity from the poor. This ethic of solidarity, thus, is not just a matter of empowering those on the margin, but of enriching the overall community through the full contributions of its diverse members.

On one level the global economy is breaking down the barriers between diverse cultures, and persons with the capacity for combining multiple identities—the verve of mestizaje—would seem to be strategically situated for success in the twenty-first century. Indeed, as noted previously, many businesses are trying to engender in their employees the virtues of fluidity and synergy. Still, the inequitable distribution of profits between haves and have-nots in the global economy, as geographically exemplified by the suburban-urban split, is a twenty-first century version of the nineteenth-century industrial company town, except that the beautiful home of the corporate magnate can no longer be seen from the dilapidated homes of the workers. If we are serious about realizing unity-*in*-diversity, the separatist challenges posed by the persistence of de facto segregation in the United States constitute a microcosm of the threats to solidarity posed by "frontier" engagements of immigration and the global economy.

Politics of Migration

The United States prides itself on being a nation of immigrants. Of course, this notion denies the existence of the indigenous peoples prior to the arrival of the European American colonists in the early seventeenth century. It also denies the fact that African Americans brought to this country as slaves obviously did not come by choice. Yet it remains true that the vast majority of U.S. Americans are the descendants of immigrants. Indeed, immigration to the U.S. in the 1990s was the highest it has been since the decade of 1900–1910.

Although the country has this immigrant heritage, in the latter 1990s a growing wave of anti-immigrant sentiment swept the country. Most notably, California's Propositions 187 (against extending welfare support to undocumented aliens) and 227 (against bilingual education) targeted immigration. In turn, the U.S. Government in the past decade has increased its efforts to thwart the access of undocumented immigrants into the country. This undertaking, ironically, has ensued during the same period in which the 1994 North American Free Trade Agreement (NAFTA) supposedly "opened up" the economic borders between Canada, the United States, and Mexico. Although Mexican and other Latino immigrants are hardly the only immigrants coming into the country, documented or undocumented, they have become the principal targets in the prevailing enforcement of U.S. immigration policy. Given that my articulation of a mestizo democracy emphasizes crossing borders—not erecting them—and that the ethos that forms this political theory is drawn extensively from Mexican American and Latino articulations of mestizaje, it is imperative that we engage the implications of this ethos for U.S. immigration policy. Indeed, since the U.S.-Mexico border is the largest in the world between the developed and developing world, the example set along *la frontera* has repercussions for North-South relations across the globe.

U.S. immigration policy has had five distinct stages. In the "open-door" era of 1820–1880 anyone could come to the United States with little or no restriction. During the "door-ajar" era of 1880–1920 some restrictions were put in place, but most people could still enter the country. The "pet-door" era of 1920–1950 used a quota system to allocate permissible immigrant totals on a country-by-country basis. The "Dutch-door" era, 1950–1985, expanded the total legal numbers of immigrants, with provisions that led to extensive refugee flows. Finally, in the "revolving-door" era—from 1985 to the present—again the total numbers of legal immigrants have been increased, but with a marked tendency for many of these persons to move back and forth between the United States and their country of origin.[49]

Although until 1970 immigrants to the United States were overwhelmingly from Europe, since 1970 immigrants from Latin America and Asia have been the two largest groups, approximately 52 percent and 34 percent, respectively, of the total number of immigrants.[50] In the past two decades over six million permanent resident immigrants have come from Latin America and the Caribbean and three and a half million of these from Mexico.[51]

The change most responsible for accelerating extensive non-European immigration to the United States was the Immigration and Nationality Act of 1965. Specifically, the quota system that had previously favored immigrants from Northern and Western Europe was eliminated. At the same time, the Act established for the first time a total cap of 120,000 on immigration from countries in the Western Hemisphere. The 1965 Act also privileged immigrants who already had family in the United States or had professional skills deemed essential for economic growth. Subsequently, in 1976, Congress established a cap of 20,000 immigrants per country, regardless of hemisphere. Nevertheless, these measures did not stem the rising tide of undocumented immigration.

Congress tried to address this latter problem through the Immigration Reform and Control Act of 1986. This law sought to penalize employers of undocumented workers while simultaneously giving legal amnesty to un-documented immigrants already in the United States although the employer sanctions proved unworkable, over three million immigrants, primarily of Mexican or Latin American origin, benefited from the amnesty. In the 1990s many of these immigrants became naturalized and are increasingly partici-pating in the political system. Despite such success stories, in 1996 Congress initiated new restrictions on the opportunities of permanent residents which, as a consequence, have increased the likelihood of undocumented immi-gration: (1) immigrants who commit felony and certain misdemeanor crimes are more likely to be deported; (2) permanent residents are denied access to many social welfare programs; and (3) minimum household income levels are set for sponsors of immigrants—a deterrent to many potential immi-grants whose families in the United States are poor. As a result, substantial increases in the budgets of the Immigration and Naturalization Service for enforcement activities, instead of service initiatives, and increased militari-zation of the border have not only explicitly deterred migration but have increased the likelihood of human rights abuses.[52]

As reviewed in chapter 2, Mexican Americans, as distinguished from many other U.S. ethnic groups, initially were *not* immigrants. At the con-clusion of the 1846—1848 war between Mexico and the United States, 125,000 Mexicans already lived in the U.S. Southwest.[53]

Migration has continually occurred back and forth between the United States and Mexico over the past century and a half due to a number of factors on both sides of the border, again as reviewed previously in chap-ter 2. Essentially, though, the United States welcomes Mexicans into the economy with open arms when the country is in need of laborers, as during World War II, and deports them when economic times turn sour, as during the Depression. In like fashion, although the 1965 Immigration Act enabled non-European peoples to immigrate much more easily into the United States, the previous year Congress terminated the bracero program that had enabled many Mexican laborers to work legally in the United States in the mid-twentieth century.

Even Samuel Huntington, whose theoretical outlook is Eurocentric, acknowledges that there are at least three factors that distinguish Mexican "immigration" to the United States from that of other groups. First, in con-trast to immigrants from other continents who have to traverse an ocean to enter the United States, Mexicans can literally walk into the U.S. Southwest and are able to sustain ties to communities both north and south of the border. Second, most Mexican immigrants still reside in the U.S. Southwest—

an area that was historically part of Mexico and thus forms "a continuous Mexican society stretching from Yucatan to Colorado."[54] Third, Mexican immigrants have shown that they are more resilient than most immigrant groups in terms of sustaining their cultural identity and resisting assimilation. Indeed, Huntington cites the furor over Proposition 187 in California in 1994 as evidence.[55]

Given this historical and geographic context, the steady movement of Latin Americans from Mexico, Central America, and other parts of Latin America into the United States is a *migration* in which the participants retain identities shaped by more than one culture and renew their bonds to multiple locales, both north and south of the border, on a regular basis. U.S. immigration policy in the twenty-first century cannot afford to ignore this long-standing nexus of Latin American and U.S. American politics, economics, and culture in the borderlands.

In addition to the deep historical and cultural ties across the U.S.-Mexico border, several contemporary developments are making the sovereignty of the nation-state and the accompanying notion of associating one's identity with one country quite dated. First, many persons are now eligible for dual citizenship—particularly in Latin America where newcomers to the United States from Brazil, Colombia, Costa Rica, the Dominican Republic, and Mexico can retain their rights to their country of origin.[56] Second, the rise of regional trading blocs like NAFTA and the European Union inevitably provides the potential, if not the need, for laborers to move freely across borders. Obviously, having open borders in terms of labor supply challenges long-standing immigration policies within many nation states. The EU actually has been much more comprehensive than NAFTA in terms of enabling free movement of laborers. Indeed, NAFTA does not allow for movement of labor across national boundaries, with the exception of highly trained professionals, and this is one of the main factors contributing to the flow of undocumented immigrants from Mexico into the United States.[57]

Third, these developments of the global economy have also led to the shifting of what were government functions to non-governmental or quasi-governmental institutions. As a consequence of the above-mentioned trading blocs and of outcomes of the General Agreement on Tariffs and Trade (GATT), nascent transnational legal and regulatory bodies have been created whose responsibilities include circulating workers and business people under these agreements. As Saskia Sassen points out, these bodies do not *formally* promulgate migration policies, but in *de facto* terms they do. Fourth and finally, international human rights covenants over the past half century have changed the focal point of political and legal participation from the citizen in a nation-state to the person in the global community. Enforcing the human rights of the latter—especially "immigrants, refugees, and asy-lum-seekers"—has not only become a prominent item on the dockets of national judiciaries but has necessarily promoted human rights—especially for migrants—to the level of normative principles for legal and judicial sys-tems increasingly across the globe.[58]

In conclusion, though it may have been the traditional locus for cre-ating and enforcing immigration policy, the nation-state is increasingly sharing this role with international business, non-governmental, and human-rights organizations. The capacity of any nation-state, including the United States, to control its borders is quickly being eroded by the global economy. That transnational systems of governance, both public and private, are having an extensive impact on migration and human rights issues is no longer a question. However, the transnational public needs to become more aware of these transnational developments as "glo-bal citizens" probe and debate what should be the contour and content of these transnational political structures that are increasingly superceding the domains of nation-states.

To effect a transnational politics, we need a transnational sense of po-litical identity. This idea is not just an abstract projection, for the mestizaje that is ensuing along the U.S.-Mexico border and in the U.S. Southwest is cultivating a sense that one can have multiple political identities. Tradition-ally, in the assimilation model of immigration, an immigrant enters the United States and within three generations has become culturally natural-ized, with few traces of previous cultural heritage remaining. However, the history of many Mexican Americans and Latinos suggests instead a circular model in which migrants remain just as oriented to their country of origin as to their new country. They retain two or more identities that can be per-sistently reinforced through the communication and transportation ad-vances of the global economy.[59]

Beyond just the notion of encouraging multiculturalism within the confines of any nation-state, as Sassen suggests, transnational identities make manifest how dated the concept of nation-states is becoming. Indeed, these transnational persons, growing in number, with roots in both Mexico and the United States pose challenges to both their country of origin and to their "new country." In contrast to either assimilationist or separatist mod-els of cultural identity, this transnational mestizaje engenders a "'third space' beyond the confines of any one nation-state."[60] Formerly easy distinctions between "place of origin" and "place of exile" are losing significance.[61]

As an example, Roger Rouse provides a case study of migration between Aguililla in Michoacán, Mexico, and Redwood City, California, since the 1940s. Migrants from Aguililla have come to Redwood City for over half a century for economic opportunities not available in Michoacán. Although many stay permanently in Redwood City, others take the wealth they earn and return to Aguililla to develop small-scale family-based operations that are incongruent to the cultural patterns of Redwood City. Rouse points out that many Aguilillians never strive for U.S. citizenship because as Mexican citizens with the right to permanent residence in the United States they can easily move back and forth. He adds that it is not unusual for these migrants in Redwood City to send their children back to Mexico for education and for vacations so as to cultivate the bilingual and bicultural skills essential for continuing this transnational life. Aguilillians on both sides of the border keep in touch and visit one another with such frequency that they retain allegiances to both locales.[62]

The Aguililla-Redwood City binary relationship is replicated over and over when members of villages from Mexico or Central America relocate virtually intact in U.S. cities. In return these migrants then send financial resources to and, in some instances, initiate infrastructure improvement—roads, utilities, and sanitation systems—for their villages. In fact, the global economy has broken down the homogeneous first world–third world demarcation. As Rouse points out, third-world realities—"extreme poverty, residential overcrowding and homelessness, underground economies, new forms of domestic service and sweatshops"—now characterize many major U.S. cities to a degree not heretofore experienced.[63] Moreover, amending the urban-suburban split accented by Goizueta, Rouse notes that even U.S. suburban areas now cannot escape the poor and the marginalized, for new housing developments are often found in relatively rural locales with long-standing populations of migrant workers.

Consequently, at a minimum, a U.S. immigration policy consistent with a mestizo democracy would consist of the following planks:

- creation of more opportunities for legal entry into the United States,
- elimination of the militarization and consequent violence ensuing along territorial boundaries,
- more regulation of workplace labor, health, and safety standards,

- providing some voting rights in school board elections for noncitizen parents of public school children.[64]

Consonant with a transnational ethos, not only should these policies be realized in the United States but also in Mexico and in other countries whose destinies are becoming increasingly entwined due to globalization. As a matter of fact migrant communities in the 1990s have engaged in political mobilization in both their home and host countries. The Southwest Voter Registration and Education Project, a renowned mobilizer of Latinos in the United States, has critically confronted both the United States and Mexican governments: the former on U.S. foreign policy toward Mexico and Central America and the latter on human-rights violations. As Purnima Mankekar argues, we need to realize a political space that transcends the host/home dichotomy, yet enables us to pursue social justice issues in both venues.[65]

By reconceptualizing immigrants into migrants—as well as frontiers into borders, assimilation/separatism into mestizaje, and nation-states into transnational political, social, and economic systems—the heritage of transnational, transcultural persons, which is frequently denigrated and marginalized in homogenized nation-states, becomes our compass through the "vivid, often violent juxtaposition" of diverse ways of life in the "borderlands" of the twenty-first century.[66] Indeed, the lives of "ordinary" people, as in the Aguililla-Redwood City nexus, have much to teach us, Rouse notes, "as we try to chart our way through the confusions of the present toward a future we can better understand and thus more readily transform."[67]

From the standpoint of a mestizo democracy, the politics of immigration is not just about green cards and deportations, but of envisioning a transnational political citizenship. Even though the ongoing extensive migration of Latin Americans into the United States reinforces the historical mestizaje of cultures in the U.S. Southwest, the temptation remains to render this movement according to the dated model of one-directional immigration from home to host countries. Instead, the juxtaposition of multiple identities accelerated by the global economy testifies to the impact of border crossings, both literal and figurative, that have been intrinsic to the mestizaje of the U.S. Southwest for most of the past two centuries. This in-depth cultural heritage provides a hermeneutical basis for projecting not just a multicultural democracy within the United States, but a transnational politics that can contend in a just fashion with the global forces that increasingly inscribe our lives.

Politics of Globalization

Pursuing this transnational politics entails a critical engagement of the pros and cons of the global economy. As the preceding discussion of migration suggests, the transnationalization of free trade is reaching into every corner of the globe, and, especially in the wake of NAFTA, the U.S.-Mexico border has become the front line of the growing intersection of the developed and developing worlds in the Americas.

Rebecca Morales contends that four assumptions underlie the onset of neoliberal trade policies and agreements such as NAFTA. First, such free trade supposedly stimulates economic growth across the Americas. Second, such "unrestrained" trade between developing and developed nations will supposedly lead to benefits for each.[68] Third, "macroeconomic policies and economic stabilization programs" by themselves can supposedly reconstruct economies.[69] Finally, international free trade supposedly entails "the mobility of factors of production."[70]

In point of fact, according to Morales, none of these assumptions has proven accurate. First, NAFTA is actually a regional agreement and thus thwarts hemispheric-wide free trade. Moreover, she notes, the confidence placed by neoliberals in economic growth belies the fact that such policies have had "a negative effect on income distribution."[71] Second, NAFTA privileges the dominant partner in the agreement—the United States; in essence, major U.S. companies have access to the expanding Mexican market to the detriment of small companies and the working classes in both countries. In practical terms, as Manuel Pastor and Carol Wise note, "the survival of the fittest" orientation of neoliberalism does not grasp the importance of "small- and medium-sized firms" to generating exports.[72] Third, Morales contends, the above macroeconomic programs need support from micro-economic initiatives, especially government programs that target technological and educational training programs. Finally, contrary to the abstract ideal of free labor flow across borders, she insists that NAFTA prevents labor markets from being able to respond to the professional and job dislocations engendered by the agreement. The rise in migration discussed in the preceding section is a direct consequence of such con-striction.[73]

Although there were partisans in the NAFTA debate who wanted to retain closed economic borders, most of the substantive arguments were not over the overall benefits wrought by free trade but over the specifics of the free-trade policy. Labor and environmental groups, both at the time of the agreement as well as today, have contended that the agreement insufficiently deals with the following components of a healthy economy: movement of labor forces, sanitary working conditions, just wages, and ecologically sound policies for dealing with industrial waste and developmental sprawl. As noted above, NAFTA engenders free trade but not free access of laborers back and forth across the U.S.-Mexico border. Vicente Fox's goal of working toward open borders is a step in the right direction, but its realization must move beyond symbolic gestures.

Not all free trade agreements are alike. The Single Europe Act of 1986 enables free movement of goods, services, *and labor* across the European Union. Its underlying philosophy is that it is better for free trade in the long run to build up consciously less developed economies within the region rather than letting them remain forever in a dependent status. By contrast, NAFTA principally decreases "the costs of trade and foreign investment" without addressing the overall disparity between the economic power of the trading partners.[74] In terms of migration policies, NAFTA does enable individuals of high educational abilities and capital to move back and forth between countries, but governments are left with the issues of coping with the diminishing possibilities for low-skilled workers and their dependents.[75] The EU is also well ahead of the United States in terms of granting rights to individuals, regardless of whether they are citizens of a particular nation-state.[76]

Despite counter-examples such as the EU, some neoliberal economists will still contend that efficiency in international free trade is at the expense of equitable distribution of wealth: supposedly short-term pain in terms of the displacement of inefficient jobs leads to long-term gain for the economy as a whole. However, there is a growing literature that suggests that economic growth and equity are actually linked. For instance, within the industrialized world those economies with the worst income distribution in the early 1980s—the United States and Switzerland—manifested less productivity and growth than those with the best income distribution—Japan, Belgium, and Sweden.[77] Chronic poverty and inequality, Morales adds, are detrimental to the economy because (1) resources are not utilized well, (2) consequent social programs prove costly, and (3) consumption is not optimized. In contrast, certain political benefits derive from greater equality:

- less squabbling between different sectors of the economy— between farmers *v.* urbanites, for instance—which thus preempts the need for inefficient government price supports;
- less "conflict-driven inflation" and the related hope that the costs of stabilization will be borne by another group;

- more willingness to make adjustments to short-term macroeconomic instability;
- more acceptance of property rights and consequent openness to
  long-term growth plans;
- more investment in health and education programs, which in
  turn creates "a productive base of human capital."[78]

In Pastor's words, inequality leads to both "bad economics as well as bad politics."[79]

Therefore, given the real possibilities for equality-driven development, we need to abandon what Jeremy Breecher has termed "downward level-ing" development.[80] Undoubtedly, neoliberal trade policies have enabled capital to move more freely throughout the globe. But the primary aim of such policies has been to lower the costs of production. Unfortunately, mi-nus the above concern for equity and equality, communities and nation-states alike get caught in a bidding war that lowers production costs to such an extent that workplace standards and conditions deteriorate to "those of the poorest and most desperate."[81]

Breecher instead advocates an "upward leveling" or a "globalization-from-below," characterized by the following notions:

- Economic development must ensue in a democratic fashion:
  "Global institutions must be democratic, transparent, account-
  able, and accessible to the public."
- Transnational rules and institutions must positively address both
  labor and environmental issues.
- Popular organizations and movements across national borders
  must be consolidated to contend with the collective power of
  multinational corporations.
- Economic standards of the poor can and must be raised, contrary
  to the prevailing transnational "race to the bottom."[82]

In essence, we need a transnational or global politics to deal with neoliberal trade policies that exploit prevailing inequalities between the rich and the poor and fail to engage the concept of pro-growth with equality. Just as the U.S. government a century ago tempered the economic excesses of the rob-ber barons by regulating trusts and monopolies and eventually establishing minimum-wage laws and maximum-hour laws for workers, the time is ripe for developing transnational political structures, both at the grassroots and formal institutional level, that foster "upward leveling." Developing global codes of economic conduct—such as the EU Social Charter's stipulation that resources be given to poorer member states so that they can comply with EU minimum-wage standards—is imperative for realizing democratic "border crossings" rather than the neo-imperialistic expansion of "frontiers."[83]

Actually, the political struggle over NAFTA has brought together labor and environmental activists, human rights advocates, and farming lobbyists from both north and south of the U.S.-Mexico border. The initiatives of such broadly based, grassroots mobilization are the initial steps toward engendering genuine democratic transnational institutions. For instance, a coalition of religious, labor, Latino, and women's organizations from both countries has drafted the "Maquiladora Code of Conduct" to deal with corporations on the Mexican side of the border.[84] It specifies standards for environmental protection—especially in terms of hazardous materials—prohibits employment discrimination, insists on just wages and the workers' right to organize, and seeks strong measures against sexual harassment.

The accelerated marginalization of poor Latinos and Latin Americans in squalid urban and rural barrios due to neoliberal trade policies has provided a fertile basis for cultivating Latino solidarity across the Rio Grande/ Río Bravo divide. Historically, established Latino organizations within the United States have been at times hostile to new migrants from Mexico and other parts of Latin America. The League of United Latin American Citizens (LULAC), in its early years, quite explicitly distinguished its membership as being Mexican American as opposed to more recent Mexican migrants.[85] Even César Chávez and the United Farm Workers as late as 1973 were reluctant to advocate for undocumented workers because they feared the expansion of the labor pool by such workers would make the task of unionizing farm workers extremely difficult.[86]

In contrast to such past resistance to migrants even within the Latino community, mobilization efforts across the border—such as the one against the *maquiladoras*—suggest that the future of political activism both within and between both countries will be through the grassroots community model. This model comports very well with the concrete relational notion of community articulated in Latino theology. Indeed, such grassroots organizations within the United States—especially as organized by the Industrial Areas Foundation—are increasingly assuming the leadership mantle held by long-standing conventional organizations such as LULAC and the GI Forum.[87]

Articulating a global politics to contend with the global economy may seem a departure from my primary focus on engendering egalitarian multicultural relations in the United States. To the contrary, the growing intersection between the world's developed and developing economies on a global scale parallels the divide between rich and poor peoples discussed earlier in the section on housing. "Crossing borders" can, first of all, be as much an issue of class as of cultural divides. Second, combining opposites, such as competing economies, seemingly in tension with each other is very much at the ethical heart of my articulation of mestizaje as a political theory. Finally, recalling Dussel's critique of modernity, most of the developed world is comprised of the Eurocentric colonial and neocolonial powers—Japan being the most notable exception—whereas the developing world is primarily comprised of peoples of color who were previously colonized by those European powers. Hence, in the global economy debate there is an overlay of the subjugated 'other' who is of a different race, ethnicity, or religion.

Samuel Huntington, in particular, has captured this connection between globalization and what he projects as a potential "clash of civilizations."[88] Although Huntington is ultimately an apologist for Western civilization, his articulation of the increasingly international political encounter between these civilizations moves the debate over globalization beyond the narrow discourse of political economy to one that engages the politics of intersecting cultures.

Huntington argues that in the post–Cold War world, there are nine key civilizations: Western, Latin American, African, Islamic, Sinic, Hindu, Orthodox, Buddhist, and Japanese. Contrary to those such as Barber who contend that modernization is providing a corporate universality to the globe—"McWorld"—Huntington contends that the resources and forces of modernization can be adapted by non-Western civilizations without contaminating their cultures.[89] Indeed, the power provided by modernization is enabling the resurgence of Islamic civilization and a further assertion of Asian civilization in global politics. Although Western civilization is losing its hegemonic grip on the world stage, Huntington maintains that it can successfully assert itself not as a universal civilization but by pursuing the following initiatives:

- consolidating political, economic and military integration among the Western countries;
- Westernizing Latin America as much as possible;
- impairing the shift of Japan away from the West and toward China;

- restricting the military development of the Islamic and Sinic nations;
- enhancing Western technological and military superiority;
- being circumspect about Western interventions in the spheres of other civilizations.[90]

In a multipolar, multicivilizational global politics, Huntington concludes, the revitalization of Western civilization is imperative for the survival of the United States and its European allies; at the same time, he continues, world security depends upon the "acceptance of global multiculturalism."[91]

Huntington's analysis of contemporary global politics manifests some features congenial to my articulation of a mestizo democracy and some that are not. Consonant with the ethos of mestizaje Huntington recognizes that no civilization can present itself as universal, for the world is constituted of many civilizations. He is particularly critical of the way in which Western civilization has projected itself: not only is Western civilization not universal, but such claims or attitudes only incite hostility in the non-Western world. In contrast to Schlesinger's spirited defense of Western civilization against multiculturalism that I reviewed in chapter 1, Huntington emphasizes the need for Westerners to understand Western civilization as just one among many. Nevertheless, Huntington, like Schlesinger, defends Western civilization as the foundation for European and U.S. power in world politics and is particularly critical of proponents of multiculturalism in the West because they erode this very foundation.

Overall, Huntington recognizes the presence of multiple civilizations and does not presume the superiority of any one of them in normative terms. Just as in chapter 2 I accented how advances in telecommunications and transportation systems are changing the dynamic of the intersection of cultures within the United States, Huntington illustrates that these same developments will lead to extensive intersections among world civilizations in the coming century. At the same time, as Huntington points out, the modernization that is ensuing in non-Western civilizations does not mean they will become Western in orientation: "We will be modern but we won't be you."[92] Instead of modernization unifying Western and non-Western cultures, according to Huntington, it actually strengthens the power of non-Western civilizations on the global stage and heightens the potential for clashes between civilizations.

Consequently, although he is sensitive to the salience of multiple civilizations in the contemporary world, Huntington does not hold much hope for their "mixing" in a constructive fashion in the manner of mestizaje. Huntington simply ignores the *transnational* identities, networks, and organizations emerging across the U.S.-Mexico border. Instead, he leaves us with a portrait of contending civilizations well steeped in the long-standing realist disposition in international relations theory: "Cold peace, cold war, trade war, quasi war, uneasy peace, troubled relations, intense rivalry, competitive coexistence, arms races: these phrases are probable descriptions of relations between entities from different civilizations. Trust and friendship will be rare."[93]

The closest Huntington comes to articulating anything resembling the lateral integration of cultures in a mestizo democracy is when he articulates the "*commonalities* rule" that "people in all civilizations should search for and attempt to expand the values, institutions, and practices they have in common with peoples of other civilizations."[94] In particular, he notes that the world's principal religions "share key values in common."[95] Although he disparages the attempt of any particular civilization to project itself as being universal—especially Western civilization—he does invoke the merit of Walzer's distinction between "thin" universal vs. "thick" particular moralities: each particular civilization has its own "thick" morality, but there remains a "thin" universal morality that is "common to most civilizations" and can serve as a basis for civilized discourse among these civilizations.[96]

One example that gives credence to Huntington's "commonalities rule," but one that Huntington never develops, is that the same global economic, communications, and transportation networks that are leading to greater interchange among the world's civilizations are also cultivating transnational peace organizations. The development of "transnational social movements and nongovernmental organizations," human rights networks, cultural interchange as a consequence of the global economy, and international news-media coverage is enabling peace activists and conflict-resolution specialists to coordinate activities across national boundaries.[97] As a result, religious leaders can more easily cooperate not only with their counterparts in other religious traditions but with political humanitarians in the pursuit of peace and the promulgation of human rights. Indeed, nongovernmental religious organizations, distinct from formal religio-political structures, have proven effective at forming partnerships with religious groups, governments, think tanks, and independent radio and television stations.[98] As Scott Appelby notes, the field is fertile for developing "regional centers for religious and cultural peacebuilding," which would systematically coordinate such networking.[99] Ultimately though, the prospect of such extensive, substantive, transnational peace building challenges the realist suppositions that otherwise inform Huntington's argument.

The merit of Huntington's work remains that it spurs the global-economy debate beyond the confines of political economy to envision a global politics among world civilizations. Conversely, the drawback of Huntington's analysis is that, except for the "commonalities rule," it does not envision the emergence of transnational political systems that could effect democratic syntheses among cultures and civilizations and also cultivate a sense of global citizenship.

Nevertheless, transnational political organizations are the future. Their growing impact is exemplified (1) by how such organizations, in general, are rapidly displacing nation-states in the creation and promulgation of migrant policies and (2) by how the EU regional trade agreement, specifically, promotes the movement of free labor across national borders and grants rights to individuals independent of nationality. Returning attention for a moment to NAFTA, one can conceive of a transnational government that would encompass the United States, Canada, Mexico, and the countries of Central America and the Caribbean. The ongoing political reforms in Mexico under the Vicente Fox administration and his advocacy of an open labor border between the United States and Mexico are initial steps facilitating such a development.

At a minimum, such a North and Central American government would operate in the manner of the Councils of Government in Texas—organizations bringing together city, county, and special districts from a specific area of Texas, such as Houston-Galveston, to discuss overlapping concerns and to coordinate overlapping public policies. COGs in Texas cannot coerce their constituent members to do anything; rather, they provide a place and space for these governmental bodies to alter contradictory policies and initiatives that work to the detriment of all. For instance, it makes perfect sense in the wake of NAFTA to provide a forum that would bring together on a regular basis the governors of the northern states of Mexico with the governors of the states of the U.S. Southwest. Potentially, a regional transnational government could pass and enforce laws on behalf of its member states and ensure the protection of human rights. The EU's evolution toward a European government suggests such a possibility.

Indeed, the preceding discussions of both migration and the global economy suggest transnational political organizations are already in process. The challenge is to have the imagination to conceive of transnational political bodies that would not just assume many of the responsibilities of prevailing nation-states, but would embody and project a both/and rather than either/or vision of political identities. For instance, take the case of the long-standing conflict in the six counties of Northern Ireland. Rather than pursuing a solution solely in Nationalist terms—a reunification of the six counties with the Republic of Ireland—or in Unionist terms—a cementing of Northern Ireland's connection to the United Kingdom, a both/and vision would suggest that this region be collaboratively governed by both the Republic and the United Kingdom. In fact, the three parts of the agreement of the Good Friday Peace Accords—a Northern Irish assembly comprised of all Catholic and Protestant factions, formal consultation between Northern Ireland and the Republic of Ireland on "all-Ireland" concerns, and a formal consultation between the Republic of Ireland and the United Kingdom on transnational concerns—move in this direction.

The contribution of mestizaje as a politics of "crossing borders" is precisely its capacity to envision lateral, collaborative interchange, if not integration, among diverse cultures and civilizations without extirpating their distinctive identities. Giving Huntington's pursuit of "commonalities" its just due, his multipolar rendering of civilizations in contest still requires the need of civilizations "to protect what distinguishes 'us' from 'them.'"[100] His articulation of "the clash of civilizations" cogently captures on a grand scale the separatist outlook of cultural identity I reviewed in the first chapter. By contrast, a mestizo democracy affirms, in Elizondo's terms, "an anthropology of inclusive and progressive synthesis" that manifests "a universality of harmony, a universality of respect for others in their differences, a universality of appreciation of differences, a universality of love, compassion, and mutual aid."[101]

Undoubtedly, if we do not cultivate an ethos by which diverse cultures and civilizations can pursue constructive, nonviolent interchange—as an alternative to one heritage simply triumphing at the expense of the other— then the sobering tones of Huntington's conclusions will prove prescient. The question is not whether there will be a global politics, for that is already underway; rather, the question is whether this will be a democratic politics that can realize "globalization from below" by stressing and engaging the compatibility of juxtaposed cultural and economic identities.

Epilogue

In this chapter I have explored what mestizaje's normative emphasis on "crossing borders" can mean for public policies regarding multilingualism, political participation, equal education and employment opportunity, housing, migration, and globalization. In this short space I have only scratched the surface of each of these policy areas.

At the same time, through each of the policies that I have proposed and/or endorsed—dual-language education, cumulative voting, diversity management, de facto integration of neighborhoods, multiple if not global citizenship, and transnational political organizations—runs a common thread: the capacity both to acknowledge and combine multiple identities. Dual-language education moves beyond sterile "English only" proposals to encourage each of us to develop the capacity to communicate on multiple levels and in diverse ways. Cumulative voting moves beyond the scripting of legislative districts on the basis of ethnicity or race to stimulate political coalitions among people of diverse backgrounds. Diversity management enables educational and employment networks to thrive and synergize by bringing together culturally diverse individuals. Pursuing integrated neighborhoods advances the notion that the well-being of democracy is dependent on the capacity of its citizens to interact as equals in close proximity, regardless of class, ethnicity, or race. Multiple citizenship demonstrates that each of us has identities that increasingly move beyond narrow nationalities and that human rights transcend the parameters of national citizenship. The politics of globalization, in turn, dares us to envision transnational political organizations and solutions to international conflicts that integrate the concerns of multiple cultures and civilizations.

Many of the challenges of the twenty-first century—such as potential environmental catastrophes; inadequate economic, educational, and health-care opportunities for the poor; and increasing tensions between cultural groups—are not easily resolved by a politics geared to conflicting self-interests or to public policies mired in the possessive sense of entitlements. Instead, a more holistic outlook that can break down the barriers that unnecessarily separate cultures and that cultivates an environment for mutual interchange is essential. If there is to be a democratic alternative to the center-periphery dynamic that characterizes so many polities, from the local to the transnational level, it will entail lateral, civil engagements between diverse cultures and peoples that do not culminate in glaring contrasts between haves and have-nots. In a shrinking world in which each of us is increasingly "crossing borders" on a growing number of issues, a mestizo democracy can engender a genuine "public happiness" among a diverse, if not global, citizenry—the focus of the concluding chapter.

Conclusion

Embracing the Future of Mestizo Democracy

*T*he preceding seven chapters have been an odyssey through which I have tried to pinpoint both the basis and justification for a mestizo democracy that can constructively engage the challenges posed by diversity from the local to the transnational arenas. In these concluding reflections, I synthesize the themes that weave in and out of these very distinct chapters and suggest further research directions for those willing to pursue the challenge of articulating a substantive sense of community through multicultural relations.

Mestizaje as a U.S. American Experience

Multiculturalism in terms of ethnicity, language, race, and religion is a given in the United States but is also increasingly a worldwide phenomenon, as advances in telecommunications and transportation networks, as well as increases in the number and complexity of intersections in the global economy, bring the world's peoples into greater contact with one another. The United States in the first decade of the twenty-first century is more multicultural than at any other time in its history, and population forecasts for the next few decades suggest this trend will persist, if not grow. As the twenty-first century proceeds, the long-standing distinction between the *majority* population of European Americans and *minority* populations of African Americans, Asian Americans, Latinos, and Native Americans will become dated (as is already the case in states such as California, Florida, and Texas), given the decreasing percentage of European Americans vis-à-vis the nation's population. As I argued in the discussions on migration and globalization in chapter 7, more and more of us increasingly have identities connected to multiple regions and cultures from across the globe.

The crucial question is not *whether* at the local, national, or transnational level we will have to deal with multiculturalism but, rather, *how* we will deal with this reality: "As more and more cultures meet and encounter one another, it becomes evident that the future is indeed mestizo, but what kind of mestizaje will it produce?"[1] The future clearly holds a heightened mixing of cultures, but will this mixing ensue according to democratic norms of justice? Unless we are vigilant in ensuring that equality of opportunity does not privilege any particular ethnic, linguistic, or racial group, a dichotomy between empowered and unempowered cultural groups may very well emerge, with the latter being heavily comprised by peoples of color. A mestizo democracy, therefore, not only projects how multiple cultures can mutually intersect and transform one another, but emphasizes that the terms on which multiple cultures intersect—collaboration as opposed to domination, lateral as opposed to vertical, and open-ended as opposed to "tightly-scripted"—are a measure of how genuinely democratic we are.

A mestizo democracy overcomes the prevailing *unum-pluribus* divide when it comes to dealing with this growing reality of multiculturalism in the United States and elsewhere. As reviewed in chapter 1, our prevailing conceptual schemes argue either for assimilation as in the "melting pot" or for some form of separatism or "utter diversity." These antipodes share a possessive, as opposed to a relational, notion of personal or cultural identity; supposedly, one is either "this" culture or "that," with no room left for the possibility of mixing cultures—the *mezcolanza* (mixture) and *otredad* (otherness) accented by Segovia. By contrast, a mestizo democracy envisions personal, cultural, and political relationships as being steeped in the intersubjectivity underscored in phenomenology and hermeneutics and in the relational character of life emphasized by the affective, aesthetic rationality articulated by Vasconcelos and refined by the Latino theologians reviewed in chapters 2 and 3. Rather than seeing the mixing of cultures as a "problem," a mestizo democracy renders such mixing as intrinsic to human relationships and indispensable for cultivating the well-being of the community, as well as that of each of its members.

But there are other competitors for reinvigorating a sense of national political community. As I reviewed in chapter 1, Geyer's and Schlesinger's individualist renderings of U.S. liberal democracy are much too Eurocentric in terms of intellectual heritage to engage multicultural reality constructively. In Barber's case, although his indictment of the universalizing consumer inclinations of "McWorld" is well taken, his call for a revitalization of nation-states is too acultural in approach to realize his credible democratic aims. More so than in the case of these other perspectives, however, the strengths and drawbacks of Bellah's communitarianism put into relief the merits of a mestizo democracy.

Bellah's most valuable insight is that to effect political community one has to speak in terms thoroughly comprehensible to the people in question. For instance, in my case study of the multicultural relations committee I broached the issue of bringing about "unity-in-diversity" in terms appropriate to and deeply felt by that particular religious congregation. Bellah, to his credit, argues for communitarianism in language that in the U.S. context is more *affective* than many varieties of Kantian, Hegelian, Marxist, or Nietzschean discourses.

Unfortunately, Bellah's communitarian languages do not capture the ongoing mestizaje among multiple cultures ensuing in the U.S. Southwest and increasingly in other parts of the country. The rhetoric of both the Biblical tradition and civic republicanism has a parochial, expired quality. These heritages beautifully convey the nineteenth-century depiction of "the American Republic," but they are too steeped in Winthrop's vision of "the-city-on-the-hill" and the frontier mentality of Manifest Destiny to reflect the breadth and vitality essential for engendering community in the post-Eurocentric multiculturalism of the twenty-first century United States.

In contrast, a mestizo democracy is steeped in the vibrant mixing of ethnicities, languages, races, and cultures that has been ensuing in the U.S. Southwest for a significant portion of our history. Building on Wolf's insight that African American, Asian American, Latino, and Native American cultures are each integral parts of U.S. culture and not something "foreign," one can see how mestizaje provides a language that engages the growing intersection of each of these cultures both with each other and with European American culture without privileging the latter. The experience of moving between cultures and combining multiple traditions has been intrinsic to the Latino experience for almost two centuries, considerably longer when one traces mestizaje to its historical origins in the intersection of African, indigenous, and Spanish cultures in Latin America. In contrast to the vista of Manifest Destiny, a mestizo democracy accents the value of crossing borders. Likewise, in contrast to the conventional east-to-west coast rendering of U.S. history, the heritage of mestizaje captures the U.S. experience as also a south-to-north migration (the Latin American presence) and a west-to-east migration (the Asian and Pacific Rim presence). In an age in which geographic boundaries are steadily giving way to transnational conceptualizations of politics and economics, this capacity to mix and match multiple directions and to combine seeming opposites is of inestimable value.

The specific qualities a mestizo democracy brings to bear for effecting unity-in-diversity in the twenty-first century in the United States are:

- an in-depth engagement of the mixing of ethnic and racial cultures, especially confronting how racial and skin-color categories have been used both in the United States and Latin America to subordinate and denigrate people;
- a heritage of lived, heart-felt traditions and stories—such as Our Lady of Guadalupe—that vividly manifest the nexus of multiple cultures without culminating in the domination of one culture over others;
- an ethical and political belief in welcoming the 'other';
- a focus on overcoming the exclusion of diverse ethnicities and races from political, social, and economic networks of opportunity;
- a gritty commitment to democratic practices that avoids the allure of romantic idealism or a preoccupation with procedural instrumentalism;
- an articulation of an affective, aesthetic yet practical rationality that emphasizes and pursues crossing borders.

This particularly U.S. American engagement of mixing cultures in the pursuit of community offers a rich heritage upon which each of us can draw as we engage diverse 'others' in our personal lives, our neighborhoods, our social activities, and our workplaces. The affective character of this heritage and language provides a particularly compelling case for why this hermeneutical legacy should be included in twenty-first century endeavors to bring about unity-in-diversity.

In addition to challenging the "Eurocentric" castings of U.S. political languages, a mestizo democracy also moves beyond the increasingly dated white *v.* black rendering of race relations in the United States without abandoning the democratic vision of the African American civil rights movement.

This long-standing white-black framework has been invaluable for coming to terms with the legacy of slavery, de jure segregation, and de facto segregation in the United States. However, it does not capture the mixing of ethnicities and races in the U.S. Southwest or the annihilation of most indigenous tribes in the westward expansion of the U.S. frontier. As race relations in the United States ensues—not just between European Americans and 'others,' but in a context mutually including African Americans, Asian Americans, European Americans, Latinos, and Native Americans—the ethos and experience of crossing borders, intrinsic to a mestizo democracy, charts a vision of integrating cultures that moves beyond master-slave dichotomies.

An Affective, Aesthetic Yet Practical Rationality

If at the level of concrete, experiential politics a mestizo democracy offers a vibrant, lived language, at the conceptual level the affective, aesthetic rationality elicited by Vasconcelos but subsequently refined by Latino theologians, such as Elizondo and Goizueta, suggests a practical rationality distinct from that of Kant or Aristotle. In particular, this alternative practical rationality can engage the "politics of identity" as taken up by postmodernism without sliding into the relativism characterizing some postmodern perspectives.

As I have previously contended through Dussel's critique of Habermas, the difficulty with neo-Kantian types of practical reason lies in their excessive reliance on developing deontological procedures of public discourse so as to test and validate our moral intuitions. The aesthetic yet practical rationality intrinsic to a mestizo democracy assumes that universal principles are not just abstractions apart from lived experience but are realized in the myths and poetic symbols of peoples. Although Rawls's "overlapping consensus" and Habermas's discursive rationality are vital concepts for any democratic discussion concerning effecting unity-in-diversity, such notions remain too abstract to be the basis for mobilizing a lived multicultural democracy.[2] Neo-Kantian practical reason resonates even less in the hearts and minds of most U.S. Americans than the languages Bellah invokes. In the context of a mestizo democracy, Rawls and Habermas instead need to focus, in the manner of Las Casas, on the terms through which people of diverse cultural backgrounds can begin to engage in democratic discourse.

Nevertheless, the aesthetic yet practical rationality of a mestizo democracy shares with Bellah's outlook and with Aristotelian practical reason the conviction that moral rationality not only be accepted by the mind but also lived by the heart, through habits, mores, and traditions continually re-shaped by community institutions. Indeed, the ethical bearings of a mes-tizo democracy are akin to politics as an end in itself, as in an Aristotelian praxis or Arendt's nonsovereign action and freedom.

The differences between the affective, aesthetic rationality of a mestizo democracy and Aristotle's and Arendt's perspectives are two fold. First, as I indicated through Goizueta's work in chapters 3 and 4, a praxis that is merely an end in itself too easily becomes passive and disengaged from pursuing what is a just distribution of political, social, and economic opportunities. As Bickford notes, Aristotle reduces how people speak and listen to their socioeconomic backgrounds, and Arendt is unwilling to address how in-equality affects how people are seen and heard in the public realm.[3] Latino theologians temper these drawbacks by persistently depicting mestizaje as involving the overcoming of the poverty and marginalization experienced by many Latinos and many 'others' in the United States.

Second, political, social, and economic inequality affect who gets to participate and who gets heard in our public forums. If we want to realize better communication and understanding among cultures, we need to examine critically how political and social practices, especially their affective dimensions, both foster and inhibit the speaking and listening skills essential to *democratic* deliberation.[4] The affective, aesthetic yet prac-tical rationality of a mestizo democracy focuses on how to achieve equal-ity among civic interlocutors, rather than presuming that such equality already exists. Consequently, a mestizo democracy moves the public dis-course emphasized by Aristotle and Arendt in a more dynamic, egalitar-ian direction.

If the abstract practical reason of Rawls and Habermas and the static rendering of public deliberation in Aristotle and Arendt insufficiently at-tend to engendering democratic discourse amid diverse cultural traditions and economic inequalities, postmodern perspectives give up too quickly on the possibility of engendering a substantive sense of democratic com-munity among supposedly incommensurable cultures. Even to suggest that diverse cultures can intersect in a lateral if not collaborative fashion sup-posedly runs the risk of constructing hegemonic identities that "become overly unified and rigid."[5] Additionally, although Deloria's tribalism, re-viewed both in chapters 1 and 5, grants the possibility of community within small geographically situated tribal groups, it eschews the notion of com-munity for political units that transcend parochial locales.

The affective, aesthetic rationality that informs a mestizo democracy, as reviewed in chapter 3, is steeped in a holistic worldview that has enabled African, medieval European, and indigenous perspectives to intertwine, especially in Latino popular religious practices, contrary to Deloria's sectarian casting of indigenous perspectives. In addition this heritage attests to how cultural identities can be juxtaposed without leading to contradictions—a both/and as opposed to an either/or outlook. I have always found amazing how the African American, Filipino, Jamaican, Mexican, and Vietnamese members of St. Nessan's choir, examined in chapter 6, could sing in multiple languages and move almost seamlessly back and forth among their diverse cultural traditions. This harmonic convergence is in large part due to this shared aesthetic rationality.

Nevertheless, some would still contend that such an aesthetic rationality has an apolitical cast.[6] To the contrary, this aesthetic rationality's emphasis on that one's identity is realized through extended relationships beyond the self has served historically as the existential basis from which the poor and the marginalized have organized political and cultural resistance to political, social, and economic elites in Mexico and in the U.S. Southwest.

Ironically, the very fact that I have, at great length, contrasted a mestizo democracy's affective, aesthetic yet practical rationality with the outlooks of Rawls, Habermas, Aristotle, Arendt, and postmodern perspectives underscores the degree to which Eurocentric perspectives still dominate our political discourses. The historical mixing of African, European, and indigenous perspectives in mestizaje, and then the normative rearticulation of this heritage by Vasconcelos and in contemporary Latino theology, anticipates that the coming century will be marked by an increasing engagement between European and other world civilizations. Raimon Pannikar, for instance, points out that the complex challenges posed by today's global reality demand the collaboration of the world's religious traditions: "No single human or religious tradition is today self-sufficient and capable of rescuing humanity from its present predicament."[7] If this is true of religions, it is even more true of the plurality of political and moral perspectives intersecting one another, from the local to the transnational level. The ethos of a mestizo democracy is that diverse cultures, philosophies, and spiritualities can engage one another in nonviolent, albeit at times agonal, ways that culminate in mutual transformation rather than in the triumph of one tradition at the expense of all others.

Both the Reformation/Counter-Reformation debate and the Enlightenment/post-Enlightenment debates in theology and philosophy, therefore, are outdated by their very Eurocentrism. Of all the approaches I have reviewed over the previous chapters, Dussel's projection of transmodernity goes the furthest in terms of moving beyond Eurocentrism to engage non-European perspectives without abandoning the Enlightenment's project of liberation. At the same time—even though Dussel perceptively uses the Las Casas-Sepulveda debate to illustrate the challenges that lie before any genuine lateral, multicultural discourse—his argument lacks the *affective* style of the aesthetic rationality contained in popular religion and recast in intellectual terms by Latino theology.

Realizing a unity-in-diversity, whether within the United States or transnationally, entails a discourse whose substantive symbols and values move people. More so than Dussel's exposition, the aesthetic yet practical rationality of a mestizo democracy, as experienced in the lives and outlooks of a growing number of U.S. Americans, offers an existential basis for a transformation of U.S. politics. In turn, this rationality provides both an experiential and conceptual bridge that provides a way of addressing the rising impact of non-European philosophies, spiritualities, and cultural perspectives.

To Dussel's credit, he still includes European intellectual traditions as being integral to the realization of democracy in the coming century; that is, he does not reject European thought categorically due to its hegemonic hold on much of human discourse for the past five centuries. Indeed, the running contrast throughout this text between the permeable intersection of borders versus the polarizing extension of frontiers could be misinterpreted as an either/or in which the Enlightenment gets inescapably linked to the domination motif of the frontier mentality. To the contrary, the liberation motif of the Enlightenment is a noble one and will not be realized short of genuine border crossings in which multiple cultural intellectual traditions are able to engage each other on terms that facilitate mutual permeation and genuine understanding. Toward this end, a mestizo democracy pursues the *affective* basis through which we can realize a polity characterized by lateral multicultural relations of mutuality, not domination.

Madison Goes Mesoamerican

Both experientially and conceptually, a mestizo democracy is a realistic engagement of the vital need to reenvision and revitalize our political processes and institutions from the local to the transnational level to meet the challenges posed by multiculturalism. In this endeavor, we have much to learn from a figure who does not ordinarily come to mind in such debates—James Madison. Madison's relevance is not so much in his prescriptions for effecting unity-in-diversity in the late eighteenth century United States—although I will review his notion of the extended republic briefly—but in his capacity to think "outside the box" within the context of his times. Such unconventional creative verve is indispensable for envisioning nascent political schemes that can affectively and effectively engage the challenges before us.

Long before discussions of multiculturalism and unity-in-diversity became fashionable, Madison projected in *Federalist* #10 and #51 a scheme that would counter the formation of oppressive natural majorities and simultaneously foster the national common good through the contest of a myriad of diverse groups—the extended republic. Such a republic extends over a larger area of land and thus incorporates a greater number of diverse individuals, groups, and interests. By expanding the sphere of popular government through an extended republic, Madison contends that "you make it less probable that a majority of the whole will have a common motive to invade the rights of other citizens; or if such a common motive exists, it will be more difficult for all who feel it to discover their own strength and to act in unison with each other."[8] Indeed, he adds, "the larger the society…the more duly capable it will be of self-government."[9]

The practical genius of Madison's republican solution is that it incorporated the thirteen states as governing entities that would reinforce the regional plurality of beliefs and interests that thwart the rise of a natural majority at the national level. The political reality of the late 1780s was that the state governments would remain key players in the United States, albeit at a diminished level in the U.S. Constitution from what was the case in the Articles of Confederation. Madison turns a seeming negative into a positive: the states rather than being a threat to national sovereignty become essential to empowering it through an extended republic. Federalism as a division of powers between the national and state governments becomes a way to foster the extended republic that supposedly serves as a deterrent to the formation of minority or majority factions. Retaining state and local governments under the U.S. Constitution also allows for diverse governing options across the country. Madison's extended republic projects a vision of unity-in-diversity. This republic avoids both the uniformity of unitary government and the anarchy of confederal schemes by enabling multiple groups and interests to engage each other on a national level without the prospect of any faction, especially a majority, becoming oppressive in the manner of parochial democracies.[10]

The degree to which Madison's republican scheme has actually thwarted factions from dominating U.S. politics over the past two centuries is highly debatable. Indeed, over the past half century interest-group pluralism has been criticized both by those who contend that the wealthy run the country—elitism—and by those who contend that too many groups have significant access to government, culminating in gridlock—hyperpluralism. The qualitative judgment that Madison hoped an extended republic would foster in our political representatives has certainly been sullied by the degree to which our elected representatives have had to pander to political action committees and rich donors in order to reach and remain in public office.

However, to get mired in the elitist-pluralist-hyperpluralist debate is to miss the relevance of Madison's example for a mestizo democracy. As much as *Federalist* #10 and #51 have become staple entries in U.S. government textbooks and readers, we easily forget how radical his concept of an extended republic was within the context of his times. Most commentators of his day, and for that matter many of his predecessors in Western political theory, had thought that either direct or indirect democracy was best conducted in small geographic communities, as in the ancient Greek city-states. Indeed, a principal preoccupation of the Anti-Federalists was preserving "likenesses" in local communities.[11] Madison had the foresight to see that a representative democracy incorporating federalism was the sensible way to realize a viable nation-state from among thirteen states comprising multiple peoples and groups and whose geographic expanse far exceeded that of previous experiments in popular government.

Given the challenges posed by multiculturalism within the United States and the increasing transnational character of daily life, we are at another critical historical juncture analogous to that experienced by Madison and the other founders of the United States. We need to dare to re-envision the U.S. scheme of unity-in-diversity at local, regional, and national levels and, in turn, to project transnational democratic initiatives capable of contending with global economic forces. Just as Madison's "extended republic" challenged prevailing thinking regarding the realization of popular government over large geographic areas and their diverse constituencies, today we need to move beyond the *unum-pluribus* divide by projecting creative democratic schemes from the local to the transnational level that welcome and combine multiple cultural identities.

A mestizo democracy challenges Madison's vision of unity-in-diversity in two ways. First, Madison's pluralism is cast too much in terms of what Isaiah Berlin terms "negative liberty"—freedom from government and social tyranny.[12] Supposedly the sheer number of distinct groups comprising the country, reinforced by diverse geographic regions and multiple state governments, will thwart the predominance of any one faction. However, Madison gives little attention to the possibility, at the center of mestizo democracy, that cultural groups can engage in mutual substantive interaction without culminating in the domination or assimilation of one group by the other. The either/or he sets up in *Federalist* #10 between curing the causes of faction or controlling its effects—with Madison opting for the latter—does not leave much room for considering the qualitative benefits of multicultural interchange for the interacting cultural groups and for the country. Madison's preoccupation with the deleterious aspects of factions prevents him from realizing that an extended republic will never be truly pluralistic unless it addresses the character of the interaction among its constituent groups.

Beyond just recognizing how the intersection of multiple groups and interests negates the likelihood of preponderant factions, a mestizo democracy underscores that such interaction, even if at times painful, expands the horizons of the intersecting groups and can engender a substantive consensus that is distinct from, yet reflective of, the contributions of the intersecting groups. Pluralism should be seen not just as a deterrent to tyranny but as an ethos of inclusion. Madison's aim to sustain unity *through* diversity is sound, but to cope with the multicultural challenges of the twenty-first century, his institutional solution must be recast in terms of the substantive pluralism of crossing borders. Unlike frontiers, borders are permeable: mestizaje as a political theory suggests that a dynamic yet democratic sense of community reflective of our multiple, not univocal, cultural identities can ensue through such crossings.

Second, in structural terms, we need to disentangle Madison's principal institutional means of fostering unity-in-diversity—the extended republic—from its tight *geographic* moorings. In a world in which reconciling multiple identities is increasingly part and parcel of daily life, the quality of our political conduct will be primarily measured by our capacity for crossing borders. State and local governments in the United States have played a vital role in fostering the political diversity sought by Madison, but they should not be the only means by which we ensure the constructive intersection of diverse perspectives, especially cultural ones. Cumulative voting, reviewed in chapter 7, is just one example of how to encourage political mobilization and coalition building among diverse interests without relying on geographic districts. On the transnational level, also as suggested in chapter 7, we need the courage to project schemes of transnational sovereignty, such as a council comprised of the northern states of Mexico and the states of the U.S. Southwest, to consider the issues of *la frontera*. A mestizo democracy retains from Madison's extended republic the notion that political representation should reflect a multiplicity of interests and groups, but it moves beyond territorial federalism to create additional ways in which our growing cornucopia of cultural groups can engage one another in egalitarian discourse.

My emphasis on moving beyond territorial boundaries and "thickly" defined cultural identities is why throughout this text I have looked askance at representation schemes that strive to increase the access of diverse groups to political forums solely through geographic districts, such as in Taylor's "asymmetrical federalism" or in gerrymandered single-member "majority-minority" districts. Particularly odious are corporatist schemes that would divide political representation strictly according to ethnic or racial groups; such schemes end up petrifying rather than mixing cultures. Consequently, more research is needed on practical ways— which are neither territorial nor corporatist in character—to foster multicultural interaction in our political processes and institutions. In turn, research is needed also on the degree to which the affective, aesthetic rationality of a mestizo democracy suggests a basis for the emergence of powerful multiethnic, multiracial political coalitions. Political leaders who grasp how to weave together a set of symbols and issues that reflect this holistic outlook could extensively transform U.S. if not transnational politics in the twenty-first century.

In the end, although the norms and structures of Madisonian pluralism may be dated, his courage to think creatively "against the grain" is not. As disparate as Barber's and Huntington's renderings of the growing global economy are, they both point to the need to develop transnational political mores and institutions that can contend in democratic terms with the expanding power structure of the global economy. Just as Madison dared to envision an extended republic beyond the pale of parochial city-states, we need to envision and realize a transnational democratic politics beyond the increasingly timeworn character of nation-states. Unfortunately, neither Barber's Manichean distinction between McWorld and jihad nor Huntington's accent on "the clash of civilizations" contribute much toward this end.

Contrary to the conventional possessive rendering of identity, a mestizo democracy emphasizes the capacity for creatively mixing and matching multiple identities. From this latter basis, we can begin to project transnational democratic processes and institutions—whether they take the shape of (1) regional associations like the EU or, hypothetically, an entity linking Canada, the United States, and Latin America or (2) scenarios of *democratic* world government. Given the rising level of protest against the lack of accountability of transnational economic bodies such as the World Trade Organization and the International Monetary Fund, the time is ripe for developing transnational political bodies that vigilantly ensure such accountability. Much more research is needed on transnational political developments already underway and on what other possibilities might be forthcoming.

Essentially, however, be it on the local or transnational level, a mestizo democracy entails recasting political mores, processes, and structures to enable distinct cultures and creeds to intersect and transform each other and the political community in a civil yet substantive fashion.

Mestizaje as a political theory specifically amplifies democracy's key characteristics of *plurality, ambiguity,* and *publicness.*[13] Contrary to those who would disparage the pursuit of a substantive consensus in an age of radically diverse groups, a mestizo democracy suggests that unity-in-diversity can be realized through the mutual interchange of diverse cultures. Contrary to those who contend that one substantive good should be uniformly shared by all or, conversely, that such substantive norms should be confined to one's particular ethnic, linguistic, racial, or religious community, a mestizo democracy maintains that moral and political debates among individuals, groups, and cultures can ensue without culminating in complete unanimity or irresolvable disunity. Finally, in view of the capacity of privileged elites to prevail in presumably "public" debates, a mestizo democracy counters that only through the inclusion of marginalized groups can we begin to realize a qualitative, public discourse.

At the same time, such arid and analytical presentations do not capture the vivid *affective,* aesthetic character of the Mesoamerican heritage of combining opposites that is at the heart of a mestizo democracy. To realize a democratic unity-in-diversity among multiple cultures, we need to temper modernity's pervasive rendering of life in materialistic, utilitarian, and even scientific terms with the holistic, mythopoeic rendering of reality, especially as captured in the mixing of African, European, and indigenous perspectives in Latino spirituality. This "indigenous turn"—a concrete cultural hermeneutical engagement of the mixing of world views in the Americas—is what distinguishes a mestizo democracy from attempts in contemporary political theory that yearn to move beyond modernity but whose affective discourse remains Eurocentric. Far from being a retreat from politics, such "tempering" refocuses our attention on pursuing terms of conversation—Las Casas's quest—through which all persons, and especially the poor, can gain access to the political, social, and economic relations that circumscribe their lives.

Ultimately, the common good is at stake in terms of the degree to which lateral, intersubjective relations between members of diverse cultures characterize our political communities. Do we really pine for a universalism in which human beings are reduced to being consumers and commodities of economic exchange? Would we prefer instead a cultural separatism in which xenophobia leads to relentless conflict among peoples? Or do we want a democracy that integrates, not assimilates, its plural constitutive cultures so as to realize a substantive unity-in-diversity? Truly, this vision leads us along a path toward a mestizo democracy.

Notes

• • •

Introduction

1. John Courtney Murray, S.J., *We Hold These Truths: Catholic Reflection on the America Proposition*, 45.
2. Robert N. Bellah et al., *The Good Society*, 300.
3. "Catholics and the Presidency," 384.
4. Sara Lawrence Lightfoot, interview by Bill Moyers, in *A World of Ideas: Conversations with Thoughtful Men And Women about American Life Today and the Ideas Shaping Our Future*, 159. Richard Rose articulates Lightfoot's point in terms of the chasm between proponents and critics of pluralism: "Proponents of the philosophy of pluralism argue that we should not expect Americans to agree about the ultimate goals of society. Agreement is necessary only about the rules of the game by which governments resolve disputes among groups advancing a plurality of demands. Variety is welcomed as a good in itself; politics becomes the means of reconciling competing efforts to define a good society. Critics of pluralism emphasize the common attributes and desires that individual members of society share. They believe that the power of government should be used to identify what is in the common good, or best for the majority, and that everyone must then share in it" (Richard Rose, *What is Governing: Purpose and Policy in Washington*, 1).
5. Lightfoot, interview by Bill Moyers, 159.
6. In scholarship of Latin American culture one finds practically as many references to *mulatez*—the mixing of Africans and Europeans—as to mestizaje. Undoubtedly, one cannot grasp the cultures of most of the countries of the Caribbean, as well as that of Brazil, without engaging this African legacy. However, Mexico actually was an important disembarkation locale for slave ships in Spanish Colonial America. Indeed, a slave rebellion ensued in Mexico as early as 1537. Slavery itself was finally done away with in Mexico in the 1820s. For further scholarship on the African legacy and presence in Mexico, *see* Gonzolo Aguirre Beltrán, *La Población negra de México*.
7. Robert N. Bellah et al., *Habits of the Heart: Individualism and Commitment in American Life*, 27–35.
8. Stephen L. Carter, *The Culture of Disbelief*.
9. Michael and Julia Mitchell Corbett, *Politics and Religion in the United States*, 387–406.

10. Carter, *Culture of Disbelief,* 105–23.
11. Kenneth D. Wald, *Religion and Politics in the United States,* 4.
12. Marvin L. Krier Mich, *Catholic Social Teaching and Movements,* 165–75.
13. Bellah et al., *Good Society,* 301.

Chapter 1

1. Arthur Schlesinger, Jr., *The Disuniting of America,* 117.
2. Georgie Anne Geyer, *Americans No More,* 101–2.
3. Ibid., 50.
4. Ibid., 107.
5. Ibid., 108.
6. Ibid., 111–13.
7. Ibid., 137–42.
8. Ibid., 54.
9. Schlesinger, *Disuniting of America,* 16–17.
10. Ibid., 76.
11. Ibid., 72.
12. Geyer, *Americans No More,* 277–317.
13. Ibid., 131.
14. Schlesinger, *Disuniting of America,* 15.
15. Ibid., 36.
16. Ibid., 117.
17. Bharti Mukherjee, interview by Bill Moyers, in *A World of Ideas II: Public Opinions From Private Citizens,* 8.
18. Schlesinger, *Disuniting of America,* 127.
19. Labeling this last example "separatist" could be misleading because hatred of non-White and non-"Aryan" peoples manifested by the Ku Klux Klan and the neo-Nazis ultimately culminates in the genocide of supposedly inferior races and religions—racial extermination not separation.
20. Vine Deloria, Jr., *God is Red,* 62.
21. Ibid., 67.
22. Ibid., 73.
23. Ibid., 274.
24. Ibid., 281.
25. Ibid., 166–67.
26. Vine Deloria, Jr., *Custer Died for Your Sins,* 176, 180.
27. Luther Standing Bear, quoted in Vine Deloria, Jr., *God is Red,* 60.
28. *God is Red,* 290–91.
29. Ibid., 194.
30. Ibid., 201.
31. I am indebted to both Benjamin Barber and Michael Walzer in for my distinction between thick and thin moral discourses. *See* Benjamin Barber, *Strong Democracy: Participatory Politics for a New Age,* and Michael Walzer, *Thick and Thin: Moral Arguments at Home or Abroad.*

32. Benjamin Barber, *Jihad vs. McWorld.*
33. Ibid., 4.
34. Ibid., 215.
35. Ibid., 8.
36. Ibid., 6.
37. Ibid., 279.
38. Ibid., 244.
39. Ibid., 224.
40. Ibid., 228.
41. Ibid., 219–20.
42. Gary Brent Madison, *The Hermeneutics of Postmodernity: Figures and Themes,* 49.
43. Hans-Georg Gadamer, *Truth and Method,* 236.
44. Madison, *Hermeneutics of Postmodernity,* 114.
45. Gadamer, *Truth and Method,* 238.
46. Ibid., 273.
47. Leslie Paul Thiele, *Thinking Politics: Perspectives in Ancient, Modern, and Postmodern Political Theory,* 19.
48. Madison, *The Hermeneutics of Postmodernity,* 191.
49. In contrast to a procedural conceptualization of pluralism, Arendt focuses on how plurality is the ontological condition for political action: "While all aspects of the human condition are somehow related to politics, this plurality is specifically the condition—not only the *conditio sine qua non,* but the *conditio per quam*—of all political life. . . . Action would be unnecessary luxury, a capricious interference with general laws of behavior, if men were endlessly reproducible repetitions of the same model, whose nature or essence was the same for all and as predictable as the nature or essence of any other thing. Plurality is the condition of human action because we are all the same as anyone else who ever lived, lives, or will live." Hannah Arendt, *The Human Condition,* 7–8.
50. Ibid., 182–84.
51. Ibid., 183.
52. Hannah Arendt, *On Revolution,* 127.
53. Susan Bickford, *The Dissonance of Democracy,* 96.
54. Arendt, *Human Condition,* 183.
55. Gadamer, *Philosophical Hermeneutics,* 16.
56. Gary Brent Madison, *Understanding: A Phenomenological-Pragmatical Analysis,* 65.
57. Maurice Merleau-Ponty, *Signs,* 115.
58. Ibid.
59. Ibid., 118.
60. Clifford Geertz, *The Interpretation of Cultures,* 16.
61. Ibid., 23.
62. Ibid., 30.
63. Madison, *Hermeneutics of Postmodernity,* 117.
64. Merleau-Ponty, *Signs,* 120.
65. Ibid., 120, 139.
66. Geertz, *Interpretation of Cultures,* 37.
67. Ibid., 44.

68. Ibid., 212.

69. Merleau-Ponty, *Signs*, 124.

70. Madison, *Hermeneutics of Postmodernity*, 70–71, 114–15.

71. Paul Ricoeur, *History and Truth*, 283.

72. Madison, *Understanding*, 45. The phrase "one best way" comes from Frederick Taylor's positivist notion of scientific management. For more on Taylor and scientific management see Robert Denhardt, *Public Administration*, 306–11.

73. Hans-Georg Gadamer, *Philosophical Hermeneutics*, 17.

74. Madison, *Hermeneutics of Postmodernity*, 51–52, 115.

75. Ibid., 102–3.

76. Thiele, *Thinking Politics*, 101.

77. Ibid., 82.

78. Stephen Eric Bronner, "Postmodernism and Poststructuralism," in *Twentieth Century Political Theory: A Reader*, 237.

79. Madison, *Hermeneutics of Postmodernity*, 70.

80. Ibid., 71.

81. Ibid., 114.

82. Ibid.

83. Ibid., 115.

84. Ibid.

85. Fred Dallmayr, *Beyond Orientalism: Essays on Cross-Cultural Encounter*, 41.

86. Hans-Georg Gadamer, "Hermeneutics and Logocentrism," quoted in Dallmayr, *Beyond Orientalism*, 49.

87. Dallmayr, *Beyond Orientalism*, 57.

88. Jacques Derrida, *The Other Heading: Reflections on Today's Europe*, quoted in Dallmayr, *Beyond Orientalism*, 58.

89. Hwa Yol Jung, *Rethinking Political Theory: Essays in Phenomenology and the Study of Politics*, 162.

90. Maurice Merleau-Ponty, *Themes from the Lectures at the College de France, 1952–1960*, quoted in Jung, *Rethinking Politcal Theory*, 163.

91. Jung, *Rethinking Politcal Theory*, 163.

92. Madison, *Hermeneutics of Postmodernity*, 115.

93. Jung, *Rethinking Political Theory*, 165.

94. Hans-Georg Gadamer, *Das Erbe Europas*, quoted in Dallmayr, *Beyond Orientalism*, 54.

95. Derrida, *The Other Heading*, quoted in Dallmayr, *Beyond Orientalism*, 57–58.

96. Thomas Pantham, "Some Dimensions of the Universality of Philosophical Hermeneutics: A Conversation with Hans-Georg Gadamer," 132.

97. Susan Wolf, "Comment," in *Multiculturalism: Examining The Politics of Recognition*, 81.

98. Mukherjee, interview by Bill Moyers, 9.

99. Schlesinger, *Disuniting of America*, 138.

100. Robert N. Bellah et al., *Habits of the Heart: Individualism and Commitment in American Life*, 27–35. It must be noted that Bellah and his consociates in *Habits of the Heart* paint a rather pessimistic portrait of the chance that these alternative discourses will

lead to a political transformation in a communitarian direction. Throughout the work they illustrate how difficult it is for the persons interviewed to articulate their framework of values in terms other than a materialistic individualism or a behavioral individualism drawn from therapeutic discourse.

101. The term "premise keepers" was used by Bettia Martinez in her remarks at a plenary session at the interdisciplinary conference "Hispanics: Cultural Locations," University of San Francisco, October 1997.

102. Lightfoot, interview by Bill Moyers, 159–60.

103. United States Catholic Conference, *Cultural Pluralism in the United States*, #22.

Chapter 2

1. Gloria Anzaldúa, *Borderlands/La Frontera: The New Mestiza*, 5.

2. Richard Nuccio, *What's Wrong, Who's Right in Central America*, 3–6.

3. Allan Figueroa Deck notes that another factor highlighting the medieval orientation of the Spanish colonies as opposed to the modern orientation of the English colonies is that the latter were literate from the outset, whereas oral communication was predominant in pre-and post-Cortés Mexico: "Individualism is not enhanced by orality since knowledge is a collective patrimony" (Allan Figueroa Deck, *The Second Wave: Hispanic Ministry and the Evangelization of Cultures*, 43).

4. Anzaldúa, *Borderlands/La Frontera*, 5.

5. Interestingly, Costa Rica, frequently held up as "the model Latin American democracy" has a history that more closely parallels the English than the Spanish colonization of the Americas. In Costa Rica the Spanish found few indigenous tribes and vanquished them quickly in battle. At the same time, the lack of mineral wealth in this colony led the Spanish to focus more on the other regions of Central America. Consequently, instead of large mining operations and landed estates being served by the indigenous population being established, in Costa Rica small family farms were the order of the day without much interference from Spain; a large but almost exclusively Spanish, not mestizo, middle class developed, as similarly occurred in the English colonies (Nuccio, *What's Wrong, Who's Right in Central America*, 25–27).

6. José Vasconcelos, *The Cosmic Race: A Bilingual Edition*, 3.

7. Ibid., 9.

8. Joseba Gabilondo, afterword to the 1997 edition, in Vasconcelos, *The Cosmic Race*, 108.

9. John Haddox, *Vasconcelos of Mexico: Philosopher and Prophet*, 12–49; Fernando Salmerón, "Mexican Philosophers of the Twentieth Century," in *Major Trends in Mexican Philosophy*, 266–70; Patrick Romanell, *Making of the Mexican Mind: A Study in Recent Mexican Thought*, 104–38.

10. Vasconcelos, *Cosmic Race*, 25.

11. Ibid., 28.

12. Ibid., 29.

13. Ibid.

14. Ibid.

15. Ibid., 30.

16. Ibid., 39.

17. Ibid., 30.

18. Didier T. Jaén, introduction to Vasconcelos, *Cosmic Race*, ix.

19. Vasconcelos, *Cosmic Race*, 32.

20. Gabilondo, afterword to Vasconcelos, *Cosmic Race*, 108.

21. Ana María Díaz-Stevens and Anthony M. Stevens-Arroyo, *Recognizing the Latino Resurgence in U.S. Religion: The Emmaus Paradigm*, 7.

22. Vasconcelos, *Cosmic Race*, 17.

23. Ibid., 38–39.

24. Ibid., 5.

25. Roberto Goizueta, *Caminemos con Jesús: Toward a Hispanic/Latino Theology of Accompaniment*, 125.

26. Vasconcelos, *Cosmic Race*, 34.

27. Jaén, introduction to Vasconcelos, *Cosmic Race*, xiv.

28. Gabilondo, afterword to Vasconcelos, *Cosmic Race*, 102.

29. Jaén, introduction to Vasconcelos, *Cosmic Race*, xxiv.

30. Carlos Fuentes, interview by Bill Moyers, in *A World of Ideas: Conversations with Thoughtful Men and Women about American Life Today and the Ideas Shaping our Future*, 506.

31. Vasconcelos, *Cosmic Race*, 10–11.

32. Gabilondo, afterword to Vasconcelos, *Cosmic Race*, 100.

33. Díaz-Stevens and Stevens-Arroyo, *Recognizing the Latino Resurgence in U.S. Religion*, 7.

34. Gabilondo, afterword to Vasconcelos, *Cosmic Race*, 110.

35. Díaz-Stevens and Stevens-Arroyo, *Recognizing the Latino Resurgence in U.S. Religion*, 7.

36. Fuentes, interview by Bill Moyers, in *A World of Ideas*, 507.

37. Geoffrey Fox, *Hispanic Nation: Culture, Politics, and the Construction of Identity*, 68.

38. Deck, *Second Wave*, 47; Fox, *Hispanic Nation*, 71.

39. Rodolfo Acuña, *Occupied America: A History of Chicanos*, 54–55; F. Arturo Rosales, *Chicano!: The History of the American Civil Rights Movement*, 154–55.

40. Fox, *Hispanic Nation*, 76.

41. Deck, *Second Wave*, 47–48.

42. United States Bureau of the Census, *Census 2000 Redistricting Data*, P.L. 94–171; "The Changing Color of America," A-14. I have substituted *Latino* for the term used by the U.S. Bureau of the Census, *Hispanic*. The Bureau of the Census considers *Hispanic* to be an ethnic not a racial classification; therefore, Hispanics can identify themselves in any of the following race categories: black, white, Asian, native Hawaiian and other Pacific Islander, American Indian and Alaska native, some other race, and two or more races.

43. "Mexicans Pace U.S. Hispanic Surge," A-4.

44. Bureau of the Census, *Census 2000*; Fox, *Hispanic Nation*, 20–21.

45. Eric Schmitt, "Census Shows Big Gain for Mexican-Americans," A-22.

46. "Mexicans Pace U.S. Hispanic Surge," A-4.

47. "U.S. to Have World's Second Largest Hispanic Population," http://efe.es/. (EFE is a

Spanish news service.) As of 1990 no other non-English language in the U.S. had more than two million speakers (Fox, *Hispanic Nation,* 37).

48. Fox, *Hispanic Nation,* 21.

49. Bureau of the Census, *Census 2000;* Steve H. Murdock et al., *The Texas Challenge: Population Change and the Future of Texas,* 22–30.

50. Murdock, et al., *Texas Challenge,* 22–30.

51. Population Estimates and Projections Program, Texas State Data Center et al., "Projections of the Populations of Texas and Counties in Texas by Age, Sex, and Race/ Ethnicity."

52. City of Houston, Planning and Development Department, *Demographic and Land Use Profile for Houston, Texas;* "Census 2000: Texas at a Glance," A-1; Bureau of the Census, *Census 2000.*

53. Murdock et al., *Texas Challenge,* 222–23.

54. Virgil Elizondo, *The Future is Mestizo: Life Where Cultures Meet,* 56.

55. Ibid., 26.

56. Ibid., 12.

57. Ibid., 20.

58. Ibid., 95.

59. Rosemary Johnston, "Theologians Ponder Meaning of Borders," 11.

60. Ibid.

61. Ibid.

62. Virgil Elizondo, *Guadalupe: Mother of the New Creation,* 135.

63. Goizueta, *Caminemos con Jesús,* 121.

64. Rigoberta Menchú, *I, Rigoberta Menchú: An Indian Woman in Guatemala,* 1–2.

65. The contradictions in the Mexican approach to race and especially skin color distinctions is captured in "The *Güera,*" in Patrick Oster, *The Mexicans: A Personal Portrait of a People,* 247–58.

66. Anzaldúa, *Borderlands,* 17–18.

67. Ibid., 16.

68. Ibid., 27–28.

69. Ibid., 31.

70. Ibid., 30–31.

71. Ibid., 31.

72. Ibid., 78.

73. Ibid., Preface.

74. Robert Maldonado. "*¿La Conquista?* Latin American (*Mestizaje*) Reflections on the Biblical Conquest," 25.

75. Anzaldúa, *Borderlands,* 62.

76. Elizondo, *Future is Mestizo,* 109.

77. Ibid.

78. Ibid., 96.

79. Ibid., 93.

80. Ibid., 94.

81. Anzaldúa, *Borderlands,* 63–64.

82. Elizondo, for instance, points out that in his early religious studies it seemed that

"anything that did not conform to U.S. [European-American] Catholicism was wrong and stupid" (*Future is Mestizo*, 58). For more on Taylor and scientific management see Robert Denhardt, *Public Administration: An Action Approach,* 306–11.

83. Anzaldúa, *Borderlands,* 78–79.
84. Elizondo, *Future is Mestizo,* 84.
85. Ibid., 26.

Chapter 3

1. Fernando F. Segovia, "Two Places and No Place on Which to Stand: Mixture and Otherness in Hispanic American Theology," in *Mestizo Christianity: Theology From the Latino Perspective,* 29.
2. In addition such divides are not just cultural but economic. As Allan Figueroa Deck notes, Latinos find themselves between the realities of the developed and developing world. Whereas most people in Latin America face poverty and economic oppression, many Latinos in the U.S. are oriented by the middle-class way of life even if they are statistically poor. Consequently, according to Deck, a liberation theology whose critique of oppression is based only on the long-standing Latin American experience, will not, regardless of its relevance, have the same *affect* among Latinos in the United States (Allan Figueroa Deck, "The Spirituality of United States Hispanics: An Introductory Essay," in *Mestizo Christianity,* 228).
3. Roberto S. Goizueta, "The Significance of U.S. Hispanic Experience for Theological Method," in *Mestizo Christianity,* 85.
4. Segovia, "Two Places and No Place on Which to Stand," 31.
5. Arturo J. Bañuelas, "U.S. Hispanic Theology: An Initial Assessment," in *Mestizo Christianity,* 59.
6. Justo L. González, *Santa Biblia: The Bible Through Hispanic Eyes,* 85.
7. Ibid., 86.
8. Ibid., 85–86.
9. Ibid., 86.
10. Carlos Fuentes, interview by Bill Moyers, in *A World of Ideas: Conversations with Thoughtful Men and Women about American Life Today and the Ideas Shaping our Future,* 513.
11. Gonzáles, *Santa Biblia,* 88. Gonzáles adopts the term "fluid identity boundaries" from Donna Nolan Fewell, "Joshua," in *The Woman's Bible Commentary.*
12. Ibid., 113.
13. Ada María Isasi-Díaz, *Mujerista Theology: A Theology for the Twenty-First Century,* 18.
14. Ibid., 19.
15. Virgil Elizondo, *Guadalupe: Mother of the New Creation,* 132–34.
16. Orlando O. Espín, "Tradition and Popular Religion: An Understanding of the *Sensus Fidelium,*" in *Mestizo Christianity,* 154.
17. Orlando O. Espín, *The Faith of the People: Theological Reflections on Popular Catholicism,* 122, 124.

18. Ibid., 127.
19. Espín, "Tradition and Popular Religion," 155.
20. Justo L. González, "Hispanics in the New Reformation," in *Mestizo Christianity*, 240.
21. Ibid., 245.
22. Ibid.
23. Ibid., 243.
24. Ibid., 253.
25. Ibid.
26. Ibid., 255.
27. Andrew Sung Park, *Racial Conflict and Healing: An Asian-American Theological Perspective*, 90.
28. Andrew Greeley, *The Catholic Myth: The Behavior and Beliefs of American Catholics*, 45.
29. Ibid., 45–48.
30. Mark Massa, *Catholics and American Culture*, 3–10.
31. Ana María Díaz-Stevens and Anthony M. Stevens-Arroyo, *Recognizing The Latino Resurgence in U.S. Religion: The Emmaus Paradigm*, 235.
32. Ibid.
33. Allan Figueroa Deck, *The Second Wave: Hispanic Ministry and the Evangelization of Cultures*, 1.
34. Virgil Elizondo, foreword, to Deck, *Second Wave*, xv.
35. Elizondo, *Guadalupe*, 116.
36. Ibid., 118.
37. Sixto J. García, "Sources and Loci of Hispanic Theology," in *Mestizo Christianity*, 119.
38. Elizondo, *Guadalupe*, 117.
39. Roberto S. Goizueta, *Caminemos con Jesús: Toward a Hispanic/Latino Theology of Accompaniment*, 160.
40. Ada María Isasi-Díaz, "*Mujerista* Theology's Method: A Liberative *Praxis*, A Way of Life," in *Mestizo Christianity*, 185.
41. Virgil Elizondo, *The Future is Mestizo: Life Where Cultures Meet*, 93.
42. Marcos J. Villamán, "*Iglesia e Inculturación*," quoted in Maria Pilar Aquino Vargas, "Directions and Foundations of Hispanic/Latino Theology: Toward a *Mestiza* Theology of Liberation," in *Mestizo Christianity: Theology from the Latin Perspective*, ed. Arturo J. Bañuelas, 197.
43. Isasi-Díaz, *Mujerista Theology*, 65. Isasi-Díaz actually is much more explicit than any of the other Latino theologians regarding the public policies reflective of a grassroots, inductive spirituality that seeks to transform decision-making structures of domination into those of collaboration. She advocates for full employment, an adequate minimum wage, redistributive inheritance and wealth taxes, comparable worth, economic democracy, preventive health care available to all, increased representation of Latinos/as in political office, and equitable refinancing of public education not tied to de facto segregation.
44. Deck, *Second Wave*, 123.

45. Gilkey casts his remarks in terms of reservations that he has about the modernizing dimension of the reforms of the Roman Catholic Church instituted by Vatican II. It would be a mistake, however, to believe that he is opting instead for a restoration of a medieval perspective. For instance, it could be argued that Vatican II, granting all of its significant accomplishments, at least initially downplayed the importance of popular religion, especially the processions, rosaries, and rituals in the Spanish-speaking tradition. But these time-hewn liturgical practices are both heartfelt and expressive of an alternative rationality to the modern worldview. Therefore, why reinvigorate Catholic liturgy with Latin so as to catalyze a sense of holistic awe when one has Latino popular spirituality, which is much more expressive of the people's spirituality and much more open to non-European views in the face of the "monolithic reason" of modernity? Goizueta, "In Defense of Reason," 25.

46. Ana María Díaz-Stevens and Anthony M. Stevens-Arroyo, *Recognizing the Latino Resurgence in U.S. Religion: The Emmaus Paradigm*, 222.

47. Deck, *The Second Wave*, 101.

48. Ismael García, *Dignidad: Ethics Through Hispanic Eyes*, 17.

49. Ibid.

50. Goizueta, "Significance of U.S. Hispanic Experience for Theological Method," 91.

51. Joseph A. Fiorenza, "*Encuentro* 2000: A Time to Address Pressing Issues," 24.

52. Deck, *The Second Wave*, 150. *Conjunto* literally means in entirety or as a whole. For more on this pastoral planing in communal style, see Ana María Pineda, "Pastoral de Conjunto," in *Mestizo Christianity*, 126–31.

53. Isasi-Díaz, *Mujerista Theology*, 27.

54. Ibid., 132–33.

55. Ibid., 65–66.

56. Ernesto Cortes, interview by Bill Moyers, in *A World of Ideas II: Public Opinions from Private Citizens*, 147.

57. Goizueta, *Caminemos con Jesús*, 17.

58. García, *Dignidad*, 17–19.

59. Pineda, "Pastoral de Conjunto," in *Mestizo Christianity*, 130.

60. Ibid., p. 130.

61. Goizueta, *Caminemos con Jesús*, 203.

62. Elizondo, *Guadalupe*, 107.

63. Ibid., 126.

64. Ibid., 135.

65. Ibid., 129.

66. García, *Dignidad*, 172.

67. Bañuelas, "U.S. Hispanic Theology," 72.

68. Although I am sympathetic to García's contention that African Americans, Puerto Ricans, and Native Americans are "conquered and colonized nations and peoples," his conclusion that the United States is therefore "a federation of nations, not just a plurality of ethnic groups" comes very close to advocating corporatism, the deleterious consequences of which I address in chapter 5 (García, *Dignidad*, 96).

69. Segovia, "Two Places and No Place on Which to Stand," 35.

70. Ibid., 36.

71. Espín, "Tradition and Popular Religion," 157.
72. Goizueta, *Caminemos con Jesús,* 32–37.
73. Elizondo, *Guadalupe,* 121.
74. Ibid., 120.
75. Deck, *Second Wave,* 54–73.
76. González, "Hispanics in the New Reformation," 250.
77. Ibid., 253.
78. González, *Santa Biblia,* 42.
79. González, "Hispanics in the New Reformation," 254.
80. Aquino Vargas, "Directions and Foundations," in *Mestizo Christianity,* 200.
81. González, *Santa Biblia,* 117
82. Ibid., 118.
83. Ibid., 55.
84. Aquino Vargas, "Directions and Foundations," in *Mestizo Christianity,* 201.
85. Ibid., 200.
86. Elizondo, *Guadalupe,* 115.
87. Ibid., 135.
88. Harold Recinos, "Mission: A Latino Pastoral Theology," in *Mestizo Christianity,* 133.
89. Segovia, "Two Places and No Place on Which to Stand," 38.
90. Goizueta, "Significance of U.S. Hispanic Experience for Theological Method," 93.
91. Elizondo, *Guadalupe,* 135.
92. Recinos, "Mission," 133.
93. Cortes, interview by Bill Moyers, in *A World of Ideas II,* 47.
94. Goizueta, *Caminemos con Jesús,* 180.
95. Bañuelas, "U.S. Hispanic Theology," 77.
96. Aquino Vargas, "Directions and Foundations," in *Mestizo Christianity,* 205.
97. Elizondo, *Guadalupe,* 136.
98. Ibid., 129.

Chapter 4

1. Enrique Dussel, *The Invention of the Americas: Eclipse of "the Other" and the Myth of Modernity,* 90.
2. Ibid., 20.
3. Ibid., 19.
4. Ibid., 33.
5. Ibid., 50.
6. Ibid., 25.
7. Ibid., 35. Other Latino scholars echo Dussel's indictment of the subject-object dichotomy in modern philosophy as culminating with the violation of the 'other'. For instance, Gloria Anzaldúa argues that "in trying to become 'objective,' Western culture made 'objects' of things and people when it distanced itself from them, thereby losing 'touch' with them. This dichotomy is the root of all violence" (Anzaldúa,

Borderlands/La Frontera: The New Mestiza, 37). In the same vein, Ada María Isasi-Díaz argues that pursuing a praxis of mestizaje entails a rejection of a rationality that leads to "a competitive individualism that destroys our sense of community and makes us see life as a win-lose situation" (Ada María Isasi-Díaz, *En la Lucha/In the Struggle: A Hispanic Women's Liberation Theology,* 196–97).

8.   Dussel, *Invention of the Americas,* 85.
9.   Ibid., 43.
10.   Leslie Paul Thiele, *Thinking Politics: Perspectives in Ancient, Modern, and Postmodern Political Theory,* 110.
11.   Ana María Pineda, "The Colloquies and Theological Discourse: Culture as a Locus for Theology," 27–33.
12.   Dussel, *Invention of the Americas,* 55.
13.   Ibid., 50.
14.   Ibid., 85. In the early 1980s it became fashionable to talk in political-economy circles about a North-South "dialogue." The term *dialogue* was a point of derision among some Latin American scholars, for it falsely projected the notion that the powers of the developed and developing world—again, note the modernist language—were on equal terms in such a dialogue. The North American Free Trade Agreement and subsequent international economic agreements are again bringing this euphemism of dialogue back into vogue without addressing what changes would really have to take place in order to accommodate a genuine dialogue between presently unevenly matched parties.
15.   Graciela Limón, *Song of the Hummingbird,* 216–17.
16.   Dussel, *Invention of the Americas,* 36.
17.   Ibid., 97.
18.   Ibid.
19.   Ibid., 101.
20.   Ibid., 103.
21.   Ibid., 116.
22.   Virgil Elizondo, *Guadalupe: Mother of the New Creation,* 28–30.
23.   Dussell, *Invention of the Americas,* 117.
24.   Octavio Paz, *The Labyrinth of Solitude,* 369.
25.   Ibid., 369–70.
26.   Ibid., 361.
27.   Ibid., 102–3.
28.   Ibid., 363.
29.   Ibid., 363–64.
30.   Ibid., 105.
31.   Ibid., 100.
32.   Ibid., 92.
33.   Ibid., 102.
34.   Ibid., 315.
35.   Ibid., 324.
36.   Ibid., 371.
37.   Ibid., 145.

38. Ibid., 372.
39. Ibid., 324.
40. Ibid., 362.
41. Ibid.
42. Ibid., 366.
43. Ibid., 339.
44. Ibid.
45. Ibid., 47.
46. Ibid., 209, 211.
47. Ibid., 370. In terms of Mexico's "plurality of pasts," see also Carlos Fuentes, *A New Time for Mexico*, 22–23.
48. Dussel, *Invention of the Americas*, 127.
49. Ibid., 128.
50. Ibid., 125.
51. Ibid.
52. Paz, *Labyrinth of Solitude*, 87.
53. Dussel, *Invention of the Americas*, 126.
54. Ibid.
55. Paz, *Labyrinth of Solitude*, 172.
56. Ibid., 170.
57. Ibid., 173.
58. Ibid., 374–75.
59. Ibid., 376.
60. Ibid., 170, 173.
61. Dussel, *Invention of the Americas*, 12–13.
62. Ibid., 112.
63. Ibid., 131.
64. Ibid., 12.
65. Ibid., 131.
66. Ibid., 72.
67. Ibid., 120.
68. Simone Chambers, *Reasonable Democracy: Jürgen Habermas and the Politics of Discourse*, 212–45.
69. Dussel, *Invention of the Americas*, 87.
70. Susan Bickford, *The Dissonance of Democracy: Listening, Conflict, and Citizenship*, 170.
71. John Rawls, "Justice as Fairness: Political, Not Metaphysical," in *Political Theory: Classic Writings, Contemporary Views*, 668.
72. Ibid., 677.
73. Dussel, *Invention of the Americas*, 132.
74. Ibid., 26.
75. Ibid., 87.
76. Ibid., 132, 26.
77. Ibid., 26.
78. Roberto S. Goizueta, "In Defense of Reason," 17.

79. Roberto S. Goizueta, *Caminemos con Jesús: Toward a Hispanic/Latino Theology of Accompaniment*, 136.

80. Goizueta, "In Defense of Reason," 23.

81. Goizueta, *Caminemos con Jesús*, 138.

82. Goizueta, "In Defense of Reason," 22.

83. Ibid., 23. Goizueta adds cynically that at the very moment Latinos are critically challenging the dominant intellectual elites, "we are advised that reason does not exist, only intuition, ambiguity, and irrationality" (*Caminemos con Jesús*, 148).

84. Goizueta, *Caminemos con Jesús*, 170–71.

85. Ibid., 172.

86. Dussel, *Invention of the Americas*, 132.

87. Ibid., 131.

88. Ibid., 70.

89. Ibid., 70–71.

90. Ibid., 69–70.

91. Ibid., 117.

92. Ibid., 132.

93. Goizueta, "In Defense of Reason," 20.

94. Ibid., 21.

95. Goizueta, *Caminemos Con Jesús*, 168.

96. Goizueta, "In Defense of Reason," 25.

97. Iain S. Maclean, *Opting for Democracy?: Liberation Theology and the Struggle for Democracy in Brazil*, 153–230. Actually, Maclean maintains that liberation theology must take a purist stand of radical critique toward liberal democracy in deference to the "preferential option for the poor" or must accommodate itself in a more temperate fashion with procedural democracy and rising pluralistic civil societies across Latin America. Unfortunately, Maclean's analysis remains too mired in either/ors—practical *v.* utopian outlooks, procedural *v.* participatory democracy, or option for the poor *v.* generation of the common good—to project how liberation theology can help realize a participatory democracy that is not utopian.

98. Gustavo Gutiérrez, *Las Casas: In Search of the Poor of Jesus Christ*.

Chapter 5

1. Bruce Ackerman, *Social Justice in the Liberal State*; Ronald Dworkin, *Taking Rights Seriously*; William Galston, *Liberal Purposes: Goods, Virtues, and Diversity in the Liberal State*; Will Kymlicka, *Contemporary Political Philosophy: An Introduction*; Will Kymlicka, *Liberalism, Community, and Culture*; Will Kymlicka, *Multicultural Citizenship: A Liberal Theory of Minority Rights*; John Rawls, "Justice as Fairness: Political not Metaphysical"; John Rawls, *A Theory of Justice*; Joseph Raz, *The Morality of Freedom*.

2. Charles Taylor, "The Politics of Recognition," in *Multiculturalism: Examining The Politics of Recognition*, 25–74; Charles Taylor, *Reconciling the Solitudes: Essays on Canadian Federalism and Nationalism*; Michael Walzer, "Comment," in *Multiculturalism*, 99–103.

3. Taylor, *Reconciling the Solitudes,* 183, 148–52.
4. Kymlicka, *Liberalism, Community, and Culture,* 151.
5. Ibid., 165.
6. Ibid., 175, 190.
7. Ibid., 146, 147.
8. Ibid., 135.
9. Ibid., 172.
10. Ibid.
11. Ibid., 255.
12. Ibid., 209.
13. Ibid., 210.
14. *Brown v. Board of Education of Topeka, Kansas,* 347 U.S. 438 (1954).
15. Kymlicka, *Liberalism, Community, and Culture,* 145.
16. Taylor, "The Politics of Recognition," in *Multiculturalism,* 40, 58.
17. Ibid., 40.
18. Ibid., 43.
19. Ibid., 56; Walzer, "Comment," in *Multiculturalism,* 99.
20. Walzer, "Comment," in *Multiculturalism,* 99.
21. Taylor, "Politics of Recognition," in *Multiculturalism,* 55.
22. Ibid., 52–53.
23. Ibid., 53.
24. Ibid., 59.
25. Ibid., 58.
26. Walzer, "Comment," in *Multiculturalism,* 99.
27. Taylor, *Reconciling the Solitudes,* 11.
28. Taylor, "The Politics of Recognition," in *Multiculturalism,* 58.
29. Ibid., 61
30. Ibid., 59.
31. Ibid.
32. Taylor, *Reconciling the Solitudes,* 165.
33. Ibid., 147.
34. Ibid., 150.
35. Ibid.
36. Ibid., 183.
37. Ibid., 102.
38. Ibid., 132.
39. Ibid., 200.
40. Ibid., 183.
41. Ibid., 183, 199–200.
42. Walzer, "Comment," in *Multiculturalism,* 101.
43. Ibid., 102.
44. Ibid., 102–3.
45. Population Estimates and Projections Program, Texas State Data Center et al., "Projections of the Populations of Texas and Counties in Texas by Age, Sex, and Race/Ethnicity."

46. Andrew Sung Park, *Racial Conflict and Healing: An Asian American Theological Perspective*, 100.

47. Carlos Fuentes, interview by Bill Moyers, in *A World of Ideas: Conversations with Thoughtful Men and Women about American Life Today and the Ideas Shaping our Future*, 506.

48. Simone Chambers, *Reasonable Democracy*, 212–45.

49. Jeremy Waldron, "Pluralism: A Political Perspective," in *The Rights of Minority Cultures*, 95.

50. Iris Marion Young, "Together in Difference: Transforming the Logic of Group Political Conflict," in *Rights of Minority Cultures*, 161.

51. Ibid., 165.

52. Ibid., 170.

53. Ibid., 165.

54. Ibid., 173.

55. Ibid., 174.

56. Homi Bhabha, "Introduction: Narrating the Nation," in *Nation and Narration*, 1–7; Homi Bhabha, "DissemiNation: Time, Narrative, and the Margins of the Modern Nation," in *Nation and Narration*, 291–322.

57. Bhabha, "Introduction," 4.

58. Ibid., 5, 4. Bhabha adapts the term "interruptive" from Gayatri Chakravorty Spivak, *In Other Worlds: Essays in Cultural Politics* (New York: Methuen, 1987).

59. Aaron Knight, "A Critical Reaction to 'Substantive Pluralism' by John Francis Burke," 70.

60. For an interpretation of Locke that challenges the conventional materialist individualism perspective, see Jerome Huyler, *The Moral Philosophy of the Founding Era*.

61. Hannah Arendt, *On Revolution*, 127; Robert N. Bellah et al., *Habits of the Heart: Individualism and Commitment in American Life*; Robert N. Bellah et al., *The Good Society*.

62. Knight, "Critical Reaction," 72.

63. John Francis Burke, "A Substantive Pluralism: Cultivating Community through Multicultural Relations," 69.

64. William Galston, *Liberal Purposes*, 225.

65. See my discussion of intersubjectivity, in the context of phenomenology, in chapter 1.

66. Alexander Hamilton et al., *The Federalist Papers*, #10, 81.

67. Michael Shapiro, "Post-Liberal Civil Society: A Critique of Neo-Tocquevillian Social Theory."

68. John Courtney Murray, S.J., *We Hold These Truths: Catholic Reflection on the America Proposition*, and Bellah et al., *Good Society*, 300–1.

69. Ana María Díaz-Stevens and Anthony M. Stevens-Arroyo, *Recognizing The Latino Resurgence in U.S. Religion: The Emmaus Paradigm*, 7.

70. Geoffrey Fox, *Hispanic Nation*, 241.

71. Duncan Earle, "The Borders of Mesoamerica," 61.

Chapter 6

1. Arnoldo made his comments in Spanish. These reflections were subsequently trans-lated into English by Mary Jane De La Rosa Burke and myself in consultation with Arnoldo.
2. Homer L. Jernigan, "Teaching Pastoral Theology from a Global Perspective," 95.
3. Allan Figueroa Deck, *The Second Wave*, 62.
4. Virgil Elizondo, *The Future is Mestizo: Life Where Cultures Meet*; "*Evangelii Nuntiandi:* Evangelization in the Modern World," 303–45; Joseph P. Fitzpatrick, S.J., *One Church Many Cultures: The Challenge of Diversity*; "*Gaudium et Spes:* Pastoral Constitution on the Church in the Modern World," 166–237; Andrew Greeley, *The Catholic Myth: The Behavior and Beliefs of American Catholics*; Alfred T. Hennelly, ed., *Liberation Theology: A Documentary History*; Jacques Maritain, *Integral Hu-manism: Temporal and Spiritual Problems of a New Christendom*; Jacques Maritain, *Man and the State*; Jacques Maritain, *The Range of Reason*; John Courtney Murray, S.J., *We Hold These Truths: Catholic Reflection on the America Proposition*; "*Octogesima Adveniens:* A Call to Action on the Eightieth Anniversary of *Rerum Novarum*," 265–86; Peter Schineller, S.J., *A Handbook on Inculturation*; Aylward Shorter, *Toward a Theology of Inculturation*. Also see my article "Cultivating Com-munity through Diversity: An Inductive, Hermeneutical Approach to Pluralism in Catholic Social Thought," 15–30.
5. Greeley, *Catholic Myth*, 45.
6. "*Octogesima Adveniens*," #4.
7. Ibid., #25.
8. United States Catholic Conference, *Cultural Pluralism in the United States*, #22.
9. [Bishops of the Diocese of Galveston-Houston], *Many Members, One Body: A Pastoral Letter on the Cultural and Ethnic Diversity of the Church of Galveston-Houston*, #26.
10. Arnoldo adds that those choosing this second course will be criticized, but that it is to their credit: "This position many times as a consequence leads to this person be-ing criticized, but this should not matter because when others speak well or ill of you, this means that you are doing something; if no one talks or says anything about you, then it means you are doing nothing."
11. Put powerfully by a Houston Catholic Latina: "A fully respected variety in unity" must look upon cultural diversity "not as a burden to be borne . . . but . . . [as] a mystery to be acknowledged and accepted." United States Catholic Conference, "Ethnicity and Race," in *Call to Action: An Agenda for the Catholic Community*, 42.
12. Historically, the number of African Americans and non-Vietnamese Asian Americans has been insufficient to warrant liturgies in their own culture or language. Ruth, a member of the committee, clarifies the situation as of the mid 1990s: "My vision as a Black female on the MRC is one of unity within diversity. Right now, our focus is primarily on the Latino and Vietnamese populations, since these two groups are the largest organized ethnic minorities in the parish. There is a strong but growing Af-rican American community, and each year we have sponsored an event for Black History Month. Some Negro Spirituals have also been included in some of our

liturgical celebrations. As this African American community grows at [St. Nessan's], the MRC will increase its focus on this community."

13. "Small Faith Communities: Theology Meets Life," 7.

14. On the "gendering" of morality" see Carol Gilligan, *In a Different Voice: Psychological Theory and Women's Development;* Lawrence Kohlberg, *Essays in Moral Development;* Lawrence Kohlberg, *The Philosophy of Moral Development: Moral Stages and the Idea of Justice;* Joan Tronto, *Moral Boundaries: A Political Argument for an Ethic of Care,* 61–97.

15. Virgil Elizondo, *Christianity and Culture: An Introduction to Pastoral Theology and Ministry for the Bicultural Community,* 170–71.

16. See Leslie Wirpsa, "Filipinos Sing, Share Festive Foods, Teach Old Ways to Young," 3, for a further discussion of the practices of Filipino spirituality and family life in the United States. The Filipino heritage of multiple languages and being colonized by the Spanish and then the United States also has some parallels to the history of Mexican Americans. More research should be done in this area, especially in terms of its implication for both liturgical and political practices in the United States.

17. [Bishops of the Diocese of Galveston-Houston], *Many Members, One Body,* #26.

18. Mark Massa, *Catholics and American Culture,* 3–10.

19. Demetria Martinez, "Chicanos Hear Conquest's Echo in Quandaries about Language," 24.

Chapter 7

1. Barbara Vobejda, "Hispanic Children Surpass Number of Black Children," A-2.

2. Enrique T. Trueba, *Latinos Unidos: From Cultural Diversity to the Politics of Solidarity,* xl.

3. James C. Stalker, "Official English or English Only," in *Point Counterpoint: Readings in American Government,* ed. Herbert Levine (New York: St. Martin's, 1998), 124–25.

4. Gloria Anzaldúa, *Borderlands/La Frontera: The New Mestiza,* Preface.

5. Ada María Isasi-Díaz, *En La Lucha/In the Struggle: A Hispanic Women's Liberation Theology,* 159.

6. James Stalker, "Official English or English Only, 129. Along the same lines the U.S. Supreme Court's overturning, in *Plyler v. Doe,* 457 U.S. 202 (1982), of the Texas law prohibiting free public school education to children of undocumented aliens was in part motivated by the fear that a permanent servant class would emerge if such legislation were upheld.

7. Nancy Cloud, Fred Genesee, and Else Hamayan, *Dual Language Instruction: A Handbook for Enriched Education,* 5. This five-point list is quoted directly from this source.

8. Ibid., 5. In addition, as Stalker notes: "There is evidence that knowing a second language increases our ability to use our first language. People who know two languages generally perform better on tests of verbal ability administered in their native language than do monolingual speakers" (Stalker, "Official English or English Only," 130).

9. *Shaw v. Reno,* 113 S. Ct. 2816 (1993); *Miller v. Johnson,* 63 U.S.L.W. 4726 (1995); *Bush*

v. Vera, 116 U.S. 1941 (1996); *Shaw v. Hunt,* 116 U.S. 1894 (1996); *Hunt v. Cromartie,* 69 U.S.L.W. 4234 (2001).

10. Tatcho Mindiola, Jr., "A Pity Local Hispanics Still on Political Sidelines," A-15.
11. Lani Guinier, *The Tyranny of the Majority: Fundamental Fairness in Representative Democracy,* 96.
12. "Cumulative Voting System Impacts Minority Precincts," A-1.
13. Guinier, *The Tyranny of the Majority,* 99–101.
14. Iris Marion Young, *Justice and the Politics of Difference,* 48.
15. Ibid., 190.
16. "California Proposition 209," in *American Political Thought,* 563.
17. Michael C. Lemay, *The Perennial Struggle: Race, Ethnicity, and Minority Group Politics in the United States,* 290.
18. Ibid., 294.
19. Jonathan Tompkins, *Human Resource Management in Government,* 131.
20. Ibid., 161–63.
21. Manning Marable, "Staying on the Path to Racial Equality," in *The Affirmative Action Debate,* 5.
22. Ibid., 14.
23. Tompkins, *Human Resource Management,* 176–77.
24. Barbara R. Bergmann, *In Defense of Affirmative Action,* 141.
25. Eleanor Holmes Norton, "Affirmative Action in the Workplace," in *Affirmative Action Debate,* 41.
26. Tompkins, *Human Resource Management,* 176.
27. Clarence Page, "Supply-Side Affirmative Action," in *Voices of Diversity: Twentieth-Century Perspectives on History and Government,* 222.
28. R. Roosevelt Thomas, Jr., "From Affirmative Action to Affirmative Diversity," quoted in Tompkins, *Human Resource Management,* 180.
29. *Human Resource Management,* 178–80.
30. Donna J. Markham, *Spiritlinking Leadership,* 13–16.
31. A. Barry Rand, "Diversity in Corporate America," in *Affirmative Action Debate,* 70.
32. Ibid., 74.
33. Charles Moskos, "Affirmative Action in the Army: Why it Works," in *Affirmative Action Debate,* 227–38.
34. Glenn C. Loury, "Achieving the 'Dream': A Challenge to Liberals and Conservatives in the Spirit of Martin Luther King," in *American Political Thought,* 543.
35. Ibid., 540.
36. Ibid.
37. Ibid, 543.
38. Ibid.
39. *Plessy v. Ferguson,* 163 U.S. 537 (1896).
40. Joan Tronto, *Moral Boundaries,* 161–62.
41. Lemay, *Perennial Struggle,* 299.
42. Ibid., 297.
43. Ibid., 298.
44. Ibid.

45. Ibid., 298–300.
46. Roberto S. Goizueta, *Caminemos con Jesús: Toward a Hispanic/Latino Theology of Accompaniment*, 197–98.
47. Ibid., 199.
48. Virgil Elizondo, *The Future is Mestizo: Life Where Cultures Meet*, 47.
49. Lemay, *Perennial Struggle*, 301–2.
50. Ibid., 302.
51. Christine Marie Sierra et al., "Latino Immigration and Citizenship," 536.
52. Ibid.
53. Juan Gómez-Quiñones and David R. Maciel, "'What Goes Around, Comes Around': Political Practice and Cultural Response in the Internationalization of Mexican Labor, 1890–1997," in *Culture Across Borders*, 30.
54. Samuel P. Huntington, *The Clash of Civilizations and the Remaking of World Order*, 206.
55. Ibid.
56. Sierra et al., "Latino Immigration and Citizenship," 538.
57. Saskia Sassen, "The Transnationalization of Immigration Policy," in *Borderless Borders: U.S. Latinos, Latin Americans, and the Paradox of Independence*, 61.
58. Ibid., 64–66.
59. Roger Rouse, "Mexican Migration and the Social Space of Postmodernism," in *Between Two Worlds: Mexican Immigrants in the United States*, 251.
60. María de los Angeles Torres, "Transnational Political and Cultural Identities: Crossing Theoretical Borders," in *Borderless Borders*, 181.
61. Ibid.
62. Roger Rouse, "Mexican Migration and the Social Space of Postmodernism," 252–55.
63. Ibid., 257.
64. Sierra et al., "Latino Immigration and Citizenship," 539.
65. Torres, "Transnational Political and Cultural Identities," 182.
66. Rouse, "Mexican Migration and the Social Space of Postmodernism," 259.
67. Ibid.
68. Rebecca Morales, "Dependence or Interdependence: Issues and Policy Choices Facing Latin Americans and Latinos," in *Borderless Borders*, 9.
69. Ibid., 10.
70. Ibid., 10.
71. Ibid., 8.
72. Manuel Pastor, Jr., and Carol Wise, "Trading Places: U.S. Latinos and Trade Liberalization in the Americas," in *Borderless Borders*, 48.
73. Morales, "Dependence or Interdependence," 8–11.
74. Ibid., 9.
75. Sassen, "The Transnationalization of Immigration Policy," 61.
76. Ibid., 65.
77. Morales, "Dependence or Interdependence," 9.
78. Manuel Pastor, Jr., "Interdependence, Inequality, and Identity: Linking Latinos and Latin Americans" in *Borderless Borders*, 23–24; Pastor and Wise, "Trading Places," 49.

79. Ibid., 24
80. Jeremy Brecher, "Popular Movements and Economic Globalization," in *Borderless Borders*, 186.
81. Ibid.
82. Ibid., 190–91.
83. Ibid., 192–93.
84. Ibid., 191.
85. Benjamin Marquez, *LULAC: The Evolution of a Mexican American Political Organization*, 30–34.
86. David Gutiérrez, "*Sin Fronteras?*: Chicanos, Mexican Americans, and the Emergence of the Contemporary Mexican Immigration Debate, 1968–1978," in *Between Two Worlds: Mexican Immigrants in the United States*, 193–94.
87. Benjamin Marquez and James Jennings, "Representation by Other Means: Mexican American and Puerto Rican Social Movement Organizations," 543.
88. Huntington, *Clash of Civilizations*.
89. Ibid., 78.
90. Ibid., 312.
91. Ibid., 318.
92. Ibid., 101.
93. Ibid., 207.
94. Ibid., 320.
95. Ibid.
96. Ibid., 320, 318.
97. R. Scott Appleby, *The Ambivalence of the Sacred: Religion, Violence, and Reconciliation*, 281.
98. Ibid., 281–82, 288–303.
99. Ibid., 303.
100. Huntington, *Clash of Civilizations*, 129.
101. Virgil Elizondo, *Guadalupe: Mother of the New Creation*, 132, 134.

Conclusion

1. Virgil Elizondo, *The Future is Mestizo: Life Where Cultures Meet, Revised Edition*, 113.
2. Similarly Jonathan Boswell's argument for political community in *Community and the Economy: The Theory of Public Co-operation* is congenial to my own, especially since he draws heavily upon Christian Democratic themes. It is nevertheless written out of the European political-economy tradition and would therefore have to be translated into U.S. American terms to have the rhetorical and transformative impact I am seeking.
3. Susan Bickford, *The Dissonance of Democracy: Listening, Conflict, and Citizenship*, 52–53, 95–96.
4. Ibid., 23–24.
5. Leslie Paul Thiele, *Thinking Politics: Perspectives in Ancient, Modern, and Postmodern Political Theory*, 108.

6. In this regard, see especially Manuel J. Mejido, "A Critique of the 'Asthetic Turn' in U.S. Hispanic Theology: A Dialogue with Roberto Goizueta and the Posting of a New Paradigm," 18–48.

7. Raimon Pannikar, *Invisible Harmony: Essays on Contemplation and Responsibility*, 175.

8. Alexander Hamilton et al., *The Federalist Papers*, #10, 83.

9. Hamilton et al., *The Federalist Papers*, #51, 325.

10. Donald S. Lutz, *The Origins of American Constitutionalism*, 84–86, 134–35, 154–55.

11. Wilson Carey McWilliams, "Ties That Almost Bind," 24–25; Dennis Hale, Marc Landy, and Wilson Carey McWilliams, "Freedom, Civic Virtue and the Failing of Our Constitution," 15.

12. Thiele, *Thinking Politics*, 176

13. Robert Denhardt, *Public Administration: An Action Approach,* 15–19.

Bibliography

• • •

Ackerman, Bruce. *Social Justice in the Liberal State*. New Haven, Conn.: Yale University Press, 1980.

Acuña, Rodolfo. *Occupied America: A History of Chicanos*. New York: HarperCollins, 1988.

Aguirre Beltrán, Gonzolo. *La Poblacion negra de Mexico*. Mexico City: Ediciones Fuente Cultural, 1946.

Anaya, Rudolfo. *Bless Me, Ultima*. New York: Warner Books, 1972.

Anzaldúa, Gloria. *Borderlands/La Frontera: The New Mestiza*. San Francisco: Aunt Lute, 1987.

———, ed. *Making Face, Making Soul Haciendo Caras: Creative and Critical Perspectives by Women of Color*. San Francisco: Spinster/Aunt Lute, 1990.

Appiah, K. Anthony. "Identity, Authenticity, Survival: Multicultural Societies and Social Reproduction." In *Multiculturalism: Examining the Politics of Recognition*, edited by Amy Gutmann, 149–64. Princeton, N.J.: Princeton University Press, 1994.

Appleby, R. Scott. *The Ambivalence of the Sacred: Religion, Violence, and Reconciliation*. Lanham, Md.: Rowman & Littlefield Publishing, 2000.

Aquino Vargas, María Pilar. "Directions and Foundations of Hispanic/Latino Theology: Toward a *Mestiza* Theology of Liberation." In *Mestizo Christianity: Theology From the Latino Perspective*, edited by Arturo J. Bañuelas, 192–208. Maryknoll, N.Y.: Orbis, 1995.

Arendt, Hannah. *The Human Condition*. Chicago: University of Chicago Press, 1958.

———. *On Revolution*. New York: Pelican Books, 1977.

Bañuelas, Arturo J. "U.S. Hispanic Theology: An Initial Assessment." In *Mestizo Christianity: Theology From the Latino Perspective*, edited by Arturo J. Bañuelas, 55–82. New York: Orbis, 1995.

Barber, Benjamin. *Jihad vs. McWorld*. New York: Times Books, 1995.

———. *Strong Democracy: Participatory Politics for a New Age*. Berkeley: University of Califonia Press, 1984

Barrera, Mario. *Beyond Aztlan: Ethnic Autonomy in Comparative Perspective*. Notre Dame, Ind.: University of Notre Dame Press, 1988.

———. *Race and Class in the Southwest: A Theory of Racial Inequality*. Notre Dame, Ind.: University of Notre Dame Press, 1979.

Bellah, Robert N., et al. *The Good Society*. New York: Vintage Books, 1992.

———. *Habits of the Heart: Individualism and Commitment in American Life*. New York: Harper & Row, 1985.

Bergmann, Barbara R. *In Defense of Affirmative Action*. New York: HarperCollins, 1996.

Bernstein, Alan. "Primary 96: Hispanic Candidates Getting a Boost at Polls." *Houston Chronicle*, March 14, 1996, A-33.

Bernstein, Richard J. *Beyond Objectivism and Relativism: Science, Hermeneutics, and Praxis.* Philadelphia: University of Pennsylvania Press, 1983.

Bhabha, Homi. "DissemiNation: Time, Narrative, and the Margins of the Modern Nation." In *Nation and Narration*, edited by Homi Bhabha, 291–322. New York: Routledge, 1990.

———. "Introduction: Narrating the Nation." In *Nation and Narration*, edited by Homi Bhabha, 1–7. New York: Routledge, 1990.

Bickford, Susan. *The Dissonance of Democracy: Listening, Conflict, and Citizenship.* Ithaca, N.Y.: Cornell University Press, 1996.

[Bishops of the Diocese of Galveston-Houston]. *Many Members, One Body: A Pastoral Letter on the Cultural and Ethnic Diversity of the Church of Galveston-Houston.* Houston: Diocese of Galveston-Houston, 1994.

Boswell, Jonathan. *Community and the Economy: The Theory of Public Co-operation.* New York: Routledge, 1990.

Brecher, Jeremy. "Popular Movements and Economic Globalization." In *Borderless Borders: U.S. Latinos, Latin Americans, and the Paradox of Independence*, edited by Frank Bonilla et al., 185–93. Philadelphia: Temple Universtiy Press, 1998.

Brimelow, Peter. *Alien Nation: Common Sense About America's Immigration Disaster.* New York: Random House, 1995.

Bronner, Stephen Eric. "Postmodernism and Postructuralism." In *Twentieth Century Political Theory: A Reader*, edited by Stephen Eric Bronner, 237–38. New York: Routledge, 1997.

Burke, John Francis. "Cultivating Community through Diversity: An Inductive, Hermeneutical Approach to Pluralism in Catholic Social Thought." *Journal For Peace and Justice Studies* 5 (spring 1993): 15–30.

———. "Hannah Arendt." In *An Introduction to Modern European Philosophy*, edited by Jenny Teichman and Graham White, 158–68. London: MacMillan, 1998.

———. "The Interreligious Dimension: A Global Ethic of Peace." In *Concilium: The Return of the Just War*, edited by María Pilar Aquino and Dietmar Mieth, 52–61. London: SCM, 2001.

———. "Phenomenology and Multiculturalism: Moving Beyond Assimilation and Utter Diversity through a Substantive Pluralism." In *Analecta Husserliana.* Vol. 55, edited by Anna-Teresa Tymieniecka, 85–94. Dordrecht, The Netherlands: Kluwer, 1998.

———. "Reconciling Cultural Diversity with a Democratic Community: *Mestizaje* as Opposed to the Usual Suspects." *Citizenship Studies* 3 (1999): 119–40.

———. "Response to 'A Critical Reaction' by Aaron Knight." *Texas Journal of Political Studies* 17 (fall/winter 1994/1995): 74–78.

———. "A Substantive Pluralism: Cultivating Community through Multicultural Relations." *Texas Journal of Political Studies* 16 (fall/winter 1993/94): 62–76.

———. "U.S. Hispanic Theology and the Politics of Border Crossings: 'We Hold These Truths.' From *La Frontera.*" *The Review of Politics* 60 (summer 1998): 563–73.

Burke, John Francis and Adolfo Santos. "We Didn't Cross the Border, The Border Crossed Us—*Otra Vez* (Again)." In *Texas Politics Today*, edited by William Earl Maxwell and Ernest Crain, 83–87. Belmont, Calif.: Wadsworth, 2000.

"California Proposition 209." In *American Political Thought,* edited by Kenneth M. Dolbeare, 563–64. Chatham, N.J.: Chatham House, 1998.

Carter, Stephen L. *The Culture of Disbelief: How American Law and Politics Trivialize Religious Devotion.* New York: Basic Books, 1993.

"Catholics and the Presidency." *Commonweal* 71 (January 1, 1960): 383–84.

"Census 2000: Texas at a Glance." *Houston Chronicle,* March 13, 2001, A-1.

Chambers, Simone. *Reasonable Democracy: Jürgen Habermas and the Politics of Discourse.* Ithaca, N.Y.: Cornell University Press, 1996.

"The Changing Color of America." *New York Times,* March 13, 2001, A–14.

City of Houston, The Planning and Development Department. *Demographic and Land Use Profile for Houston, Texas.* Houston: City of Houston, 1992.

Cloud, Nancy, Fred Genesee, and Else Hamayan. *Dual Language Instruction: A Handbook for Enriched Education.* Boston: Heinle & Heinle, 2000.

Corbett, Michael, and Julia Mitchell Corbett. *Politics and Religion in the United States.* New York: Garland, 1999.

Cortes, Ernesto. Interview by Bill Moyers. In *A World of Ideas II: Public Opinions from Private Citizens,* edited by Andie Tucher. 141–48. New York: Doubleday, 1990.

"Cumulative Voting System Impacts Minority Precincts." *Amarillo Globe News,* May 7, 2000, A-1.

Dallmayr, Fred. *Beyond Orientalism: Essays on Cross-Cultural Encounter.* Albany: State University of New York Press, 1996.

Deck, Allan Figueroa, S.J. *The Second Wave: Hispanic Ministry and the Evangelization of Cultures.* New York: Paulist Press, 1989.

———. "The Spirituality of United States Hispanics: An Introductory Essay." In *Mestizo Christianity: Theology From the Latino Perspective,* edited by Arturo J. Bañuelas, 226–35. Maryknoll, N.Y.: Orbis, 1995.

Deloria, Jr., Vine. *Custer Died for Your Sins: An Indian Manifesto.* Norman: University of Oklahoma Press, 1988.

———. *God is Red: A Native American View of Religion.* Golden, Colorado: Fulcrum, 1994.

Denhardt, Robert. *Public Administration: An Action Approach.* Belmont, Calif.: Wadsworth, 1995.

Díaz-Stevens, Ana María, and Anthony M. Stevens-Arroyo. *Recognizing the Latino Resurgence in U.S. Religion: The Emmaus Paradigm.* Boulder, Colo.: Westview, 1998.

Dunn, Timothy J. *The Militarization of the U.S.-Mexico Border, 1978–1992: Low-Intensity Conflict Doctrine Comes Home.* Austin: University of Texas at Austin Press, 1996.

Dussel, Enrique. *The Invention of the Americas: Eclipse of "the Other" and the Myth of Modernity.* Translated by Michael D. Barber. New York: Continuum, 1995.

———. *The Underside of Modernity: Apel, Ricoeur, Rorty, Taylor, and the Philosophy of Liberation.* Edited and translated by Eduardo Mendieta. Atlantic Highlands, N.J.: Humanities, 1996.

Dworkin, Ronald. *Taking Rights Seriously.* Cambridge, Mass.: Harvard University Press, 1977.

Earle, Duncan. "The Borders of Mesoamerica." *Texas Journal of Ideas, History, and Culture.* 20 (fall/winter, 1997): 54–61.

Elizondo, Virgil. *Christianity and Culture: An Introduction to Pastoral Theology and Ministry for the Bicultural Community.* San Antonio: Mexican American Cultural Center, 1983.

———. *The Future is Mestizo: Life Where Cultures Meet*. Bloomington, Ind.: Meyer-Stone, 1988.

———. *The Future is Mestizo: Life Where Cultures Meet, Revised Edition*. Boulder, Colo.: University Press of Colorado, 2000.

———. *Galilean Journey: The Mexican-American Promise*. Maryknoll, N.Y.: Orbis, 1991.

———. *Guadalupe: Mother of the New Creation*. Maryknoll, N.Y.: Orbis, 1997.

Espín, Orlando. *The Faith of the People: Theological Reflections on Popular Catholicism*. Maryknoll, N.Y.: Orbis, 1997.

———. "Tradition and Popular Religion: An Understanding of the Sensus Fidelium." In *Mestizo Christianity: Theology from the Latino Perspective*, edited by Arturo J. Bañuelas, 148–74. Maryknoll, N.Y.: Orbis, 1995.

"*Evangelii Nuntiandi*: Evangelization in the Modern World." In *Catholic Social Thought: The Documentary Heritage*, edited by David J. O'Brien and Thomas A. Shannon, 303–45. Maryknoll, N.Y.: Orbis, 1992.

Fernández, Eduardo C. *La Cosecha: Harvesting Contemporary United States Hispanic Theology (1972–1998)*. Collegeville, Minnesota: Liturgical Press, 2000.

Fiorenza, Joseph A. "*Encuentro 2000*: A Time to Address Pressing Issues." *National Catholic Reporter* 36 (April 28, 2000): 24.

Fitzpatrick, Joseph P., S.J. *One Church Many Cultures: The Challenge of Diversity*. Kansas City, Mo: Sheed & Ward, 1987.

Fox, Geoffrey. *Hispanic Nation: Culture, Politics, and the Construction of Identity*. Tucson, Az.: University of Arizona Press, 1996.

Freire, Paulo. *Pedagogy of the Oppressed*. Translated by Myra Bergman Ramos. New York: Continuum, 1993.

Fuentes, Carlos. Interview by Bill Moyers. In *A World of Ideas: Conversations with Thoughtful Men and Women about American Life Today and the Ideas Shaping our Future*, edited by Betty Sue Flowers. 506–13. New York: Doubleday, 1989.

———. *A New Time for Mexico*. Translated by Marina Gutman Castañeda and Carlos Fuentes. New York: Farrar, Straus & Gircux, 1996.

Gabilondo, Joseba. Afterword to the 1997 edition. In *The Cosmic Race: A Bilingual Edition*, translated by Didier T. Jaén, 99–117. Baltimore: Johns Hopkins University Press, 1997.

Gadamer, Hans-Georg. *Philosophical Hermeneutics*. Edited and translated by David E. Linge. Berkeley: University of California Press, 1976.

———. *Truth and Method*. Translated by Garrett Barden and John Cumming. New York: Crossroad, 1982.

Galston, William. *Liberal Purposes: Goods, Virtues, and Diversity in the Liberal State*. New York: Cambridge University Press, 1991.

Garcia, F. Chris, ed. *Latinos and the Political System*. Notre Dame, Ind.: University of Notre Dame Press, 1988.

———. *Pursuing Power: Latinos and the Political System*. Notre Dame, Ind.: University of Notre Dame Press, 1997.

García, Ismacl. *Dignidad: Ethics through Hispanic Eyes*. Nashville: Abingdon, 1997.

García, Sixto J. "Sources and Loci of Hispanic Theology." In *Mestizo Christianity: Theology from the Latino Perspective*, edited by Arturo J. Bañuelas, 105–24. Maryknoll, N.Y.: Orbis, 1995.

"*Gaudium et Spes:* Pastoral Constitution on the Church in the Modern World." In *Catholic Social Thought: The Documentary Heritage,* edited by David J. O'Brien and Thomas A. Shannon, 166–237. Maryknoll, N.Y.: Orbis, 1992.

Geertz, Clifford. *The Interpretation of Cultures.* New York: Basic Books, 1973.

Geyer, Georgie Anne. *Americans No More.* New York: Atlantic Monthly Press, 1996.

Gilligan, Carol. *In a Different Voice: Psychological Theory and Women's Development.* Cambridge, Mass.: Harvard University Press, 1982.

Goizueta, Roberto S. *Caminemos con Jesús: Toward a Hispanic/Latino Theology of Accompaniment.* Maryknoll, N.Y.: Orbis, 1995.

———. "In Defense of Reason." *Journal of Hispanic/Latino Theology* 3 (February, 1996): 16–26.

———. "The Significance of U.S. Hispanic Experience for Theological Method." In *Mestizo Christianity: Theology From the Latino Perspective,* edited by Arturo J. Bañuelas, 83–103. Maryknoll, N.Y.: Orbis, 1995.

Gómez-Quiñones, Juan and David R. Maciel. "'What Goes Around, Comes Around': Political Practice and Cultural Response in the Internationalization of Mexican Labor, 1890–1997." In *Culture Across Borders,* edited by David R. Maciel and María Herrera-Sobek, 27–65. Tucson: University of Arizona Press, 1998.

González, Justo L. "Hispanics in the New Reformation." In *Mestizo Christianity: Theology From the Latino Perspective,* edited by Arturo J. Bañuelas, 238–59. Maryknoll, N.Y.: Orbis, 1995.

———. *Santa Biblia: The Bible Through Hispanic Eyes.* Nashville: Abingdon, 1996.

Greeley, Andrew. *The Catholic Myth: The Behavior and Beliefs of American Catholics.* New York: Charles Scribner's Sons, 1990.

Guinier, Lani. *The Tyranny of the Majority: Fundamental Fairness in Representative Democracy.* New York: Free Press, 1994.

Gutiérrez, David G. "*Sin Fronteras?*: Chicanos, Mexican Americans, and the Emergence of the Contemporary Mexican Immigration Debate, 1968–1978." In *Between Two Worlds: Mexican Immigrants in the United States,* edited by David G. Gutiérrez, 175–209. Wilmington, Delaware: Scholarly Resources, 1996.

Gutiérrez, Gustavo. *Las Casas: In Search of the Poor of Jesus Christ.* Translated by Robert R. Barr. Maryknoll, N.Y.: Orbis, 1993.

Habermas, Jürgen. *Communication and the Evolution of Society.* Translated by Thomas McCarthy. Boston: Beacon, 1979.

———. "Struggles for Recognition in the Democratic Constitutional State." In *Multiculturalism: Examining the Politics of Recognition,* edited by Amy Gutmann, 107–48. Princeton, N.J.: Princeton University Press, 1994.

Haddox, John. *Vasconcelos of Mexico: Philosopher and Prophet.* Austin: University of Texas Press, 1967.

Hale, Dennis, Marc Landy, and Wilson Carey McWilliams. "Freedom, Civic Virtue and the Failing of Our Constitution." *Freedom At Issue* 84 (May/June 1985): 12–16.

Hamilton, Alexander, John Jay, and James Madison. *The Federalist Papers.* New York: New American Library, 1961.

Hennelly, Alfred T. S. J., ed. *Liberation Theology: A Documentary History.* Maryknoll, N.Y.: Orbis, 1990.

Herrick, Thaddues. "U.S.-Mexico Border Taking On Iron Curtain Look." *Houston Chronicle*, June 15, 1998, C-1.

Herzog, Lawrence A. *Where North Meets South: Cities, Space, and Politics on the U.S.-Mexico Border*. Austin: University of Texas Press, 1990.

Huntington, Samuel P. *The Clash of Civilizations and the Remaking of World Order*. New York: Touchstone, 1996.

Hulyer, Jerome. *The Moral Philosophy of the Founding Era*. Lawrence: University Press of Kansas, 1995.

Isasi-Díaz, Ada María. *En La Lucha/In the Struggle: A Hispanic Women's Liberation Theology*. Minneapolis: Fortress, 1993.

——. *Mujerista Theology: A Theology for the Twenty-First Century*. Maryknoll, N.Y.: Orbis, 1996.

——. "Mujerista Theology's Method: A Liberative Praxis, A Way of Life." In *Mestizo Christianity: Theology from the Latino Perspective*, edited by Arturo J. Bañuelas, 177–90. Maryknoll, N.Y.: Orbis, 1995.

Jaén, Didier T. Introduction to *The Cosmic Race: A Bilingual Edition*, translated by Didier T. Jaén, ix–xxxiii. Baltimore: Johns Hopkins University Press, 1997.

Jernigan, Homer L. "Teaching Pastoral Theology from A Global Perspective." *Journal of Pastoral Theology* 5 (1995): 95.

Johnston, Rosemary. "Theologians Ponder Meaning of Borders." *National Catholic Reporter* 33 (July 4, 1997): 11.

Jung, Hwa Yol. *Rethinking Political Theory: Essays in Phenomenology and the Study of Politics*. Athens, Ohio: Ohio University Press, 1993.

Klineberg, Stephen L. *The Houston Area Survey, 1982–2001: Public Perceptions during Twenty Years of Remarkable Change*. Houston: Sociology Department, Rice University, 2001.

Knight, Aaron. "A Critical Reaction to 'Substantive Pluralism' by John Francis Burke." *Texas Journal of Political Studies* 17 (fall/winter, 1994/1995): 70–73.

Kohlberg, Lawrence. *Essays in Moral Development*. New York: Harper & Row, 1981/1984.

——. *The Philosophy of Moral Development: Moral Stages and the Idea of Justice*. San Francisco: Harper & Row, 1981.

Kymlicka, Will. *Contemporary Political Philosophy: An Introduction*. Oxford: Clarendon Press, 1990.

——. *Liberalism, Community, and Culture*. Oxford: Clarendon Press, 1989.

——. *Multicultural Citizenship: A Liberal Theory of Minority Rights*. Oxford: Clarendon Press, 1995.

"L.A. Is Burning: Five Reports from a Divided City." *Frontline*, Public Broadcasting Service, April 27, 1993.

Lemay, Michael C. *The Perennial Struggle: Race, Ethnicity, and Minority Group Politics in the United States*. Upper Saddle River, N.J.: Prentice-Hall, 2000.

Lightfoot, Sara Lawrence. Interview by Bill Moyers. In *A World of Ideas: Conversations with Thoughtful Men and Women about American life Today and the Ideas Shaping Our Future*, edited by Betty Sue Flowers. 159–60. New York: Doubleday, 1989.

Limón, Graciela. *The Song of the Hummingbird*. Houston: Arte Público, 1996.

Loury, Glenn C. "Achieving the 'Dream': A Challenge to Liberals and Conservatives in the Spirit of Martin Luther King." In *American Political Thought*, edited by Kenneth M. Dolbeare, 538–48. Chatham, N.J.: Chatham House, 1998.

Lutz, Donald S. *The Origins of American Constitutionalism.* Baton Rouge: Louisiana State University Press, 1988.

Maclean, Iain S. *Opting for Democracy?: Liberation Theology and the Struggle for Democracy in Brazil.* New York: Peter Lang, 1999.

Madison, Gary Brent. *The Hermeneutics of Postmodernity: Figures and Themes.* Bloomington: Indiana University Press, 1988.

———. *The Logic of Liberty.* Westport, Conn.: Greenwood, 1986.

———. *Understanding: A Phenomenological-Pragmatical Analysis.* Westport, Conn.: Greenwood, 1986.

Maharidge, Dale. *The Coming White Minority: California's Eruptions and America's Future.* New York: Times Books, 1996.

Maldonado, Robert D. "*¿La Conquista?* Latin American (*Mestizaje*) Reflections on the Biblical Conquest." *Journal of Hispanic/Latino Theology* 2 (May, 1995): 5–25.

Marable, Manning. "Staying on the Path to Racial Equality." In *The Affirmative Action Debate*, edited by George Curry, 3–15. New York: Addison-Wesley, 1996.

Marcel, Gabriel. *Being and Having: a Translation by Katharine Farrer of Etre et Avoir.* Translated by Katharine Farrer. Westminster (London): Dacre, 1949.

Markham, Donna J. *Spiritlinking Leadership: Working Through Resistance to Organizational Change.* New York: Paulist Press, 1999.

Maritain, Jacques. *Integral Humanism: Temporal and Spiritual Problems of a New Christendom.* Translated by Joseph Evans. New York: Charles Scribner's Sons, 1968.

———. *Man and the State.* Chicago: University of Chicago Press, 1951.

———. *The Range of Reason.* Translated by Pierre Brodin. New York: Charles Scribner's Sons, 1952.

Marquez, Benjamin. *LULAC: The Evolution of a Mexican American Political Organization.* Austin: University of Texas Press, 1993.

Marquez, Benjamin, and James Jennings. "Representation by Other Means: Mexican American and Puerto Rican Social Movement Organizations." *PS: Political Science and Politics* 33 (September, 2000), 541–46.

Martinez, Bettia. Plenary presentation at Hispanics: Cultural Locations, an interdisciplinary conference, University of San Francisco, October 1997.

Martinez, Demetria. "Chicanos Hear Conquest's Echo in Quandaries About Language." *National Catholic Reporter* 34 (July 3, 1998): 24.

Martínez, Oscar J., ed. *U.S.-Mexico Borderlands: Historical and Contemporary Perspectives.* Wilmington, Del.: Scholarly Resources, 1996.

Marty, Martin E. *America's Struggle for the Common Good.* Cambridge, Mass.: Harvard University Press, 1997.

Marzal, Manuel, et al. *The Indian Face of God in Latin America.* Maryknoll, N.Y.: Orbis, 1996.

Massa, Mark. *Catholics and American Culture: Fulton Sheen, Dorothy Day, and the Notre Dame Football Team,* New York: Crossroad, 1999.

McGaa, Ed, Eagle Man. *Native Wisdom: Perceptions of the Natural Way.* Minneapolis: Four Directions, 1995.

McWilliams, Wilson Carey. "Ties That Almost Bind." *Commonweal* 74 (August 15, 1997): 24.

Mejido, Manuel J. "A Critique of the 'Asthetic Turn' in U.S. Hispanic Theology: A Dialogue with Robert Goizueta and the Posting of a New Paradigm." *Journal of Hispanic/Latino Theology* 8 (February, 2001): 18–48.

Menchú, Rigoberta. *I, Rigoberta Menchú: An Indian Woman in Guatemala.* Edited by Elisabeth Burgos-Debray and translated by Ann Wright. New York: Verso, 1984.

Merleau-Ponty, Maurice. *Signs.* Translated by Richard C. McCleary. Evanston, Illinois: Northwestern University Press, 1964.

"Mexicans Pace U.S. Hispanic Surge." *Houston Chronicle,* May 10, 2001, A-4.

Mich, Marvin L. Krier. *Catholic Social Teaching and Movements.* Mystic, Conn.: Twenty-Third Publications. 2000.

Mindiola, Tatcho, Jr. "A Pity Local Hispanics Still on Political Sidelines." *Houston Chronicle,* April 8, 1996, A-15.

Morales, Rebecca. "Dependence or Interdependence: Issues and Policy Choices Facing Latin Americans and Latinos." In *Borderless Borders: U.S. Latinos, Latin Americans, and the Paradox of Independence,* edited by Frank Bonilla et al., 1–13. Philadelphia: Temple University Press, 1998.

Moskos, Charles. "Affirmative Action in the Army: Why it Works." In *The Affirmative Action Debate,* edited by George C. Curry, 227–40. Reading, Mass.: Addison-Wesley, 1996.

Mounier, Emmanuel. *Personalism.* Translated by Philip Mairet. Notre Dame, Ind.: University of Notre Dame Press, 1952.

Mukherjee, Bharati. Interview by Bill Moyers. In *A World of Ideas II: Public Opinions From Private Citizens,* edited by Andie Tucher. 3–10. New York: Doubleday, 1990.

Murdock, Steve H., et al. *The Texas Challenge: Population Change and the Future of Texas.* College Station: Texas A&M University Press, 1997.

Murray, John Courtney, S.J. *We Hold These Truths: Catholic Reflections on the American Proposition.* New York: Sheed & Ward, 1960.

Norton, Eleanor Holmes. "Affirmative Action in the Workplace." In *The Affirmative Action Debate,* edited by George C. Curry, 39–48. Reading, Mass.: Addison-Wesley, 1996.

Nuccio, Richard. *What's Wrong, Who's Right in Central America.* New York: Holmes & Meier, 1989.

"*Octogesima Adveniens:* A Call to Action on the Eightieth Anniversary of *Rerum Novarum.*" In *Catholic Social Thought: The Documentary Heritage,* edited by David J. O'Brien and Thomas A. Shannon, 265–86. Maryknoll, N.Y.: Orbis, 1992.

Oster, Patrick. *The Mexicans: A Personal Portrait of a People.* New York: Harper & Row, 1989.

Page, Clarence. "Supply-Side Affirmative Action." In *Voices of Diversity: Twentieth-Century Perspectives on History and Government,* edited by Pat Andrews, 220–22. N.p.: Dushkin/McGraw-Hill, 2000.

Pannikar, Raimon. *Invisible Harmony: Essays on Contemplation and Responsibility.* Minneapolis: Fortress, 1995.

Pantham, Thomas. "Some Dimensions of the Universality of Philosophical Hermeneutics: A Conversation with Hans-Georg Gadamer." *Journal of the Indian Council of Philosophical Research* 9 (1992): 132.

Parekh, Bhikhu. *Rethinking Muliticulturalism: Cultural Diversity and Political Theory.* Cambridge, Mass.: Harvard University Press, 2000.

Park, Andrew Sung. *Racial Conflict and Healing: An Asian-American Theological Perspective.* Maryknoll, N.Y.: Orbis, 1996.

Pastor, Jr., Manuel. "Interdependence, Inequality, and Identity: Linking Latinos and Latin Americans." In *Borderless Borders: U.S. Latinos, Latin Americans, and the Paradox of*

Independence, edited by Frank Bonilla et al., 17–33. Philadelphia: Temple University Press, 1998.

Pastor, Jr., Manuel and Carol Wise, "Trading Places: U.S. Latinos and Trade Liberalization in the Americas." In *Borderless Borders: U.S. Latinos, Latin Americans, and the Paradox of Independence*, edited by Frank Bonilla, et al., 35–51. Philadelphia: Temple University Press, 1998.

Paz, Octavio. *The Labyrinth of Solitude and Other Writings.* Translated by Rachel Phillips Belash, Lysander Kemp, and Yara Milos. New York: Grove, 1985.

Pineda, Ana María. "The Colloquies and Theological Discourse: Culture as a Locus for Theology." *Journal of Hispanic/Latino Theology* 3 (February 1996): 27–42.

———. "Pastoral de Conjunto." In *Mestizo Christianity: Theology From the Latino Perspective*, edited by Arturo J. Bañuelas, 126–31. Maryknoll, N.Y.: Orbis, 1995.

[Population Estimates and Projections Program et al.] "Projections of the Populations of Texas and Counties in Texas by Age, Sex, and Race/Ethnicity." College Station: Texas State Data Center, Texas Agricultural Experiment Station, Texas A&M University System and The Center for Demographic and Socioeconomic Research and Education, Department of Rural Sociology, Texas Agricultural Experiment Station, Texas A&M University System, 1996.

Rand, Barry. "Diversity in Corporate America." In *The Affirmative Action Debate*, edited by George C. Curry, 65–76. Reading, Mass.: Addison-Wesley, 1996.

Rawls, John. "Justice as Fairness: Political, Not Metaphysical." In *Political Theory: Classic Writings, Contemporary Views*, edited by Joseph Losco and Leonard Williams, 668–83. New York: St. Martin's, 1992.

———. *Political Liberalism.* New York: Columbia University Press, 1993.

———. *A Theory of Justice.* Cambridge, Mass.: Harvard University Press, 1971.

Raz, Joseph. *The Morality of Freedom.* Oxford: Clarendon Press, 1986.

Recinos, Harold. "Mission: A Latino Pastoral Theology." In *Mestizo Christianity: Theology From the Latino Perspective*, edited by Arturo J. Bañuelas, 133–45. Maryknoll, N.Y.: Orbis, 1995.

Ricoeur, Paul. *History and Truth.* Translated by Charles A. Kelbley. Evanston, Illinois: Northwestern University Press, 1965.

Rodriguez, Jeanette. *Our Lady of Guadalupe; Faith and Empowerment Among Mexican-American Women.* Austin: University of Texas Press, 1994.

Romanell, Patrick. *Making of the Mexican Mind: A Study in Recent Mexican Thought.* Lincoln, Nebraska: University of Nebraska Press, 1952.

Rosales, F. Arturo. *Chicano! The History of the Mexican American Civil Rights Movement.* Houston, Texas: Arte Público, 1996.

Rose, Richard. *What is Governing: Purpose and Policy in Washington.* Englewood Cliffs, N.J., Prentice-Hall, 1978.

Rouse, Roger. "Mexican Migration and the Social Space of Postmodernism." In *Between Two Worlds: Mexican Immigrants in the United States*, edited by David G. Gutiérrez, 247–63. Wilmington, Delaware: Scholarly Resources, 1996.

Salmerón, Fernando. "Mexican Philosophers of the Twentieth Century." In *Major Trends In Mexican Philosophy*, translated by A. Robert Caponigri, 246–87. Notre Dame, Ind.: University of Notre Dame Press, 1966.

Sassen, Saskia. "The Transnationalization of Immigration Policy." In *Borderless Borders:*

U.S. Latinos, Latin Americans, and the Paradox of Independence, edited by Frank Bonilla et al., 53–67. Philadelphia: Temple University Press, 1998.

Schineller, Peter, S.J. *A Handbook on Inculturation*. New York: Paulist Press, 1990.

Schlesinger, Arthur M., Jr. *The Disuniting of America*. New York: W. W. Norton, 1992.

Schmitt, Eric. "Census Shows Big Gain for Mexican-Americans." *The New York Times*, May 10, 2001, A–22.

Segovia, Fernando F. "Two Places and No Place on Which to Stand: Mixture and Otherness in Hispanic American Theology." In *Mestizo Christianity: Theology From the Latino Perspective*, edited by Arturo J. Bañuelas, 29–43. Maryknoll, N.Y.: Orbis, 1995.

Shapiro, Michael. "Post-Liberal Civil Society: A Critique of Neo-Tocquevillian Social Theory." Paper presented at the annual meeting of the Northeastern Political Science Association, Boston, November 1996.

Shorter, Aylward. *Toward a Theology of Inculturation*. Maryknoll, N.Y.: Orbis, 1988.

Sierra, Christine Marie, et al., "Latino Immigration and Citizenship." *PS: Political Science and Politics* 33 (September 2000): 535–40.

"Small Faith Communities: Theology Meets Life." *Call to Action News* 14 (December 1992): 7.

Stalker, James C. "Official English or English Only." In *Point Counterpoint: Readings in American Government*, edited by Herbert Levine, 124–33. New York: St. Martin's, 1998.

Taylor, Charles. *The Ethics of Authenticity*. Cambridge, Mass.: Harvard University Press, 1991.

———. *Philosophy and the Human Sciences*. Cambridge: Cambridge University Press, 1985.

———. "The Politics of Recognition." In *Multiculturalism: Examining The Politics of Recognition*, edited by Amy Gutmann, 25–74. Princeton, N.J.: Princeton University Press, 1994.

———. *Reconciling the Solitudes: Essays on Canadian Federalism and Nationalism*. Montreal and Kingston: McGill-Queen's University Press, 1993.

———. *Sources of the Self: The Making of Modern Identity*. Cambridge, Mass. Harvard University Press, 1989.

Thiele, Leslie Paul. *Thinking Politics: Perspectives in Ancient, Modern, and Postmodern Political Theory*. Chatham, N.J.: Chatham House, 1997.

Tijerina, Andrés. *Tejanos and Texas Under the Mexican Flag, 1821–1836*. College Station: Texas A&M University Press, 1994.

Tompkins, Jonathan. *Human Resource Management in Government: Hitting the Ground Running*. New York: HarperCollins, 1995.

Torres, María de los Angeles. "Transnational Political and Cultural Identities: Crossing Theoretical Borders." In *Borderless Borders: U.S. Latinos, Latin Americans, and the Paradox of Independence*, edited by Frank Bonilla et al., 169–82. Philadelphia: Temple University Press, 1998.

Tracy, David. *The Analogical Imagination: Christian Theology and the Culture of Pluralism*. New York: Crossroad, 1981.

Tronto, Joan C. *Moral Boundaries: A Political Argument for an Ethic of Care*. New York: Routledge, 1994.

Trueba, Enrique T. *Latinos Unidos: From Cultural Diversity to the Politics of Solidarity*. Lanham, Md.: Rowman & Littlefield, 1999.

United States Bureau of the Census. *Census 2000 Redistricting Data*. P.L. 94–171. Washington, D.C., April 2, 2001.

United States Catholic Conference. *Cultural Pluralism in the United States.* Washington, D.C.: United States Catholic Conference, 1980.

———. "Ethnicity and Race." In *Call to Action: An Agenda for the Catholic Community.* Washington, D.C.: United States Catholic Conference, 1976.

"U.S. to Have World's Second Largest Hispanic Population," http://efe.es/. Forwarded by the "Center for the Study of Latino/a Catholicism," University of San Diego, http://acusd.edu/theo/latino-cath.html.

Vasconcelos, José. *The Cosmic Race: A Bilingual Edition.* Translated by Didier T. Jaén. Baltimore: Johns Hopkins University Press, 1997.

Vento, Arnoldo Carlos. *Mestizo: The History, Culture and Politics of the Mexican and the Chicano, The Emerging Mestizo-Americans.* Lanham, Md.: University Press of America, 1998.

Vobejda, Barbara. "Hispanic Children Surpass Number of Black Children." *Houston Chronicle,* July 15, 1998, A-2.

Wald, Kenneth D. *Religion and Politics in the United States.* New York: St. Martin's, 1987.

Waldron, Jeremy. "Pluralism: A Political Perspective." In *The Rights of Minority Cultures,* edited by Will Kymlicka, 139–54. Oxford: Oxford University Press, 1995.

Walzer, Michael. "Comment." In *Multiculturalism: Examining The Politics of Recognition,* edited by Amy Goodman, 99–103. Princeton, N.J.: Princeton University Press, 1994.

———. "The Communitarian Critique of Liberalism." *Political Theory* 18 (1990): 6–23.

———. *The Company of Critics: Social Criticism and Political Commitment in the Twentieth Century.* New York: Basic Books, 1988.

———. *Interpretation and Social Criticism.* Cambridge, Mass. Harvard University Press, 1987.

———. *Radical Principles: Reflection of an Unreconstructed Democrat.* New York: Basic Books, 1980.

———. *Spheres of Justice: A Defense of Pluralism and Equality.* New York: Basic Books, 1983.

———. *Thick and Thin: Moral Arguments at Home and Abroad.* Notre Dame, Ind.: University of Notre Dame Press, 1994.

Weber, David J. and Jane M. Rausch, eds. *Where Cultures Meet: Frontiers in Latin American History.* Wilmington, Del.: Scholarly Resources, 1994.

Williamson, Chilton, Jr. *The Immigration Mystique: America's False Conscience.* New York: Basic Books, 1996.

Wirpsa, Leslie. "Filipinos Sing, Share Festive Foods, Teach Old Ways to Young." *National Catholic Reporter* 34 (August 14, 1998): 3.

Wolf, Susan. "Comment." In *Multiculturalism: Examining The Politics of Recognition,* edited by Amy Gutmann, 75–85. Princeton, N.J.: Princeton University Press, 1994.

Young, Iris Marion. *Justice and the Politics of Difference.* Princeton, N.J.: Princeton University Press, 1990.

———. "Together in Difference: Transforming the Logic of Group Political Conflict." In *The Rights of Minority Cultures,* edited by Will Kymlicka, 155–78. Oxford: Oxford University Press, 1995.

Index

• • •

ABC (American Broadcasting Company), 66

Ackerman, Bruce, 146

affirmative action, 26, 216–18

Africa, 6, 7, 49, 175; and influences in Mexico, 9, 261n.6

African American civil rights movement, 5

African Americans, xiv, 8, 15, 49; and equal employment opportunities, 216, 223–24; and housing, 224–25; and issue of slavery, 25, 250; and segregation, 150; in the U.S. Army, 221; voting issues, 211–13

Aguililla, Michoacán (Mexico), 234

Alamo, 69

Albuquerque, 65

Alinsky, Saul, 102, 108, 109

Amish, 28, 30

Anglo (as term), xiv

Anglo-Protestant (WASP), 6, 7

Anglo-Saxon, 21; and civic spirit, 23

Anti-Federalists, 255

Anzaldúa, Gloria, 11, 51, 53, 71, 83, 84, 161, 168, 271n.7; and the affective, aesthetic rationality, 95–96; and Catholicism, 92; and the difficulties of cultural conflict, 75–82; and language issues, 206, 210; and women's issues, 87–88

Apel, Kart-Otto, 136, 141

Appleby, Scott, 242

Aquino Vargas, María Pilar, 83, 107, 110

Arendt, Hannah, 20, 41, 45, 251, 263n.49; and plurality and equality, 36–38, 215; and practical rationality, 252; and public happiness, 102, 109

Aristotle, 23, 120, 250, 251, 252

Arizona, 63

Arkansas, 66

Articles of Confederation, 254

Ash Wednesday, 95

Asia, 6, 7, 49, 175; immigrants from, 230

Asian Americans, xiv, 15, 49, 224

assimilation *v.* separatism, 6–8, 10, 11, 12, 27, 39, 40, 172; contrasting views of, 19–22, 31, 33–35; and the melting-pot theory, 7–8, 15, 20–22, 25, 26, 49, 58, 72, 94, 157, 171, 247; as opposed to a lateral view of relationships, 45–46; rejection of, 53, 83, 115, 156, 204, 233

AT&T, 66

atheism, 15

Augustine, Saint, 143

Austin, Stephen F., 62

Aztecs, 30, 52, 117, 118–20, 124–28, 130, 134

Aztlán, xiv, 28

Balkans, 8

Bañuelas, Arturo, 104, 109

Barber, Benjamin, 20, 165, 248; and capitalist/consumerist ethos, 58; and McWorld *v.* jihad, 31–34, 45, 61, 79, 81, 99, 103, 130; and moral discourse, 262n.31; and transnational political institutions, 257

Battle of San Jacinto (1836), 64

Baylor University, 193

Belgium, 237

Bellah, Robert, 5, 49, 166, 250; and community, 20, 84, 111, 102, 143, 165, 248; *The Good Society,* 48; *Habits of the Heart,* 47–48, 264n.100; and lifestyle communities, 99; and political/spiritual interplay, 13, 166

Bergmann, Barbara: *In Defense of Affirmative Action,* 218

Berlin, Isaiah, 256

Bhabha, Homi, 12, 276n.58; and colonialism, 164; and hybridity, 62, 147, 160, 161–63, 169

Bickford, Susan, 135, 251

Birmingham, 224

Black History Month, 191

Black Muslims, 28

black nationalism, 27

Bolívar, Simón, 128

Bosnia, 164

Boswell, Jonathan, 281n.2

Brazil, 142, 232, 261n.6

Breecher, Jeremy, 238

Brimelow, Peter: *Alien Nation,* 3, 8, 22

Brown v. Board of Education, 150

Buddhism, 15, 74, 144

Buffalo, New York, 224

Burke, Francisco, x

Burke, John Francis, ix

Burke, Mary Jane De La Rosa, x, 180, 182, 191

Burke, Sean, x

California, 4, 24, 167, 247; and the cultural bond to Mexico, 63; Latino presence in, 50; pre-1848 inhabitants, 9, 65; and voter propositions: #187, 69, 82, 159, 229, 232 #209, 69, 82, 159, 216, 220 #227, 69, 82, 159, 229

Californios (people), 64

Canada, 4; and European immigrants, 9; and the French Canadian culture, 152–54, 156, 157, 158, 159, 164; and rights of indigenous people, 28, 148–50, 156; Supreme Court of, 152; and the U.S. border, 229

Canadian Charter of Rights (1982), 152

capitalism, 23, 32, 33, 120

Carranza, Venustiano, 59, 125

Caribbean, 230, 261n.6

Carter, Stephen, 13–14; and culture of disbelief, 13

Catholic Hispanic Pastoral Plan, 100

Catholicism, 15, 74, 268n.82; the Charismatic movement of, 91, 197; and the Encuentros movement, 100; in contrast to Protestant social/political outlook, 79, 93; and the genesis of modernity, 123–25; and the Multicultural Relations Committee (Houston parish), 180–96; and the popular church, 78, 89, 90–93, 123, 197, 270n.45; and treatment of indigenous people, 133, 170. *See also* Roman Catholic Church

CBS (Columbia Broadcasting System), 66

Central America, 265n.5

Chambers, Simone, 135, 159

Chávez, César, 14, 72, 239

Chiapas (Mexico), 60, 126, 133

Chicago: African American population of, 224; Latino population of, 66, 225

Chicano (as term), xiv;

Chicano movement, 61, 84, 158

China, 45, 240

Chinese Americans, 25

Chinese Exclusion Act of 1882, 25

Christian Coalition, 14

Christianity, 29, 57; and the Charismatic movement, 199, 123 (*see also* Catholicism: the Charismatic movement of); and indigenous peoples/spiritualities, 92, 133–34, 73–74, 78–79

Cincinnati, 224

citizenship, 23–24; and cultural parochialism, 33; in a democracy, 31; dual citizenship, 232; effects of economic globalization upon, 26–27, 30, 31, 33–34, 232; global, 243, 245; and the politics of commodity, 33; politics of resentment, 33; procedures for, 24–25, 26

civil rights, 14, 26, 219, 223–24

civil rights movement, 25, 106, 249–50

Civil Rights Act: of 1964, 217; of 1968, 225
civil society, 31–34, 45
Cleveland, 224
Cold War, 142, 157
Colombia, 232
colonialism, 26, 94, 129, 147, 164
Colorado; and the cultural bond to
    Mexico, 63
commercialism. *See* global economy
Commonweal, 6
communitarianism, 12, 146, 147, 160, 165;
    and cultural *v.* political membership,
    148–49, 156; and materialism, 107; and
    mestizo democracy, 168–69, 172–74;
    and individualism, 103. *See also*
    community
Communities Organized for Public Service
    (COPS), 101–102
community, 99–103; global, 233; and
    majority/minority contrast, 157;
    Mexican celebrations of, 126–27;
    political, 36–37. *See also* commun-
    itarianism
conjunto/encuentro process, 102–103
consumerism, 31, 80, 158. *See also* global
    economy
corporatism, 107, 167, 214, 257, 270n.68
Cortes, Ernesto, 101–102, 108
Cortéz, Hernán, 53, 117, 120, 124–25, 129
cosmopolitanism, 160, 162, 163
Costa Rica, 232, 265n.5
Council of Trent, 89, 93, 197
Counter-Reformation. *See* Reformation:
    Reformation–Counter Reformation
    debate
Croce, Benedetto, 62
crossing borders (defined), 10, 11, 16, 80, 82
Cuban Americans, 64
cultural identity, 8, 10, 19, 45, 47, 166, 244;
    and citizenship, 34; as divisive, 31;
    heterogenity/homogenity of, 164, 232;
    Mexican identity, 126; and multiple
    identities, 65, 72, 74, 171, 206, 213, 255–57;
    as possession, 20, 22, 49, 159, 165, 167; as
    a relational dynamic, 22, 34, 46, 164, 165,
    217, 233, 247, 252; and U.S. identity, 93

Cursillo prayer movement, 186
Cypress, 164

Dallas, 68
Dallmayr, Fred, 42–43, 44, 45
Darwinism, 82
De Tocqueville. *See* Tocqueville, Alexis-
    Charles-Henri Clérel de
Deck, Allan Figueroa, 83, 94, 105, 181,
    265n.3, 268n.2
deconstruction, 39, 40, 42, 44, 119, 144
Deloria, Vine, Jr., 20, 28, 31, 49, 95, 159, 165,
    252; and atonement motif, 28; and
    significance of place, 28–30, 78, 92, 251;
    and tribal responsibility, 34–35
Depression (of 1930s), 65, 231
Derrida, Jacques, 40, 42, 43, 44–45, 165; *The
    Other Heading: Reffiection on Today's
    Europe*, 42
Descartes, 35, 41, 42, 117, 121–22, 190
Detroit, 224
Dewey, John, 32, 149, 151, 156, 166
Día de los Muertos (Day of the Dead, All
    Souls' Day), 89, 95
Díaz, Porfirio, 54, 59, 125
Díaz-Stevens, Ana María, 83, 93–94, 98, 170
Diego, Juan, 72–73, 105, 129
Diocese of Galveston-Houston, 183
diversity management, 220–24, 245
Dominican Republic, 232
Dominicans, 90
DuBois, W. E. B., 217, 224
Dussel, Enrique, 12, 164, 220, 250, 271n.7;
    and affective, aesthetic rationality, 253;
    and dialogue, 133–35, 147, 169; and
    Eurocentrism, 180, 253; and the
    European-indigenous divide, 129; *The
    Invention of the Americas*, 116, 129, 131,
    140, 144; and modernity, 115–21, 127–45,
    157, 240
Dworkin, Ronald, 146, 149, 151, 152, 156

economic globalization. *See* global
    economy
El Paso, 66. *See also* Ysleta
El Salvador, 65

Elizondo, Virgil, 11, 51, 53, 105, 107, 168; and anthropology on inclusion, 88, 244; and community, 103; and cross-cultural changes/mestizaje, 70, 71–84, 129, 143, 184; and the *divina providencia*, 95–96; and European response to indigenous religions, 90, 108, 110, 121; *The Future is Mestizo*, 194; and living in process, 190, 192; and practical rationality, 250

Encuentro 2000: Many Faces of God's House, 100

England, 23

Enlightenment, 46, 141, 197, 199; and colonialism, 26, 94, 129; Enlightenment/post-Enlightenment debate, 123, 252; and individualism, 23; and liberation, 122, 128, 131, 139, 253

Equal Pay Act (1963), 217

Esperanto, 201

Espín, Orlando, 83, 89–91, 93, 105, 127, 197

Esprit, 179

ethnicity, 24. *See also* cultural identity

Eurocentrism, 45, 252–53; of conquest, 121–28, 134; and liberation theology, 143; moving beyond, 115, 147, 164, 180, 249; and unity-in-diversity, 47, 175

European Americans, xiv, 15

European Union (EU), 232, 237, 239, 243, 258

Federal Housing Administration, 225

Federal National Mortgage Association, 225

federalism, 254–57

Federalist Papers: #10, 254, 255, 256; #51, 254, 255

Fewell, Donna Nolan, 268n.11

Filipino Americans, 186, 192, 194, 199, 252, 278n.16

Florida, 167, 247; Latino population of, 66

Foucault, Michel Paul, 40, 44, 165; *The Archaeology of Knowledge*, 43

Fox, Geoffrey, 171

Fox, Vicente, 126, 237, 243

Franciscans, 90

frontier *v.* border mentality, 83–88, 94, 110, 123, 134, 166, 199, 250

Fuentes, Carlos, 59, 87

Gabilondo, Joseba, 61

Gadamer, Hans-Georg, 20, 38, 43, 44–45, 165; and dialogue, 35–36, 40, 42; *Truth and Method*, 42

Galilee, 72

Galston, William, 146, 167–68

García, Ismael, 83, 98, 103, 104, 270n.68

García, Sixto, 83, 96

Garveyites, 27

Gary, Indiana, 224

Geertz, Clifford, 38–39

General Agreement on Tariffs and Trade (GATT), 232

genocide, 262n.19

Georgia: Latino population of, 66

Geyer, Georgie Anne, 20, 48, 49, 165; *Americans No More*, 22, 23–27, 38, 86; and citizenship, 130, 28–31, 33–34, 46; and community, 84; and individualism, 37, 247; other cultures as threat, 47

G.I. Bill programs, 225

G.I. Forum, 239

Gilkey, Langdon, 98, 270n.45

global economy, 44–45, 58–61, 69–70, 77, 147; and citizen as consumers, 97, 141, 158; and cultural homogeneity, 130–31, 175, 229; and integration of races, 54; and multiple identities, 235, 258–59; and NAFTA, 70; politics of, 236–45; and transference of wealth, 121. *See also* transnationalism

Goizueta, Roberto S., 57, 83, 84, 108, 251; and community, 99, 102, 115; and empowerment, 109; and liberation theology, 105, 143–45; and the marginalized, 103; and postmodernism, 137–39, 141, 169; and practical rationality, 250; and the urban-suburban split, 226–27, 234

González, Justo L., 83, 268n.11; and frontier *v.* border mentality, 85–88, 123, 134, 199;

and the marginalized, 107; and religion, 90–92, 106, 142

Good Friday, 95, 105

Good Friday Peace Accords, 244

Greece, 23, 27

Greeley, Andrew, 92, 94, 96, 98, 111, 183, 200

Green, Thomas Hill, 149

Guadalupe (Our Lady of), 14, 78–79, 170, 249; appearance of, 72–73, 90, 107; feast of, 67, 95; and indigenous/Mexican spiritual or mythical entities: la Chingada, 76, Coatlicue, 76, la Llorona, 76, la Malinche, 76, 118, 129, Tonantzin, 72, 76, 90, 126; symbolic importance of, 76, 105, 108, 121, 126, 129. *See also* Quetzalcóatl

Guatemala, 65, 75

Guinier, Lani, 212, 214, 215

Gutiérrez, Gustavo, 84, 143–44

Habermas, Jürgen, 49, 98, 141, 250; and neo-Kantian liberalism, 115, 135–36, 139, 143, 165; and practical reason, 251, 252

Harvard University, 218

Hasidic Jews, 28

Hegel, Georg Wilhelm Friedrich, 116, 140

Heidegger, Martin, 42

Herberg, Will, 92, 94

hermeneutics, 35–36, 38–39, 42, 46

Hidalgo y Costilla, Miguel (Father Hidalgo), 125

Hinduism, 15, 74, 144

Hispanic: defined, xiii

Hispanos, 64

Hobhouse, Leonard Trelawney, 149

Housing and Urban Development programs, 226

Houston, 67, 101; Latino population of, 66, 68–69; voting practices in, 211

Houston, Sam, 64

Howard University, 217

human rights, 233

Huntington, Samuel, 231–32, 240–44; and transnational political institutions, 257

Immigration and Nationality Act: of 1965, 230, 231; of 1976, 230

Immigration and Naturalization Service, 231

Immigration Reform and Control Act (1968), 230

immigration, 4, 6; European, 9; governmental policies toward, 22, 24, 27, 34, 70, 86, 230, 234; illegal, 4, 229; immigration/migration distinction, 158; and moving borders, 63. *See also* citizenship; migration

Incas, 30, 52, 117

India, 45

indigenous (as term), xiv

individualism, 23, 98–99, 103, 165–66; individual *v.* community, 6–8, 11, 35, 172, 271n.7. *See also* communitarianism; community; personalism

Industrial Areas Foundation (IAF), 102, 108, 109, 239

International Monetary Fund, 258

intersubjectivity, 20, 100; and community, 98, 166; and cultural diversity, 34–38, 50, 112, 155–57, 247, 259; and cultural identity, 41–45, 103, 164, 213; as opposed to subjectivity, 141, 168; and postmodernism, 138

irrationalism, 138

Isasi-Díaz, Ada María, 83, 96, 107, 179, 269n.43, 272n.7; and *mujerista* theology, 88, 101

Islam, 15, 31, 74, 92, 95, 116, 144, 200

Jansenism, 122

Japan, 45, 237, 240

Japanese Americans, 25

Jernigan, Homer L., 180

Jesuits, 90

Jesus (of Nazareth), 72, 73, 103, 105

John Paul II (Pope), 90

Johnson, Lyndon, 217

Joseph (son of Jacob), 87

Joshua (book of the Bible), 87

Journal of Pastoral Theology, 179

Judaism, 15, 74
Jung, Hwa Yol, 43

Kallen, Horace, 25–26
Kant, Immanuel, 116, 140, 143, 250
Kennedy, John F., 5
Kennedy, Ruby, 92, 94
King, Martin Luther, 210
Kohlberg, Lawrence, 98
Ku Klux Klan, 262n.19
Kymlicka, Will, 146, 163, 173; and cultural
    rights, 12, 147–51, 155, 164; and group
    rights, 219; and purposive liberalism,
    156–60, 165, 166, 167–68

Lamy, Jean Baptiste, 91
Las Casas, Bartolomé de, 141, 142, 180, 198,
    217; in defense of indigenous people,
    117–18, 143–43; and political access of the
    marginalized, 250, 258; and the
    Valladolid debate, 133–35, 140, 253
Latin America, 4, 6, 7; immigrants from, 230
Latin American Episcopal (Catholic)
    Conference, 78, 90
Latino, 15, 49, 64, 225, 266n.42; defined, xiii–
    xiv; and discrimination against, 16; and
    equal employment opportunities, 216
League of Nations, 150
League of United Latin American Citizens
    (LULAC), 239
Lebanon, 8
Lemay, Michael, 225
liberalism, 12, 146–49, 165, 167–68, 172–74;
    dual 152–55, 157; materialistic, 166;
    neutral, 149–50, 156; purposive, 151, 156,
    164, 166–68
liberation philosophy, 115, 127–28, 133, 140–45
liberation theology, 12, 84, 111, 268n.2;
    Eurocentrism of, 95; and preferential
    option for the poor, 90, 105, 274n.97;
    reevaluation of, 115, 142–44
Lightfoot, Sara Lawrence, 6–7, 261n.4
Limón, Garciela: The Song of the Hum-
    mingbird, 118–19
Locke, John, 166

Lopez, Jennifer, 138
Los Angeles, 63, 67, 101, 224
Los Angeles (L.A.) Metropolitan Organiza-
    tion, 101
Loury, Glenn, 223

Maclean, Iain S., 274n.97
McCullough, David, 24
Madison, Gary, 36, 41, 42, 43
Madison, James, 13, 168; and the extended
    republic, 254–57
Madrid, Miguel de la, 125
Manifest Destiny, 85, 106, 248
Mankekar, Purnima, 235
Maori (people), 161
Maquiladora Code of Conduct, 239
Marable, Manning, 217
Maritain, Jacques, 182
Markham, Donna: Spiritlinking Leadership,
    180
Martí, Jóse, 59, 60
Martin, Ricky, 138
Martínez, Antonio José, 91
Martinez, Bettia, 265n.101
Martinez, Demetria, 198
Massa, Mark, 93
Maximilian (Ferdinand Maximilian
    Joseph), 159
Maya (people), 117, 120, 134
MCI (telecommunications), 66
Meech Lake Accords, 152
melting-pot theory. See assimilation v.
    separatism: and the melting-pot theory
Mercedarians, 90
Merleau-Ponty, Maurice, 20, 39, 41, 43, 44,
    45, 135, 165
Mesoamerica, 52, 63, 175
mestizaje, 10, 11; defined, ix, 9, 52
mestizos (as term), 9
Metropolitan Organization, The, (TMO), 101
Mexican American Cultural Center
    (MACC), 71
Mexican Americans, xiv, 9, 25, 64
Mexican Revolution (1910), 54, 59, 64, 125
Mexican (as term), xiv

Mexico, 4, 49, 68, 72, 170; during colonialization, 122–25; pre-1848 inhabitants of, 9, 52, 231; slave rebellion of 1537, 261n.6; and the U.S. border, 229, 232; and the U.S.-Mexico War of 1846–1848, 59, 63, 64. *See also* Mexican Revolution (1910)

Miami, 66, 67

migrants/migration, 4, 65, 94; and maintaining cultural ties, 67; and undocumented workers, 4. *See also* immigration

Mill, John Stuart, 149, 151, 156, 166

Milwaukee, 224

Misa de las Américas (Mass of the Americas), 192

miscegenation, 28

Mississippi Delta, 182

Moctezuma, 120, 125

modernity (modernism), 12, 97, 115, 117–18, 120–23, 126–28, 136–37; myth of, 130–31, 135. *See also* postmodernism; transmodernity

Monterrey (Mexico), 67

Monticello, 23

Morales, Rebecca, 236, 237

Mormons, 30

Moskos, Charles, 221

Mother's Day celebration, 95

Mounier, Emmanuel, 179

Mukherjee, Bharati, 26, 47

mulatez, 261n.6

Multicultural Relations Committee (Houston parish), 181, 198; cessation of, 193–96; creation of, 181–87; as diversity model, 199–201; and multicultural choir, 191–93, 199; workings of 187–88, 202–203

multilingualism, 13. *See also* public policy issues: education, language

Murray, John Courtney, 5–6, 10, 15, 48, 74, 169, 182

Native Americans, xiv, 8, 15, 25; and discrimination against, 16; and spirituality of place, 28–30

NBC (National Broadcasting Company), 66

neocolonialism, 147, 164

neoliberalism, 59, 107

neo-Nazis, 262n.19

Neo-Thomism, 122

New Mexico, 4, 67; and the alternative Catholic Church, 91; and the cultural bond to Mexico, 63; pre-1848 inhabitants of, 9, 65

New York City, 66

New Zealand, 161

Nicaragua, 65

North American Free Trade Agreement (NAFTA), 4, 60, 62, 70, 229, 232, 236–37, 239, 243, 272n.14

North Carolina: Latino population of, 66

Northern Ireland, 243–44

Nuevo Laredo (Mexico), 67

Pachon, Harry, 204

Page, Clarence, 220–21

Pakeha (people), 161

Pannikar, Raimon, 252

Pastor, Manuel, 236, 238

pastoral de conjunto, 103, 270n.45. *See also* Catholicism: and the Encuentros movement

pastoral theology, 180

Paul VI, Pope, 183

Pax Romana, 23

Paz, Octavio, 12, 115, 123–27, 132, 135; and the European-indigenous divide, 129; *The Labyrinth of Solitude*, 122, 131

Pentecostalism, 91–93, 123, 197, 198

personalism, 166

phenomenology, 35–36, 38, 41–47

Philadelphia, 224

Phoenix, 66

Pineda, Ana María, 83, 103, 118

Plato, 119

Plessy v. Ferguson, 224, 226

pluralism, 13, 35–38, 40, 261n.4, 263n.49

Plyer v. Doe, 278n.6

politics and theology, 14, 104–108

posadas, las, 89

positivism, 125, 127, 129
postmodernism, 12, 20, 115, 141, 147, 165, 172–74, 252; and mestizo democracy, 169–70; myth of, 136–38; and personal identity, 40–42, 250; and subjectivity, 43–45
poststructuralism, 44
Princeton University, 218
Protestantism, 15, 74, 93, 197; in Latin America, 106
Protestant Reformation, 23, 29, 89, 122
public policy issues: affirmative action, 216–18; education, 204, 245: bilingual and dual language programs, 208–209, 278n.8, Robin Hood plans, 228; employment, 216–24: equal employment opportunity (EEO)204; cultural code-switching, 206, 208–209; globalization, 204, 228, 234–44, 245; housing, 204, 224–29, 245; language, 204–10; migration/immigration, 204, 229–35; patriotism, 205; political participation, 204, 207–208; transportation, 226–27; voting, 210–17, 245, 256
Puerto Rican Americans, 64
Puerto Rico 104
Putnam, Robert, 102, 111

Quebec, 135, 152, 155, 156, 157
Quetzalcóatl, 120

Rand, Barry, 221, 224
rationality, 39, 133, 137, 270n.45, 271n.7; aesthetic/affective/holistic rationality, 14, 57, 70, 73, 82, 83, 95–98, 104, 108, 112, 119–20, 137, 141–45, 146, 180, 197, 247, 249, 250–53; Aristotelian, 13 (*see also* Aristotle); Kantian, 13 (*see also* Kant, Immanuel); of modernity, 129, 138–39; practical, 13, 112; scientific, 41
Ravitch, Diane, 25
Rawls, John, 49, 98, 149, 151, 251, 252; and neo-Kantian approach, 115, 135, 139, 165; and neutral liberalism, 156; and overlapping consensus, 250; *Theory of Justice*, 136

Raz, Joseph, 146
raza cósmica, la, 54–62, 73–74, 77–78, 80, 84, 95, 97, 111, 199
Recinos, Harold, 83
Redwood City, California, 234
Reformation: and individualism, 23, 197–99; its influence in Latin America, 123; Reformation–Counter Reformation debate, 79, 93, 122–23, 144, 197, 252; as Western tradition, 26–27, 46, 94
relativism, 39–40, 42, 138
religious fundamentalism, 32
Republic of Ireland, 244
Republic of Texas, 64, 68. *See also* Texas
Ricoeur, Paul, 39
Rio Grande, 64, 65
Rio Nueces, 64
Rodó, Jóse Enrique, 59, 60
Rodriguez, Jeanette, 83
Roman Catholic Church, 90, 105, 115, 270n.45; papal documents of, 183; the Vatican, 115, 142. *See also* catholicism
Roman Empire, 23, 27, 29
Rorty, Richard, 137, 141
Rose, Richard, 261n.4
Rouse, Roger, 234–35

Salinas, Carlos, 125
San Antonio, 63, 65, 68, 71, 101, 105, 225
San Diego, 63
San Fernando Cathedral (San Antonio), 192
San Francisco, 63, 224
Santa Ana, California, 66
Santa Anna, Antonio López de, 64
Santeria, 89
Sassen, Saskia, 232–33
Schlesinger, Arthur, Jr., 20, 34; and citizenship, 28; and community, 30–31; *The Disuniting of America*, 22–27; Eurocentrism of, 47, 49, 241, 247–48
Segovia, Fernando, 83, 84–85, 105, 108, 247
separatism. *See* assimilation *v.* separatism
Sepúlveda, Juan Ginés de, 133–35, 140, 253
Single Europe Act, 237
slavery, 14, 25, 261n.6

Soliván-Román, Samuel, 83
Southwest Voter Registration and Education Project, 235
Sowell, Thomas, 219
Spain, 60, 63, 68; and conquest of Mesoamerica, 53, 57, 75–76, 117–21, 123, 170; and modernity, 122–23
Spanish American War (1898), 59, 104, 106
Spencer, Herbert, 54
spirituality: of place, 28–29; and the political debate, 14–15
Spivak, Gayatiri Chakravorty, 276n.58
St. Louis, 224
Stalker, James, 207, 278n.8
Standing Bear, Luther, 29
Stevens-Arroyo, Anthony, 83, 94, 98, 170
Stockton, California, 224
Strategy Research Corporation, 66
Sweden, 237
Switzerland, 237

Taylor, Charles, 12; and cultural rights, 151–60, 164, 257; and communitarian approach, 146, 147, 163, 165; and individual choice, 150
Taylor, Frederick, 80, 264n.72
Tejanos, 64; music of, 67
Telemundo (television network) 66
Tenochtitlán (Mexico City), 118
Tepeyac, 90
Texas A&M University, 68, 69, 158, 192
Texas, 4, 167, 247; colonialization of 63–64; Councils of Government (COG) in, 243; and the cultural bond to Mexico, 63; Latino presence in, 50, 68–69; pre-1848 inhabitants of, 9, 65. *See also* Republic of Texas
Thiele, Leslie Paul, 36, 117
Thompkins, Jonathan, 221
Tlacaélel, 120
tlamatinime, 119–20, 133
Tocqueville, Alexis-Charles-Henri Clérel de, 27, 102
Tomás Rivera Policy Institute, 204
Toronto, Joan, 224

Tracy, David, 93, 96, 111, 183, 200
transmodernity, 139, 140, 141, 143
transnationalism, 61–62, 232–33, 235, 236–39, 242, 245, 249, 253, 257, 258
Treaty of Guadalupe-Hidalgo (1848), 25, 64
tribalism, 12, 28, 165, 170–71, 172–74
Trueba, Enrique, 204
Tucson, 63

U.S. Americans (as term), xiv; as hybrid people, 29
U.S. Army, 221
U.S. Census Bureau, 66, 67–68, 266n.42; 1980 census of, 68; 1990 census of, 68, 212; 2000 census of, 3, 68, 69
U.S. Conference of Catholic Bishops: documents of, 183
U.S. Constitution, 254; first Amendment (Establishment Clause), 5, 14; fifteenth Amendment, 210
U.S. Department of Transportation, 226
U.S. District Court (District of Columbia), 210
U.S. Justice Department, 210
U.S. Supreme Court, x, 212, 224, 278n.6
U.S.-Mexico War of 1846–1848, 59, 63, 64, 91 104, 106
Ulster (Northern Ireland), 164
United Farm Workers of America, 14, 72, 239
United Kingdom, 244
United States: and cultural identity/ citizenship, 154–55; imperialism of, 59–61
unity-in-diversity, 6, 31, 143, 144, 229, 253, 255–59; in Catholicism, 182–84, 201, 148; and cultural identity, 10–11, 15, 20, 24; and intersubjectivity, 35, 37, 40, 45–46; and mestizo democracy 15, 49, 79, 110–11, 83, 128, 138, 156, 167, 169, 251, 249, 250
universalism, 29–31, 39
Univision (television network), 66

Valladolid debate, 133, 140
Vallejo, California, 224

Vasconcelos, José, 11, 51, 84, 123; and
affective, aesthetic rationality, 70–71, 73–
75, 95, 247, 250; and Elizondo, 77–82;
and Eurocentrism, 170, 111; and
integration of cultures, 53–63, 97, 199,
252; *La raza cósmica,* 54
Vatican II, 90, 195, 197, 270n.45; *Gaudium et
Spes,* 183
Villa, Pancho, 59
Villafañe, Eldín, 83
Villista revolutionaries, 125
Voting Rights Act (1965), 167, 210, 213–14

Waldron, Jeremy, 12, 147, 161; and cosmopolitanism, 160, 162–63, 167
Walzer, Michael, 12, 165; and cultural
rights, 151–52, 155, 163–64; and deep
diversity, 156–58; and morality, 30, 242,
262n.31; and politics of nation-states,
146
Western civilization, 240–42

white supremacy, 28
Williamson, Chilton: *The Immigration
Mystique,* 22
Winthrop, John, 93, 197, 248
Wise, Carol, 236
Wolf, Susan, 47, 48, 49, 248
World Trade Organization, 258
World War II, 25, 231

xenophobia, 4
Xerox Corporation, 221, 224

Yale University, 218
Young, Iris Marion, 12, 147, 162; and group
rights, 219; and relational group theory,
160–61, 163, 164; and the heterogenous
public, 215
Ysleta (El Paso), 63

Zapatistas, 50, 60, 125, 126
Zedillo, Ernesto, 125

ISBN 1-58544-346-8